# INFLUENCE IN PARLIAMENT: CANADA

## PUBLICATIONS OF THE CONSORTIUM
## FOR COMPARATIVE LEGISLATIVE STUDIES
## Malcolm E. Jewell,
### *General Editor*

G. R. Boynton and Chong Lim Kim, Editors, *Legislative Systems in Developing Countries*

Abdo I. Baaklini, *Legislative and Political Development: Lebanon, 1842–1972*

Allan Kornberg and William Mishler, *Influence in Parliament: Canada*

Peter Vanneman, *The Supreme Soviet: Politics and the Legislative Process in the Soviet Political System*

Albert F. Eldridge, *Legislatures in Plural Societies*

*Forthcoming titles to be announced*

# INFLUENCE IN PARLIAMENT:

# CANADA

**ALLAN KORNBERG**

and

**WILLIAM MISHLER**

Duke University Press, Durham, North Carolina 1976

*For Robert Taylor Cole,*

*James B. Duke Professor of Political Science, Emeritus*

*Colleague and friend*

Publication of this book has been assisted by funds from the Duke University Center for Commonwealth and Comparative Studies.

# CONTENTS

# FOREWORD

This study is important, first, because it adds significantly to our knowledge about the Canadian Parliament. Based on indepth interviews and a quantitative analysis of legislative activity, it is the latest and most impressive in a series of recent studies that have applied systematic and behavioral techniques of analysis to one of the most important but least studied legislative bodies in the western world.

This study is also important because of the contributions it makes to the comparative study of legislative systems and behavior. The questions that it poses, the methodology that is used, and the conclusions of the study are all useful to students of other legislative bodies, particularly in the western world, and to those who are interested in the comparative analysis of legislatures across national boundaries. This study of the Canadian Parliament is comparable in importance to other major studies of parliamentary bodies in recent years, such as Loewenberg's study of the German Bundestag, MacRae's analysis of parties and the French National Assembly, Jackson's study of party discipline in the British House of Commons, and Debuyst's book on the Belgian parliament.[1]

The scholarly interest in comparative legislative studies implies a rejection of the theory that parliaments and other legislative bodies in the western world are declining, that they are hollow shells without any important functions in modern governments. As Gerhard Loewenberg has pointed out, "repeated prophecies of the demise of parliament have proven to be premature if not clearly mistaken. Old parliaments survive and new ones are constantly established." Loewenberg argues that these premature obituaries often result from the failure of observers to recognize that the functions of parliamentary bodies continue to change over time:

> The long history of parliament helps to explain the conflicting expectations of the institution which have caused successive generations of observers to conclude that representative assemblies were declining in quality and in political importance. Such judgments were often the result of applying the

standards of a previous stage of institutional development to the parliamentary behavior of the moment. Late-nineteenth-century criticism of democratically elected parliaments, for example, applied standards of eloquence in debate, courtesy among members, and independence of party which were derived from the bourgeois, oligarchical parliaments of the eighteenth century. Twentieth-century criticism of specialized, committee-ridden parliaments used standards derived from nineteenth-century parliaments operating in political system of limited scope. . . . Decline, in short, is in the eye of the beholder and depends on his analytical perspectives.[2]

In short, we have begun to realize that we should approach the study of parliaments without preconceived notions about what they ought to do, and instead try to understand what they do and what functions they perform in the larger political system.

The Canadian Parliament is a good source of examples for anyone who wants to demonstrate the decline of parliaments. As political parties have grown in importance and the Cabinet has assumed responsibility for initiating most public policies, the Parliament has become less important as an independent policy-making body. The institution has been slow to adopt reforms that would strengthen its policy-making role and improve its efficiency. A high rate of turnover reduces the proportion of experienced members and consequently erodes the political effectiveness of Parliament.

The purpose of this study, however, is not to prove or to disprove that the Canadian Parliament has declined in importance. The purpose is to understand how the Parliament actually operates and, more specifically, what factors determine the patterns of influence that develop among members of Parliament. This goal requires the authors to examine in considerable detail what the MPs actually do and to determine how the MPs perceive their roles and activities. The data shed light on the operation of the parliamentary parties and the committee system, levels of participation in debate, leadership structure, and the opportunities available to individual backbench members of Parliament. Although we learn much about how the institutional structures work, the perspective is consistently that of the individual member.

In order to demonstrate the utility of this study for the comparative study of legislatures, we should focus our attention on a few of the major themes of the book that are closely related to major themes in the comparative legislative literature. The authors seek to show how the attitudes and behavior of Canadian MPs are shaped by their social backgrounds, their political socialization, and their recruitment into the legislature. Political scientists have devoted a great deal of attention to studying these characteristics of legislators, in Congress and state legislatures, in western parliaments, and in the legislatures of some of the developing countries. As Patterson has pointed out, "One of the firmest generalizations which can be made about the social composition of legislatures is that they do not mirror their populations." Legislators are much better educated and represent higher level occupations and social classes than their con- stitutents. Longitudinal studies in both western and nonwestern legislatures, however, have led to the conclusion that "the develop- mental tendency in parliamentary bodies has been their occupational democratization over time." An aristocratic elite has been replaced by more middle-class legislators, many of whom are professionals (such as lawyers) or are party or interest group politicians.[3]

Students of legislative system can not be satisfied with collecting data on the background, socialization, and recruitment of legislators. They must try to determine the consequences of variations in these factors for the attitudes, roles, and behavior patterns of legislators. It is not obvious what those consequences should be or even whether every one of these independent variables has some measurable effect on how legislators think and behave. It is easy to understand why individuals who develop an interest in politics from their family during childhood are more likely to seek political office than indi- viduals who become socialized as young adults. But it is not obvious what differences in legislative activity we might expect from two MPs who were socialized at different times and in different ways. Part of the task is to identify those independent variables that are most likely to affect (in measurable ways) how legislators think and act. Those background characteristics that are available in published form may not be the ones most pertinent; similarly, the aspects of sociali- zation most often recalled by respondents are not necessarily the ones most useful for research purposes. A second job is to identify those dependent variables most likely to be affected. Political sociali- zation might affect members' career patterns and motivations for seeking leadership positions without having any significant impact on their skill in debate or their tendency to vote with their party.

This is not the place to attempt a comprehensive summary of the efforts to establish these linkages, but it may be useful to mention a few of the problems encountered and conclusions drawn by scholars. Searing has studied the relationships between a large number of social background characteristics and political attitudes of elites in different countries, and has concluded that those characteristics that are useful in one country have little relationship to attitudes in another.[4] A survey of studies in various countries on the correlates of legislative representational roles found wide variations in the social background, recruitment, and district characteristics that were most closely related to particular roles.[5]

One of the more fruitful approaches to studying background characteristics, socialization, and recruitment is to examine their effects on the approaches that legislators take to their job: their career choices, efforts to seek leadership positions, levels and areas of activity within the legislature. Matthews, in his 1960 study of the U.S. Senate, examined the effects of such variables on career patterns and on levels of floor activity and specialization.[6] Barber, in his study of Connecticut legislators, showed that background characteristics and the wide variety of motivations associated with recruitment can help to explain both the willingness to pursue a legislative career and the types of activities that members choose to devote their time to in the legislature—and consequently their effectiveness as lawmakers.[7] Several scholars, notably Fenno and Bullock, have examined the factors that determine which committees the members of Congress seek and what factors may cause them to shift from one committee to another.[8] Loewenberg's study of the West German Bundestag demonstrated that members with a professional political background have dominated the positions of leadership and have established the norms of that parliamentary body.[9]

This study of the Canadian Parliament adds further evidence to support the conclusion from other studies that those legislators who take a more active part in legislative activities and those who seek positions of leadership can be identified on the basis of variables antecedent to their entrance into the legislature, including some background variables, aspects of socialization, and circumstances and motivations of recruitment. It is also true, as the authors point out, that the opportunities legislators have to assume leadership positions depend on political circumstances, just as such political factors help to determine which potential legislators will have the opportunity to run for office and to win.

One feature of this study, though not its central focus, is the examination of legislators' representational roles. Ever since the seminal work on four American state legislatures by Wahlke, Eulau, Ferguson, and Buchanan,[10] legislative scholars have been using role analysis extensively. Examples can be found in studies of national, state, and local legislative bodies in the United States, a number of the western legislatures, and a growing number of nonwestern legislatures.[11] Kornberg's earlier book on *Canadian Legislative Behavior* is one of the earliest and best studies of roles in a parliamentary setting.[12] Role analysis, if used skillfully and imaginatively, has several advantages. Information on the degree of role consensus among legislators, and their tolerance of nonconforming roles, may provide a good measure of legislative institutionalization. Data on legislators' perceptions of purposive rules can provide clues to the functions that the institution is serving. For example, if most legislators give priority to a constituency service role, it suggests that this is an important function of the legislature. Information about the client roles of legislators is important for understanding the relationships between the legislators and outside groups, such as parties or interest groups. If we also had information about the role perceptions of members of those groups (party leaders and lobbyists, for example), these relationships would be even clearer.[13]

Role analysis offers pitfalls, as well as advantages. In the past one weakness of some legislative role studies has been that they have followed too closely the model established by Wahlke and his associates for the study of Ohio, New Jersey, California, and Tennessee. There is no reason to expect that exactly the same roles will be found in European or Asian nations, nor is it very useful to count exactly how many trustees, delegates, facilitators, or resisters are found in each legislature. Despite the large number of legislative role studies, some ambiguities and contradictions remain in the definition of terms and the interpretations of findings.[14]

The study of legislative career patterns and roles has brought about a recognition that members of legislative bodies have the opportunity to make choices about the allocation of their time and attention to a variety of activities. The range of these opportunities is greater in some legislatures than it is in others, but choices appear to exist in any legislative body. In legislatures that contribute significantly to the making of policy, members may seek positions of leadership where their influence over policy will be great or they may choose to be followers. They may also choose how much and in which fields to specialize. In legislatures that have a smaller impact on policy-making the opportunities for participating significantly in policy-making are reduced. Nevertheless, individuals may choose to become advocates of particular viewpoints or interests in debate.

They may seek to gain an influential voice in party councils. Or, they may leave policy questions to others, and concentrate their attention on other activities, such as constituency service.

In some legislative bodies, such as the U.S. Congress and the Canadian House of Commons, an active constituency role appears to be essential for any member who aspires to reelection. But the American congressman has some choice about leaving such matters to his staff or devoting personal attention to them and some choice about priorities among service projects. Given the relatively small staff available to Canadian MPs their choices are more limited. Consequently, as the study indicates, a great deal of almost every members' time and attention are given to constituency-related work. Nonetheless, members do have some room to choose, and an important finding is that a preference for constituency work is one of the factors that best distinguishes followers from leaders in the Canadian House of Commons. Another finding, or more accurately, another contention is that through a variety of methods party leaders in the House have been able to use their backbenchers as a kind of functional equivalent of personal staff. Although this latter assertion may be arguable, the above mentioned statement regarding latitude in choosing activities has solid empirical support. Thus, a recent series of studies of Third World parliaments in which constituency service is not so widespread or institutionalized demonstrated that many members still choose to spend their time on such activities in order to enhance their prospects for reelection or because their opportunities for accomplishment appear greater in this area than in policy-making.[15]

An analysis of the choices that legislators make may contribute to our understanding of the legislative institution. If the question period is monopolized by a few members and committee attendance is low, it may be because members find it more productive to spend a greater proportion of their time in the constituency, trying to deal with local problems. Another of the useful findings of this study is that the committee system in the Canadian Parliament, which has been reformed and revitalized in recent years, provides an outlet for the activities of MPs who have some interest in policy questions but do not hold positions of leadership in their parliamentary parties. This finding gives us some perspective on both possibilities for further strenthening of the committee system and the upper limits of that growth.

As the title indicates, the main theme of this volume is the study of influence in the Canadian Parliament. The influence of individual members is measured by asking other MPs to list the most influential members, and the model that is tested posits that influence results from participating in various forms of activity and from holding leadership positions.

Students of American and some other western legislatures have approached the study of legislative influence in a variety of ways. One general approach is theoretical and often mathematical. There have been efforts to define power and influence in very precise terms and to develop a formal index of power in the legislature. There have been a number of efforts to apply coalition theory to legislative bodies. In coalition theory, the influence of an individual may depend on the likelihood that he will provide the vote that turns a losing coalition into a winning one. In American legislatures, coalition theory is usually applied to the effort to create a winning coalition of legislators on a particular issue; in European studies, attention has been focused on the process by which a governing coalition is formed from the political parties, with each party treated as a unit of analysis.[16]

Another approach to the study of influence, particularly in American legislatures, emphasizes cue-taking: the process by which legislators seek the advice of other legislators on issues in committee or on the floor of the house. Several efforts to conduct simulations of roll call voting have given particular attention to cue-taking within the legislature.[17] This approach does not ignore influences from outside the legislature, but seeks to document more precisely the conditions under which the viewpoints of one legislator directly influence the opinion and vote of another. It relies much less on theories of influence and coalitions and much more on observation and interviews of legislators. This general approach to legislative influence may not be limited to voting on bills but may extend to other decisions that legislators make, such as the decision to investigate activities in an agency or to criticize aspects of foreign policy.

Those who have tried to determine what makes one legislator more influential than another have concentrated their attention on several factors. Some of those who have studied legislative norms, beginning with Matthews in the U.S. Senate, have sought to show that those who conform to well established norms are more influential than those who do not. Some legislatures, however, appear to be much more tolerant than others of nonconformist behavior.[18] Norms obviously change with time, and the congressional norm that has assigned only a lowly apprentice role (and thus limited influence) to newcomers appears to be fading in importance.

Most studies of influence have concluded that one important source is the formal positions of authority, including the presiding officer, the leadership positions in legislative parties, and the chairmanships of committees. It generally appears to be true that influence is more associated with formal positions in larger legislative bodies. The relative importance of various positions such as party and committee leadership, can be expected to vary from one legislature to another. Any study of legislative influence must pay attention to the formal structure of the legislature and to trends that affect the patterns of influence. For example, as Ripley has noted, the decentralization trend in the U.S. Senate in recent years has gone so far that "significant legislative power is spread among virtually all senators in both parties."[19] More recently, in the U.S. House, changes in rules and practice regarding subcommittees and seniority have reduced the power of subcommittee chairmen and rank and file members. One consequence has been to make the influence of committee chairmen more dependent on their own skills.

What makes the holder of a formal position influential? In some cases it is the formal authority derived from the rules, such as the presiding officer's power of recognition during debate or the committee chairman's authority to schedule bills for hearings and discussion. Leaders may have resources, such as staff, at their disposal. In some cases legislative norms mandate a certain deference to leaders. Leaders may benefit from being at the center of the communications network, and therefore better informed than most members of the legislature. Leaders often have certain rewards and sanctions that they can utilize and that are not available to most members.[20]

Almost every study of legislative leadership has concluded that effectiveness depends in large part on the skills with which individuals use these powers, resources and opportunities. A leader has greater potential for influence than a non-leader, but different individuals holding the same position have much different degrees of influence. (Influence is also dependent, of course, on environmental factors, such as the size of partisan majorities.) What is true for leaders is also true for rank-and-file members. Some of them are unusually influential because of their experience, knowledge of parliamentary rules, skill in bargaining, facility in personal relationships, and familiarity with issues. Studies of cue-taking have generally shown that some members who do not hold formal positions of power are a source of voting cues on particular issues where their knowledge and good judgment are recognized. Legislators themselves probably attach greater importance than political scientists do to the personal element in explaining legislative patterns of influence.[21]

The political scientist may recognize the importance of personal, idiosyncratic factors in explaining influence within the legislature, but he also recognizes the difficulty of incorporating such factors in a systematic, comparative study of legislative influence. In this respect, as in others, the challenge to legislative scholars is to develop theories that can contribute to systematic analysis but that take into account the realities of legislative practice. Happily, the present study has tried to do both and undoubtedly, the utility of the sophisticated methodologies that are employed and the validity of the findings will be tested in future comparative legislative research.

Malcolm E. Jewell, General Editor

Comparative Legislative Studies Series

# AUTHORS' PREFACE

This book is dedicated to our colleague, Robert Taylor Cole, James B. Duke Professor of Political Science, Emeritus. Professor Cole was born in Bald Prairie, Texas in 1905 and received an A.B. (1925) and a M.A. (1927) from the University of Texas. He received his doctorate from Harvard University. Although he taught at both Harvard and Louisiana State University, virtually all of his professional career (other than wartime service) was spent at Duke University. His contributions to the University, to political science, and to the comparative study of politics in particular are so numerous they almost defy cataloging. By way of illustration, the British Commonwealth-Studies Center was founded at Duke because of his initiative. The Committee on International Studies of Duke University and its several subcommittees, all of which have made a notable contribution to the intellectual life of the University, also were established because of his initiative and generosity in sharing a very large research grant he had received. Professor Cole also served as chief academic officer (Provost) of Duke University from 1960 to 1969.

Insofar as the discipline of political science is concerned, he has been an active member of both the American and Southern Political Science Associations throughout his career. He served as President of the Southern Political Science Association in 1951–52, and as President of the American Political Science Association in 1958–59. He edited the *Journal of Politics* from 1945 to 1949, and the *American Political Science Review* from 1950 to 1953. In addition to editing two of the most important journals of the discipline and serving on the editorial boards of a number of other professional journals he was a long time member of both the Social Science Research Council and the International Political Science Association.

His scholarly accomplishments have been equally meritorious. A career-long student of bureaucracies and of federal systems, he published numerous scholarly papers in these two areas. More recently, he turned his attention to some of the countries of the Third World, especially to Nigeria. In addition, the wave of student unrest in the late 60s and early 70s, and his own experience as a high-level academic administrator led to an interest in conducting research on the politics of higher education. His recent study of higher education in Canada complements and enriches his earlier research on federalism and the bureaucracy in that country. Given his long-time and continuing interest in all aspects of the Canadian political process, it is particularly fitting that this book on influence in the Canadian House of Commons be dedicated to him.

Finally, not only has Professor Cole enriched the discipline with his own published research, he also has had a significant impact on the research of graduate students and many of his departmental colleagues at Duke. His incisive, but gentle, questioning of their theoretical assumptions, their methodologies, and interpretations of findings while playing his favorite role of "devil's advocate," helped sharpen and clarify the research efforts of literally scores of scholars over the years. Happily, he has continued to share his knowledge and insights with us since his recent retirement. As his colleagues, former students, and legion of friends throughout political science will gladly testify, the designation, "scholar and gentleman," undoubtedly was coined with Taylor Cole in mind.

Allan Kornberg

William Mishler

## ACKNOWLEDGEMENTS

We are pleased to acknowledge the assistance and financial support of the Duke University Research Council and the University's Comparative Legislative Studies and Canadian Studies Program. The University's Center for Commonwealth and Comparative Studies provided a subsidy which facilitated the publication of this book.

We also are pleased to acknowledge the assistance that the Political Science Department of Carleton University, Ottawa, Ontario gave us during the conduct of the field work. A number of undergraduate and graduate students in the Carleton Department assisted in the collection of some of the data that are presented.

The efforts of Ms. Donna Giles, Lenora Chambers, Kay Shaw, and Mr. David Campbell were of great value during the various stages of data processing. Ms. Alice Falcone lent us her considerable editorial skills during the preparation of our manuscript and Professors Ian Budge, Harold Clarke, Malcolm Jewell, Gerhard Loewenberg, and Michael Rush read it in draft form. Although we are grateful for the many helpful suggestions they made, the responsibility for any errors of fact or interpretation is ours alone. Messrs. Gregory Mahler and David Campbell helped prepare the index for this book and Ms. Dorothy Weathers typed the many versions through which each of the several chapters passed with unerring skill and unfailing good humor. Finally and most obviously, without the generous cooperation of the 189 Members of Parliament who agreed to be interviewed there would be no book. We are, indeed, grateful to them for their assistance.

# INFLUENCE IN PARLIAMENT: CANADA

# INTRODUCTION

> In all societies—from societies that are very meagerly developed and have barely attained the dawnings of civilization, down to the most advanced and powerful societies—two classes of people appear—a class that rules and a class that is ruled. The first class, always the less numerous, performs all political functions, monopolizes power and enjoys the advantages that power brings, whereas the second, the more numerous class is controlled and directed by the first . . . [Gaetano Mosca, *The Ruling Class*, trans. by Hannah D. Kahn (New York: McGraw-Hill Book Co., 1939), p. 50].

## THE MEMBERS OF THE GOVERNMENT

"Harry Fesler," "Brewster O'Dare," and "Roger Cyr" are all Liberals, members of the party that formed the government during the lifetime of the 28th Canadian Parliament, 1968–1972.

The representative of a partly suburban, partly rural, highly competitive constituency, Harry Fesler claims he has been in politics literally all of his life. Political meetings, he recalls, were often held in his home ("Dad was the bag man for Mr.____, you know") and politics was the subject most frequently discussed over dinner. A graduate of his province's oldest university, he was a staunch campus Liberal as an undergraduate. After receiving his law degree he involved himself in community affairs and in the civic organizations of the city of 15,000 in which he established his law practice. Fesler was elected to the local school board at age twenty-five, served a three-year term as chairman of the board, was twice president of his local Chamber of Commerce, and in the spring of 1968, won his party's nomination over four other candidates in a nominating meeting that he says lasted until three o'clock in the morning.

He has been a fairly active member of the Miscellaneous Estimates Committee and also has spoken frequently, and (he feels) effectively, in party caucus about the threat posed by inflation. He is in frequent contact with certain cabinet colleagues; he has established a good working relationship with at least two deputy-ministers and has made use of these contacts in pursuing the interests of constituents. Given the party's weakness in his province, its overall national strength, and the Canadian custom of including a representative in the cabinet from each province, Fesler feels there is a very good chance that he will become a cabinet minister if he is reelected.

In spite of both his background and his assumption that he will become a minister, there is little evidence that Fesler's colleagues share his favorable self-evaluation. Only one of them (a party colleague serving with him on the Miscellaneous Estimates Committee) listed Fesler as one of the "ten most influential" men in the 28th Parliament and as a member whose "advice and good judgment" he particularly valued. Nor, apparently, were Fesler's constituents impressed with his performance; he was defeated soundly in the 1972 federal election.

Brewster O'Dare is short, muscular, and immaculately groomed. He bounces in and out of chairs and paces incessantly about his office which is large and well furnished as befits a senior member of the Liberal cabinet. During an interview, O'Dare delivers a lecture on the importance of observing "the rules of the game" if one is to have a "Chinaman's chance" of getting into the cabinet. It obviously is a subject he relishes and one that he probably has had cause to lecture on previously. "Do the right thing in caucus and in the House to come to the attention of the heavyweights. Give the impression that you speak for someone or something other than yourself. Then do a decent job when they give you something to do."

Mr. O'Dare, it would appear, has followed his own advice. Elected in 1962 from a metropolitan working class constituency, he was not initially regarded, according to a number of his party colleagues, as "cabinet material." In the words of one of these colleagues "there are two categories of members, the annointed and everyone else. Brewster definitely was in the latter category but he was shrewd and realistic enough to realize that if you want to get out of that category you not only have to work your tail off, you also have to have a sponsor and say and do things for that sponsor that an intelligent and sensitive person normally would prefer not to do or say. Brewster was _____'s boy and did and said whatever _____ told him to."

O'Dare has definite views on differences among backbenchers: "There are MPs and there are MPs. There are the hardworking, aggressive ones who really want to participate in the legislative process and represent their constituents and those who simply want to be here, for a variety of reasons, collecting a salary. The former need more staff and research and clerical help—a lot of help. The latter don't need what they already have." On the need of backbenchers to become specialists: "If they would only realize that specialization is the key. An ordinary member can and will have influence if he wants to work hard enough and specialize enough to get it. It's not just a question of what the government can do for the backbencher, but also, what is he willing to do for himself? Say, that sounds a little like John Kennedy's inauguration address, doesn't it?"

Although O'Dare realizes that he is very much a part of the parliamentary establishment, he feels strongly that one has to earn admission to this select group rather than be appointed to it. Referring to another powerful Liberal cabinet minister, he recalls "we were freshmen, you know, and shared an office during that first year. I spent half of my time answering the phone and taking messages for him. They already were talking about him as a future Prime Minister, although we were in opposition at the time and he had yet to demonstrate that he could do anything but dance well."

At the time he was interviewed, Roger Cyr was serving his second term in the House, having won reelection over his Creditiste opponent in 1968 by a margin of some 17% of the vote. He had delivered two brief speeches and never had asked a single oral question in the House during the three years the 28th Parliament had been in session. He had, however, spoken fairly frequently in two of the House committees of which he was a member, Northern Affairs and Justice. He said he "always" had been aware of politics. "My parents talked about Bourassa, whom they approved of, and Duplessis, whom they disapproved of, all the time but I don't think I became interested in politics until I was 16 or 17."

Mr. Cyr's interest in politics quickened during his undergraduate years and he became active in constituency party organization work after receiving his law degree. He initially sought a parliamentary seat in the federal election of 1957 but did not receive the Liberal nomination. Nor was he successful in winning a nomination in the provincial election of 1960. Somewhat discouraged by these two experiences, he nonetheless decided to remain in the party and to try to build up an organized base of personal support within it. "I felt that I had a role to play in society. I was lucky enough to go through the university and I felt I had to participate in public life. Besides, I was a lawyer from a working class district and it was a personal challenge to be a professional and try to win an election in a working class district."

He enjoys being an MP and says he would run again even if he were defeated in some future election. His goals are "to help eliminate the atmosphere of hate, discord, and misunderstanding in this country. I would like to see a harmonious life, with diversity, in which we can live together in friendship as two different people. I also would like to eliminate poverty. It would be hard for a person who has never lived there to realize the poverty that exists in a great city and the problems that many people face just looking after themselves. I think I can best accomplish both these things by working quietly on my own as I have done in committee, in caucus and by constantly being in touch with my constituents. I don't speak much on the floor because I feel you have to be responsible. If everyone spoke as much as they wanted to, no laws would ever be passed." Although his parliamentary colleagues may have appreciated his dedication and his responsible behavior, he received no nominations for being influential, or for being a member whose advice and good judgment are particularly valued.

Harry Fesler, Brewster O'Dare and Roger Cyr (the names are fictitious but the men and the sketches are not) are three of the very special men and women who were members of Canada's 28th Parliament. Although each successfully traversed the difficult path to membership in this elite institution, their political fortunes since then have differed vastly. Fesler has been returned to private life; Cyr currently is serving his fourth term in office although he still is virtually unknown, even to many of his parliamentary colleagues; and O'Dare, although seemingly no better prepared for leadership, remains a cabinet minister and one of the most influential men in Canadian public life. Their parliamentary careers bear witness to the validity of Mosca's famous dictum, for even in a "society of peers," apparently, some members attain positions of power and influence, whereas others do not. This study tries to explain why. Before taking up the question, or acquainting the reader with the procedures we employed in answering it, some vignettes illustrating characteristics of opposition MPs may further acquaint the reader with the people who are the subjects of this book.

## FOUR MEMBERS OF THE OPPOSITION

One of these MPs, a power by any standard, is "Thomas W. Chaney," a sixty-eight-year-old member of the Progressive-Conservative frontbench, and a parliamentary veteran of some twenty years standing. His father, the late Donald W. Chaney, had been a member of several provincial cabinets and his grandfather, the late Weldon H. Chaney, had been a Conservative member in one of Canada's first parliaments. After a long career in municipal and provincial politics (he twice was mayor of the city in which he still resides) he entered parliament by winning a special by-election for a parliamentary seat that had been held by his party since Confederation. ("Mr. _____, the sitting member, personally picked me to succeed him.") He has a reputation for being one of the Conservative's most effective but least publicized frontbenchers. And, although he feels he may not contest the next election, he is an extremely active member of his caucus and a vigorous critic of the current government's programs. The words "decent," "humane," "gentlemanly," "honest," "honorable," and "trustworthy" are most frequently invoked by the members of his own and other parties to explain his influence and the value they ascribe to his advice. According to one of his warmest admirers, a Liberal cabinet minister, "Tom Chaney is the kind of man whose office you like to slip up to for a drink after a tough day. A hell of a decent man, a fine gentleman."

Another Conservative MP, though substantially less influential, is "Matt Reznowski." Reznowski is a huge man; six feet tall and weighing over three hundred pounds, he has fingers like sausages. Seated behind a desk in his parliamentary office, Reznowski looks like a huge smiling Buddha. It is only when he stands up and moves across a room with quick, almost graceful strides, that he reveals traces of the athletic ability that took him from an ethnic ghetto to the campus of a famous American university, and then to a career in professional athletics. He is a successful businessman who had never been even mildly interested in politics until he was approached in 1967 by some friends in the Conservative party and by a Catholic woman's group to contest the Conservative nomination in a newly formed constituency. He became his party's candidate for parliament, but only after two nominating conventions had been held: "I got a draw with three others the first time out. Two dropped out and I beat the 'establishment' candidate the second time."

He feels that parliament is not unlike an athletic contest. "You get along by playing ball. If you put out, and play fair, you're respected. If you play dirty and make yourself a pain in the ass, you're treated that way." Although he enjoys "working with people" and helping them "cut through the red tape," he feels this is not the way to "get ahead" in parliament. He is uncertain whether he will run for parliament again because he dislikes traveling to and from his constituency. Although he does not dwell on it, another reason for his indecision may be his frustration with what he perceives as his exclusion from the inner circle of his party. "Some of my esteemed colleagues think I'm a clown, great for playing Santa at the Christmas party, but that's all. But I get the job done, which is a sight more than can be said for some of them."

More sanguine about his personal influence, perhaps naively so, is "Paul Cloutier." A Creditiste MP and one of the youngest members of Canada's 28th Parliament, Cloutier's first rememberance of politics is the night his father left the Liberal party and became a supporter of Social Credit. Despite his father's defection, Cloutier thought of himself as a Liberal until June 8, 1962. "I was spending my holidays in _____. A cousin of mine came and got me to attend a meeting for Mr. _____, a Social Credit candidate for parliament that year. Since I was well educated and since well educated people are not supposed to understand Social Credit it really was supposed to be a big joke. But I was fascinated. It seemed to make such good sense, I spoke to Mr. _____ after the meeting and began to read anything about Social Credit I could get my hands on. I also began to canvas for the party although I must say I certainly didn't agree with Caouette (i.e., Real Caouette, national leader of the Social Credit party) at the time. In 1964 I got a job working part time for the party in Ottawa during the school year. I did research, I prepared questions for question period, helped write speeches—anything I was asked to do. I got to know people in the party and got their support at a nominating convention in 1964, before the 1965 election. Of course, I lost to _____ and went back to work for the party. But I tried again in 1968 and here I am."

For a first term MP, Cloutier speaks fairly often in the House but is only marginally involved in the activities of the three committees of which he is a member ("They are not important; they are shadow institutions of no influence at all on legislation."). His immediate goal is to elect fifty Creditiste members of parliament from the province of Quebec, a rather formidable goal given the historic strength of the Liberal party in that province. Cloutier is convinced that if he were a Liberal he would assuredly be a cabinet minister. ("You know what everyone says. Cloutier is smart, Cloutier is an excellent speaker. If he were a Liberal, he would be in the cabinet for sure.") However, there is some evidence to indicate that Cloutier's parliamentary colleagues did not entirely share his high opinion of himself. Not one included him in a list of ten most influential MPs and only one, a party colleague, felt that Cloutier's advice, opinions, and judgment were particularly valuable.

Not quite a power but certainly no one to be ignored, "George Rempel" is a member of the New Democratic Party. He is forty-nine years old and has fifteen years of parliamentary experience, having been elected initially in the mid-50s after two unsuccessful attempts to unseat an incumbent Liberal. He acknowledges that he takes pride in being something of a maverick and a prodder of the conscience of parliament. Indeed, he regards himself as the *enfant terrible* of both parliament ("I think I have been influential in changing the rules, the committee structure, and much of the House's ideas about decorum by screwing things up. I may not be the smartest person here, but I know the rules and how to use them") and his party ("There have been times when _____ wouldn't even look at me, let alone speak to me. Sometimes the rest of the caucus, other than _____, made me feel like a pariah. It's been lonely but I've tried not to let it bother me"). Rempel feels he has become an expert on parliament's procedures, that he is an extremely competent opposition MP, but doubts he would be a desirable or effective member of a governing party. ("I have developed a gift for being negative and for smelling out and exposing phonies. I feel I am a very competent opposition member but I would have a son-of-a-bitch of a time being a member of a Government. I tend to rebel against things that I feel are forced on me.")

He was both admired and disliked by the eight MPs who named him one of the ten most influential MPs. One of his nominators, a highly educated veteran Conservative MP, said of him, "Rempel is a demagogue and a bit of a bigot, a windy one at that. On the other hand I think there are a great many Canadians who are much happier today and enjoy life more because of George Rempel's presence in this House. I think it is fair to say that he and _____ affected a fundamental change in _____ legislation. He may be something of a character because he will stand up and say things that should be said—unpopular things, sometimes—and because he has the tenacity to keep saying them until something is done about them. So all-in-all I think the people of Canada have been well served over the years by George Rempel and those of his stripe."

## A CONCEPTUAL FRAMEWORK FOR EXPLAINING PARLIAMENTARY INFLUENCE

These vignettes reveal a number of interesting differences in the backgrounds and personalities of the men and women who become Canadian members of parliament. We find that some, like Mr. Chaney, are the scions of wealthy families that have been politically prominent in Canada for generations while others, like Messrs. Rempel and Reznowski, are reared in more modest and less politically stimulating circumstances. Some attend exclusive preparatory schools and take graduate and professional degrees in prestigious universities at home and abroad. Others, undoubtedly, are fortunate if they complete high school and spend a year or two at a local college. Some are interested and even actively involved in party politics in their teens. Others initially became active virtually on the eve of their candidacies. Some members work hard on all aspects of their jobs while others, like Mr. Cloutier, are quite selective in the application of their energies. Finally, some like Mr. O'Dare, attain highly visible positions of power in parliament and in the country; others, like Mr. Cyr, remain virtually unknown and without influence after years in office. Still others, like Mr. Fesler, despite their excellent preparation for the parliamentary position, their hard work, and their ambition for high office, are returned rather quickly to private life by a restless electorate.

As interesting and informative as these biographical sketches are from a literary point of view, they contribute very little to the systematic description and explanation of the behavior of individual members of parliament. Nor do they tell us much about why a few MPs attain power and position within parliament whereas the majority do not. In our view, we can shed more light on such matters if we develop an interrelated series of hypotheses whose validity can be tested by collecting and analyzing the appropriate data. Accordingly, we present for the reader's consideration a conceptual framework of the determinants of the influence attributed to members of a British model parliamentary system. It is derived from a somewhat mixed bag of theoretical assumptions, empirically-grounded generalizations and more-or-less informed speculations about the nature of mass and elite politics and the functioning of, and individual behavior within, the Canadian parliamentary system. The concepts and their relationships to one another are depicted schematically in figure 1. The framework postulates that the influence ascribed to Canadian MPs is a consequence of their holding formal positions of leadership and their participation in the several activities of parliament. Position-holding and participation, in turn, are seen as products of an extended process that has its origins in MPs' backgrounds and early life experiences.

More generally, the social backgrounds of MPs are assumed to affect how they will be socialized politically and both of these influences contribute to the ways they are recruited into the political system. In turn, recruitment (and political socialization) experiences are assumed to determine political attitudes and motivations that MPs develop. However, the current political environment also influences these attitudes and both affect opportunities to participate in parliamentary affairs and/or occupy a position of leadership. Opportunity acts as a kind of filter. On the one hand MPs who aspire to leadership positions and who want to participate in parliament's affairs must have the opportunity to do so. On the other hand

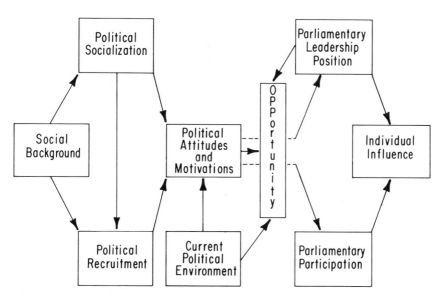

**FIGURE 1.1. A CONCEPTUAL FRAMEWORK OF THE DETERMINANTS OF INFLUENCE IN THE CANADIAN HOUSE OF COMMONS**

participation creates the opportunity to hold a leadership position, and occupancy of a leadership position provides the opportunity to participate. Finally, the attribution of influence to a MP is assumed to be a joint function of his occupancy of a leadership position and the extent to which he participates in parliamentary affairs.

This last statement may trouble some readers for two reasons. They may feel that the relationships between parliamentary participation and leadership positions on the one hand and parliamentary influence on the other are reciprocal. Alternatively, they may feel that participation and position simply are surrogate measures of influence. Regarding the first possibility, it may well be that leadership positions and the opportunity to participate extensively in parliament's affairs derive as much (or more) from being influential as being influential is a consequence of holding a leadership position and participating extensively. If subsequent tests of the model that will be generated from the conceptual framework suggest this is the case, then both the framework and the model will have served their principal purpose; the theoretical assumptions embedded in the framework can be revised to make them more congruent with reality. Similarly, if our analyses indicate that rather than being distinct the three concepts really are alternative measures of the same phenomenon, we will have made a valuable contribution to the way in which we should think about individual influence in a British-model parliamentary system.

Before we can test these two or any other theoretical assumptions underlying the conceptual framework schematized in figure 1, we first must operationalize the several concepts. For this purpose we have devised what, in our view, are appropriate indicators of concepts such as social background, political socialization, recruitment, and so forth. For example, ethnicity and religion are assumed to be good predictors of Canadian political behavior at all levels and thus are included among our social background indicators. The development of political interest and a psychological identification with a political party also are assumed to affect political behavior and are among the variables that are used to operationalize and measure the concept of political socialization. Only a minute proportion of the population of most Western societies ever holds an elected public office, but since office-holding experience, even at the local level, has been assumed to be an important predictor of whether political actors will aspire to higher public offices, office-holding experience, both public and party, are among the variables that we employ to operationalize the concept political recruitment. Among the variables that we used to operationalize the attitudes and motivations concept are the representational role perceptions of MPs, their aspirations for cabinet positions, their goals as parliamentarians, their desire for a public office other than member of parliament, and their attitudes toward making parliament a career. The concept of political environment has been operationalized with variables that previous research indicates are particularly salient for the behavior of members of parliament in free societies (e.g., the relative competitiveness of their constituencies, the length of their experience as parliamentarians, and their political knowledge and sophistication). We have operationalized leadership positions in terms of their relative importance, while participation is operationalized in terms of both formal activity on the floor of the House and in committee and informal, or behind-the-scenes, communications with constituents, cabinet ministers, and high level bureaucrats. Finally, influence is measured as the number of nominations each MP receives for being one of the ten most influential members of the House.

From the description immediately above the reader will have observed that we will be testing the causal and temporal order of relationships depicted in the conceptual framework with data that were derived largely from interviews with MPs taken at one point in time. This may have introduced an element of bias into the data. By way of illustration, we have hypothesized that attitudes and motivations will help determine whether or not a MP acquires a formal leadership position. The respondents' assessments of their attitudes and motivations, however, may have been affected by the fact that some already were leaders at the time the interviews were taken. There is greater potential for bias and error in the data that were used to operationalize the concepts of political socialization and recruitment. These data rely on the respondents' recollections of events that in some instances had occurred many years ago. The recognized hazards involved in this procedure have been most succinctly outlined in a paper by Richard Niemi.[1] We were cognizant of these hazards and accordingly included a number of probes in our survey instrument to check the accuracy of the events and the time periods recalled by the respondents. Even if there is bias or recall error present in the data, however, it can be argued that the inclusion of such biases may be important for properly assessing the residual or indirect effects of a variable—such as the age of a first awareness of politics—on some aspect of adult political behavior (indirect effects together with direct and spurious effects are assessed and reported in chapter 9). The nature of the current impact of an earlier event or experience may be determined largely by one's perceptions or recollections of the event, however inaccurate or biased these recollections may be. John Honigmann says as much when he reminds us "that the past doesn't operate from the past like a physical force continuously extending into the present. The past is gone and currently can do nothing except as its traces continue here and now to act in the minds and bodies of men."[2]

A more pragmatic reason for utilizing data largely gathered at one point in time to test relationships that develop over an extended time period is that their use has enabled us to study, and hopefully to better understand, the complex process through which, over time, a very exclusive subpopulation of current adults has acquired influence in an elite political institution. Because there is no way of predicting which of the thousands of Canadians born annually will become influential members of parliament, to have studied the process longitudinally—by, let us say, following a group of children through to the stage of life at which we encountered the MPs—would have required a population sample of immense size and the commitment of the whole of our professional lives. Parenthetically, financial support for such a vast and extended undertaking might have been rather difficult to find.

### INFLUENCE IN PARLIAMENT: NOTES ON THE ORGANIZATION OF THE STUDY

Strictly speaking, figure 1 is a conceptual framework, not an operational model. Its value is that it identifies and relates broad clusters of variables believed to be determinants of individual influence in parliament. It does little, however, to enable us to predict or explain influence in a systematic and empirical fashion. This objective can best be achieved by transforming the conceptual framework in figure 1 into an operational model in which the variables (analogues of each concept) are explicitly defined and measured, and the relationships between and among them are specified and estimated. Much of this study is devoted to these tasks.

Chapter 1 begins by describing the basic features of the parliamentary system and by surveying the historical development of these structural features during the 100 plus years of parliament's existence. Following an attempt to relate the formal structures of parliament both to the distribution of influence in parliament and to the evolving role of parliament in society, chapter 2 presents statistical profiles of the members of the 28th Parliament and of the members of each of the four parties.

In chapter 3, we begin the process of converting the conceptual diagram in figure 1 into a model of individual influence. Chapter 3 is concerned with operationalizing and measuring the concept of influence and with the manner in which it is distributed in parliament as a whole and among various party and regional subgroups of members. Chapters 4 and 5, like chapter 3, are given over largely to questions of measurement and description. In chapter 4 we examine the structure of individual participation in the formal activities of parliament. Our purpose here and in chapter 5 (in which we consider the informal dimensions of participation) is two-fold. First, we attempt to identify and measure the several forms of individual activity in parliament. Second, we delineate the extent to which different categories of MPs engage in the different types of activities available to them.

Having concentrated upon operationalizing the primary concepts of influence, position, and participation in chapters 3 through 5, chapter 6 begins our assessment of the extent to which these concepts are related. Employing two multivariate analytical procedures, we try to determine the relative independent effects upon individual influence of the several forms of participation and types of parliamentary leadership positions. Chapter 7 is concerned with the determinants of parliamentary participation and, in particular, with the operationalization and measurement of the impact of attitudes and motivations and of current and early life political experiences upon variations in participation in the formal activities of the House—debate on the House floor, participation in committees, and the introduction of private members' bills and debatable resolutions in the House. Chapter 8 is identical to 7 in organization and purpose except that its concern is with delineating the factors that distinguish leaders from nonleaders. More specifically, we not only will compare the social and political backgrounds of leaders and nonleaders in the four parliamentary parties, but we also will try to determine whether their recruitment experiences and their current attitudes and perspectives differ. We will extend these comparisons to Conservative frontbenchers and Liberal cabinet members. Finally, we will compare top echelon leaders in the governing Liberal party (cabinet ministers) with their cohort of middle-level leaders, the chairmen of the several standing committees of parliament. In chapter 9 we attempt to summarize and integrate the information developed in the preceding chapters by constructing and validating a number of causal models based upon our framework. We employ these models to elaborate the network of direct and indirect pathways to influence followed by members of the Liberal and Conservative parliamentary parties.

In our concluding chapter we try to suggest how the data and the models contribute to an increased understanding of the way that parliament functions in Canadian society.

*Chapter* 1

## THE EVOLUTION OF THE CANADIAN HOUSE OF COMMONS: AN OVERVIEW

This is a book about the Canadian House of Commons, one of the oldest continuously functioning parliamentary bodies in the world. More specifically, this book describes and tries to explain variations in the extent and character of individual participation in the formal and behind-the-scenes activities in which members of parliament engage; how these are affected by the backgrounds, the values and perspectives of members, and the formal positions they hold; and how these, in turn, are related to the amount of influence they enjoy.

The institution of parliament and virtually all of the procedures it initially followed were transported from Great Britain via the legislative bodies[1] of the Crown colonies that united in 1867 to form the new Dominion of Canada. In the hundred plus years that have passed since Canada formally became a nation, the country has changed from a small, economically underdeveloped, largely rural society to an advanced urban-industrial country of some twenty-two million people currently enjoying a standard of living that is one of the highest in the world. During this same period parliament also has experienced some notable changes. For one thing its membership has increased from 181 members in the first House to 264 in the 28th—the House that is the subject of this book. For another, the House of Commons long has exercised primary responsibility for making public policy in the form of legislation, despite the fact the Senate still retains (at least in theory) the formidable set of legislative muscles with which that body was equipped by the British North

America Act. Because this is the case, we will use the terms parliament and House of Commons interchangeably.

Since this book is concerned with individual as well as collective behavior in the 28th Parliament, we can describe only briefly selected aspects of the major dimensions of change that have occurred during the past century. Nonetheless, even this limited description can provide a useful background against which the analyses and discussions that follow can be interpreted. In this chapter we first will briefly describe some of the changes that have occurred in the composition of the House membership since 1867, since these can suggest some of the changes in the skills and experiences that members have brought to the institution over time. Next we will describe some of the changes that have been made in formal procedures and the evolution of informal arrangements under which the House has functioned. Rules of procedure help maintain the viability of legislative organizations by regularizing and making predictable the behavior of legislators. Procedures also constrain and systematize the activities of the legislature as an organization. In so doing, however, they help determine—to borrow Harold Laswell's phrase— "who gets what, when and how." Thus, an examination of the directions and of the patterns of procedural changes also may shed light on some of the changes that have occurred over the years in the relative statuses of governing versus opposition parties and of cabinets as opposed to private members.

Any consideration of these matters, of course, involves us in a discussion of changes that have occurred in the structure and function of the cabinet and particularly the office of the prime minister; in a consideration of the growth of standing committees and of what these committees currently do that they did not do in the past; and in a discussion of changes that have taken place in the ways that legislative parties operate. These admittedly cursory descriptions are intended to inform this chapter's concluding speculations on whether or not the Canadian parliament has declined in power and importance duringing the past century.

### THE MEMBERS: 1867–1972

A number of empirical studies of the social and political backgrounds of Canadian MPs have made clear that in comparison to a cross section of the population MPs always have been an elite group. Indeed, in an intensive analysis of the freshman members of the

House of Commons from 1867 to 1963 Roman R. March found that a significant proportion of 19th century freshman members were what he termed "Notables."[2] Although the proportion of Notables who were elected to parliament declined as the suffrage was extended to previously excluded groups, other studies have indicated that the House remains an institution with a membership that is remarkably atypical of the Canadian public.[3] For example, the proportion of MPs enjoying high status occupations has never been less than 60% whereas no more than 15% of the public ever has enjoyed such occupations. Moreover, differences in educational attainment between MPs and members of the public always have been great, and given the correlation between occupation, education, and income, we may infer that social background differences between MPs and average citizens extend to income levels as well.

As one might expect, the level of political involvement of MPs before their election to parliament also has differed drastically from the political involvement of average citizens. Longitudinal studies indicate that substantial proportions of MPs have held local and provincial public offices (either elective or appointive) before winning election to parliament.[4] Even larger numbers of MPs have been active in party politics, holding offices at either the constituency, provincial, or national levels. Many have been important organizational figures at all three levels. Although we lack the kinds of historical data on mass political participation that we could use to compare the general public with MPs, recent studies strongly suggest that differences in the political backgrounds and experiences that have existed between MPs on the one hand and the Canadian public on the other are at least as great as are the socioeconomic differences that always have characterized them.[5] Clearly then, MPs, in comparison to the Canadian population, are a socioeconomic and political elite and always have been.

Not unexpectedly, members of the several federal cabinets may be said to constitute an "elite-within-an-elite" in that they stand in approximately the same relationship to backbenchers as do the latter to the general public.[6] With regard to differences in political background, for example, cabinet members generally have tended to be younger men than those who were not appointed to the cabinet. Yet, on the average, they have had more tenure in the House and more extensive office-holding experience before becoming MPs than non-cabinet colleagues. Moreover, the kinds of offices they have held before their election to parliament have tended to distinguish them from the rank and file members: cabinet members are more likely to have held offices in provincial legislatures whereas noncabinet members have tended to have held local public offices. Insofar as social status differences are concerned, cabinet members have tended to be better educated and have enjoyed more prestigious occupations at the time of their election to parliament.

If, then, MPs generally and cabinet members in particular always have constituted a socioeconomic and political elite, in what ways has the social composition of the membership of the Commons changed in the past century? The answer is that it has not changed very much. Certainly it has not changed much in comparison to the social and economic changes that have characterized Canadian society as a whole during the past century.[7] But there have been some changes in their socioeconomic backgrounds and the most important may be summarized as follows. (1) Given the decline in the election of "Notables," the occupational prestige scores of MPs (although not of cabinet ministers) have declined somewhat. It should be emphasized, however, that the majority of each House has been made up of men who are business executives/proprietors and members of the several professions, principally lawyers. Indeed, about one-third of the members of any House have been lawyers. (2) The educational level of the House has increased over time. (3) Members' ages at the time of their first election to parliament have risen. (4) The ethnic composition of the House has changed somewhat to reflect the substantial increase in Canadian immigration from Eastern, Central and Southern Europe which began in the last decade of the 19th century.

The most striking changes are those that have occurred in the political rather than the social backgrounds of members. First, an increasingly smaller proportion of members—both cabinet and backbenchers—have held public offices prior to their election to parliament. Indeed, fewer MPs today have had the experience of being a candidate, let alone winning a public office, before their election to parliament. Second, their tenure in parliament has tended to decrease. Third, over time the proportion of members who have retired voluntarily (rather than because of electoral defeat) has decreased. Fourth, the number of members who gained their parliamentary seat in an uncontested election has declined precipitously, a reflection, undoubtedly, of the growth of party organizations within the electorate during the 20th century. Fifth, and consonant with the growth and increasing importance of party organization both within and outside of parliament, the number of independents elected to parliament and the switching of party loyalties after elections have declined.[8] In fact, so rare has it become for members to cross the aisle that on the occasions when this does occur, the incident is widely reported and discussed.

## FORMAL PROCEDURAL CHANGES

If the social composition and the political attributes of House members have not changed radically in the past century, the formal procedural rules that govern the activities of MPs certainly have.[9] These changes until very recently have tended to be asymmetrical. That is, they have been largely in the direction of limiting both the time and the formal opportunity available to private members to participate in the process of drafting and evaluating legislation. As has been indicated, the first Canadian parliament accepted British-model parliamentary government and its rules of procedure almost in total. Those rules had their origins in the 17th and early 18th centuries, a period which, in comparison to the present, afforded almost unlimited opportunities for individual MPs to represent the unique interests of their constituencies, to participate in a leisurely fashion in parliamentary deliberations, and to look over the shoulder of the executive. These rules were appropriate in preconfederation provincial legislatures and in 19th century Canadian parliaments for many of the same reasons that they had been suited to the parliament of the mother country a century earlier (e.g., the society was largely rural and agricultural, the population was small, the electorate was limited, party organization was skeletal, and the scope of governmental activity was narrow). From 1867 to 1906, the House operated under a set of rules that permitted fairly broad participation by individual members in all stages of the legislative process: the introduction and discussion of private member bills consumed a considerable proportion of the House's time; private member bills dealing with particularistic subjects constituted a substantial proportion of the legislation receiving Royal Assent; and the government made no serious moves either to increase its control of the House's time or to accelerate the pace at which legislation made its way through the House.

It labors the obvious to note that in this century the Canadian population has increased greatly and shifted from rural to urban and suburban areas, three new provinces have been added, internal communications and industry have developed, trade has increased and the scope of governmental activities has broadened to include areas that were part of the private domain in the 19th century. Both parliamentary executives and parliamentary scholars[10] have tended to cite the demands created by these changes to explain the ascendancy of the executive over the legislative branch of government in almost all liberal and social democracies. It is proper that a government's policy proposals be carefully scrutinized, that the interests of minorities be protected, and that the opposition be given adequate opportunity to put its views and perspectives before the public. But it is equally proper that a government which has won an election will have the opportunity to carry its programs and policies through parliament—or so it is generally argued.[11]

In Canada successive governments have tried to carry out their perceived mandates in four related ways: (1) by insuring that the consideration of government legislation takes calendar and time precedence over private members' proposals; (2) by controlling the time the House may debate and discuss each bill; (3) by limiting the opportunities available to private members of the House either to initiate legislative proposals or to participate in their evaluation; and (4) by controlling access to information for members both in active restraint and passive nonresponse to requests. The first serious steps to control what legislation would be considered, by whom and under what conditions were taken during the period 1906–1913. Very briefly, Standing Order 26 (hereafter we will use the letters S.O. for Standing Order), which was modified in 1906, restricted both the numbers of times and the circumstances under which private members could offer motions for adjournment of the House in order to discuss matters they considered important. These changes at one and the same time enhanced the government's control over the House's business and restricted the speaking opportunities available to private members. Another rule change required that speeches be "relevant" while still others placed limits on the numbers and the kinds of motions that could be debated. Since 1927 time limits also have been imposed on members' speeches. These limits subsequently have been reduced and varied according to the type of business before the House.

During the period 1927–1961 numerous changes were made in the rules governing the introduction and discussion of private member bills. Not only did such bills lose the preeminence they sometimes had enjoyed over government bills during the 19th century, but the opportunities available to introduce and discuss them were so severely restricted that their utility as a vehicle for initiating legislation was effectively ended.[12] Other procedural changes placed restrictions on the time and opportunities available to private members to participate in the debates on the Budget, the Throne speech and on motions to move into Committee of the Whole to consider government requests for Supply. Such debates long had afforded members an opportunity to offer general criticism of the policies of a government.

Many of the most sweeping changes, proposed by a select Committee on Procedure, were implemented in 1969. The principal ones were: (1) the "streamlining" of the several processes through which prospective legislation passes while not unduly restricting individual opportunity to participate in these processes;[13] (2) the formalization of previously informal arrangements between the House Leader of the government party on one hand and the House Leaders of the opposition parties on the other regarding the substance of business and the order in which it would be taken up by the House; (3) the potential limitation of each of the several stages of debate by guillotine-like procedures (i.e., S.O. 75 a, b, c)[14] (formerly a government had only two procedural measures available for terminating debate on an issue, the draconian and infrequently used "Closure" and "Previous Question" motions);[15] (4) the virtual abandonment of the use of the Committee of the Whole both for debate of broad policy questions (e.g., by means of motions to consider Supply, Ways and Means, etc.) and for clause-by-clause consideration of legislation; and (6) the formal limitation of question time to one hour on Mondays and to 40 minutes on all other days.[16]

In place of the opportunity Supply and Budget motions formerly provided for the discussion of broad policy questions, there are now 28 allotted days in each parliamentary session in which opposition members may discuss Supply or, for that matter, any other subject within parliament's jurisdiction. An additional six days are allotted to a general debate on the Budget. Moreover, eight days also are given over to a general policy debate following the Throne speech. All other prospective legislation is routinely sent to one of 18 standing committees or to an ad hoc special committee.[17] We shall comment on the committee system shortly. For the present it should be noted that although a time limit was placed on question period, (S.O. 39[5]) any member who feels his question has been unsatisfactorily answered has been provided with an opportunity to raise the matter again (S.O. 39[6] and S.O. 40) during an adjournment debate from 10:00–10:30 p.m. on any Monday, Tuesday, or Thursday, labeled "the late show."

More important perhaps than the changes that have been made in formal procedures are the myriad informal arrangements that have arisen to facilitate the performance of old tasks and the assumption of new ones. These informal arrangements derive from the access to cabinet members and senior bureaucrats afforded private members as a consequence of all three groups working on or near Parliament Hill. The most frequent interactions probably occur between members of the governing party, but opposition MPs enjoy the same access and reasonably may expect a certain number of favorable decisions from the ministers and bureaucrats they petition. Not only do bureaucrats try to avoid the unprofessional and imprudent posture of partisanship, but the governing party hesitates to alienate the opposition needlessly by refusing to consider requests or rendering unfavorable decisions in areas of low salience. Some of the forces mentioned earlier that help explain the current preeminence of executive over legislature also help explain the modification in the role of the MP since the 19th century. The average population of the constituency he represents, for example, has grown from 19,133 in 1867 to 75,514 in 1966. While the population increased, the socioeconomic structure of the society also has changed dramatically. The average proportion of population between five and nineteen years of age attending school increased from 51% in the period 1871–1901 to 76% in the period 1941–1966.[18] These educational increases helped produce occupational heterogeneity among other changes which strongly affected the structure of Canadian society. Concomitant with these societal changes, government moved into areas that were previously the preserves of other agencies. All of these factors combined to modify the role of the MP in three significant ways. First, because the electorate is larger and so much more varied than was the case in the 1800s, the MP has had to spend an increasing proportion of his time and resources monitoring grass roots opinion. As will be demonstrated later in this book, a variety of survey research techniques are used to tap representative views from the major population groups. The results often become the basis of an MP's inputs into caucus discussions and occasionally affect the policy positions his parliamentary party takes in the House. Second, for a variety of reasons, increased political efficacy has accompanied the rising socioeconomic status of the voters in Canada as in other Western liberal and social democracies.[19] Larger numbers of people write MPs requesting information and assistance and expect replies than was the case even as recently as a generation ago. Consequently, a greater portion of an MP's day must be devoted to responding to requests of this kind. Finally, because government affects so many facets of modern life, the MP has been forced to assume ombudsman-like tasks for his constituents and to help them wend their ways through what they regard as ever-increasing layers of bureaucratic red tape. As a result of these new demands on their time and energies, MPs have less time to devote to the preparation of speeches dealing with the great issues of the day for delivery on the floor of the House or for the consideration of major policy alternatives to those presented by government and opposition although these historically have been the primary tasks of MPs in parliamentary systems of the British model.

## QUEST FOR INFORMATION: RESEARCH FACILITIES

"To live effectively'" Norbert Wiener has written, "is to live with adequate information."[20] Adequate information also is necessary if legislatures, or, indeed, if complex social organizations of any kind, are to function effectively. Traditionally there have been three ways in which the members of most Western legislative bodies have acquired information: (1) through independent research or through the research efforts of a competent personal staff or a structure such as a legislative reference service; (2) by asking questions of and soliciting information from the executive and the administrative bureaucracy; and (3) by means of discussion and testimony offered at hearings and meetings of special and standing legislative committees. Members of parliament, of course, vary with respect to their intellectual ability, their interest in their work and their willingness to seek information that would facilitate the performance of their tasks. Consequently, it is reasonable to assume that even without any staff assistance, members still would do (and, in fact, are doing) a great deal of their own information-gathering. In Canada, however, for over 100 years these efforts have been facilitated by a Library of Parliament that was initially formed by amalgamating the legislative libraries of Upper and Lower Canada after these two provinces were united into the province of Canada in 1841.

Control of the Library of Parliament[21] is vested in the Speaker of the Senate and the Speaker of the House of Commons, assisted by a joint committee appointed by the members of each body. The library serves the Senate and the House in both a reference and research capacity. The Reference Branch of the library tries to respond to the many daily routine requests for information and assistance from MPs. Thus, for example, the staff provides source materials for use in speeches, prepares bibliographies, indexes and abstracts and maintains and makes available to MPs a vertical file and clipping service. The Research Branch, established in 1965, handles more complex and time-consuming requests for assistance from Senators and MPs. It maintains a staff of approximately 35 people that includes lawyers, political scientists, economists, and other professionals. These researchers prepare relatively lengthy and comprehensive research papers on a variety of topics.[22] When time permits, the Research Branch also provides direct staff assistance to standing and special parliamentary committees and to parliamentary associations.

In addition to the assistance provided by the two branches of the parliamentary library, every MP has two secretaries. Whenever he requires, he also can secure additional clerical help from a secretarial pool maintained for the House. The Leader of the Opposition is provided with a staff of three. Cabinet members, as might be expected, are provided with public funds with which they generally hire three of four administrative assistants, a personal secretary, and three or four clerk-typists. In comparison to the staff and research resources available to an American Congressman, the services provided to Canadian MPs are meager. In comparison to the staff and research resources available to the members of most other Western legislative bodies, however, the Canadian MP is rather well served.[23]

Canadian MPs now have available additional staff to gather and organize information. In 1969, $125,000 of public funds were allocated to the official opposition, the Progressive-Conservatives, and $35,000 each to the New Democratic and Creditiste parties. These funds were to be used for the salaries of research assistants. In the spring of 1970 an additional $130,000 of public funds were provided for research staff for the Liberal party caucus. According to Edwin R. Black, the governing Liberal party was willing to use public funds for these purposes because Prime Minister Trudeau recognized that MPs, especially in the opposition parties, required additional assistance if they were to perform their tasks more effectively.[24] The prime minister also recognized that the governing party's position vis-a-vis the opposition is enhanced by the fact that the leaders of the former can draw upon and make use of the human and technical resources of the administrative bureaucracy in a variety of ways whereas the latter cannot.[25] According to Prime Minister Trudeau,

> ... the intent of this measure is to enable leaders of the opposition parties to avail themselves of some technical facilities, to resort to the services of economists, sociologists, jurists, and to alleviate their difficult duty in criticizing the government's legislative measures. . . . The intention is, of course, not that these funds be employed for political organization or narrow partisan purposes but that they be employed directly as an aid to parliamentary work.[26]

Although Mr. Trudeau may very well have intended that the research assistance that was being provided not be used for "various partisan purposes," in fact, the parties have varied considerably in the extent to which they have used their research staff for precisely those purposes. By way of illustration, the Research Office of the Liberal party is primarily made up of young social scientists. Each of the six committees of the Liberal caucus (economic, social policy, cultural, foreign affairs, national and human resources, and environment and urban affairs) has one of these young social scientists assigned to it and, in effect, the researcher works for the committee under the direction of its chairman. The staff member prepares background papers on current and prospective legislation, provides the committee with data on the distribution of public attitudes on matters of concern to it and so forth. When parliament is not in session, however, the research office staff also will service the needs of individual members. Presumably the purpose of at least some of these requests from members is political.

The initial intention of the first Director of Research for the Conservative party caucus was to organize his staff in much the same way as the Liberals have done. However, almost immediately intense pressure was brought on him to service the requests of individual members, particularly to write speeches for members. The party's national organization also put pressure on the Research Office to coordinate its activities in ways that would enhance the political status of the Conservative party in and out of parliament. Although the Research Director and his successor tried to resist these pressures, it seems that the Conservative caucus has used its research staff primarily for political purposes. And, although the use of the staff in this manner may have upset its first director,[27] it can be argued that a basic principle underlying the operation of a parliamentary system of the British model is that the same party will not always control the instruments of government. Thus, any staff work that helps make this principle a reality by facilitating the political defeat of a current government may be justified as being consonant with the theory of parliamentary democracy.

The research offices of both the New Democratic and Creditiste parliamentary parties also appear to be employed for partisan purposes, but primarily to help realize the objectives of their respective party leaders. Secondarily, they have tried to assist the party caucus as a whole, and to the extent that time and resources have permitted, they also have tried to satisfy individual requests for service from MPs. Given the relatively short time since the establishment of research facilities for the use of the several parties, it is difficult to predict the manner and the extent to which they will develop. If Black's description of the problems that arose in the Conservative caucus because of its use of the staff can be generalized to the other parties, we may assume that conflicting demands will continue to be made upon research personnel and that the latter's view of their roles and the roles that MPs ascribe to them will continue to differ. That is, the research people, since most of them are professionals, probably will want to devote the bulk of their effort to developing comprehensive, in-depth, reports that can become the basis of party positions on major policy issues. However, the MPs, subject as they are to the vicissitudes of electoral fortune, will probably want to engage them in tasks that will improve their chances of reelection.[28]

### QUESTIONS

A second vehicle that members of parliament use to obtain information is question period. Indeed, this is one of the most important procedures in British-model parliamentary systems. Technically, questions to the administration are asked before the first "Order" for any day and are referred to as "Questions asked on the Orders of the Day." As is well known, during this time any member who catches the eye of the Speaker can ask any cabinet minister a question. Although in theory these questions should seek information from the government, and should be "concise, factual, and free of opinion and argument which might lead to debate,"[29] in practice, opposition members have tried, at least some of the time, to use this device to embarrass cabinet members individually and the governing party collectively. Consequently, it is not surprising that over time the several governments have implemented a series of procedural changes whose purpose is to limit the opposition's opportunities to elicit potentially embarrassing information. Thus, for example, in 1906 ministers were permitted to treat certain oral questions as notices of motions that could be transferred to different sections of the Order papers. Once transferred, they could be answered at the pleasure of the minister. In 1910 the rules were changed again to enable a minister to offer a written reply to a question unless a member specifically asked for an oral reply. Another change permitted a minister at his own discretion to turn an oral question into an order for a written reply to be tabled in the House at a later date. As might be expected, this tactic was used either to delay answering a question or to bury answers to potentially embarrassing questions. More important, a minister simply could refuse to answer any question and his refusal could not be made the subject of a second question nor could it be raised as a matter of privilege.

Generally, rather than refusing outright to answer a question, ministers will offer the more expedient reason of the "public interest." Questioning of cabinet ministers periodically has brought to light and helped to rectify administrative abuses. However, students of Canadian politics are generally agreed that the question period falls short of being an instrument that could elicit the kind of information that would afford parliament any substantial measure of control over a government. Largely because of the high rate of turnover of members and a lack of expert staff assistance, questions frequently tend to be clumsily and inappropriately worded; they tend also to be based on limited or incorrect information. Consequently, a substantial proportion are ruled out of order by the speaker. Many questions also tend to be trivial.[30] Nonetheless, opposition members continue to value the question period highly and questions continue to produce periodic heated exchanges—not only between government and opposition members but also between members of the opposition parties. Because they do, the spectator galleries invariably are packed for the beginning of an afternoon sitting, a very clear indication that question period continues to be regarded both by members of the public and representatives of the media as the most interesting and popular part of the legislative day.

## COMMITTEE SYSTEM

The vehicle that legislative bodies often have used to gather information that can be employed to formulate and evaluate public policy and to scrutinize the actions of a government has been the legislative committee. Legislatures, like other complex social organizations, vary in size, and the size of the House of Commons has grown steadily over the years—from 181 members in 1867 to 200 members in 1872, to 211 in 1882, to 213 in 1892, to 214 in 1903, to 234 in 1914, to 245 in 1924, to 265 in 1952.[31] Although larger size makes available more human resources, it also decreases opportunities for individual participation. This is especially true of legislatures, since legislatures tend to be oriented toward the achievement of specific goals within reasonable time limits. Given this orientation, it follows that the greater the number of individuals who participate in the legislature's requisite deliberations and activities, the longer the time required to realize specific goals. The use of committees, however, tends to vitiate the effects of large size on opportunities for individual participation in parliament's work because it increases both the number of opportunities and the length of time available for individuals to participate. At least this is one way in which the creation and utilization of parliamentary committees has been rationalized. Thus, the Canadian parliament always (or almost always) has had legislative committees. These generally have been of three kinds: Committees of the Whole House,[32] Special Committees, and Standing Committees. The number of committees and their titles have been governed by the Standing Orders of the House.

Unfortunately, in the view of most parliamentary scholars, committees have had relatively little impact on the work of parliament. For example, in evaluating the work of standing committees before 1965, Dawson and Ward noted that not only did most standing committees meet infrequently, but indeed that years passed in which committees never met.[33] Their assessment of ad hoc special committees also was negative.[34] There are a number of reasons why committees in the Canadian House of Commons may have played less important roles over the years than they have in other legislative bodies. First, their membership has tended to be large. For example, in 1887 the average membership on parliamentary committees was well over 100 and although the number of members on committees occasionally was reduced somewhat, they were still large enough (an average of 35–60 members until 1965) to severely limit opportunities available for members to participate. Second, in Canada many MPs have been reluctant to delegate certain functions that in theory are the prerogative of all members to committees made up of only a few members. Third, cabinets, regardless of their party label, have been extremely reluctant to countenance rivals, to permit committees to develop too great a power of initiative for fear they might evolve into something like United States Congressional committees. Rightly or wrongly the concern has been that a strong committee system would usurp the powers and responsibilities that in Canada by custom belong to the cabinet.[35] Fourth, the Canadian parliament (in part because of the aforementioned unwillingness to delegate power and responsibility to a few) historically has made great use of the Committee of the Whole, a device not particularly suited either to the enhancement of individual participation or to speedy deliberations. As one minister noted in explaining and defending the substantial procedural changes implemented in 1969,

> We were trying to do certain kinds of very important business in highly unsuitable forums or theatres. We were trying to examine the spending estimates for each fiscal year, department by department, vote by vote, in the Committee of Supply, a committee composed of all the Members of the House. This meant that about 260 Members were being asked to focus their attention on a vast spectrum of topics, to listen to the speeches delivered for the benefit of the voters back home, and to cover all the work thoroughly and expeditiously. A vainer, more unrealistic request is hard to imagine. We were trying also to conduct the clause-by-clause analysis of all public bills in a committee of the whole House.[36]

Yet another impediment to the more extensive and effective use of committees by the Canadian House of Commons is that they have not had the assistance of specialized staff. As another former minister noted in commenting on changes proposed in the committee system in 1960,

> You can have all the committees you want . . . but if you do not have the facilities for them to do their work, what are they going to do? . . . we have not got the clerical staff . . . we have not the translators, we have not even the committee rooms.[37]

Since in addition to lacking adequate staff, the opportunities available for committees to meet also were restricted, their efforts generally produced reports such as the one described by the former MP, Douglas Fisher:

> The report was a pastiche of the ideas, even whims, of six or seven of the more active members, including myself. It was pieced together in parts in an atmosphere of hurry, 'let's have done with it!'; the evidence, 100 pages in print, was not digested by the committee or even by smaller subcommittees.

In sum, it was uneven and amateurish, finished with a rush, and unrelated to the overall policy of the government and its financial position.[38]

There was wide-spread agreement that the committees, as they then were functioning, were contributing little to the work of parliament, and a number of changes in their structure and operation were proposed in 1965 and again in 1968 by the Committee on Procedure. As a consequence of these suggestions certain changes eventually were implemented. First, the number of standing committees was reduced to 18, each with no more than 20 members except the Committees on Agriculture and External Affairs which have no more than 30 members, and the Committee on Private Bills and Standing Orders and on Procedure and Organization which have 12 members each.[39]  Second, all clause-by-clause evaluation of legislation is now conducted by the appropriate standing committees after which the bill is sent back to the House for a third and final reading without again being considered by Committee of the Whole.[40]  Third, estimates of expenditures proposed by the several ministries also are sent to standing committees for consideration. Finally, committees may consider general social issues, may conduct investigations and acquire information relevant to these issues, and may prepare reports for consideration by the whole House.

With respect to their current operation, the composition of each committee reflects (more-or-less) the distribution of party strength in the House. A member of the governing party chairs all but the Public Accounts Committee (which functions as a watch dog of government spending). Cabinet ministers, the speaker and his deputy, and the leader of the opposition are not normally members of standing committees although parliamentary secretaries are. In fact, the parliamentary secretary on each of the committees acts as a kind of government whip. Officially, the members of the several standing committees are appointed by a Committee of Selection composed of party whips. In practice, the committee merely endorses the choices that previously have been made by individual MPs and agreed to by their respective whips. A member is free to change committees, the only requirement being that he notify the government whip who in turn notifies the Clerk of the House. Unlike the chairmen of standing committees of the American Congress, Canadian committee chairmen largely tend to be presiding officers. Their principal task is to insure that each committee member has an opportunity to speak, to question expert witnesses, etc. Generally the staff of each committee currently is limited to a clerk,[41] who, under the chairman's direction, arranges the meeting, calls witnesses, and performs all the necessary clerical work related to the committee's work.

As was indicated, committees not only engage in clause-by-clause evaluation of prospective legislation and scrutinize the estimates of the several departments of government, they also are free to investigate and report on matters relevant to the substantive policy area with which the committee is concerned. A reasonable estimate is that the standing committees now spend about 50% of their time considering the estimates of the departments and divide the remainder of their time between scrutinizing current legislation and conducting investigations, collecting information on particular problems and preparing reports for the consideration of the House. Their reports, when submitted, are not normally debated. Since the government is free to ignore any policy recommendations they may contain, it has permitted the committees a relatively free hand in these matters, to date.[42] Understandably the government is far less inclined to accept amendments to the legislation it proposes. In fact, some concern has been expressed that the committees at times generate collegial attitudes that cut across party lines and thereby pose a potential threat to cohesive party action. According to Thomas A. Hockin,

> The Minister of Agriculture and the Minister of Justice spent many hours in the summer of 1969 consulting with committee members on proposed legislation thus recognizing the political reality that both the Agriculture and the Justice Committees were developing attitudes of their own; attitudes sometimes at variance with government policy. The price to a government of a standing committee becoming conversant, even expert, in a policy area may be the establishment of a policy-idea source which is independent of party and of the public service. The price for excessive collegiality might be to break down party lines on policy altogether.[43]

Whether the changes that have been made in the structure and operation of the Canadian committee system ultimately may threaten the current institution, or whether, instead, the changes are largely cosmetic but highly functional in the sense they provide members (especially the government's backbenchers) with "busy work" and leave Cabinet freer to govern than in the past, are interesting questions. Unfortunately, the changes that have been made are of such recent origin that answers cannot be posited with any degree of confidence. Although this is one of the questions we will address in this study, more certain is the fact that Cabinet, and particularly the office of the prime minister, has changed in ways that have markedly affected the operation of parliament. We will now briefly describe the substance and direction of the most important changes.

## CABINET AND PRIME MINISTER

> There shall be a Council to aid and advise in the Government of Canada to be styled the Queen's Privy Council for Canada; and the Persons who are to be Members of the Council shall be from Time to Time chosen and summoned by the Governor-General and sworn in as Privy Councillors, and members thereof may be from Time to Time removed by the Governor-General. (Section II, BNA Act)

As may be observed, the British North America Act makes no mention of any entity termed "cabinet." Nevertheless, the cabinet[44] is the Canadian Executive, while apart from two or three ceremonial occasions the privy council never has met. The distinctions among terms such as privy council, committee of the privy council, and cabinet have been made a number of times by constitutional experts and need not concern us here. It is sufficient to note that the terms "cabinet" and "cabinet council" are employed as synonyms and that in Canadian usage the terms "ministry," "administration," "executive," and "government" are also used interchangeably.[45] The cabinet is a legislative, executive, and administrative body. Each of the several departments of government is headed and administered by a cabinet minister. Collectively it decides upon the content of the legislative program the government will pursue during any parliamentary session. It executes decisions in the form of Orders-in-Council and Treasury Board Minutes and also makes judicial and other highest level appointments to public office. Collectively, the cabinet also is responsible to parliament for the conduct and the administration of governmental departments.

The cabinet is headed and presided over by a prime minister. The British prime minister used to be described as primus inter pares and as the keystone of the cabinet arch. Bernard Crick contends these labels are no longer adequate. "He is not merely the keystone, but the foundation stone and the cement for all other stones as well."[46] He observes that the prime minister's current exalted status is a direct consequence of the expansion of the electorate. With the achievement of universal suffrage, the electorate more and more chooses among party leaders rather than local party candidates or the parties themselves. No political party can afford to choose a leader who does not promise it a reasonable chance to succeed at the polls. His importance is magnified by the fact that he also is the only member of the government who is highly visible to the public. [47] Although parties are able to project fairly well defined images, these images do not depend on the public's capacity to distinguish figures in each party's cadre of secondary leaders. Thus, a prime minister justifiably can argue with cabinet colleagues that insofar as the public is concerned, he is the government.[48] The same claim, more-or-less, has been made for Canadian prime ministers, although given the secrecy surrounding cabinet deliberations, the claim generally is tinged with partisanship and rests on inside dopester revelations [49] rather than on empirical evidence.[50] Nonetheless, one can argue that the Canadian prime minister's institutional position always has given him certain built-in advantages over his cabinet colleagues. More recent structural changes in the operation of the cabinet and its supporting institutions seem to have increased these inherent advantages.[51] Four are worth noting.

First, the size of the prime minister's personal staff (prime minister's office) has increased greatly—especially since the beginning of World War II.[52] Although the size of the personal staffs of other members of the cabinet also has increased, this increase has not kept pace with the growth of the prime minister's office. Like most personal staffs, the men and women in the prime minister's office perform such routine tasks as answering mail, drafting speeches, organizing appointments, and arranging travel schedules. The principal function of the prime minister's office, however, is to enhance the personal political status of the prime minister in every area and with every important group in the country, including the cabinet. [53]

Second, as the cabinet has grown in size, committees of cabinet increasingly consider and help establish policy priorities.[54] The prime minister decides which of his colleagues will sit on these committees, who will chair each committee, and to a great extent, with what matters each committee will be concerned.

Third, as the size of each of the departments of government that cabinet members administer has increased, so has the proportion of working time that they must allocate to the basic concerns of departmental administration. Although Canadian cabinet ministers still are expected to be generalists, it is safe to assume that demonstrated administrative ability will help a man enter and remain in cabinet. In contrast, prime ministers (although they historically have had a special interest in foreign affairs) have rarely, if ever, been the administrative heads of operating departments. Thus, they have been free and they currently are freer than other members of the cabinet to concern themselves with both broad and specific policy matters and to collate and evaluate information that bears on these matters. Put another way, the prime minister not only enjoys a critical advantage over his colleagues in occupying a position of centrality in the cabinet's information network, he enjoys an additional advantage in being able to make effective use of his central position.

Fourth, although the cabinet may be collectively responsible to parliament for the conduct and administration of the several departments of government, each minister is personally responsible to the prime minister. In practice this means that ministers normally will not take significant actions in their departments without first consulting the prime minister, an overt acknowledgment that the prime minister is the boss and his colleagues, although colleagues, are also his agents.[55]

Although a Canadian prime minister always may have been something more than the first among equals, he never has been, nor is he today, a free agent in his behavior toward his cabinet. Some of his actions toward them are constrained by convention. For example, although the prime minister decides who will be in his cabinet, in this century he has been expected to federalize his cabinet and include a party colleague who is a representative from each of the provinces. A further expectation, grounded in custom, is that representatives of major social groups (e.g., religious, ethnic, economic) also will be included in a cabinet. Over the years relatively precise formulas have been worked out to insure adequate representation for these groups. In short, the cabinet long has been the forum for the representation and articulation of the demands of major regional and socioeconomic group interests tempered by the prime minister's own policy preferences.[56] One consequence of this convention is that over the years a certain number of very able individuals have been left out of the cabinet because they represented the "wrong" province or group. We shall have more to say about this in our discussion of influence in chapter 3.

Other constraints on the actions of a prime minister vis-a-vis his cabinet colleagues are political. Principal rivals for the party's leadership mantle generally are included in a cabinet and although a prime minister's power to dismiss them or any other colleague is unquestioned, wholesale dismissals threaten his own tenure as leader. Too many dismissals or resignations of ministers project an image of both a divided government and a divided governing party—an appearance that is supposed to have deleterious consequences for party fortunes in the next election. Whether the Canadian public (or the public of any other democratic political system) really ascribes any value to governmental and legislative party unity is a question that need not concern us here. Legislative elites seem to believe that it does, however, and the belief probably constrains prime ministers (and the leaders of opposition parties as well) and leads them to seek accommodations in the case of serious intra-party divisions. In addition, the prime minister's actions are circumscribed by what might be termed "environmental" variables. For example, although every Canadian prime minister of this century has said he wanted to reduce the size of his cabinet, not only has it not been reduced, it has continued to grow. As governments have increased the scope of their activities, there has been a concomitant growth in the number of new bureaucratic units. Combinations of these units soon require political heads to administer and be responsible for them. Some of these political heads eventually have had to be included in the cabinet, where they currently share decision-making power with the prime minister.

Finally, the behavior of any prime minister toward his cabinet colleagues will be affected in great part by his personality and their own. Thus, for example, despite the political acumen, the ability to manipulate people, and the desire for political control that the late W. L. Mackenzie King is said to have possessed,[57] he supposedly still found it difficult to control the independence of powerful colleagues such as the late C. D. Howe. Undoubtedly, the same has been true, to a greater or lesser extent, of all cabinets.

In summary, then, the scope of authority exercised by both cabinet and prime minister has increased over the years as has their power and importance vis-a-vis parliament. However, the power and influence of the prime minister probably has increased more than has the influence of the cabinet. Consequently, even if a Canadian prime minister cannot claim that he is the government, at least he will retain his status as leader as long as: (1) he continues to enjoy the support of his parliamentary party caucus; and (2) the members of his party caucus continue to receive the required public support at the polls. Accordingly, we will now direct our attention to the growth and development of political parties in Canada.

## THE PARTY SYSTEM

The two major parties, the Liberal and Progressive-Conservative, have their roots[58] in the socioeconomic and political cleavages that existed in Quebec and Ontario during the first three decades of the 19th century. The roots of the two minor parties, the CCF-NDP and the Social Credit, are in the sectional strife that beset Western Canada 100 years later. The Progressive-Conservative party grew out of the business-professional and Established Church (Anglican) elites who held sway in Ontario and to a lesser extent in Quebec in the early 19th century. Indeed, they exercised such a monopoly over the available administrative and judicial offices that in derision they were termed the "Family Compact" in Upper Canada (Ontario) and the "Chateau Clique" in Lower Canada (Quebec). John A. Macdonald's successful leadership of the confederation movement and his subsequent tenure as prime minister rested largely on his ability to bring together this English-speaking protestant oligarchy with the ultramontane catholic hierarchy of Quebec and to keep them united in a conservative coalition that governed (except for a five-year period, 1873–1878) until 1896.

The ancestors of the present Liberal party were anti-Catholic, non-Established Church, and radical reform groups in Ontario, and antibusiness, anticlerical elements in Quebec. Denied victory at the national level, the Liberals concentrated their efforts on winning control of provincial governments. Under the leadership of a French-Canadian, Wilfred Laurier, they eventually gained control of the federal government and retained that control for 15 years. The Liberal ascent to power in 1896 was greatly facilitated by Laurier's skill in broadening the base of the party's public support in Quebec and making the once-radical "Parti Rouge" acceptable to the Catholic Church hierarchy and the traditional doctor-lawyer elites of the small towns.

Both the Social Credit and the CCF-NDP parties grew out of agrarian-based populist movements that led first to the formation of "United Farm" parties in the Western provinces and Ontario and then to the short-lived Progressive party. According to historian William Morton, the Progressive party "was a revolt against a concept of Canadian economic policy and of Canadian political practice." [59]

In the view of Progressives, the largely rural and agriculturally-oriented West was being thoroughly and ruthlessly exploited in the best colonial fashion by the financial and industrial elites of the urban East. The two political parties functioned as a kind of "executive arm" of these elites and the large Eastern majorities in the parliamentary caucuses of both parties were employed to articulate the interests of the exploiters and to throttle the protests of the oppressed. The Progressive party revolt, then, was supposedly as much a revolt against disciplined party government as it was against the economic policies articulated by the parties.

Interestingly, party lines had not always been so sharply drawn. For one thing, relatively severe property restrictions sharply limited the size of the electorate before 1885. For another, it must have been notoriously difficult to organize the portion of the public that was eligible to vote, because until 1878 voting was open and non-simultaneous so that partisan and ideological considerations probably often gave way to a pragmatic desire on the part of certain segments of public to vote for the expected winners. At any rate, party organization in the electorate probably was skeletal during the first two decades of nationhood since the first four elections witnessed the selection and election of substantial numbers of candidates who were independents.[60] These elections also produced individuals whom John A. Macdonald supposedly labeled "loose fish"–MPs generally elected by acclamation who were not especially amenable to party discipline nor particularly concerned about the necessity of acting cohesively to achieve party goals. One indication of this lack of cohesion is the relatively high defection rate on roll-calls that characterized voting in early parliaments, many of whose members labeled themselves Independent-Liberals, Independent-Conservatives or Liberal-Conservatives.[61] Another indication of the lack of party organization in the electorate during the 19th century is that as late as 1880 only about 50% of the federal constituencies had even paper party associations. Moreover, the Liberal party did not hold its first national convention until 1893 and did not establish a national party office until 1912. The Conservatives lagged even further behind than the Liberals in both these areas.[62]

Party scholars are generally agreed that the hardening of party lines in legislatures and the striving for more-or-less cohesive party action therein were associated with the expansion of the electorate and the need to deliver on at least some of the electoral promises made to newly enfranchised groups. In turn, relatively cohesive

legislative parties required a continuing supply of "safe" candidates—
individuals who would come to the legislative position with favorable
attitudes toward acting in concert with party colleagues. Such a
continuing supply of properly socialized candidates could be better
achieved if electoral party organizations were developed; if the selection and election of candidates for parliament were vested in these
organizations; and if elections were sharply contested, even in constituencies in which the prospects of victory seemed very slim.

In Canada, it would appear that party lines began to harden after
the election of 1878. This calcification was rooted in support for or
opposition to Macdonald's "national policy"—a modernization program based upon the development of internal communications and
transportation, the enhancement of industrial capacity, and the expansion of internal and external trade through the imposition of
protective tariffs.[63] With regard to the development of party organizations outside of parliament, we may infer from the Liberal party's
success in winning control of provincial governments that the "outs"
(i.e., the Liberals) organized the electorate at the constituency level
first and that the Conservatives countered with organizations of their
own. Certainly, the sharp drop in the number of independents
elected to parliament after 1899 and the decline of candidates
elected by acclamation suggests this may have been the case. It is
doubtful, however, that within a period of only twenty years discipline in the Liberal and Conservative parties became so stringent that
it led Western MPs to revolt and join forces with the Progressives.
Nor was the Eastern bias to which Western MPs objected necessarily
an indication that the Liberals and Conservatives were the spokesmen
of special interests from that region. It is possible that the positions
taken and the legislative policies adopted first by Liberal, and then
by Conservative and Union (a coalition of Conservatives and Liberals
in favor of the war) governments, had an Eastern bias because they
reflected the will of a majority of Canadians; after all, approximately
two-thirds of the population lived (and continues to live) in the
provinces of Ontario and Quebec.

Another possible explanation for the rise of the Progressive party—
beyond the Eastern exploitation and excessive party discipline theories—is that it benefited from the votes of newly enfranchised
groups in provinces whose populations were rapidly increasing (something approaching universal suffrage was achieved by 1921). Whatever the reasons, the Progressives were able to elect 65 members to

parliament. Their presence forced W. L. Mackenzie King, elected to the leadership of the Liberal party in 1919, to form a minority government. King, who was to serve as prime minister for about a quarter of a century, spent his first years in office trying to resolve differences between Liberals and Progressives and to bring some of the Liberals turned Progressives back into the party fold. Apparently such a task was consistent with King's political philosophy. He viewed a party primarily as a mechanism for mediating and resolving intergroup conflicts and only secondarily as a vehicle for generating and implementing public policy. Thus, R. M. Dawson wrote of him,

> He considered that the parties in Canada had two major functions: the propagation and carrying out of ideas and policies, and the bringing together of diverse and even conflicting groups and interests so as to secure a working agreement and a measure of common action. The second function was in his eyes even more important than the first.[64]

J. M. Beck and D. J. Dooley perceived King only in the role of "broker." According to them,

> In King's view a Canadian political leader could not be doctrinaire; he had to balance one pressure group against another, and he had to prevent issues becoming so clearly defined that they caused deep divisions.[65]

If King really preferred the honest broker role, and if he really was reluctant to generate policies that might result in conflict and thereby threaten a supposedly fragile national unity, his preferences seemingly were shared and continued to be shared by other members of the Canadian political elite—or so a recent systematic and empirical study of the role of interest groups in the Canadian political process suggests.[66] Even if King's style was to react rather than to innovate, the foundation of much of Canada's welfare program was laid during his period as prime minister. This program, together with other reallocative measures, as well as proposals intended to broaden the industrial base of the Canadian economy, were pursued by King's successors during the years 1948–1957. With regard to industrial and economic expansion policies, it was the insistence of the Liberals (particularly of King's long-time cabinet colleague, C. D. Howe) on pursuing what they regarded as a necessary and highly desirable development policy, but one which the opposition parties regarded as a raid on the Treasury that would principally benefit a small group of "insiders," that led to the famous "Pipeline" debate, the invoking of Closure, and the Liberals' subsequent defeat in the election of June, 1957.

In that year, John Diefenbaker,[67] a small-town Saskatchewan lawyer, who had recently (1956) been chosen leader of his party, led the Conservatives to a close victory. The next year, largely as a result of his personal charisma ("Follow John" was the Conservatives' principal campaign slogan) the Conservatives won the greatest electoral victory in Canadian history. Although the Conservatives suffered so sharp a reversal in electoral fortunes in 1962 that they were again reduced to forming a minority government, they, nevertheless, generated some important changes in the nature of party representation in parliament. First, Mr. Diefenbaker[68] and a handful of close associates inside and out of parliament literally were able to redirect the Conservative party from a primary orientation to urban and industrial Ontario, to upper-middle class interests, and to Canadians of Anglo-Celtic origins,[69] into a party whose electoral strongholds are the "have not" Prairie and Atlantic provinces in which they also receive disproportionate support from "lower" class and "hyphenated" (i.e., ethnic) Canadians.[70] Second, because of Conservative successes in the Prairie and Atlantic regions, the Liberals, who for years (and with considerable justification) claimed to be Canada's only national party, now have difficulty sustaining that claim. [71] Third, the undisputed hegemony that the Liberals enjoyed in Quebec national politics was severely disrupted by the Conservative victory of 1958. And, although the fortunes of the Conservatives in Quebec again have declined, a substantial other-than-Liberal vote has persisted from which the Creditistes principally have benefited (i.e., the Creditiste won nine of Quebec's parliamentary seats in 1965, 14 in the 1968 election and 15 in 1972).

As for the two minor parties, both (as was indicated above) grew out of the short-lived Progressive party. The Social Credit, under the leadership of William Aberhart, was able to parlay strong support from former Progressives and from members of the United Farmers of Alberta into victory in the Alberta provincial election of 1935 and to maintain itself in office for over 35 years.[72] In 1952 the party gained control of the British Columbia provincial government and stayed in power for 20 years. Despite this regional success at the provincial level the party has made virtually no headway either nationally or provincially—other than in Quebec—in other parts of Canada. In Quebec, the party under the leadership of Real Caouette has been an important force in Quebec national politics since 1962.

Ironically, Mr. Caouette's success in the rural areas and small towns of Quebec has rested in great part on Social Credit appeals and slogans that the Western section of the party long ago abandoned (e.g., "poverty in the midst of plenty"; "prosperity through the creation of social credit"; the "corruption and moral bankruptcy of the two old parties").[73] In contrast to its Quebec wing, the Western branch of Social Credit for over a decade has been a solidly conservative party whose leaders continually "point with pride" to the stability and responsibility of the provincial administrations of Alberta and British Columbia and to the unprecedented prosperity these provinces enjoyed under Social Credit governments.

Just as the Western branch of the Social Credit party largely has abandoned many of the more radical financial panaceas advocated during the 1930s, so has the CCF-NDP soft-pedalled its original goal of establishing a socialist commonwealth in Canada.[74] Like Social Credit, the CCF experienced substantial initial success in the West. Unlike the Social Credit, however, it also has had considerable appeal for the voters of other regions. The party's first electoral victory came in Saskatchewan[75] where it won control of the provincial government in 1944 and maintained its hegemony for 20 years. After several years in opposition the party again was victorious in Saskatchewan and subsequently also won control of the provincial governments of Manitoba and British Columbia. In the interim between its initial victory in Saskatchewan and the other subsequent provincial electoral successes the party has had difficulty securing broadly-based support for its candidates in federal elections, never having elected more than 28 members to parliament. In part because of the party's inability to compete successfully with the Liberals and Conservatives in national elections (especially in the search for funds to finance electoral campaigns) and in part because the party's leaders long had enjoyed strong support from and had close ties to the leaders of organized labor, these ties were formalized in a national convention in 1961 and the CCF (Cooperative Commonwealth Federation) became the NDP (New Democratic party). T. C. Douglas, then premier of Saskatchewan, became the party's first national leader.

To date the party has benefited in a number of ways from this union: more of the financial and human resources needed to wage electoral campaigns are now available; the attractiveness of the candidates the party has been able to recruit for parliamentary races has increased markedly; and the party's share of the vote in urban and metropolitan areas also has risen. On the other hand, the conservative, "bread-and-butter" influence organized labor supposedly has had on the party's programmatic direction and ideological orientation has engendered some relatively serious internal strains. A group of disaffected younger party leaders (many of them intellectuals and academicians) terming themselves the "Waffle" has questioned the direction the party has taken since 1961 and has tried to move the party leftward along the ideological continuum—toward the socialist goals that originally were its inspiration.

Unfortunately, we know relatively little about parliamentary parties' links, either with their party organizations in the electorate or of the nature of the interactions among members of the respective party caucuses. The research findings available suggest there are fairly close ties and frequent communications between MPs in the several parties and key organizational workers (some of whom are themselves local elected public officials) in the several constituencies.[76] Whether these contacts stem from a feeling on the part of MPs that local party leaders and workers are important and reliable reference groups,[77] or whether they regard it simply as "good politics" to consult with them (in that interactions of this kind help maintain the morale and the support of individuals whose efforts will be required in future campaigns) is as yet undetermined. There may be a variety of other reasons as well. Whatever the case, large proportions of MPs in each of the parliamentary parties spend a part of their time trying to explain and interpret to organizational supporters the parliamentary party's position on current major issues. They also try to relay to their parliamentary colleagues the feelings and attitudes of grassroots organizational workers and supporters. Caucus traditionally has served as a vehicle for exchanging and discussing this kind of information. Again, unfortunately, relatively little systematic research has been conducted on the functions performed by party caucuses in the Canadian House of Commons. The data currently available suggest that caucus has four principal uses: (1) it provides an opportunity for MPs to exchange information gleaned from constituency party supporters, from surveys or from other studies conducted by subcommittees of the caucus; (2) it provides an opportunity for party members to discuss current strategies and tactics that will be employed in discussions in the House and in committees; (3) it provides members with an opportunity to achieve a kind of catharsis of their grievances against the leadership and against other party colleagues by providing a forum for their expression; and (4) it provides members with a mechanism for discussing and achieving agreement on longer-range party programs and organization.[78] The extent to which the caucus is utilized for different purposes, however, varies substantially by party and is one of the matters with which we will be concerned in chapter 5 of this book.[79]

## WHAT PARLIAMENT HAS DONE

The bare-bones of what parliament has done, insofar as debating and passing legislation is concerned, can be described very briefly. The first 27 parliaments (1867–1968) were in session a total of 16,171 days and actually sat on 9,699 of those days, or 60% of the time. During this period 13,499 bills were introduced into parliament, an average of 1.4 bills each sitting day. Of these 69% were enacted into law.[80] In comparison to the 598 sessional and 359 sitting days of the average parliament during the period 1867–1968, the 28th parliament, with which this book is concerned, was in session 718 days and actually sat on 565 days, 47% of the time. Fully 1031 bills were introduced into the 28th parliament, or 531 more than were introduced, on the average, in each preceding parliament. Of these, 216 (21%) received Royal Assent, 131 fewer, on the average, than the number receiving Royal Assent in preceding parliaments. Thus, although twice as much legislation was introduced into the 28th parliament as was introduced, on the average, in preceding parliaments, the average number of bills that passed each day (.32 bills) in the 28th Parliament was considerably smaller than the average number of bills that passed each sitting day in the first twenty-seven. The members of the 28th Parliament thus continued a well established trend. That is, over time the number of days parliament has been in session and is sitting and the average number of bills introduced into each parliament have increased greatly, but the average number of bills that have passed each parliament has sharply declined.[81]

Assuming that the cabinet is part of parliament—in practice as well as in theory—the first 27 parliaments also ratified 282,446 Orders-in-Council[82] and Treasury Board Minutes—administrative regulations and legislative interpretations—which although often trivial, nonetheless, still can have a marked impact not only on the administration but also on the substance of public policy. Of these Orders-in-Council slightly over 17% were promulgated during World War II when Prime Minister King and his cabinet colleagues virtually dispensed with parliament.[83] Thus, approximately 29 Orders-in-Council have been promulgated for every piece of legislation that parliament has passed during the period 1867–1968. And, even if the 48,782 Orders-in-Council of 1940–1945 are excluded from this total, there still are approximately 25 Orders-in-Council that have been promulgated for every piece of legislation passed until 1968. The 28th Parliament again continued and, indeed, extended this well established trend toward the delegation of legislative powers. During the 28th Parliament 19.6 Orders were promulgated each sitting day and 62 Orders were ratified for every piece of legislation that received Royal Assent.

Although no attempt ever has been made to systematically analyze the content of Orders-in-Council, two recent studies have tried to delineate and to classify the kind of legislation that was passed by the first 27 Canadian parliaments.[84] Their principal findings with respect to the overall pattern of legislation passed and the expenditures made by parliament for the period 1867–1968 may be summarized as follows.

(1) "Regulative" legislation (i.e., bills that regulate interactions between and among major groups) comprises the bulk of the outputs of parliament. Interestingly, the highest proportion of regulative legislation was passed during the period when Canada was least modernized. The authors speculate that getting a new country off the ground is somewhat analogous to organizing any other complex form of social endeavor. In the early stages of nation-building, rule-makers within a polity must be concerned with regularizing, stabilizing, and making predictable the interactions among the several social groups and with the relationship of public authority to society. The fact that "government," the "general public," and the various "regions" more often were the subject of regulative enactments during the period of 1867–1904 would tend to support this speculation.[85]

(2) Regardless of the time period considered, only minute proportions of legislative outputs are "extractive" (i.e., outputs that provide the fiscal and human resources upon which governments draw) or "symbolic" (i.e., legislation concerned with national symbols such as flags, seals, coats of arms). The authors observe that both extractive and symbolic outputs are highly salient for and visible to the public. They evoke intense feelings in people and tend to raise the level of tension within society. From a system-stability perspective, there-

fore, eschewing the passage or even frequent consideration of these kinds of policies is quite understandable.

(3) In comparison to other Western countries with more limited resources, the proportion of national revenue expended over the years on "welfare" policies has been relatively low. Moreover, although Canada has never aspired to military greatness (other than during the two world wars of this century), the proportion of the budget spent for "defense" purposes in this century exceeds welfare expenditures by a substantial margin.

(4) The proportion of "redistributive" outputs (i.e., legislation that reallocates the general resources of society to specific groups or regions in a country) passed by Canadian parliaments has increased over time. However, in not one of the 27 parliaments considered do redistributive bills amount to even one-half of the nonroutine public bills receiving Royal Assent.

(5) Over time (and not unexpectedly) major economic groups and foreign powers are increasingly the objects of parliamentary outputs. From 1867 onward, however, "business" has been the object of nonroutine legislation far more often than either "agriculture" or "labor."

(6) Although changes in both the social and economic environment exert a substantial and independent effect on legislative outputs, the relationship of social changes to legislative outputs is stronger than is the relationship of economic changes to legislative outputs.

(7) Over time, changes in the political environment are substantially less important in determining legislative outputs than are social and economic changes in the environment. The authors conclude (but qualify their conclusion in a number of ways) that although variations in political factors (such as changes in the composition of the membership of the several parliaments) exercise some influence on the conversion of social and economic inputs into legislative outputs, they tend to be intervening rather than additive predictors of outputs.

## FACTORS CONSTRAINING PARLIAMENT'S DECISIONS

Although the findings of Kornberg, Falcone and Mishler may not surprise students of United States public policies, the fact is that in Canada (other than for sixteen powers expressly delegated to the legislatures of the provinces) parliament has the constitutional right (Section 91, BNA Act, 1867) to make or amend any law that it wishes. Thus, it could be argued that both the type of legislation passed by parliament over time and the amount of public funds allocated to different substantive areas are as they are because of the particular configurations of members in the several parliaments and cabinets. If, over the years, other individuals had become MPs, or, if other than Liberal and Conservative cabinets had governed the country, then both the content of the legislation that has been passed and the amount of money spent for various purposes might well have been quite different. Although this is a plausible and theoretically possible speculation, an equally compelling argument can be made that certain economic, sociocultural, political, and legal factors limit and constrain what any parliament can do, regardless of the composition of its membership.

With respect to legal limitations, for example, because of the original distribution of powers between the national and provincial governments and, more important, because of the subsequent development of Canadian federalism, the provinces exercise legislative jurisdiction in major policy areas that in other Western countries are the sole prerogatives of a national government. Thus, unless parliament had been willing to replace or drastically alter these arrangements, the substantive areas in which it was able to legislate were limited.[86]

Insofar as economic constraints are concerned, both the economy and the population of Canada have grown in an incremental fashion over the years. Thus, the level of socioeconomic development at any point in time has set fairly strict limits on the range of policy alternatives that parliament realistically could consider. With regard to sociocultural and political constraints, the maintenance of national integrity in the face of (a) sharp internal regional cleavages based upon cultural and economic particularism, and (b) a giant neighbor with ten times Canada's population, very likely has set both psychological and physical limits on the policies that parliament has felt able or willing to pursue. We may reasonably assume that legislation that might have antagonized particular ethnic or religious groups or development policies that might have been good for the public or beneficial in the long run but which might have exacerbated current regional cleavages also had to be avoided—regardless of how rational or eminently desirable such policies might have appeared at the time. Similarly, Canadian governments (regardless of their political composition) undoubtedly have had to anticipate the likely response of the United States to any Canadian policy that might seriously affect that country. Given the disparity in size and strength between them, and given also the complexity of economic, military and cultural interactions that have characterized relationships between the two countries, the possibility that an American government might react negatively to Canadian policies that impinged on American interests has been one that no Canadian government ever has been able to take lightly. Prime Minister Trudeau probably summarized the latter problem most succinctly when he noted that "sharing a continent with the United States is rather like sleeping with an elephant—he may not know you're there, but you must be sensitive to his every twitch."[87] A substantial group of Canadian scholars go beyond this. They argue that not only has concern over the anticipated response of the United States constrained the actions and limited the options available to Canadian governments in many critically important policy areas, but also, because of the unprecedented level of control over major segments of the economy exercised by multi-national United States corporations, some of parliament's policy-making prerogatives have been usurped by the United States; decisions that should have been made in Ottawa instead were made and continue to be made in Washington and in corporate board rooms in New York.[88]

Canada's political culture has been described many times from different perspectives, most often, in terms of comparisons with the political culture of the United States. Although scholars differ in the emphasis they give to particular facets of the culture, its major dimensions appear to be conservatism, pragmatism, and a tendency to emphasize the values of corporativism, collectivism, and deference for and compliance with the edicts of authority, both public and private.[89] If these scholarly assessments of the principal components of the Canadian political culture are accurate, we may assume that the demands made upon parliament by other than a number of particularly powerful elite groups have not been unusually heavy over the years. Nor have the general public's reactions to parliament's outputs in the form of legislative decisions—other than for the Conscription bills—ever been notably severe. But if the alternatives that parliament has considered have not been constrained by heavy and intense demands made by the general public, there is reason to believe that its actions have been strongly affected by the aforementioned powerful elite groups. This position has been most effectively argued by John Porter in his provocative analysis of social stratification and the distribution of power in Canada. Porter has contended that the elite segments of the two Canadian "charter groups" (British and French) have exercised far more influence on virtually every aspect of Canadian public life than have elite groups in the United States. This is particularly the case with the British charter group elite. It is small, easily defined, and frequently exercises overlapping influence over the economy, the media, the academic and religious communities, the public bureaucracy and the political system. In addition to being disproportionately of Anglo-Scottish-Irish descent the elite members of the British charter group share other characteristics: they tend to be members of high status protestant churches; they tend to derive from upper-class and upper-middle-class social origins; they tend to be graduates of a small number of select prep schools and Eastern Canadian universities; they tend to be informally linked by ties of kinship and marriage and formally linked through common membership on major corporate boards, public commissions, key service and charitable organizations, etc. The most powerful and socially prestigious members of these groups do not themselves enter politics, but they are directly and intimately linked to the parliamentary and bureaucratic elites and to the organizational leaders of the major political parties (Liberal and Conservative) by corporate lawyers. These lawyers are the most likely members of the charter group elite to have overt political affiliations (equally divided between the Liberal and Conservative parties); to have held elected or appointed public offices; and to have held top offices in the organizations of the two major parties.

Porter's analysis assumes that the influence of these elites is so powerful and pervasive, that they are able to make decisions (having important public consequences) from outside of parliament and be certain that their decisions will be ratified within parliament.[90] Alternatively, key decisions are seen as being made by private elites acting in concert with members of the cabinet and the top bureaucracy, and only then being ratified by parliament.[91] We may speculate that the ability of elites to exercise so powerful an influence on policy decisions that are made as well as not made is facilitated by the relative quiescence of the public, its deference to authority, its low level of politicization, and its willingness to accept the activities and the power exercised by elites as legitimate and proper. In other words, the ability of elites to exercise disproportionate influence on the content of public policy is facilitated and sanctioned by the political culture. This latter speculation has received considerable support from Robert Presthus' recent study of interest group activity in Canada.[92] Presthus observes, for example, that the central features of the Canadian political culture "culminate . . . in a national political process . . . in which major decisions regarding national socio-economic policy are worked out through interactions between governmental (i.e., legislative and bureaucratic) elites and interest group elites."[93]

Even if the process by which elites have influenced national public decision-making in Canada has not been either as neat or as cut-and-dried as Porter and others[94] have suggested, it still is reasonable to assume that there are frequent contacts between cabinet members, senior bureaucrats, other members of parliament and representatives of elite groups in the economy, the media, etc. We further may assume that just as the actions of parliaments and of cabinets have been constrained by the need to anticipate the response of the United States, so have they also been affected by the need to consult with and anticipate the responses of the leaders of major domestic interest groups.

Finally, the actions of parliaments and cabinets of this century undoubtedly have been affected, and hence constrained, by the growth of a professional bureaucracy. John Porter writes,

> It is generally accepted by students of Canadian government that the senior public service has had a crucial position in the overall structure of power, particularly after the appointment in 1932 of W. C. Clark, an Economics professor from Queens University.[95]

Of Professor Clark, R. Taylor Cole has said:

> Dr. Clark was the center of a small coterie of Deputy Ministers and of permanent and temporary "civil servants" and officials, mostly economists, who constituted the inner spring of the governmental mechanism in Canada and largely determined its economic policies from 1939–1945.[96]

With respect to the interaction between economists and cabinet members, John Meisel remarked that the Liberal party leaders "appeared mesmerized by the cult of the Gross National Product."[97] He went on to suggest that the 1957 Liberal party election platform was generated not by the Liberal party organization in the electorate, or by the Liberal parliamentary caucus, but rather, by certain high level bureaucrats. And, if the scholarly consensus reflected in Van Loon and Whittington's recent book is accurate, senior bureaucrats continue to exercise a predominant influence on resource allocation initiatives today.[98] Van Loon and Whittington and many other scholarly observers feel that even if the cabinet does decide among priorities in resource allocation, their decisions largely are circumscribed by: (a) what senior advisors in the bureaucracy define as priority areas; and (b) the data advisors marshall for cabinet to use in deciding among alternatives. The role they ascribe to parliament in the policy process is one of refining legislation, making minor changes in substance and language.

## PARLIAMENT: ADAPTATION OR DECLINE?

Assuming for the moment (regardless of the social and political composition of its membership) that the cabinet's role in the policy process has been limited and constrained by the above mentioned factors, and assuming also that the role of private members is largely confined to refining legislation that reflects already decided policies, we might extrapolate from these points to the more general assumption that the Canadian parliament has declined over the years.[99] It is tempting to make this assumption and to conjure an image of a golden age of parliament in 19th century Canada. As has been indicated, several studies of early post-Confederation parliaments strongly suggest that the average private member had at least the potential for a more fundamental role in formulating public policy than his successors have had. Data indicate that in these 19th century Houses of Commons relatively large numbers of members frequently participated in parliamentary debates; that government bills, even supply bills, were amended; that private members were less circumscribed in their actions by a demanding executive than is currently the case; that a more substantial proportion of the public bills passed were initiated by private members; and that House committees performed a number of functions "in a manner which today would be remarkably independent but which were possible then because the executive had not yet assumed control of virtually everything, either directly or through the slavish support of its majority in the Commons."[100]

Although it may be tempting, in light of these findings, to conceive of a golden age of parliament—an age when a private member's policy preferences were no less important than the government's; when the majority of members were fully involved in every stage of

the legislative process; when committees shaped legislation and reviewed its administration; when the policies adopted by parliament
reflected its own thinking instead of the dictates of special interests
within and outside of the country—it also may be unrealistic to think
of parliament in this way. For one thing, as K. C. Wheare has observed,
"Parliament's golden age recedes as we approach it." [101] For another,
it should be recalled that fifty years ago, when Lord Bryce
wrote of the decline of parliaments in Western democracies, he did
not include the Canadian House of Commons (or the Australian
House of Representatives) in his list of institutions that had suffered
such a fate. This was not because the Canadian House of Commons
was more powerful than other parliaments, but because, in Bryce's
view, it had never attained a status from which decline would be
possible. More seriously, as Gerhard Loewenberg points out in his
evaluation of the decline-of-parliament literature, "decline . . . is in
the eye of the beholder and depends upon his analytic perspectives." [102]

If this is the case, then a more realistic assessment of parliament's
current status may be that as an institution and as a political
subsystem it has not suffered any great decline from what it was in
the 19th century. Rather, the manner in which its traditional functions are performed has been changing and is continuing to change in
response to general changes in society and in the political environment in which parliamentarians operate. Relatedly, it may be more
realistic to think of parliament as an institution that still is evolving
because in addition to the changed ways in which its members are
performing traditional tasks, they have added new ones. Some of the
latter are very time-consuming but are discharged in ways that are
relatively invisible to the majority of the public, hence the perceptions of decline. It may well be, however, that for at least a generation the average MP has worked much harder at being a MP than his
predecessors ever did.

John Mackintosh, in discussing the situation in Great Britain, puts
the matter of parliamentary evolution, the changes in the tasks
performed by individual MPs, and the ambiguity, uncertainty, and
confusion that have resulted thus: "We are in a first-class muddle
about our politicians, about the kind of people we want and the way
they ought to behave." [103] He observes that the 19th century view
of parliament and of the parliamentary position was that the job of a
MP was a part-time one. The assumption was that MPs had income
from another occupation and that their parliamentary activities were

an addition to their normal occupational pursuits. The 19th century perspective further assumes that the principal task of MPs was to express their individual views on the great issues of the day. The positions of those who could argue their views most cogently and effectively prevailed. They were not supposed to act as local welfare officers or ombudsmen. Indeed, they had no special position of authority in dealing with the affairs of constituents. Letters that they might address to civil servants and other public officials on behalf of constituents, for example, could claim no more attention than letters written by any other citizen. If the 19th century perspective of the proper function of MPs is accepted, it follows that MPs have no need for private offices, for telephones, for postal allowances, for secretarial assistance and so forth.

A second perspective, what might be termed the 20th century view, contends that the job of being a MP is a full-time one, that parliament is a profession just as medicine and law are professions. The principal task of MPs is to be concerned with and to take action on local, largely personal, problems that are brought to their attention by their constituents. The assumption is that constituents are less and less concerned about what actions their MPs take on national issues and these should be left to a handful of parliament's leaders. If this perspective is accepted—and Mackintosh observes that, in fact, it is by an increasing number of the members of all parties—it follows that MPs do need office space within and outside of parliament to conduct surgeries. They do need clerical and technical support, and their interventions on behalf of constituents should be accorded special status.

Both perspectives have the support of substantial numbers of MPs and important elements of the public not only in Great Britain but in Canada as well. The relative popularity of these essentially contradictory positions and the claims that are made for their appropriateness as models of parliamentary behavior are difficult to evaluate because of the paucity of detailed and accurate data on what, in fact, parliament does. In particular, there have been almost no systematic studies of the activities in which individual MPs engage and of the emphasis they give, in terms of time and energy, to various activities. One might ask, for example: How much speaking does an average backbencher as opposed to frontbencher do during a parliamentary session? To what topics do they address themselves? How many and what kinds of questions are addressed to the cabinet? How many bills and debatable resolutions do non-cabinet members of parliament introduce during a parliamentary session? How frequently do MPs attend meetings of committees of which they are members? To what extent do they participate in committee deliberations? How frequently do they contact ministers and civil servants on behalf of constituents? With what effect? To the best of our knowledge questions such as these have never been systematically addressed in a study of a parliamentary system either in Canada or elsewhere. The almost total absence of such data was one of the major factors motivating the present study. [104] As was indicated in the introduction, we have gathered data from several sources that not only can help fill this informational void but also can be used to test our theoretical assumption that power and influence within the Canadian parliament are ascribed, in great part, to those MPs who participate the most extensively (and by inference most effectively) in parliamentary activities.

First, however, we would like to elaborate the assumption made previously that the Canadian parliament may not have declined in importance as an institution and as a component in the political system from what it was in the 19th century but rather that the things its members do and how they do them have changed considerably in the past 100 years. It may be true that private members of the 19th century parliaments initiated more public bills than do current members. However, a substantial proportion of these probably were "dog and cat" (i.e., special interest) bills. They dealt with the very local problems of selected individuals—peers of the member. Not only was the range of problems rather narrow and uncomplicated, but the amount of information required to act on them probably was quite limited. Moreover, the bulk of the legislation generated by private members of earlier parliaments did not have consequences that extended very far. It is almost a cliché to note that the problems with which new nations must cope become increasingly complex as these nations evolve into modern urban-industrial societies. Nor is it necessary to labor the point that the degree of interdependence in a society increases as it becomes more developed. It should be remembered, too, that Canada did not conduct her own foreign relations until 1931. Given these conditions, we may assume that not only has there been a huge increase in the amount of information Canadian MPs require to deal in a reasonably intelligent way with problems that face parliament, but also that the consequences ensuing from policy decisions they help make have greatly increased. Because of this and the paucity of resources that private members have had available to them, one can understand (although not necessarily condone) the reluctance of 20th century cabinets to accord to private members the same roles in the initiation and priority allocation stages of the policy process that they may have enjoyed in the generation after Confederation.

It also may be that far from having their initiation and priority allocation roles usurped by executives and administrative bureaucracies, private members have relinquished them and opted instead for roles they are better able to perform. Specifically, they currently may be concentrating on influencing the final content of legislation and monitoring the ways in which the administration of that legislation affects individuals or groups that are of particular concern to them. This is not to say that all or even the great majority of private members willingly have relinquished their roles as initiators of legislation. The substantial number of policy proposals introduced into each session of a parliament in the form of debatable resolutions urging the government "to consider the advisability of" adopting them indicates that this is not the case. Moreover, if the continuing lament of opposition parties that governments, regardless of their political composition, have stolen their ideas and proposals has any validity whatsoever, it is reasonable to assume that some of these debatable resolutions introduced into parliament eventually did become part of a government's legislative program and of parliament's outputs. In this regard, parliamentary scholar J. R. Mallory has claimed that "it would not be an exaggeration to say that practically every significant measure of reform in the last forty years has been introduced in parliament by a private member, usually, but not invariably from the opposition." [105] However, private members' bills and debatable resolutions are only two rather limited means that MPs with policymaking aspirations currently can use to realize their objectives. Formal debates in the House and in standing committees not only provide more frequent opportunities for members to critically evaluate and offer alternatives to government policies, but also to oversee the administration of that which is already the law of the land. From a traditional and symbolic perspective, this is, after all, what parliament is all about.

To recapitulate, we have suggested that even though the range of policies parliament can pursue may be somewhat constrained and the role that individual members can play in the process of policy formation increasingly may be restricted to refining legislation initiated by the bureaucracy and decided upon by the cabinet, parliament has not necessarily suffered a precipitous decline in its political power and importance over time. Instead we have suggested it simply may have changed the way it performs traditional functions and added a variety of new ones at which members spend an increasing proportion of their time. These changes are a product of, and a response to, changes that have occurred in Canadian society as a whole and in the more immediate environment in which parliament operates. More specifically, because of the democratization and modernization of Canadian society, private members may have had the part they play in formal parliamentary deliberations constrained and reduced. On the other hand, the informal mechanisms available to them to influence the content of public policy and the administration of legislation may well have increased so that currently they may be more important than the formal means. In addition to the time spent on legislative policy matters, we have suggested that MPs spend substantial proportions of their working days performing ombudsmen-service-representational tasks. They do so because a much greater proportion of the general population than was the case in the 19th and early 20th centuries now expects members of parliament to be primarily engaged in these activities and because an increasing number of the backbenchers and leaders of the parliamentary parties share the public's expectations. It may be the case that these latter roles are at least as important as the traditional legislative role and that a MP's status and influence with his parliamentary peers rest, in great part, upon how effectively and diligently he performs them. This is one of the principal assumptions that we will test in the chapters that follow.

## Chapter 2

# THE MPs: AN OVERVIEW

## INTRODUCTION

As was noted in the first chapter, Canadian MPs are not now nor have they ever been representative of a cross-section of the nation's population in either social or political background terms. There have been a number of empirical studies that have documented this assertion; enough, in fact, so that the point need not be labored. Rather, we will present a statistical profile of the members of the 28th Parliament together with a profile of each party group. A comparison of party profiles should help clarify the manner in which individual experiences and motivations interact with the organizational needs of political parties and result in the recruitment of different but still relatively homogeneous groups of elite political actors. Specifically, we first shall describe and compare the social and political milieus from which the parliamentary members of the four parties derive. Then we will present a scenario based on the data that describes how an average MP might have become a candidate for parliament. We focus next on the experiences of MPs during the first year in office, considering matters such as their expectations for the position, the extent to which these expectations were realized, and whether and how they learned the rules of the parliamentary game. Following this we: (1) delineate what they regard as their principal accomplishments; (2) compare these with their aspirations for the future; and (3) determine whether they feel their goals (past and future) conflict with the expectations of significant groups. The matter of conflict over goals with others leads us to consider whom MPs feel they represent, their feelings regarding the manner in which representation is carried out, and their views concerning to whom MPs should be accountable. The chapter concludes with a brief section on whether and why they view parliament as a place in which they can enjoy a career.

We have a two-fold objective in presenting these data. First and most important, they enable us to acquaint the reader with many of the variables that we will use to try to explain variations in individual influence and participation and why some members become leaders whereas others remain backbenchers. Second, the data provide a composite social and political portrait of the membership as a whole as well as a profile of the members of each of the four parliamentary parties. Of course, it could be argued that there are other profiles whose comparisons might have illuminated understanding of the Canadian House of Commons and the people who give it life. For example, we might have compared the profiles of newly-elected and veteran members, of MPs in different age cohorts, or of MPs from different geographic regions. The decision to restrict our focus can be explained in part by limitations of space. Our decision also rests on the theoretical assumption that parliamentary party affiliation has been and continues to be a singularly important predictor of attitudes and behavior in parliamentary systems and hence is deserving of special attention.[1]

It should be noted that our attempts to compare the members of the four parties have been hampered by the small size of the New Democratic and, particularly, the Social Credit parliamentary parties.[2] Anticipation of the difficulties that we would encounter in analyzing data for small but important subgroups led us to try to interview every member of parliament rather than a sample. During the fall of 1971 and the winter of 1972 individual letters explaining the purpose of the study and asking for cooperation were sent to each member; scores of phone calls were made to establish and to reestablish appointments for interviews; follow-up letters were sent to individuals who initially refused to be interviewed; the good offices of friendly MPs, cabinet ministers, colleagues in Canadian universities, and even members of the media, were used to try to persuade recalcitrant MPs to change their minds and participate in the study. Because of these efforts, eventually we succeeded in interviewing 189 of the 264 MPs. In terms of party affiliations, the interviews were distributed thusly: 100 Liberals (66.6%); 60 Conservatives (84.5%); 22 NDPs (88%); and 7 Creditistes (53.8%).[3] In terms of region, we secured interviews with 84% of the MPs from British Columbia and the three prairie provinces, 81% of the members from the Atlantic provinces, 76% of Ontario's MPs, but only 51% of Quebec's MPs.[4]

It was our conscious decision to trade off possible additional interviews for a rich and varied data set, but we then were faced with analyzing these data for (what in some instances are) very small groups of people. The problem of small group size was less acute in the analyses of behavioral data on the members' participation in House and standing committee activities (presented in chapter 4). These data were derived from content analyses of Hansard and other public records and were available for all 264 members. The small size of the Creditiste and NDP parliamentary groups did present a real problem, however, for the analyses of our interview data.

When findings are reported numerically (as so many of our's are), the question arises whether their statistical or substantive significance has any theoretical meaning. It is generally understood that conventional statistical use of the term "significance" refers to whether a finding is likely to differ by chance from some alternative at an arbitrarily selected level of probability. Unavoidable errors can arise in the sampling process or in the process of measurement and can lead to discrepancies between observed values and the true values of a population under study (in the present case, all 264 MPs). Hence, it is possible that statistical significance may not have theoretical significance. For example, if there had been two more men than women elected to the House of Commons in 1968 it would have been accurate to state that there were more men than women in the population of the 28th Parliament. But it would have been silly to assign theoretical significance to this finding because what would be important about such a distribution would be the similarity in number rather than the presence of two more men. Another relevant aspect of statistical significance suggested by this example is that the larger the size of the sample, the greater the likelihood that a small difference is real. Consequently, we confined some of the analyses in this study to the members of the Liberal and Progressive-Conservative parliamentary parties because we were more confident that observed differences between these two large groups, in fact, were real.

Clarification of substantive significance requires clarification of our conventional understanding of explanation. To illustrate: imagine two groups of MPs of the same sex and socioeconomic backgrounds. One group of MPs has had an average of four years of parliamentary experience whereas the average tenure of the second group is nine years. If this difference is to be explained, other characteristics of the two groups must be observed. The more experienced group has an average age of 45 years, full heads of hair, an average weight of 165 pounds, and represents parliamentary constituencies in which the average difference in votes received by the winning and runner-up candidates in the last five parliamentary elections was 8%. The less experienced group of MPs has an average age of 36 years, all are bald, they have an average weight of 205 pounds and they represent constituencies in which the average difference in the votes received by the winning and runner-up candidates in the last five parliamentary elections was 1.5%. Any of these factors may provide a statistically significant explanation of differences in parliamentary tenure. However, since there are a number of reasons, based upon previous research, to believe that the electoral competitiveness of constituencies is causally related to the tenure of members of parliament, this variable is most noteworthy and provides the most satisfying explanation. Indeed, even if the differences in the competitiveness of their constituencies were not quite statistically significant, and those between their weights, ages, and amounts of hair were, it still would be reasonable to emphasize the first rather than the last three differences in our explanation. On the other hand, if there were reasons to suspect that the images candidates project on television affect the propensity of the public to vote for them, then factors such as age, slimness of physique, or fullness of hair might take on theoretical significance.

In this study we generally will report statistically significant differences that we believe are of substantive import. Occasionally, however, we also will report differences that are statistically insignificant because, in our view, these differences are substantively or even theoretically interesting. Before presenting any of the data, however, we will briefly describe the content of the interview schedule from which they were derived.

## THE INTERVIEW

The interview (reproduced in Appendix D) began with a series of questions that were intended to delineate three dimensions of early political socialization: the age of and the circumstances surrounding first awareness of politics and public affairs; the age of and agents associated with first psychological partisan identification and any subsequent changes of identification; and the age of and circumstances surrounding a first interest in politics and public affairs. In this portion of the interview an attempt also was made to ascertain the level of politicization of the environment in which respondents were reared. The last question in this section asked the respondents to make an assessment of the forces, influences, experiences, and events that were particularly important in inducing them to become politically active. This question served as the lead-in to a series of questions concerned with the conditions under which individuals are recruited into the political system. Included were questions on the numbers and kinds of public offices (elected or appointed) respondents held before their election to parliament; the numbers and kinds of offices for which respondents had been candidates but to which they were not elected; the age at which respondents became active in party organizations; the number and the levels of the offices they held in their party organizations; the circumstances that initially led them to become candidates for elected public offices; their motives for becoming candidates; and the relative importance of local, provincial, and federal party organizations in the parliamentary nominating process.

The questions on recruitment were followed by a series of questions that probed the reactions of respondents to their first year in office. Included were questions on: the learning of rules of the game; the degree of congruence between their expectations for the parliamentary position and the realities of being a freshman MP; the activities that they found most gratifying and those they found most onerous; and the nature of any adjustments they made during that first year.

The bulk of the interview was concerned with delineating current attitudes and behavior. Questions probed: the extent of their interactions with cabinet members, parliamentary secretaries, and highest level civil servants; the nature of these interactions; the extent of their interactions with constituents and constituency party organizations; and both how and to what extent they try to discern the distribution of public opinion in their constituencies. This section also included a number of questions on their attitudes toward parliamentary committees, the extent of their participation in committee activities, their accomplishments, their future goals, and to whom they feel accountable for their actions as parliamentarians. This section of the interview was followed by a series of questions on what the reactions of the respondents would be to an electoral defeat, why some MPs retire voluntarily, whether there are other public positions to which they aspire and what they would miss about the parliamentary position if they had to leave for some reason. Also included in this latter portion of the interview was a request that respondents nominate: (a) the ten most influential MPs, regardless of whether they hold a formal position of leadership; and (b) the three parliamentary colleagues to whom they turn for advice and assistance. Finally, in addition to the customary questions about their social backgrounds, the interviewees were asked to respond to: (1) a battery of "agree-disagree" questions regarding matters such as the style and focus of representation appropriate for MPs and a series of questions that were intended to delineate their ideological positions on major policy issues as well as their images of the locations of their parliamentary parties on these same issues. In the section immediately below we begin our report of the data acquired from these interviews.

## SOCIAL AND POLITICAL BACKGROUNDS OF CANADIAN MPs

Examination of the data in table 2.1 indicates that the Social Credit (Creditiste) MPs who were members of the 28th Parliament were a rather distinct group. All were French-Canadian Catholics. Six of seven were at least second generation Canadians reared on farms and in small towns of Quebec. Their rural Quebec roots were reflected also in the fact that six of seven had attended school only in that province. In contrast, the Liberals—the second most native, French-Canadian, Catholic party—were relatively equally distributed, in terms of birthplace, through Western Canada, Ontario, and Quebec. Half had been raised in large metropolitan areas and (in contrast to the Creditiste MPs) 46% were the sons of professionals and executives and proprietors of businesses. Liberal MPs also were far better educated than were Creditiste MPs: 80% had attended a college or university; 72% were university or college graduates; 29% had attended a graduate school; and 53% had attended professional schools (with 43% holding law degrees). Given their favored socioeconomic origins and the extent and quality of the education they had enjoyed (a quarter of the Liberal MPs who were university graduates had received their undergraduate degrees from Canada's big

## TABLE 2.1
## SOCIAL BACKGROUNDS OF MPS BY PARTY

| | NDP (N = 22) | Liberal (N = 100) | Conservative (N = 60) | Creditiste (N = 7) | All (N = 189) |
|---|---|---|---|---|---|
| Both parents born in Canada | 40.9% | 74.0% | 66.7% | 85.7% | 68.3% |
| MP born in Canada | 86.4 | 95.0 | 90.0 | 100.0 | 92.6 |
| Anglo-Celtic and Northern European ethnic origins | 59.1 | 45.0 | 63.3 | – | 50.8 |
| French-Canadian ethnic origins | – | 29.0 | 5.0 | 100.0 | 20.6 |
| Central and Eastern European ethnic origins | 4.5 | 9.0 | 10.0 | – | 8.4 |
| "Other" Canadian[a] | 36.5 | 17.0 | 21.7 | – | 20.1 |
| MP born in Western Provinces | 63.6 | 24.0 | 31.7 | – | 30.2 |
| MP born in Ontario | 21.7 | 37.0 | 23.3 | 14.3 | 30.2 |
| MP born in Quebec | – | 28.0 | 3.3 | 85.7 | 19.0 |
| MP born in Atlantic Provinces | – | 6.0 | 31.7 | – | 13.1 |
| MP grew up in large city | 41.0 | 50.0 | 4.0 | – | 35.5 |
| MP grew up in small town | 46.0 | 39.0 | 60.0 | 57.0 | 47.1 |
| MP grew up on farm | 5.0 | 10.0 | 25.0 | 43.0 | 15.4 |
| Religious affiliation is Protestant | 50.0 | 36.0 | 77.0 | – | 49.5 |
| Religious affiliation is Catholic | 5.0 | 53.0 | 18.0 | 100.0 | 38.0 |
| Religious affiliation is Jewish | 9.0 | 3.0 | 1.7 | – | 3.2 |
| Other religious affiliations | – | 4.0 | 1.7 | – | 2.6 |
| No formal religious affiliations | 36.0 | 2.0 | 1.7 | – | 4.2 |

| | | | | | |
|---|---|---|---|---|---|
| $\bar{X}$ SES of father | 37.2 | 50.0 | 41.3 | 21.1 | 44.7 |
| % whose fathers were professionals and business proprietors and executives | 22.7 | 46.0 | 41.6 | — | 40.2 |
| % whose fathers were unskilled blue collar and service workers | 9.1 | 13.0 | 13.3 | 28.6 | 13.2 |
| $\bar{X}$ years of formal education | 15.2 | 17.0 | 15.9 | 12.6 | 16.3 |
| % who attended schools outside the province in which they were reared | 45.5 | 40.0 | 48.3 | 14.3 | 42.3 |
| % who attended a college or university | 77.3 | 80.0 | 70.0 | 42.9 | 75.1 |
| % who are university graduates | 54.5 | 72.0 | 58.3 | 28.6 | 64.0 |
| % who graduated from Toronto, McGill, and Queen's universities | 4.5 | 24.0 | 5.0 | — | 14.8 |
| % who graduated from older, established provincial universities | 50.5 | 27.0 | 43.3 | — | 34.4 |
| % who attended graduate school | 22.7 | 29.0 | 21.7 | — | 24.9 |
| % who attended a professional school | 13.6 | 53.0 | 45.0 | — | 43.9 |
| % who have law degrees | 9.1 | 43.0 | 27.3 | — | 32.8 |
| % who were professionals, business proprietors, and executives when they entered politics | 64.5 | 83.0 | 71.7 | 42.9 | 74.6 |
| $\bar{X}$ SES when entering politics | 61.3 | 76.1 | 61.7 | 60.2 | 69.4 |

a. Respondents indicated their origins were "Canadian." Interviewers were instructed not to probe respondents on this point.

three—Toronto, McGill, and Queen's), it is not surprising that the Liberals primarily were members of professions or business executives/proprietors at the time they entered politics.

With respect to the substantially higher socioeconomic statuses of Liberal MPs, the present findings are consonant with previously reported research on the recruitment of Canadian parliamentary candidates.[5] The present data do differ, however, in that in the 20th through the 27th parliaments the socioeconomic statuses of MPs of both major parties were significantly higher than were the SESs of MPs in the two minor parties. There were no marked differences in this regard between current Conservatives and MPs in the Social Credit and New Democratic parties. Social Credit MPs, for example, appear to have narrowed the SES gap that separated them from Conservative MPs during the period 1945—1965.[6] Also in contrast to the earlier period is the finding that a majority of the members of the NDP, like a majority of the Conservatives, are now university graduates. Despite this narrowing of social background differences, however, the members of the Creditiste parliamentary party still tended to have the most "proletarian" social backgrounds, the Liberals tended to have the most "elite," and the social origins of Conservative and NDP MPs tended to fall somewhere in between.

When we compared the political backgrounds of the four party groups, we found that differences among them were neither particularly sharp nor consistently in the same direction (see table 2.2). The only exceptions were the monotonic relationships between left-right party affiliations and the ages at which major socializing events occurred. Age of first identification with a political party was the variable that tapped the greatest difference between parties; the average member of the NDP identified with a party fully 5.5 years earlier than his counterpart in the Social Credit party.

The fact that MPs report becoming politically aware and psychologically identified with a party at later ages than have been reported by investigators who have studied the political socialization experiences of cross-sections of the population is worth noting.[7] The relatively late stage in life at which, for example, identifications with a political party are reported, may be due to MPs interpreting partisan psychological identification as a consequence of a conscious choice. Samples of the general population seem to translate party identification as a simple feeling of oneness with a party, or as an association with, or an affective attachment to, a party label, as previous studies of the development of a partisan identification have

TABLE 2.2
## POLITICAL BACKGROUNDS OF MPS BY PARTY

| | NDP | Liberal | Conser-vative | Credi-tiste | All |
|---|---|---|---|---|---|
| $\overline{X}$ Age of first awareness | 10.0 | 10.5 | 11.3 | 13.7 | 10.8 |
| $\overline{X}$ Age of first identification | 16.5 | 17.8 | 20.0 | 22.0 | 18.5 |
| $\overline{X}$ Age first political interest | 18.6 | 18.9 | 19.4 | 20.4 | 19.1 |
| % Father strongly or quite strongly interested in politics | 59.1 | 61.0 | 65.0 | 57.2 | 61.9 |
| % Mother strongly or quite strongly interested in politics | 22.7 | 39.0 | 45.0 | 14.3 | 38.1 |
| $\overline{X}$ Parental political interest score | 5.0 | 5.2 | 5.4 | 5.0 | 5.2 |
| % Where there was a great deal of political discussion at home | 45.5 | 39.0 | 40.0 | 57.1 | 40.7 |
| % Whose father active in politics | 27.3 | 41.0 | 48.3 | 57.1 | 42.3 |
| % Whose mother active in politics | — | 13.0 | 8.3 | 14.3 | 10.1 |
| % Whose father held elected or appointed public office | 18.1 | 24.0 | 30.0 | 28.6 | 25.4 |
| % Whose father held party office and/or campaigned for party | 27.3 | 41.0 | 42.4 | 28.6 | 32.3 |
| % Whose interest in politics initially high and remained high | 54.5 | 61.0 | 45.0 | 71.4 | 55.6 |
| % Whose first identification congruent with both parents' identifications | 22.7 | 54.0 | 53.3 | 14.3 | 48.7 |
| % Who belonged to political groups in high school and college | 40.9 | 47.0 | 31.6 | 42.9 | 41.3 |
| % Who belonged to political groups outside of school | 27.3 | 34.0 | 20.0 | 28.6 | 28.6 |
| % Whose friends interested in politics | 31.8 | 24.0 | 21.7 | 14.3 | 23.8 |
| $\overline{X}$ PRIMP scores (importance of politics to "R") | .14 | .05 | −.18 | .80 | .06 |
| $\overline{X}$ Age became active in party work | 28.1 | 29.5 | 28.6 | 24.6 | 28.9 |
| % Who never held a formal party office | 22.7 | 33.0 | 50.2 | 42.9 | 32.6 |
| % Who held one party office at constituency, provincial, or federal levels | 31.8 | 43.0 | 21.7 | 42.9 | 34.9 |
| % Who held two or more party offices | 45.5 | 24.0 | 28.4 | 14.3 | 27.5 |

made clear.[8] It may well be the case that MPs formed an identification with their political party in the same way. But what may have occurred to make their responses different is that, because they are educated and highly politicized, the MPs insisted on structuring and interpreting the process in rational and cognitive rather than in affective terms. The case is strengthened by other data in table 2.2. In comparison to average-man populations in Canada, we find that Canadian MPs report what can only be termed an extraordinary degree of political interest and participation on the part of their parents. For example, 62% reported that their fathers were strongly interested in politics; 38% reported having had a politically interested mother; 41% reported a great deal of political discussion at home; and one fourth of the MPs indicated that their fathers had held a public office. One third also reported that their fathers had held a formal office in a political party organization and/or had actively campaigned on behalf of a party.[9] Given these backgrounds, it is not surprising that 41% of the MPs belonged to political groups when they were in high schools and universities, that 28% belonged to political groups outside of school, that, on the average, they became active party workers at age 29, and that 62% had held one or more formal offices in their party organizations before they became candidates for parliament. We will examine the circumstances under which they became candidates.

## RECRUITMENT[10]

The data presented in Tables 2.1 and 2.2, in studies of the 25th and 26th Canadian parliaments,[11] as well as in a diachronic analysis of the relationships between social and economic development on the one hand and changes in parliamentary recruitment patterns and parliament's policy outputs on the other,[12] document the fact that Canadian members of parliament constitute both a socioeconomic and political elite. The paper by Kornberg, Falcone, and Mishler also notes that: (1) as the Canadian party system developed, the proportion of MPs "crossing the aisle" dropped sharply; and (2) as the political system became more participatory, the number of Notables elected to parliament declined. Since Notables had tended to monopolize the holding of public office at the local and provincial levels, when their numbers declined, so did the overall level of preparliamentary public office-holding experience among 20th century MPs. Our data indicate that many of the trends noted in earlier studies continued in the 28th Parliament. With regard to the stability of party preferences, for example, 83% of the MPs had identified psychologically only with their current parties and on the average they had maintained their identifications for over 28 years. However, a somewhat larger proportion of current members had held public offices before their elections to parliament (40%) than was the case for members of the 20th through the 27th parliaments (34%), and an additional 20% of the current respondents had unsuccessfully sought elected office (see table 2.3).

With respect to the process by which they are inducted into the political system, the data in table 2.1 through 2.3, together with data derived from a previous study[13] and from off-the-record interviews with MPs and high ranking local party officials, suggest the scenario that follows is a reasonably accurate description of the parliamentary recruitment process. The average member of parliament, whom we shall call "Bill Hill," unlike the average Canadian, was reared in an upper-middle class home in which politics was a normal topic of conversation among family members. His father, an executive with a large department store chain, long had been active in the Liberal party in "Prairie City," Manitoba, and was personally acquainted with the longtime Liberal premier of the province. As Bill grew older, his interest in politics deepened, and by the time he was an undergraduate at the University of Manitoba, he was sufficiently committed psychologically to the Liberal party to gravitate to the campus Young Liberal Club, to work in the campaign of a family friend who was running for the provincial legislature, and to serve as a delegate to two provincial conventions and one national meeting of the Young Liberal Association. His decision to study law was motivated in part by a sincere interest in law as a profession, and in part by the realization that a law practice could be combined quite readily with an interest and involvement in politics.

After completing his legal studies in Toronto at Osgoode Hall, Bill returned home, opened a law practice with two lifelong friends who also were mildly interested in politics, and became active in the Liberal party organization in his riding. During the next decade (to the extent that increasing professional and familial responsibilities permitted) Bill was active in civic affairs, in the Liberal party, and even won election to a two-year term on the Prairie City school board. By 1965, he was financial chairman for the second of "John Forsythe's" close, but unsuccessful, attempts to unseat the riding's incumbent Conservative MP. When Forsythe announced after the election (even though he had come within 380 votes of unseating the incumbent) that he would not contest a parliamentary election again, Bill was asked to chair a party committee that would search for suitable candidates to carry the party's standard in the next federal election. It was Bill's wife and then two of Bill's friends whom he had appointed to his committee who first suggested, over

## TABLE 2.3
### CIRCUMSTANCES SURROUNDING THE RECRUITMENT OF MPS BY PARTY

| | NDP | Liberal | Conser-vative | Credi-tiste | All |
|---|---|---|---|---|---|
| Circumstances Surrounding Recruitment | | | | | |
| $\overline{X}$ number of years lived in constituency represented | 28.5 | 31.6 | 40.6 | 31.7 | 34.2 |
| % said family encouraged them to get into politics | 4.5 | 13.0 | 1.7 | – | 7.9 |
| % said friends and neighbors encouraged them | 13.6 | 28.0 | 15.0 | 28.6 | 22.2 |
| % said interest groups encouraged them | 13.6 | 13.0 | 15.0 | 14.3 | 13.8 |
| % said party encouraged them | 45.5 | 43.0 | 50.0 | 28.6 | 45.0 |
| % said decision to enter politics encouraged by others | 31.8 | 42.0 | 45.0 | 42.9 | 41.8 |
| % who said decision was their own | 22.7 | 30.0 | 33.3 | 42.9 | 30.7 |
| % who said decision was a product of both encourage-ment and personal decision | 36.4 | 27.0 | 20.0 | 14.3 | 25.4 |
| Motives for Running for MP | | | | | |
| % motivated by party pressure | 36.4 | 34.0 | 50.0 | 42.9 | 39.7 |
| % motivated by pressure from others | 22.7 | 38.0 | 28.3 | 42.9 | 33.3 |
| % motivated by ideological considerations | 45.5 | 41.0 | 63.3 | 71.4 | 49.7 |
| % motivated by "good government" considerations | 63.6 | 66.0 | 60.0 | 57.1 | 63.5 |
| % motivated by "challenge of office" considerations | 45.5 | 60.0 | 46.7 | 42.9 | 53.4 |

Candidacy

| | | | | | |
|---|---|---|---|---|---|
| $\bar{X}$ number of public offices held | 2.2 | 1.6 | 2.1 | 3.3 | 1.9 |
| % who volunteered their services when they became a candidate for an elected office | 27.3 | 42.0 | 36.0 | 42.9 | 38.6 |
| % who were recruited to run for the office | 54.5 | 46.0 | 55.0 | 57.1 | 50.3 |
| % who were already active party workers when they first became a public office candidate | 90.9 | 80.0 | 83.3 | 100.0 | 83.1 |
| % who unsuccessfully tried to get nomination for MP | 13.6 | 10.0 | 10.0 | 14.3 | 10.6 |
| % who had been elected to public office before becoming MP | 40.9 | 38.0 | 43.3 | 42.9 | 40.2 |
| % who had been unsuccessful candidates for public office before becoming MP candidate | 27.3 | 16.0 | 18.3 | 57.1 | 19.6 |
| % who had opposition when they were successful in becoming candidate | 77.3 | 70.0 | 61.7 | 57.1 | 67.7 |
| Which Level of Party Organization Most Important in Securing Nomination for MP | | | | | |
| Constituency | 45.5 | 51.0 | 35.0 | 71.4 | 46.0 |
| Provincial | 9.1 | 6.0 | 10.0 | – | 7.4 |
| Federal | – | 14.0 | 10.0 | 28.6 | 11.6 |
| Combination of two of the above | 13.6 | 17.0 | 21.7 | – | 17.4 |
| Factors Instrumental in Securing Nomination | | | | | |
| Personal characteristics of candidate | 90.9 | 78.0 | 83.3 | 85.7 | 81.5 |
| Circumstantial factors | 45.5 | 70.0 | 66.7 | 42.9 | 65.1 |

a. Percentages may total more than 100% because multiple responses were permitted.

coffee, that Bill himself would be the best candidate the party could find. After all, he long had worked on behalf of others in the party, he was widely known because of his school board and civic club service, he was well established professionally, and he undoubtedly would receive at least as much support as had Forsythe (who, they recalled, was not really the kind of man with whom the voters could identify). Flattered, but not yet convinced, Bill informally discussed his possible candidacy for parliament with his two law partners. He was pleasantly surprised by their genuinely warm and enthusiastic response. Nonetheless, for the next six months Bill and his committee continued to search for suitable candidates while Bill considered his own potential candidacy. He was certain that if he could secure the nomination, he would win the election. He knew from years of working in the party that there were many things he could do in his campaign that would bring him victory—things that Forsythe had never done. And, because the party was sure to form the government again, there were many, many things he, a government member, could do for the riding (which understandably had been neglected since the voters had insisted on returning a Conservative since 1958).

His excitement continuously increasing, Bill announced his intention to stand for the nomination in January of 1968 after: (1) the word had been passed from Ottawa that the prime minister would dissolve parliament and call an election either in the spring or late fall of the year; (2) a weekend trip to Ottawa and discreet talks with key people in the party's national office; and (3) an all-day discussion with his two law partners. National party officials assured him, although naturally they could not become overtly involved if opposition to his nomination developed, that they would be delighted if he were nominated. In the event he was nominated, they would do whatever they could to help Bill win the election. For, they agreed, the incumbent Conservative could be taken, and Bill was precisely the kind of Liberal candidate who could take him. His partners agreed that he could retain his partnership in the firm if he were nominated, although they would insist upon a new division of profits should he be elected. Having made his decision, Bill and his two friends on the committee "searching" for a candidate arranged a series of small, informal meetings between Bill, key people on the constituency party's executive committee, and all the well-known, long-time Liberal supporters in the constituency. Bill repeatedly emphasized to these groups that: if nominated, he was confident he could win the election; a strong new Liberal voice from the district was needed in Ottawa; as an MP he would work unceasingly on behalf of all people in the riding; he would be a loyal member of the Trudeau team, but would do his best in party caucus to stop what he regarded as the dangerous leftward drift of the party; although he was sympathetic to the aspirations of Quebec, the national interest must supersede any provincial interest; and, if a Conservative government were elected, it truly would be a national disaster. As a consequence of these meetings, Bill secured promises of support in both the nominating meeting scheduled for the next month and his future electoral campaign. Although gratified by these promises of assistance, he was surprised and irritated to learn that Forsythe, the former candidate, had changed his mind at virtually the last moment and would seek the party's nomination for a third time. Happily, on the night of the nominating meeting Bill's nomination speech was extremely well received by his many friends and supporters who, true to their promises, were present in the audience. After four tied votes (Forsythe also had friends) he finally was declared the party's candidate. Forsythe then graciously moved that his nomination be made unanimous and also agreed to become honorary chairman of Bill's campaign committee.

Although obviously the pathways to parliament taken by the several members of the 28th Parliament differed markedly from our mythical Bill Hill, the scenario is sufficiently grounded in reality to be a reasonably accurate description of the Canadian parliamentary recruitment process. Having described how most members journey to parliament, let us now consider what they do when they finally arrive.

## ON BECOMING A MEMBER OF PARLIAMENT

The position of Member of Parliament is a highly visible one and the set of behaviors associated with it may be said to constitute a role. Limits of the role are determined by the expectations held for the position by incumbents, by the incumbents of related positions, and by codes of formal (procedural rules) and informal (rules of the game) behavior. Although the rules of the legislative game have been delineated for American congressmen,[14] state legislators[15] and Canadian MPs,[16] other than for American legislators, to our knowledge no systematic empirical attempts have been made to determine precisely what expectations new members have for their roles. To fill this gap, we asked respondents whether, before they took office, they had "any ideas about what the job of an MP entailed"; what these expectations were; and whether, and in what manner, their expectations for the position differed from the reality of their first year in office. We also asked them what they regarded as the most gratifying and the least gratifying aspects of their first year.

Considering first their expectations for the position of Member of Parliament, we may note that 80% of the interviewees said that they did have an idea of what the position of MP entailed.[17] The expectations of 35% were based on personal and fairly frequent interactions with sitting MPs and on their frequent past visits to Ottawa. Another 21% said their expectations for the position derived from previous personal experience as incumbents of local and provincial public offices. And, although they did not say so explicitly, we may infer that at least some of the remaining 44% who said they knew something about the position derived their knowledge from personal observations of parliament at work, from media reports, and from textbooks and lectures on the functions of parliament that are a part of every basic high school and university course on Canadian government.

Nonetheless, when they were probed about specific expectations, about half the MPs were rather vague. Despite their excellent educations, their political sophistication, and their previous occupational experiences, 26% said they had only "general ideas, but no really specific knowledge about the job." Another 12% could only say that they expected "to work hard" or "to do a lot of work." Still others, when pressed, said things such as they expected to "make laws" (6%), "to work to achieve certain policies that I am interested in" (4%), to "travel a lot" (4%), to "work for and with parliamentary party colleagues" (4%), and "to answer mail and help constituents" (4%). Interestingly, 3% said they expected to be engaged in important enterprises because they knew the position of MP was a very important one, while at the other end of the spectrum, 6% said they really didn't expect to do much because they knew that individual MPs cannot hope to accomplish much. The most concrete expectations of the largest group of MPs (34%) were those of being "representatives of the people" or "ombudsmen."[18]

In response to the question on whether or not their expectations were fulfilled, 37% said they were. An additional 27% qualified their responses noting, for example, that "in general, they were, but there were a few surprises." The remaining 36% said either that matters did not go as they had expected, or that the reality of being a MP was completely different from their expectations for the position. Concerning the manner in which expectations differed from reality, 21% of those who said there were differences indicated that they were disappointed to learn there was very little they could accomplish as individuals. On the other hand, 13% said they were surprised and gratified to learn that they could grapple with and contribute to the solution of major national issues. Still another 20% said they were surprised to learn that the job of being a MP took up so much time, particularly that entailed in attending House debates. The remaining responses were structured in terms of the unexpected impact that becoming a MP had had on personal life styles (e.g., being separated from families for long periods of time, loss of privacy, the cost of maintaining two residences, etc.).

We may infer from these findings that most, although certainly not all, MPs learn what the specific aspects of their jobs are by watching and imitating the behavior of veteran MPs. They also learn from formal and informal interactions with the latter—interactions in which both the content and style of appropriate parliamentary behavior are communicated by the veterans to the new hands.[19]

## RULES OF THE GAME

Previous studies of legislative bodies have suggested that the stylistic dimension of roles often takes the form of informal behavioral norms, termed rules of the game. In order to determine the content of these rules, and to understand both how individual MPs become aware of them, and why they are inclined to adhere to them, we elicited the respondents' reactions to the now familiar statement: "We have been told that every legislature has its unofficial rules of the game, certain things that members must do and certain things they must not do if they want the respect and cooperation of their legislative colleagues." A second frequently employed statement, "I imagine that things could be made rather difficult for anyone who didn't observe these rules," was included to identify sanctions. Finally, we asked respondents when (i.e., before or after taking office) and from whom they had learned the rules of the game.[20]

Using an identical set of questions in his 1962 study of the 25th Parliament,[21] Kornberg found that the rules of the game and the sanctions that were available to enforce them fell into two categories: (a) those applying to behavior on the floor of the House; and (b) those applying either to behavior outside of the House but within parliament, or to behavior entirely outside of parliament. Moreover, the rules could be further categorized according to the functions they appeared to perform. Thus, rules affecting behavior within the House appeared to perform six functions. These were: (1) they helped to decrease and control conflict among parties and individual members; (2) they helped expedite the passage of legislation through the House; (3) they discouraged conduct by individual MPs that would invite criticism of the House as an institution; (4) they helped maintain party cohesion and disciplined party action; (5) they encouraged members to develop expertise in particular areas; and (6) they reinforced respect for the formal rules. The rules operating outside of the House appeared to perform four functions: (1) they helped decrease and control conflict among individual members; (2) they discouraged conduct that would subject the institution and its members to criticism; (3) they encouraged individual members to perform their tasks efficiently; and (4) they discouraged conflict within individual parliamentary parties. Insofar as sanctions were available in the House, these came from parliamentary colleagues and from the speaker. Outside of the House, sanctions could be invoked by the members of one's parliamentary party, by members of other parties, and by the constituency party organizations. The most frequently applied sanction appeared to be the social ostracism of an offending member.

We found that the rules and sanctions articulated by members of the 28th Parliament also could be classified in this manner. Table 2.4 presents a comparison of the relative frequency with which the members of the 25th and 28th parliaments articulated the several categories of rules and sanctions. The rules most frequently cited by members of the 28th Parliament were intended to promote party solidarity in the House chamber. Many members stated unequivocally that a member must vote with his party in the House, although they added that he was free to argue his case in caucus. Rules that channel conflict in the House also received attention; the most frequently mentioned was the injunction against personal attacks on members of other parties or bringing personality into House debates. Rules intended to encourage expertise were the only others mentioned with any frequency. Expertise was valued by members of all parties. Liberal backbenchers observed that a conspicuous display of expertise was a way of attracting the attention of party leaders in caucus and thus was an avenue for advancing to the frontbench.

TABLE 2.4

## A COMPARISON OF THE RELATIVE FREQUENCY WITH WHICH THE SEVERAL CATEGORIES OF RULES AND SANCTIONS WERE MENTIONED BY MEMBERS OF THE 25TH AND 28TH CANADIAN PARLIAMENTS

|  | 25th Parliament, 1962–63 | 28th Parliament 1968–72 |
|---|---|---|
| Rules in the House Chamber by Primary Functions | | |
| Rules to decrease conflict | 35.2% | 24.3% |
| Rule to expedite legislative business | 10.0 | 5.3 |
| Rules to discourage conduct that would invite criticism | 10.9 | 3.2 |
| Rules to maintain disciplined, cohesive party system | 14.0 | 45.5 |
| Rules to encourage expertise | 10.4 | 19.0 |
| Rules to reinforce respect to formal rules | 3.4 | 5.8 |
| Others | — | 2.6 |
| Rules Outside the House Chamber by Primary Functions | | |
| Rules to decrease conflict | 21.3 | 35.4 |
| Rules to discourage conduct that would invite criticism | 48.9 | 27.0 |
| Rules to encourage work and task performance | 6.2 | 2.6 |
| Rules to discourage intra-party conflict | 6.2 | 6.3 |
| Others | — | 10.6 |
| Sanctions Applied in the House Chamber | | |
| Sanctions from colleagues | 11.7 | 17.5 |
| Sanctions from speaker | 4.7 | 4.2 |
| Others | — | 1.5 |
| Sanctions Applied Outside the House Chamber | | |
| Sanctions from party colleagues | 7.6 | 38.6 |
| Sanctions from other members | 11.8 | 33.3 |
| Sanctions from constituency party | 1.3 | 2.6 |
| Social ostracism | 31.7 | 25.9 |
| Others | — | 2.6 |

a. Percentages may total more than 100% because multiple responses were permitted.

Outside of the House, stress was laid on the importance of being "friendly," "courteous," "respecting other members as people," "working harmoniously in committees," and "mixing" with members of all parties at social affairs. The other category of "outside" rules most frequently cited (i.e., rules discouraging conduct that would invite criticism) stressed avoiding behavior that would make another member "look bad" or "get another member into trouble." MPs mentioning these rules indicated that members of the media are regarded with considerable suspicion (e.g., "Those . . . reporters are a bunch of vultures. All they are interested in is scandal and personality, not the serious business of the House").

Table 2.4 indicates that the most important sanctions are political ones that are invoked outside the House. The most frequently mentioned were denial of advancement in the parliamentary party hierarchies or (in the case of the governing party) to the cabinet, the withholding of both campaign funds and help from the national party organization during elections (e.g., "They [party leaders] won't come and campaign for you"). Respondents also noted that those who broke the rules could expect no cooperation from party colleagues in legislative matters. For example, cabinet members, it was claimed, were unavailable to offending members. Further, rule-breakers would receive no help with constituency-related problems. Social ostracism of offending members also was frequently mentioned, although this most often was employed by the opposition parties. The government had other sanctions at its disposal (e.g., trips abroad were awarded other MPs, offenders were assigned small, remote offices, committee chairmanships and parliamentary secretary positions were withheld). It is interesting to note that respondents almost always perceived that the other parties punished their rule-breaking members more severely than did their own parties. However, opposition party MPs were united in their belief that the Liberals more often muzzled their members and were more likely to discipline offenders by cutting off campaign funds and intervening in nominating proceedings to prevent the renomination of any member who continuously and conspicuously flouted the rules.

Also of interest is the finding that approximately 9% of the respondents felt that while sanctions could successfully be invoked against others, they personally were immune because they did not regard the actions customarily taken as punitive (e.g., "If you don't care about trips, office space, or their lousy committee chairmanships, then things really aren't too difficult." "If you have guts, ability, and can finance your own campaign, then you can afford to grandstand, be unorthodox, a maverick. You can get away with anything, they can't hurt you. Hell, Trudeau was a maverick. With his millions he could afford to be, although he is now an expert at co-opting mavericks"). Apparently, there are few sanctions that can be invoked against members on the floor of the House. Only three were mentioned: the House leaders of the several parties leave the names of rule-breaking members off the speaker's list, the speaker neglects to recognize offenders during Question Period, and members greet a member who continuously ignores the rules with derisive remarks and catcalls when he attempts to speak.

A comparison of the types of rules and sanctions articulated by MPs in 1962 and in 1971–1972 indicates they were similar. What differs is the frequency with which the categories are cited. Members of the 28th Parliament seemingly were more concerned with maintaining disciplined parties and less concerned with controlling interparty conflict than were their predecessors a decade earlier. The latter were more concerned with blunting external criticism and less concerned with mitigating individual and interparty conflict outside the House. As far as sanctions are concerned, the members of the 28th Parliament more often perceived sanctions coming from their colleagues in the House, particularly the members of their own parties, than did members of the 25th Parliament. This difference can be explained largely by the fact that current respondents were more aware of sanctions than were the earlier members; only 17% of the 1962 members (in contrast to 67% of current respondents) were aware of sanctions that could be applied in the House chamber and only 53% (as opposed to 67% of members of the 28th Parliament) were aware of sanctions available outside the House. Another 8% of the current interviewees acknowledged that sanctions were available but claimed these were ineffective insofar as they personally were concerned. Only 16% said there were no sanctions, while the remaining 8% acknowledged that although sanctions might be available, they were unaware of any specific ones.

It is more difficult to explain why the members of the 28th Parliament so frequently cited rules whose purpose is to maintain disciplined party action in the House. Moreover, on the one hand they more often cited rules whose function is to control interparty conflict outside the House, but on the other, they were less concerned than were their predecessors with rules that are intended to help control such conflict in the House. Although current respondents were more aware of rules, this probably does not explain differences of the magnitudes indicated in table 2.4. The new committee system may offer a partial explanation. We can speculate that in order for the new system to function effectively, members of the several standing committees, regardless of their party affiliations, have had to cooperate. This may have encouraged them to cite rules such as "don't be overly or stupidly partisan," and, "collaborate in committee work." Since, however, such interparty collaboration can pose a threat to party discipline, they also cited rules that clearly are intended to facilitate discipline and cohesive action in the House (e.g., "vote with your party or get the hell out of it"). In other words, they may have been citing rules that function to facilitate and reinforce partisanship in situations in which partisan behavior is deemed appropriate (i.e., on the floor of the House) while at the same time citing rules whose purpose is to encourage nonpartisanship in settings in which that kind of behavior is considered appropriate (i.e., in committees).

Turning from the rules themselves to how these rules are learned, we may note that the majority of MPs (59%) other than the members of the Social Credit party, said they learned the rules after rather than before their election to parliament. But among the 59% who said they learned the rules of the game after their election, only 20% said they learned them from other MPs. The others said they learned them "on their own." The latter emphasized that: (a) the learning of rules of the game entails no great difficulty (e.g., "It's no big deal, they're widely known"); and (b) the rules are not unique to legislatures, but are particular applications of general norms that structure behavior in most hierarchically organized, complex organizations. Many of the MPs who said they learned the rules before their election to parliament also stressed these two points. For example, some said they had learned the rules when they were members of provincial legislatures and that the parliamentary rules of the game were somewhat, but not drastically, different. As one such respondent noted, "You have to get along, be honest, trustworthy, mix with everybody, be guarded in your remarks to the press when you are a MLA. The situation is no different there than it is here. Understandably, it is a lot easier getting along with people on a day-to-day basis if you assume they are honest, trustworthy, and reliable. It makes things predictable."

## THE FIRST YEAR

We assumed that a MP's first year in office might have been particularly memorable so we asked: (a) what aspects of the first year in office were found most gratifying; and (b) what aspects were most burdensome and onerous. We found that the aspect of their work that they most frequently (45%) found gratifying was to successfully complete a specific task—no matter how minor—given the heavy demands that were made upon their time. This was particularly true of members of the Liberal and Conservative parties. Members of the NDP most frequently found the role of ombudsman gratifying; 60% of the NDP MPs and 31% of the MPs in the other parties specifically referred to this in their responses. Another 23% of the respondents felt their work on standing committees was the most gratifying part of their first year in office. Still another frequently mentioned source of gratification was the excitement of parliament (e.g., "Just being here was gratifying. I couldn't get over it the first few months. I loved it. It seemed that one day I was reading about people like Trudeau, Sharp, and Diefenbaker, the next day I was one of them"). The two other gratifying experiences that were mentioned were meeting a great variety of people and traveling through the country and overseas.

The two most frequently cited first year burdens were the heavy work load and the frustration experienced in trying to deal successfully with problems that faced them. Some 40% of the MPs said they simply were unprepared for the volume of work with which they were faced upon taking office, while 34% said they were frustrated with the red tape, with the bureaucracy, and with their inability to help constituents who had problems. Closely related to work load and the inability to help constituents were complaints about the volume of paper work, the lack of staff, the amount of time spent and the boredom and tedium that resulted from sitting hour after hour in the House, and the inability to visit constituencies or to maintain adequate communication with constituents. Other aspects of their first year in office that MPs found burdensome were social dislocations that resulted from moving their families to Ottawa or traveling to see them, the additional expenses that resulted from having to maintain two homes, the loss of privacy and the disruption of the lives of their children. Although respondents were more often able to cite specific examples of the burdensome tasks, there is some indication that, on balance, they found their first year's experience in office more psychically gratifying than trying. Thus, whereas not a single respondent said there was nothing gratifying about their first year in office, 12% did say that they found absolutely nothing that was onerous or burdensome during their first year in parliament. The words of one such MP, "Not a thing. It was a ball!" best reflect this perspective.

## ACCOMPLISHMENTS AND FUTURE GOALS

Historically, about 40% of the members of each Canadian parliament have been novices. Although this pattern held for the 28th Parliament (39.9% of the members were freshmen), there also was a solid cohort of experienced MPs. Thus, 16% of the members had fifteen or more years of experience at the time these interviews were taken (i.e., during the third session of the 28th Parliament). The median number of years of experience for all MPs was 7.2. The Conservative parliamentary delegation contained the most experienced group of MPs (median = 13.7 years). The parliamentary experience of the members of the other three parties was considerably less; the medians for the governing Liberals and the opposition Creditiste and New Democratic Party groups were, respectively, 6.8, 7.0 and 6.8 years. During their tenure in office the majority of the MPs had been concerned, as one would expect, with the formulation and evaluation of public policy, with serving their constituents, or with both the policy process and their constituents. In response to the question, "Apart from looking after your constituents, what are the most important things you have tried to accomplish as a MP?", 30% were able to cite at least one specific accomplishment, 54% cited two to four accomplishments, and 13% mentioned five or more specific things they had accomplished during their years in office. [22] Since constituency service was taken for granted, the expectation was that most MPs would make general or specific references to their accomplishments in one or more areas of public policy, and indeed 60% did make such references. Nonetheless, 11% referred only to things accomplished on behalf of individuals or groups within their constituencies and 22% referred to legislation that concerned both policy and constituency. Eight other respondents referred to accomplishments that affected parliament as an institution. It should be noted that the majority of those who referred to some policy accomplishment did not claim personal responsibility for the passage or defeat of legislation. Rather, their more modest claims were that they "had something to do with" a specific piece of legislation or that they had been "active" and/or "interested" in a particular policy area.

TABLE 2.5

## MEAN YEARS OF SERVICE, PERCEIVED ACCOMPLISHMENTS, AND POLICY ORIENTATIONS OF MPs BY PARTY

|  | NDP | Liberal | Conser-vative | Credi-tiste | All |
|---|---|---|---|---|---|
| Accomplishments |  |  |  |  |  |
| Accomplishments concern public policy | 68.2% | 63.0% | 55.0% | 28.6% | 59.8% |
| Accomplishments concern constituents | 9.1 | 11.0 | 8.3 | 42.9 | 11.1 |
| Accomplishments concern both policy and constituents | 18.2 | 19.0 | 30.0 | — | 21.7 |
| Accomplishments concern neither policy nor constituents | 4.5 | 3.0 | 5.0 | 14.3 | 4.2 |
| N.A. | — | 4.0 | 1.7 | 14.3 | 3.2 |
| Policy Orientations[a] |  |  |  |  |  |
| Orientation is international | 18.2 | 15.0 | 13.3 | — | 14.3 |
| Orientation is national | 81.8 | 70.0 | 75.0 | 28.6 | 71.4 |
| Orientation is provincial | 4.5 | 23.0 | 31.7 | — | 22.8 |
| Orientation is constituency | 22.7 | 19.0 | 21.7 | — | 19.6 |
| $\overline{X}$ years of experience | 9.5 | 7.4 | 11.2 | 8.3 | 8.5 |

a. Some columns may total more than 100% because respondents could mention more than one orientation.

In his 1962 study Kornberg found that the members of the Liberal and New Democratic parties were more concerned with public policy matters than were their counterparts in the Conservative and the Social Credit parties. An examination of the data indicates this also was the case in the 28th Parliament. Approximately two-thirds of the members of both the New Democratic and Liberal parties made references to public policy in evaluating their accomplishments whereas 55% of the Conservatives and only 29% of the Social Credit MPs made such references. Although they sometimes combined it with concern for their provinces and constituencies, the level of government to which MPs who structured their accomplishments in policy terms most frequently referred was the national government. Thus, fully 71% of the respondents who made references to policy talked about national policy accomplishments; 23% referred to policies that had been aimed at their constituencies; and 14% talked about their international policy accomplishments (i.e., foreign trade, Canada's role in the United Nations, Canada's contribution to peace-keeping, and so forth). The NDP MPs primarily had been concerned with national policy and secondarily with constituency and foreign policy. The principal concern of Liberal MPs had been national policy; foreign, provincial and constituency policies all had been of secondary interest. The Conservative hierarchy of policy concerns had been national, provincial, constituency-related and international. And, to the extent they had been concerned with public policy, the Creditiste orientations had been national.

We followed this question with one on aspirations for the future (i.e., "What are the most important things you want to accomplish in the future?"). Six respondents said there was "nothing" they wanted to accomplish and nine others said they really hadn't thought about what they wanted to accomplish in the future; they were too worried about or too busy with the present. However, 43% were able to articulate at least one specific future goal. Another 42% articulated two to four goals, and 7% referred to five or more goals. As one might expect, a considerable number (22%) of the respondents who answered this question referred to the same matters they had talked about in their responses to the previous question; future goals were a continuation of their past work. Another 34% mentioned some of the same matters that they had already worked on but also voiced new concerns, whereas the future goals of fully 38% seemingly were unrelated to their previous activities.

In his 1962 study of the House of Commons Kornberg found that 47% of the MPs whom he interviewed had goals "that in some way were oriented toward the formulation or evaluation of legislative policies."[23] An even larger proportion of current MPs (55%), in response to our question on what they hoped to accomplish in the future, expressed the same kinds of goals. This is a particularly interesting finding given the fact that very few of them included policymaking as an expectation for the position of MP. It would appear, therefore—despite the literature on the decline of the private member as a policymaker in a parliamentary system—that sometime during his tenure in office the average MP comes to believe that he does have some role to play in the policy process.

As was the case in 1962, some of the MPs expressing policy goals were able to articulate them clearly, while the goals of others were amorphous and very general. Moreover, the concerns they reflected ranged from the narrow and esoteric to the broad and public—from their constituencies (even specific groups within their constituencies, 17%) to the international arena (10%). The majority however, reflected a concern with the nation as a whole (57%). The New

Democratic parliamentary party had the largest (69%) and the Liberals the smallest (52%) proportion of members who had goals that reflected an interest in national policy. Indeed, the NDP group had the largest proportion of members (64%) who expressed what we have termed "policy goals"; the Conservatives had the smallest proportion (48%), while approximately 55% of the Liberal and Social Credit MPs expressed these kinds of goals.

Turning from MPs who were concerned with future public policy to those who hoped to accomplish something specifically for their constituency, we may note that the proportion of such constituency-oriented MPs had decreased from 23% in 1962 to 15% in 1971–1972. And, whereas 30% of the 1962 sample had combined an interest in policy with a concern for their constituency–expressing what Kornberg termed "mixed goals"–only 16% of the current interviewees expressed goals of this kind. The remaining respondents (13%), most of whom were members of the Conservative and Social Credit parties, articulated what might be termed party and ideology-oriented future goals; the future welfare of their parties, the support of party activities, and the defeat in the next election of the current government or of individual ministers whose actions they found particularly objectionable.

We asked respondents whether they perceived differences between what they wanted to accomplish and what they felt significant others (i.e., their constituents, party colleagues in the House, their local, provincial and national party organizations and important interest groups in their constituency and province) wanted. We found that the members of the two more policy-oriented parties, the NDP and the Liberal, more frequently perceived the existence of conflict between their goals and what they felt significant others wanted than did the members of the Conservative and Social Credit parties. Indeed, only one member of the latter party perceived a difference between his goals and those of others (i.e., his provincial party). Although approximately 55% of the members of both the Liberal and New Democratic parties perceived conflict over goals with at least two important groups,[24] the NDP MPs were more inclined to see conflict with important interest groups, whereas Liberal MPs most often tended to perceive differences with parliamentary party colleagues (see table 2.6). Conservative MPs also tended to perceive differences over goals occurring more often with parliamentary party colleagues than with interest groups, with constituents, or with their party organizations in the electorate.

**TABLE 2.6**

## MPs' PERCEPTIONS OF CONFLICT WITH SIGNIFICANT OTHERS BY PARTY[a]

|  | NDP | Liberal | Conser-vative | Credi-tiste | All |
|---|---|---|---|---|---|
| % Perceived conflict with constituency | 40.9 | 30.0 | 23.3 | — | 28.0 |
| % Perceived conflict with parliamentary party colleagues | 31.8 | 53.0 | 48.3 | — | 47.1 |
| % Perceived conflict with local party organization | 9.1 | 20.0 | 13.3 | — | 15.9 |
| % Perceived conflict with provincial and/or national party organization | 22.7 | 37.0 | 16.7 | 14.3 | 28.0 |
| % Perceived conflict with interest groups | 68.2 | 36.0 | 36.7 | — | 38.6 |

a. Some columns total over 100% because respondents could cite more than one conflict.

The tendency of the members of both major parties to see differences over goals occurring more often with parliamentary party colleagues may be a function of both the larger size and the more representative character of their parliamentary groups. We may speculate that in large parliamentary parties there are fewer opportunities to get to know one's colleagues and/or to determine whether their goals and aspirations are congruent with one's own. Secondly, the Liberal and Conservative parties both have MPs who represent constituencies in the four principal regions. These broad electoral bases—relative to those of the New Democratic and Social Credit parties—make it highly probable that within-party policy preferences will be different and occasionally contradictory.

## REPRESENTATION AND ACCOUNTABILITY

Intraparty conflict over purposes and goals may have its roots in the debate over what takes precedence in a representative democracy—the nation or the several constituencies of which it is composed. The dilemma in which this nation/local representational imperative can place parliamentarians probably was best articulated by Edmund Burke in his famous speech to the electors of his Bristol constituency. But, as Heinz Eulau noted,[25] Burke's arguments were structured not only in terms of the focus of representation, but also in terms of appropriate representational style. Burke's predilections, Eulau reminds us, were not simply for national over local interests, but also for his own over his constituents' definition of what such interests were. An analysis of the representational roles of members of the 25th Canadian Parliament revealed that at least some MPs shared Burke's views.[26] It also revealed that there were two inter-related dimensions to the role styles of MPs—consultation and service. At one end of the continuum were MPs who felt they neither were required to consult with constituents nor to perform services for them (Burkean-Trustees). At the other end were MPs who felt they had to do both (Delegate-Servants). The group in the middle (Politicos) felt it was both desirable and necessary to consult with constituents, but they also wanted to rely on their own judgment; they were not averse to performing services, but they wanted to do more for their constituencies than merely run errands for individuals. Although the relationship was far from perfect, Kornberg found that role style was correlated with primary representational focus. However, in comparing Canadian MPs with a group of American congressmen studied by Roger Davidson,[27] it was apparent that the American congressmen fit Burke's model of the good representative better than Canadian MPs in terms of style, while the MPs adhered more closely to Burke's prescription concerning the propriety of focusing their representational efforts on national rather than on local interests. Kornberg also found that the representational role preferences of Canadian MPs varied with their party affiliations; the members of the Liberal and NDP parties tended to prefer the Trustee and Politico representational role styles and to focus their representational efforts on the nation, while members of the Conservative and Social Credit parties more often preferred the delegate role style and focused their representational efforts on their constituencies.[28]

Kornberg's 1962 findings were derived almost entirely from MPs responses to open-ended questions. In the present study we used direct quotations from some of their answers to try to delineate the role styles and the foci of representation of the members of the 28th[29] Parliament. These statements and the percentage of MPs by party who agreed with them are reported in table 2.7.

The first five statements in this table are concerned with both the focus and the style of representation. Our assumption was that MPs who agreed or tended to agree with these statements were oriented toward the instructed delegate role style and regarded the constituency rather than the nation as the geographical area to which they owed their most vigorous representational efforts. Insofar as representational role styles were concerned, our assumption was that

## TABLE 2.7
## REPRESENTATIONAL ROLE PERCEPTIONS OF MEMBERS BY PARTY
### (PERCENT WHO "AGREE" OR "TEND TO AGREE")

| | NDP | Liberal | Conservative | Creditiste | All MPs |
|---|---|---|---|---|---|
| 1) "The job of a MP entails being a sounding board for constituency opinion and then acting on it. I always attempt to find out what my constituents feel and make my decisions accordingly." | 19.0 | 42.2 | 59.6 | 100.0 | 47.1 |
| 2) "My first duty is to my constituency; they are the ones who elected me." | 25.0 | 37.4 | 57.9 | 83.3 | 44.2 |
| 3) "Let's face it. Insofar as people care about parliament, what they care about is what you as a MP can do for them in the way of services and favours; not what comes before parliament in the way of issues and legislation." | 33.3 | 23.9 | 34.5 | 50.0 | 29.4 |
| 4) "I am not at all certain that doing favours, running errands, or serving your constituents, call it whatever you wish, really helps get you elected. I am certain that *not doing these things* when asked will assure that you don't get elected." | 70.0 | 64.4 | 74.1 | 50.0 | 67.8 |
| 5) "The most important part of a MP's job—that is if he is interested in coming back to parliament—is to go to bat for his constituents in their dealings with government, which usually means the civil service. Even statesmen have to be reelected and for that you have to look after your constituents." | 71.4 | 73.3 | 89.5 | 83.3 | 78.7 |

| | | | | | |
|---|---|---|---|---|---|
| 6) "I can't see why there is any incompatibility between serving your constituency and the nation. I was elected to serve my country, but this is not and has never been inconsistent with serving my constituency and its people." | 80.9 | 84.2 | 86.2 | 100.0 | 85.0 |
| 7) "My job as a MP entails fighting for what I think is right. It also entails being a representative of the people in my constituency. I accept the fact that I have to deal with their problems but I also have to fight for the integrity of parliament and for a program of legislation that is in the national interest." | 100 | 96.7 | 94.8 | 100.0 | 96.5 |
| 8) "Even if a MP wanted to find out what his constituents felt about a major public issue, it would be impossible. The majority of people don't know. They don't have any information on these things. The rest, or most of the rest, simply don't care." | 28.6 | 37.4 | 37.5 | — | 35.0 |
| 9) "A MP seldom has to sound out his constituents because he thinks so much like them that he knows how they would react to almost any proposal." | 28.6 | 23.1 | 34.5 | — | 26.7 |
| 10) "My primary responsibility is to the nation as a whole. I am elected to serve the country." | 61.9 | 64.0 | 62.1 | 50.0 | 62.6 |
| 11) "My primary responsibility as a MP is to do as good a job as I can for the country—to act according to my conscience. The alternative is to toady to voters." | 70.0 | 70.6 | 73.7 | 100.0 | 72.6 |
| 12) "If anyone tells you he makes his decisions here in parliament on the basis of what his constituents want, assuming he knew what they want, he is either kidding you or himself." | 60.0 | 44.3 | 29.8 | 33.3 | 40.9 |

instructed delegates also would tend to be constituency errand boys and thus should be more likely to agree with the statement that people care more about services than the public policy decisions of MPs. They also should agree more often with the two statements that MPs who do not perform services and who do not go to bat for constituents will not be reelected. Statements six and seven were intended to tap the politico representational role orientation whereas statements eight through twelve were intended to reveal MPs who found the Burkean-Trustee role an especially congenial one. The assumption was that Politicos would be most likely to agree with statements six and seven while Trustees would agree with statements eight through twelve.

In order to make a more systematic determination of the extent to which the members' responses to these statements reflected a structured and consistent set of role beliefs, we factor analyzed the twelve representation style and focus items. Table 2.8 presents the resulting matrix of unrotated factor loadings and indicates that the responses to these items were relatively consistent and constrained. Specifically, although four factors with eigenvalues greater than 1.0 were produced by this procedure, factor I clearly was dominant accounting for almost 45% of the common variance in the twelve items. Five of the twelve role statements had loadings of .50 or more on factor I. In contrast, no more than two items loaded as strongly with any other factor, and none of these factors accounted for more than 25% of the common variance in the data.

With respect to the interpretation of the factors, inspection of the pattern of item loadings suggests that factor I is a general, summary dimension of the members' representational role orientations whereas factors II–IV appear to tap essentially idiosyncratic properties of several individual items. Supporting our interpretation of factor I, three of the five delegate style/constituency focus items (statements 1–5) load positively and strongly on this dimension while two of the Burkean style/national focus items (statements 10 and 12) load strongly and negatively. Consistent also with the hypothesis that politico role types fall midway on a representation continuum between delegates and trustees, the two politico items in the analysis (statements 6 and 7) load very close to zero. The strong, negative loadings of items 6 and 7 on factor IV and the more moderate, negative loadings of three of the Trustees items (statements 9–11) on factor III suggest that these factors, when reflexed, can be interpreted, respectively, as a politico and a Burkean role orientation. That each accounts for only 16% of the total variance explained by the four factors further suggests that they are residual dimensions and tap largely that variance in role perceptions left unexplained by factor I. Finally, the common denomination of the three items with fairly strong loadings on factor II appears to reflect the belief of some members that their constituents are politically apathetic and poorly informed. Although somewhat stronger than factors III and IV, we can speculate that this "perception of constituency capability" dimension may be more important as an explanation of the representational role perceptions of certain members than as an integral component of those roles.

Because representation is such a complex and multidimensional concept, we tried to explore it as fully as time and the patience of the interviewees would permit. Thus, during this portion of the interview, each MP was presented with a card on which was printed a list of institutions that one might reasonably assume would be represented by members of parliament in a society as socially heterogenous as Canada. They were asked, "To which, if any, of the following do you consider yourself accountable as a MP?"

1. Your party colleagues in the House
2. The leadership of your party in the House
3. Your local party organization
4. Your provincial party organization
5. Your national party organization
6. The people of your district who voted for you
7. The people of your district regardless of who they are
8. The people of your province
9. The people of Canada
10. Your conscience
11. The House as a whole
12. Others

After the respondents had checked this card, we presented them with a second copy of the same card. MPs then were asked, "Which of these is the most important to you?" Their responses to these two questions are presented in table 2.9.

As is evident, MPs rankings were similar in both cases. In order of frequency checked they were: their consciences; their constituents— (regardless of whether their constituents voted for them); and the people of Canada. In table 2.10 we have collapsed the several categories of the list into: (1) conscience; (2) people in the district; (3) people outside the district (their province and the rest of the nation); (4) the House of Commons as a whole; (5) party colleagues

## TABLE 2.8
## MATRIX OF FACTOR-LOADINGS OF 12 REPRESENTATIONAL ROLE ITEMS

| | Factor I | Factor II | Factor III | Factor IV | Communality $h^2$ |
|---|---|---|---|---|---|
| 1) "The job of a MP entails being a sounding board for constituency opinion and then acting on it. I always attempt to find out what my constituents feel and make my decisions accordingly." | .53 | −.26 | −.25 | .01 | .41 |
| 2) "My first duty is to my constituency; they are the ones who elected me." | .76 | .19 | −.07 | .02 | .62 |
| 3) "Let's face it. Insofar as people care about parliament, what they care about is what you as a MP can do for them in the way of services and favours; not what comes before parliament in the way of issues and legislation." | .30 | .54 | .00 | −.15 | .30 |
| 4) "I am not at all certain that doing favours, running errands, or serving your constituents, call it whatever you wish, really helps get you elected. I am certain that *not doing these things* when asked will assure that you don't get elected." | .15 | .12 | −.18 | .12 | .08 |
| 5) "The most important part of a MP's job—that is if he is interested in coming back to parliament—is to go to bat for his constituents in their dealings with government, which usually means the civil service. Even statesmen have to be reelected and for that you have to look after your constituents." | .54 | .20 | −.16 | .12 | .37 |

| Statement | | | | | |
|---|---|---|---|---|---|
| 6) "I can't see why there is any incompatibility between serving your constituency and the nation. I was elected to serve my country, but this is not and has never been inconsistent with serving my constituency and its people." | .02 | -.23 | -.21 | **-.52** | .37 |
| 7) "My job as a MP entails fighting for what I think is right. It also entails being a representative of the people in my constituency. I accept the fact that I have to deal with their problems but I also have to fight for the integrity of parliament and for a program of legislation that is in the national interest." | .08 | -.02 | -.05 | **-.50** | .26 |
| 8) "Even if a MP wanted to find out what his constituents felt about a major public issue, it would be impossible. The majority of people don't know. They don't have any information on these things. The rest, or most of the rest, simply don't care." | .14 | **.58** | .07 | -.28 | .44 |
| 9) "A MP seldom has to sound out his constituents because he thinks so much like them that he knows how they would react to almost any proposal." | .04 | .20 | -.33 | -.06 | .15 |
| 10) "My primary responsibility is to the nation as a whole, I am elected to serve the country." | **-.59** | -.15 | -.46 | -.07 | .59 |
| 11) "My primary responsibility as a MP is to do as good a job as I can for the country—to act according to my conscience. The alternative is to toady to voters." | -.20 | .19 | -.45 | .14 | .30 |
| 12) "If anyone tells you he makes his decision here in parliament on the basis of what his constituents want, assuming he knew what they want, he is either kidding you or himself." | **-.50** | .48 | -.05 | .17 | .51 |
| Percentage of Common Variance Explained | .43 | .25 | .16 | .16 | |

TABLE 2.9

DISTRIBUTION OF RESPONSES TO QUESTIONS ON THE
ACCOUNTABILITY OF MPs

| | Most Frequently Selected by MPs[a] | Most Important to MPs[a] |
|---|---|---|
| Your party colleagues in the House | 35.4% | 11.6% |
| Your party leaders | 35.0 | 11.0 |
| Your local party organization | 36.0 | 7.0 |
| Your provincial party organization | 11.0 | 2.6 |
| Your national party organization | 19.0 | 3.0 |
| People in your district who voted for you | 36.0 | 10.5 |
| People in your district regardless of who they are | 62.0 | 37.5 |
| People in your province | 20.2 | 4.2 |
| People of Canada | 48.3 | 22.7 |
| House as a whole | 17.0 | 2.0 |
| Your conscience | 64.5 | 44.0 |
| Others[b] | 8.0 | 8.0 |

a. Percentages total more than 100 because multiple responses were permitted.
b. Prime Minister, the Cabinet, Depends on the Issue.

in the House; and (6) party organizations in the electorate. The table compares the members of each of the four parties in terms of the frequency with which they selected these options and rank-ordered the importance of each. We find that the members of three of the four parties (Social Credit, Conservative, and Liberal) most often felt accountable and felt it was most important to be accountable to the people in their district. The NDP members most frequently selected their party organization in the electorate as the group to whom they felt accountable, but when asked to identify to whom or to what it was most important to be accountable, they selected their consciences.

Looking at the members of parliament as a group, without regard to party, the data indicate that first and foremost they feel accountable to their constituents and to themselves for their actions. Secondarily, they feel accountable to the nation as a whole and to their party colleagues in the House. These additional data help clarify why so many MPs found the politico role orientation so congenial (table 2.7, statements 6 and 7). It is, after all, a role that attempts to

# TABLE 2.10
## DISTRIBUTION OF RESPONSES TO QUESTIONS ON ACCOUNTABILITY BY PARTY[a]

| | NDP | | Liberal | |
|---|---|---|---|---|
| | Most Frequently Selected | Most Important | Most Frequently Selected | Most Important |
| Your conscience | 59.1% | 50.0% | 60.0% | 43.0% |
| People in your district | 63.6 | 40.9 | 75.0 | 45.0 |
| People outside district | 45.5 | 4.5 | 52.0 | 31.0 |
| House as a whole | 22.7 | — | 17.0 | 4.0 |
| Party colleagues in House | 45.5 | 22.7 | 39.0 | 20.0 |
| Party organization in the electorate | 72.7 | 27.3 | 36.0 | 8.0 |
| Others | 18.2 | 13.6 | 5.0 | 5.0 |

| | Conservative | | Creditiste | |
|---|---|---|---|---|
| | Most Frequently Selected | Most Important | Most Frequently Selected | Most Important |
| Your conscience | 78.3% | 45.0% | 28.6% | 28.6% |
| People in your district | 83.3 | 45.0 | 85.7 | 71.4 |
| People outside district | 48.3 | 21.7 | 71.4 | 28.6 |
| House as a whole | 16.7 | — | — | — |
| Party colleagues in House | 65.0 | 18.3 | 14.3 | 14.3 |
| Party organization in the electorate | 46.7 | 6.7 | 14.3 | 14.3 |
| Others | 3.3 | 10.0 | — | — |

a. Percentages total more than 100 because multiple responses were permitted.

combine disparate styles and representational foci and facilitates the reduction of any dissonance MPs may feel as a consequence of trying to serve simultaneously a variety of masters (their country, conscience, constituency, and party) in a variety of ways (as trustees, tribunes, errand-boys and ombudsmen).

## PARLIAMENT AS A CAREER

The importance of political ambitions as determinants of elite behavior is well established.[30] In order to understand further the motivations and political aspirations of members of parliament, we asked the MPs in our sample a series of questions concerning their attitudes toward parliamentary service as a career, their motivations for remaining in parliament and their aspirations for other public office positions. We found, in response to the question, "Do you expect to make a career out of parliament?" that over one-third of the respondents did want to make a career out of being a member of parliament, approximately one of five did not, while the remainder refused to say. It should be noted that this question and those that follow produced an abnormally high rate of nonresponse. The interviewees were reluctant to discuss these matters and tended to become irritated when probed by interviewers. For example, over half of the members of the Conservative (55%) and Social Credit (57%) parties either refused to respond to this question or would not give an unqualified positive or negative response. Among MPs who did respond, the NDP members appeared to be more interested in the possibility of a parliamentary career than did the members of the other parties.

We asked the 131 MPs who either said they would run again even if defeated, or who would not say whether they would or would not run, a follow-up question, "What are the kinds of things, other than defeat at the polls, that make a MP like yourself think twice about remaining in parliament?" A frequently cited reason for voluntary retirement was related to one's family life (e.g., the disruption of normal family life, long separations and the loss of privacy by members of the family [17%]). Another was financial and was structured in terms of the lack of congruence between the heavy demands the position made upon them and the relatively low salaries they received (20%). A few (10%) said that disillusionment with the position, particularly with respect to what a non-cabinet member can

TABLE 2.11
ATTITUDES TOWARD PARLIAMENTARY CAREER BY PARTY

| | NDP | Liberal | Conservative | Credi-tiste | All |
|---|---|---|---|---|---|
| Expect to make career out of Parliament | | | | | |
| Yes | 45.5% | 41.0% | 28.3% | 42.9% | 37.6% |
| No | 9.1 | 31.0 | 16.7 | — | 22.8 |
| Wouldn't say | 45.5 | 28.0 | 55.0 | 57.1 | 39.6 |
| Would run again, even if defeated in an election | | | | | |
| Yes | 36.4 | 14.0 | 23.3 | 42.9 | 20.6 |
| No | 4.5 | 40.0 | 23.3 | 42.9 | 30.7 |
| Wouldn't say | 59.1 | 46.0 | 53.4 | 14.2 | 48.7 |

accomplish, leads MPs to retire. Another 8% said that advancing age and problems of health made it difficult for some members to continue in office because the work load was so physically, as well as mentally, taxing. The remaining 45% either gave answers such as "Oh, a lot of things" (without specifying what these things were); "Well, I'm not really sure, different things, I suppose"; or "I guess you just get tired"; or simply refused to answer.

In response to the question, "Are there any other public offices, elected or appointed, that you would like to hold sometime in the future?", 37% said yes there were, 35% said no, and the remaining 28% would not reply. A comparison of the distribution of responses to this question with the responses of MPs a decade earlier would seem to suggest that current respondents do not regard the position of MP as highly as did their predecessors in 1962. Referring to the earlier group, Kornberg notes that, "fully 75% said there were no other public offices in which they were interested; 9% were interested in judgeships or appointments to the senate; 7% wanted to return to provincial politics; 6% said they would like to be the mayors of the cities in which they resided; and an additional 3% said they were interested in other public offices but they would not reveal what these were."[31] In comparison, 12% of the current respondents were interested in judgeships and appointments to the Senate; 4% wanted to return to provincial politics; 5% wanted to be mayors; but the largest proportion (58%) wanted a federal office. However, 34 of these 40 individuals wanted to hold an appointed federal office. Indeed, 45 of the 69 MPs (65%) who said they were interested in other public offices were interested in appointed offices.

Finally, in response to the question, "Let us suppose that next week for some reason you had to give up being a MP, what would you miss most about not being in office?" 7% said there was nothing they would miss and that, indeed, they probably would retire when the current parliament was dissolved.[32] On the other hand, the same proportion said they would miss everything, and proceeded to eulogize the office and those who held it. As was the case a decade earlier, when this question was used to determine motives for sustaining a parliamentary career, the majority of respondents seemingly were motivated to maintain their careers because of the social and psychological gratification they derived from being a MP. The most frequently cited sources of gratification were the glamour, challenge, and excitement of the position, the gratification one derived from serving the people, and the opportunity to make or participate in the making of public policy. Other sources of gratification most often mentioned in conjunction with the challenge and excitement of holding a parliamentary office were the friendships, the camaraderie, and the feeling that one is a member of the country's most exclusive club; the ritual associated with the position (e.g., the debates, the Speech from the Throne); and the ability to use the position as a national forum or platform for the expression of ideological positions. An examination of table 2.12 indicates that members of the two major parties, the Liberal and the Conservatives, were somewhat more inclined to cite the glamour and excitement as well as the friendships as things they would miss most, whereas members of the two minor parties were somewhat more likely to refer to the opportunity to use the position as a national forum for expressing their ideological views. Generally, however, the reasons MPs gave for continuing in office were relatively similar, regardless of party.

## SUMMARY

In this chapter we have presented data that provide us with a sociopolitical portrait of MPs as a group. In some instances we also have provided statistical profiles of the members of each of the parties. With regard to social origins, these data have indicated that the members of the Liberal party derived from the most elite and the

TABLE 2.12
**WHAT RESPONDENTS WOULD MISS MOST IF NO LONGER MPs BY PARTY**[a]

| Aspects of Position that Would Be Missed | NDP | Liberal | Conser-vative | Credi-tiste | All |
|---|---|---|---|---|---|
| Glamor, Excitement, Challenge of Office | 27.3% | 37.0% | 38.3% | — | 34.9% |
| a. Friendship and camaraderie | 13.6 | 26.0 | 26.7 | 14.3% | 24.3 |
| b. Ritual | 9.1 | 13.0 | 6.7 | — | 10.1 |
| c. National forum | 27.3 | 8.0 | 6.7 | 28.6 | 10.1 |
| Service-Representational aspects | 27.3 | 32.0 | 35.0 | 28.6 | 32.3 |
| Policymaking aspects | 22.7 | 31.0 | 21.7 | 28.6 | 27.0 |

a. percentages total more than 100 because multiple responses were permitted.

members of the Social Credit from the most proletarian back-grounds. There were no really sharp or consistent differences in the political backgrounds of the members of the four party groups, however.

The scenario we sketched to describe the parliamentary recruit-ment process pointed out that Canadian MPs frequently use past services to their parties and key positions in constituency party organizations as resources to advance their own candidacies. Given their relative political sophistication, it was not surprising that four out of five respondents said they had developed expectations for the position of MP before they actually were elected. However, the expectations of about half of them, despite their excellent educa-tions, their political sophistication, and their previous successes in business and in the professions, were rather vague. To the extent that they did have structured expectations, the principal ones were that they would be representatives and ombudsmen rather than policy-makers. We may infer from responses to this series of questions that a substantial number of MPs learned what specific functions MPs perform and the manner in which to perform them after rather than before their election. They learned what to do and how to do it by watching and imitating the behavior of veteran MPs.

Previous studies of legislative bodies have suggested one way in which legislators learn how to perform their tasks is by learning the rules of the parliamentary game. Consequently, we briefly described the content of these rules, compared the frequencies with which functional categories of rules were articulated by current respondents and by members of the 25th Parliament (1962–1963), and described the sanctions that are available to enforce adherence to the rules.

On the assumption that their first year in parliament might have been a particularly memorable one, we asked respondents which aspects of their first year in office they found most gratifying and which aspects they found most burdensome and onerous. The most frequent sources of gratification were the ability to successfully complete a specific task and the performance of the ombudsman function. The principal burdens were the unexpectedly heavy work load and the inability to successfully deal with problems they encountered.

Although historically approximately 40% of each Canadian parliament has been made up of newly elected members, a substantial cohort in each party had been MPs for years. As might be expected, a majority of the MPs we interviewed had been concerned with both policy formulation and evaluation and constituency service during their years in office. Fully 60% were able to cite one or more specific accomplishments in the public policy area. In response to a question concerning future goals, we found that the goals of about one-fourth of the respondents were oriented toward, and a continuation of, their work in the past, but almost 40% had goals that seemingly were unrelated to their former interest and activities. As was the case in 1962, approximately half (55%) of the current respondents had goals that were concerned with public policy. Of these, the great majority had goals that would affect the nation or the provinces rather than their individual constituencies. The members of the two major parties tended to perceive conflict between party colleagues and themselves over goals whereas the NDP members more often perceived that their goals were in conflict with the expectations of major interest groups in their constituencies. All but one of the Social Credit members felt their personal goals were consistent with the expectations of significant other groups such as party colleagues, and their party organizations in the electorate. We speculated that the reasons the members of the two major parties more often perceived conflict with parliamentary colleagues over goals was that they both were larger and contained representatives from each of the four principal geographic regions of Canada—regions that historically have had different interests and needs.

An analysis of the responses to a series of agree-disagree statements intended to determine their representational role preferences reveals, with respect to their foci of representation, that MPs perceive their primary responsibilities to be to represent their consciences, the nation and their constituencies. With respect to specific role orientations, the members of the Social Credit and Conservative parties seemingly found the Delegate-Servant role more congenial than did the members of the New Democratic and Liberal parties. The great majority of MPs, regardless of party, preferred the Politico role and, although the members of the New Democratic and the Liberal parties found the Burkean-Trustee role somewhat more attractive than did Social Credit and Conservative members, the interparty differences were not significant.

Insofar as the question of accountability is concerned, the members of three parties (Social Credit, Conservative, and Liberal) most often felt accountable, and felt it was most important to be accountable, to the people of their districts. The members of the New Democratic parliamentary party most often selected their party organization in the electorate as the group to whom they were accountable, and felt it was most important to be accountable to their consciences for their actions. The NDP members also differed somewhat from other MPs in that they were more likely to consider themselves professional parliamentarians. They wanted more often to make a career of parliament and were more willing to run for a parliamentary seat even if they were defeated in a future election. With respect to motives for sustaining a parliamentary career, the data suggest that MPs, regardless of party, are motivated by the social and psychological gratification they derive, by a desire to serve the people of Canada, and (despite the fact that very few initially expected to be policy-makers) by a desire to participate in the making of laws.

## Chapter 3

# POWER IN THE 28TH PARLIAMENT

## MEASURING POWER AND INFLUENCE

Power is a concept that has fascinated and frustrated both students of politics and political practioners.[1] Since every society has had to maintain some form of both internal and external order, power came to be identified with coercion and as the nation-state came to have a monopoly on the use of coercive instruments, power increasingly was identified with the state. There emerged, therefore, a concern with how and under what conditions power could or should be exercised by the state. Political philosophers usually treated the concept as an attribute of executive institutions although in some instances power also was viewed as a kind of transcendental force peculiar to certain political leaders.[2] Concomitant with more recent attempts to explain power in a systematic fashion there was a shift toward conceptualizations that could be operationalized and measured.

For a variety of reasons the bulk of the empirical-quantitative research on power and influence has focused on community power.[3] Unfortunately, as Heinz Eulau noted in 1962 and as is generally true today, there is little information about power and influence within legislatures other than anecdotes about the supposed dictatorial power exercised by certain legislative leaders.[4] One reason for this lack of systematic knowledge may be that the members of legislative bodies supposedly "are formally equal to one another in status"—an attribute that distinguishes parliaments from other hierarchically ordered organizations.[5] Nonetheless, legislatures in Western societies such as Canada do have leaders who do exercise at least some degree of power and authority. Eulau speculates that their ability to do so derives from the ascription of values to them by legislative colleagues, and "insofar as legislative leaders have some of these characteristics attributed to them more frequently than other legislators, their authority may be said to be rooted in such value attributions."[6] Three of these values, according to Eulau, are respect, affection, and expertise. He tests the hypothesis that greater degrees of these values are ascribed to legislative leaders than to rank-and-file members. Eulau does acknowledge, however, that his analyses, in a sense, beg the question of whether legislative leaders are ascribed these values because they occupy positions of power or whether they achieve their offices (at least in part) because they are ascribed these values.[7]

Although Eulau's question is an interesting one, our feeling is that his conceptualization of the problem in either-or terms is misleading and an oversimplification. Power in a legislature, in our view, derives both from the objective importance of formal leadership positions and from the subjective ascription to those who hold these positions of certain valued qualities. The particular mix of objective and subjective components of power and authority varies with structural and procedural differences among legislatures and with the expectations that both legislators and members of the public hold regarding the manner in which legislative leaders shall exercise power. Thus, for example, in a British-model parliamentary system a great deal of authority and influence will be attributed to the leaders of legislative parties and to the members of the cabinet. They occupy positions that are invested with authority and the members of the legislature as well as the general public expect them to exercise their authority to insure the proper functioning of the parliamentary system. On the other hand, in legislative systems in which there is a formal separation of power between the legislative and executive branches and/or in which the executive does not control the timing and substance of collective deliberations, there are likely to be more opportunities for individual legislators to exercise policy initiatives and to assert their independence of party and of the executive. Members of such a legislature (and its public) are less likely to assume that the legislative system will break down if leaders do not exercise their authority. Indeed, there may even be an expectation that the legislature will function better if rank-and-file members occasionally assert their independence of the leadership, demonstrating that they are not simply errand-boys. Power and influence in this case are likely to be attributed to people who have qualities of leadership such as those singled out by Eulau even if they are not formal leaders. Relatedly, power is less likely to be attributed to leaders merely on the basis of the offices they hold. The task of the legislative scholar, therefore, is not only to map the distribution of influence patterns in a legislature but also to explain the basis of this influence.

Given these assumptions, we included two questions in our interview that were intended both to delineate the distribution of generalized influence in the Canadian House of Commons and to explain why influence was attributed to particular individuals. In addition, we were interested in comparing the influence attributed to specific groups of MPs such as the four parties, the leaders of the government and the opposition parties, and the delegations from the four principal regions of Canada—the West, Ontario, Quebec, and the Atlantic provinces.[8] The question that we used to delineate the distribution of influence was:

> One finds, particularly through political biographies of Canada's leaders, that some MPs are mentioned consistently as being more influential in parliament than others, despite the fact that a number of these were never in cabinet, or even in the front benches of their parties. Who, in your mind, are the 10 most influential members of this Parliament—regardless of party?

To ascertain the bases of influence, interviewees were handed a list containing 12 attributes and asked a second question: "Which of the things on this list would you say contributes most to the influence that each of these individuals has in parliament?" Then, beginning with the first person named we asked: "Now, how about Mr. ____, which of the things on this list would you say contributes most to his influence?" Since the first question does not explicitly refer to the kinds of qualities that Eulau assumed were the bases of influence, we will present data from a third question which asked respondents to nominate three men from any party whose judgment they especially valued. We will demonstrate that a strong relationship exists between the two distributions of nominations. Finally, we will try to suggest the reasons power and influence are not automatically ascribed to all incumbents of formal leadership positions.

The reader already has noted that we use the terms power and influence interchangeably. We did not employ the word power in the questions we asked, but we did use the words influential or influence at several points and feel justified in assuming that those nominated in response to the questions satisfied a necessary if not a sufficient condition for the possession of power; namely, that they were recognized as powerful by others. The questions also make it clear that we were asking for nominations of MPs who are influential, whether or not they hold formal leadership positions. We may assume, therefore, that the nominees have identified themselves to their colleagues by actually exercising power, a second indication of its possession. However, a nominee may have power even if he never overtly uses it. Power and influence may be measured by the influencer's achievement of his goals following not only his visible efforts but also the adjustments made by others to what they anticipate to be his wishes. In brief, it is a moot question whether influential people need actually wield their influence to earn their reputations.

For each MP, then, influence has been defined reputationally and is measured as the number of times the person is nominated as one of the ten most influential members of parliament by the 189 MPs in our sample. This influence measure constitutes the dependent variable in tables 3.1 through 3.3. Before presenting these data, it should be noted that we are aware of the considerable controversy that surrounds the use of the reputational method for delineating power (or influence) within social groups.[9] In spite of the questions this technique raises, however, previous research has convinced us that the game is well worth the candle—that by using this method we can shed light on the distribution of power in a Canadian parliament. Moreover, we can illuminate and clarify the reasons for the attribution of power in a more systematic fashion than heretofore has been possible in legislative studies.

## FINDINGS: THE DISTRIBUTION OF INFLUENCE

32 (16.9%) of the 189 MPs would not answer the influence question although only two MPs said they could not answer because they did not know who exercised influence. The nonrespondents offered a variety of explanations, the most frequent being that it would be inappropriate for them to comment on party colleagues' influence and even less appropriate to evaluate the relative influence of MPs in other parliamentary parties. The 155 interviewees who did answer made 1298 nominations. Although, in theory, members of legislatures may be equal in status, the distribution of the nominations indicates that they certainly are not equal in influence—at least not in the Canadian House of Commons. Indeed, 57.8% of the

members did not receive a single nomination as influentials. Another 27% received at least one but not more than five nominations; 6.5% received six to ten nominations; 1.5% received eleven to twenty nominations; 2.4% were nominated twenty-one to forty times; and 4.9% received forty-one or more nominations.

As is evident from table 3.1, the official opposition, the Conservative parliamentary party, contained the largest group of unnominated MPs whereas the NDP parliamentary delegation had the smallest. The relatively high regard in which NDP members were held also is reflected in the high mean number of nominations the average NDP member received.[10]   A third indicator of influence is the difference between the percentage of NDP House population (9.5) and the percentage of NDP influence nominations (14.4). No other party group received a proportion of the total nominations that was greater than the proportion of their membership in parliament; the Liberal party made up 58.5% of the parliamentary population and received 56.5% of the nominations. The Conservatives made up 27% of the population and received 25.4% of the nominations; and the equivalent figures for the Social Credit party were 4.9% and 3.6%.

Eulau, it will be recalled, had hypothesized that legislative leaders would be regarded as more influential (as measured by the values of respect, affection, and expertise) than were rank-and-file members of American state legislatures. We assumed that if this were the case in legislatures that enable individual members to act independently of their party leaders and provide rank-and-file members with significant opportunities to initiate major pieces of legislation, then, in a highly structured system such as the Canadian House of Commons, one in which holders of formal leadership positions are invested with both great authority and the opportunity to exercise it, the disparity in the influence ascribed to formal leaders and to other MPs should be much greater. The data indicate that this is indeed the case. If we compare the influence ascribed to the 31 MPs who (at one time or another during the life of the 28th Parliament) were members of the Liberal cabinet with the influence ascribed to their party colleagues who were never in the cabinet, we find that less than 10% of the cabinet members failed to receive at least one influence nomination whereas 65% of all other Liberal MPs were not considered influential by a single respondent in this study. Indeed, 42% of the Liberal cabinet received between 11 and 116 nominations whereas not one of the Liberals outside of cabinet ranks received as many as 11 nominations. Nor was the situation appreciably different in the

**TABLE 3.1**

**A COMPARISON OF THE INFLUENCE ASCRIBED TO HOLDERS OF HIGHEST ECHELON LEADERSHIP POSITIONS AND OTHER MPs IN EACH PARTY[a]**

| Number of Nominations Received | All MPs | | NDP | | Liberal | | Conservative | | Creditiste | |
|---|---|---|---|---|---|---|---|---|---|---|
| | Leaders | Others | Leaders | Others | Cabinet | Others | Leaders | Others | Leaders | Others |
| 0 | 10.3% | 65.6% | — | 56.5% | 9.6% | 65.0% | — | 69.1% | 33.3% | 70.0% |
| 1–5 | 30.8 | 26.3 | — | 34.8 | 35.5 | 30.9 | — | 16.2 | 33.3 | 30.0 |
| 6–10 | 12.8 | 5.4 | — | 4.3 | 12.9 | 4.1 | 33.3% | 8.8 | — | — |
| 11–40 | 15.4 | 2.2 | — | 4.3 | 19.4 | — | — | 4.3 | — | — |
| 41+ | 30.8 | 0.5 | 100.0%[c] | — | 22.6 | — | 66.7 | 1.5 | 33.3 | — |
| N | (39)[b] | (224) | (2) | (23) | (31) | (123) | (3) | (68) | (3) | (10) |
| Party Mean | 4.9 | | 7.5 | | 4.8 | | 4.6 | | 3.6 | |

a. Some columns may not total 100% due to rounding errors.

b. The Speaker, Hon. Lucien Lamoureux, is formally designated an Independent.

c. One NDP member held both the House Leader and the Whip positions.

other parties. For example, if we restrict our definition of leaders only to party leader, the chief whip, and the house leader of each of the opposition parties and compare the influence ascribed to them with that attributed to their party colleagues, we find that only 5 of the 101 opposition MPs who did not hold these highest positions received as many as 11 nominations but that 5 of the 8 top leaders each received more than 40 influence nominations.

Illustrative of the differences in the influence levels ascribed to leaders and rank-and-file members in the House of Commons and in the four state legislatures studied by Eulau and his colleagues, the mean number of nominations received by American state legislative leaders was generally about twice as great as that received by rank-and-file members.[11] In contrast, Liberal cabinet ministers on the average receive 23 times as many nominations as their noncabinet colleagues. The average number of nominations received by the highest echelon Conservative party leaders is 18 times as great as that received by other Conservatives and the disparity is even greater in the two minor parties (28 times as many in the Social Credit and 33 times as many in the NDP). Obviously, in this comparison we have defined leadership rather narrowly. If we expand our definition to include a cadre of middle echelon leaders (e.g., parliamentary secretaries in the Liberal party and frontbenchers in the opposition parties), the influence gap between leaders and followers narrows somewhat. Nonetheless, it remains substantial.

With respect to the two minor parties, we find that a considerably larger proportion of their nominations come from MPs who are not party colleagues, 59% in the case of the NDP and 68% in the case of the Social Credit. Liberal and Conservative MPs who were considered influential, in contrast, received only 32% of their nominations from MPs outside of their respective party caucuses. NDP and Conservative influentials tended to receive more of their nominations from back-benchers (72% and 77.5% respectively) than did Liberal and, particularly, Social Credit influentials (62% and 31% respectively). So, to the extent that Social Credit MPs were viewed as influential, it was the leaders of parliament who so regarded them.

Conventional wisdom long has emphasized and social scientists have confirmed the importance in Canadian politics of both regionalism and federalism. It often is noted, for example, that the two super-provinces of Ontario and Quebec enjoy a status in the Canadian federal system that the other eight provinces do not share. We felt the favored status that Ontario and Quebec supposedly enjoy might be reflected in the influence ascribed to the members of their provincial parliamentary delegations generally and, in particular, to the ministers who represented them in the cabinet. We assumed that not only might Ontario and Quebec private members and ministers receive a larger proportion of the number of influence nominations than their colleagues from the Atlantic and Western provinces [12] (since the parliamentary and ministerial delegations from Ontario and Quebec each are greater than the combined delegations from either the four Western or the four Atlantic provinces), but also that the average member and the average minister from Ontario and Quebec would be ascribed more influence than their counterparts from the West and the Atlantic regions. Table 3.2 compares the total number of influence nominations as well as the mean number of nominations received by Quebec and Ontario MPs with those received by the Atlantic and Western provincial parliamentary groups. The data indicate that although the Ontario and Quebec MPs did receive the lion's share (56.8%) of the nominations, they constituted 61.1% of the parliamentary population. Moreover, neither the average MP from Quebec nor Ontario was considered as influential as the average MP from the Atlantic region. The average Western MP, although not ascribed as much influence as the average member of the Quebec delegation, was considered more influential than the average MP from Ontario.

With regard to the influence differences among ministers from the four regions, again we find that those from the two super-provinces received the majority of the nominations (see table 3.3). Indeed, the Quebec ministers alone received 55.6% of all the influence nominations made of cabinet members. But, the Ontario ministers, like the Ontario private members, received a smaller proportion of the nomi-

TABLE 3.2
**A COMPARISON OF THE DISTRIBUTION OF INFLUENCE NOMINATIONS RECEIVED BY THE PARLIAMENTARY GROUPS OF FOUR REGIONS**

| Region | N | % of Parliamentary Population | % of Total Nominations | $\overline{X}$ Nominations Received | S.D. |
|---|---|---|---|---|---|
| Atlantic MPs | 32 | 12.2% | 19.5% | 7.9 | 17.4 |
| Quebec MPs | 74 | 28.1 | 31.9 | 5.7 | 18.3 |
| Ontario MPs | 87 | 33.0 | 24.9 | 3.6 | 10.6 |
| Western MPs | 70 | 26.7 | 23.7 | 4.5 | 13.0 |

## TABLE 3.3

## DISTRIBUTION OF INFLUENCE NOMINATIONS OF CABINET MEMBERS AND PRIVATE MEMBERS WITHIN REGIONS [a]

| Regions | Nominations Received by Ministers (N = 634) | Nominations Received by Private Members (N = 664) | Total Nominations Received (N = 1298) | $\overline{X}$ Nominations of Ministers | $\overline{X}$ Nominations of Private Members | $\overline{X}$ Nominations of All Members |
|---|---|---|---|---|---|---|
| Atlantic | 79(12.4%) | 174(26.2%) | 253(19.5%) | 26.3 | 6.0 | 7.9 |
| Quebec | 352(55.6%) | 62( 9.3%) | 414(31.8%) | 35.2 | 1.0 | 5.7 |
| Ontario | 172(27.0%) | 151(22.8%) | 323(24.8%) | 15.6 | 1.9 | 3.6 |
| West | 31( 5.0%) | 277(41.6%) | 308(23.7%) | 4.4 | 4.5 | 4.5 |
| All | | | | 20.4 | 2.9 | 4.9 |

a. Some columns may not total 100% due to rounding error.

nations than their numbers warranted. A comparison in table 3.3 of the mean number of nominations received by the cabinet and the private members of each of the four regions suggests the following generalizations. First, the special status that Quebec is said to enjoy in the Canadian federal structure may be reflected in the disproportionate power attributed to the ministers but not to its private members. (Quebec private members were ascribed less influence, on the average, than private members from any of the other major regions.) Second, the power that Ontario is said to exert on the Canadian federal system was not reflected in the influence attributed to its parliamentary delegation. The influence of Ontario ministers, on the average, was not as great as the influence of the average minister from the Atlantic provinces. Moreover, the average private member from Ontario was not ascribed as much influence as the average member from either the Atlantic region or the West. The Atlantic region's average may have been inflated by the fact that Mr. Robert Stanfield, the leader of the Official Opposition, represented a New Brunswick constituency. Even if Mr. Stanfield's many nominations are not taken into account, however, the average MP from the Atlantic provinces still received 3.3 nominations, a significantly greater number than the average number received by either Quebec or Ontario private members. A third generalization these data suggest, therefore, is that, although there may be reasons for the less favored status supposedly enjoyed by the Atlantic provinces, they do not include impotency of either the ministers or the private members who represent them in parliament. On the other hand, the relative lack of influence of Western cabinet ministers may offer a partial explanation—partial because we assume they have not always lacked influential ministers and because there may be a variety of other reasons—for the "have not" status of their provinces. The seeming lack of influence of the men who represented the Western provinces in the Liberal cabinet of the 28th parliament is really striking. Although they did not hold prestigious posts in the cabinet, another more important reason, in our view, lies in the tradition of the federalized Canadian cabinet.[13]  In the Canadian House of Commons a prime minister customarily includes party colleagues from each of the ten provinces in his cabinet. Since the governing Liberal party (although it enjoyed a comfortable parliamentary majority) included relatively few members from Manitoba, Saskatchewan, Alberta, and British Columbia, there was only a small pool of Western MPs from which Mr. Trudeau could make cabinet selections. Consequently, we may speculate that at least some of the Western ministers were included in the cabinet because they represented constituencies in the "right" provinces and not because they possessed the kind of characteristics and skills that Heinz Eulau suggests explain the influence that is exercised by legislative leaders. It is to this topic that we now direct our attention.

## THE BASES OF INFLUENCE

It will be recalled that we presented the respondents with a list of twelve attributes and asked them to indicate which of these contributed to the influence of the MPs they had nominated. The list with which we presented them recognized, since our question was about an individual member's general influence in parliament, that the bases of that influence were rooted in aspects of the parliamentary environment. But it also recognized that an individual's influence might derive from his personal status and from his contacts with individuals and groups outside of parliament. In addition, respondents were given the opportunity to suggest additional reasons and some MPs did so. For example, a Liberal cabinet minister explained why a certain Western MP was influential: "Because he's tough and tenacious. He never quits. Ideologically he's back in the 18th Century but in a crazy kind of way, he's effective as hell. I've seen him bring the whole place to a screeching, grinding halt almost by himself."

We added 7 categories to our 12 existing codes and were able to include all but 2 of the other explanations. The resulting 19 attributes are grouped under the general headings presented below:

    I. Attributes that reflect position
       1. Formal position in the House
       2. The importance of the district MP represents
       3. Experience in Parliament
   II. Attributes that reflect special knowledge and expertise
       1. Knowledge of parliamentary procedure and "rules of the game"
       2. Expertise in domestic affairs generally
       3. Expertise in foreign affairs
       4. Expertise in a particular area
       5. Feel for or knowledge of public opinion
       6. Bilingual
  III. Attributes that reflect skillful role performance
       1. Persuasiveness in speaking—the logical force of his arguments
       2. Ability to get along with people
       3. Accomplishments in the past

IV. Attributes that reflect valued personal characteristics
    1. Willingness to help colleagues in his own and in other parties
    2. Decency and humanity
    3. Integrity
    4. Personality in general
V. Attributes that reflect status and interaction with significant others
    1. Personal contacts with influential people outside the House
    2. Closeness to other MPs
    3. Closeness to some one in parliament who is influential

Table 3.4 presents the distribution of reasons given by our respondents for the influence nominations they made, and indicates, as we expected, that on the average the occupancy of a formal position of leadership is the reason most frequently given to explain influence. The second most frequently cited characteristic is the ability to speak and debate. Expertise (in parliamentary procedures and informal rules of the game, in domestic affairs generally, in particular policy areas) and parliamentary experience also are cited frequently. Attributes mentioned less often but of some importance are decency and humanity, feel for public opinion, and willingness to assist colleagues, regardless of party affiliation. On the other hand, expertise in foreign affairs and contacts with influential individuals seemingly can less often be translated into influence. Personal qualities such as personality, integrity, ability to get along with people, ability to speak English and French, and (most surprisingly) past performance apparently are unrelated to influence[14] (see the right most column of table 3.4).

As one would expect, the influence of cabinet ministers appears to depend on formal position, the ability to speak and defend one's policies well, and expertise in domestic affairs generally as well as in the area in which one is a minister. Although the table does not show it, ascriptive bases of influence were most often assigned to French-speaking cabinet ministers. Personal contacts with influential people outside of parliament also were cited to explain their power more often than they were the power of English-speaking members of the cabinet. Moreover, closeness to someone who is influential is cited only to explain the influence of French-Canadian ministers. Respondents who gave this reason made it clear that the influential person to whom the nominee was close was the prime minister himself.[15] In other words, a distinction seemingly was made by MPs between the bases of influence of English- and French-speaking ministers. Thus, although both groups are ascribed influence because

## TABLE 3.4
## A COMPARISON OF THE MEAN NUMBER OF REASONS GIVEN TO EXPLAIN THE INFLUENCE ASCRIBED TO HIGHEST ECHELON LEADERS AND OTHER MPs IN EACH PARTY

| Reasons | Liberal Cabinet | Liberal Non-Cab. | Con. Leaders | Con. Others | NDP Leaders | NDP Others | Cred. Leaders | Cred. Others | All |
|---|---|---|---|---|---|---|---|---|---|
| Attributes that reflect position | | | | | | | | | |
| Formal position in the House | 10.07 | .16 | 22.00 | .48 | 28.00 | .56 | 7.66 | .10 | 1.95 |
| The importance of the district MP represents | 1.25 | .11 | .75 | .11 | .75 | .09 | 1.00 | .10 | .28 |
| Experience in Parliament | 2.40 | .12 | 6.75 | .78 | 22.50 | .69 | 2.70 | — | .87 |
| Attributes that reflect special knowledge and expertise | | | | | | | | | |
| Knowledge or parliamentary procedure and "Rules of the Game" | 2.53 | .11 | 10.25 | .52 | 30.50 | .30 | 1.67 | — | .89 |
| Expertise in domestic affairs generally | 3.50 | .19 | 5.00 | .48 | 11.00 | .56 | 2.00 | .10 | .82 |
| Expertise in foreign affairs generally | 1.50 | .01 | .25 | .25 | .50 | .13 | — | — | .25 |
| Expertise in a particular area | 3.43 | .22 | 1.25 | .67 | 7.00 | .39 | 2.33 | .30 | .79 |
| Feel for or knowledge of public opinion | 1.90 | .17 | 2.00 | .39 | 4.00 | .22 | 3.70 | — | .50 |
| Bi-lingual (speaks English and French) | — | — | — | — | — | — | .33 | — | — |

| | | | | | | | | | |
|---|---|---|---|---|---|---|---|---|---|
| **Attributes that reflect skillful role performance** | | | | | | | | | |
| Persuasiveness in speaking—the logical force of his arguments | 4.75 | .28 | 3.50 | .69 | 13.00 | .52 | 3.00 | .10 | 1.05 |
| Ability to get along with people | — | .01 | — | — | — | — | — | — | — |
| Accomplishments in the past | — | — | — | .01 | — | — | — | — | — |
| **Attributes that reflect valued personal characteristics** | | | | | | | | | |
| Willingness to help colleagues in his own and in other parties | 1.90 | .07 | 2.25 | .24 | 4.50 | .13 | 1.33 | .10 | .40 |
| Decency and humanity | 2.03 | .20 | 7.50 | .34 | 6.50 | .52 | 1.62 | .30 | .64 |
| Integrity | .18 | .04 | — | .01 | .50 | .13 | — | .10 | .06 |
| Personality in general | .50 | — | .75 | .03 | 2.00 | — | .67 | — | .09 |
| **Attributes that reflect status and interaction with significant others** | | | | | | | | | |
| Personal contacts with influential people outside the House | 2.90 | .11 | 2.25 | .16 | 4.00 | .09 | 1.00 | .10 | .49 |
| Closeness to other MPs | 1.53 | .01 | .75 | .03 | 1.00 | — | — | — | .19 |

of the formal positions they hold, ministers from Quebec are more often ascribed influence because of who they know, whereas English-speaking ministers are cited for personal attributes or for who they are.

When we compare the reasons given to explain the influence attributed to cabinet ministers with those given to explain the influence of the top leaders of the opposition parties we find there are some interesting but not unexpected differences in emphasis. It is to be expected, for example, that the influence of cabinet ministers largely will derive from their collective status as the Government. Since their formal positions require them to present and defend the policies and actions of the governmental departments they head, it also is to be expected that their influence will derive from their speaking and debating effectiveness that rests in part upon the possession of superior information provided by the bureaucracy. The data in table 3.4 tend to support these expectations. They reveal, on the average, that formal position, effective speaking, and expertise (in domestic affairs generally and in the particular areas for which they have responsibility) are the reasons most frequently given to explain cabinet influence. It also is to be expected that the leaders of the opposition parties—lacking both the status of being the government and the expert knowledge that is provided by the administrative bureaucracy—will employ whatever resources they do have to enhance the influence they enjoy among parliamentary colleagues. For example, most of the top leaders of the Conservative, New Democratic, and Social Credit parties have been members of parliament for many years. Over the years they undoubtedly have become very knowledgeable not only about substantive matters but also about the way in which the rules of parliament can be exploited for their advantage. Again, the data tend to support these expectations. We find that the influence of opposition party leaders does derive from their formal positions, their long parliamentary experience, their knowledge of, and ability to use, parliamentary procedure, their expertise in domestic affairs, and their "nice guy" images (i.e., of being decent and humane individuals). What is somewhat unexpected is the esteem in which the top leaders of the NDP appear to be held. One indication of this esteem is that their influence is attributed as much or more to their knowledge of the rules of the parliamentary game and to their long parliamentary experience as it is to the formal positions they hold. They also receive very high marks for speaking and debating ability, and for their expertise in a variety of policy areas. A comparison of the number of times, they, as opposed to top

Creditiste party leaders, are cited for these general qualities is particularly striking.

Also of interest is the importance of being a member of the cabinet in a governing party. For example, formal position, on the average, was cited 10.1 times to explain the influence of Liberal cabinet members whereas speaking ability, the second most frequently cited reason, was offered only 4.7 times. There were no such sharp differences in the frequencies with which formal positions, as opposed to other qualities, were offered to explain the influence of Liberal party nominees who are not cabinet ministers—a number of whom, nonetheless, held formal positions of leadership (e.g., parliamentary secretaries, committee chairman, caucus chairman, deputy whips). To be sure some Liberal nominees who were not cabinet ministers were ascribed influence because of their positions. But this reason was less often given than were qualities such as speaking ability, expertise in a particular area, and parliamentary experience.

The data in table 3.4 strongly suggest that the answer to the question Eulau proposed regarding the basis of influence exercised by legislative leaders is that their authority derives from occupying formal positions and from seeming to have certain desirable qualities and skills (e.g., effective speaking, parliamentary experience, and expert knowledge). Other characteristics and skills such as a pleasant personality and the ability to interact harmoniously—although they may be nice to have—are of less importance in explaining influence.

Given the sharp differences in the frequencies with which formal position as opposed to all other factors is suggested as an explanation of influence, the reader may feel that we should have made an unqualified statement that leaders in a parliamentary system of the British model have influence because they currently occupy positions from which the exercise of influence is legitimate and expected. (Indeed, some readers might go further and argue that in such a system leadership positions are synonomous with influence and really are an alternative measure of the same phenomenon.) The finding that a number of former Conservative ministers were not considered influential by MPs could be viewed as supporting the validity of such a statement and its corollary, that when an MP no longer holds such a position, he ceases to be influential. We have not interpreted our findings in this way for two reasons. First, not all of the holders of formal leadership positions—even in the cabinet—really were considered influential whereas a number of nonposition-holding MPs were. It will be recalled that three of the men who were Liberal cabinet ministers were not nominated even once and ten others received only 1 to 5 nominations. In addition, some former holders of high level positions (e.g., a former Conservative party leader, a former Liberal cabinet minister and a former leader of the New Democratic parliamentary party) were regarded as extremely influential although they were private members at the time of our study. Second, we felt that the relationship between holding a formal position of leadership and being ascribed influence may be far more complex and subtle than the data in table 3.4 suggest. The MPs' replies to the question, "What do you think are the principal criteria applied to select cabinet ministers?" buttressed this feeling. They revealed that MPs explained the selection of cabinet members in terms of many (although certainly not all[16] ) of the same attributes they had used to explain their influence. For example, over half (58%) mentioned merit, or what-you-know criteria such as "intelligence," "knowledge in depth," "ability to make decisions," and "administrative skills" while another 22% cited who-you-know criteria such as being a personal friend of the prime minister. With respect to the subtleties of the relationship between position and influence, although table 3.4 indicates that desirable personal qualities do not provide much of an explanation of why some MPs are influential, such qualities do explain why some MPs are appointed to the top level positions that are the basis of so much influence. Thus, almost a quarter (24%) of the MPs made reference to personal qualities such as "honesty," "integrity," "humanity," "congenial personality," "ability to get along with people," and "ability to accept criticism gracefully" to explain cabinet appointments. Because this is the case, because the relationships among leadership positions, individual performance, personal attributes, and ascribed influence are extremely complex, we will continue to investigate them in a series of multivariate analyses in chapters 6 through 9.

## THE ASCRIPTION OF GOOD JUDGMENT TO MPs

The importance that was ascribed to desirable personal attributes made us wonder whether the influence question we had used was tapping influence as Heinz Eulau had conceptualized it. Happily, our instrument also contained a nominating question intended to delineate friendship groups within and between parties. Although the question did not contain the words "power" or "influence" it did imply that the individuals listed would possess qualities such as those

Eulau assumed would generate respect, deference, and affection [17] among their colleagues. The question was: "Who are the three men, whether in your own party or in other parties, whose advice, opinion, and good judgment you especially value?" As was the case with the influence question, a substantial number (36) of MPs refused to nominate anyone. Although their reasons varied, the principal one was that this was a personal matter and they did not choose to comment on such matters publicly (even though we already had assured them that the confidentiality of all participants in the study would be respected).

The distribution of the responses of those who did answer, however, is remarkably similar to the distribution of responses to the influence question. We find that a majority (61.6%) of the MPs do not appear on respondents' lists. The marginals reveal that 25.1% of the MPs were named one to two times; 4.2% three to four times; 9.1% five or more times. As was the case with influence, the ascription of good judgment varied with party affiliation and with formal leadership position. The NDP parliamentary group had the smallest proportion of MPs receiving no nominations for good judgment and the highest receiving five or more. The Conservative MPs had the largest proportion receiving no nominations and the Creditiste had the lowest receiving five or more (see table 3.5). Of particular interest is the fact that good judgment, like influence, was attributed disproportionately to cabinet ministers and top leaders of the opposition parties. For example, 41.6% of the cabinet members in the Liberal party received five or more nominations for having good judgment but less than 1% of their noncabinet party colleagues received as many. In fact, the nominations received by Liberal ministers com-

TABLE 3.5

**THE DISTRIBUTION OF NOMINATIONS OF MPs IN EACH PARTY WHOSE ADVICE AND JUDGMENT ARE VALUED[a]**

| Number of Nominations Received | NDP | Liberal | Con- servative | Creditiste | Total |
|---|---|---|---|---|---|
| 0 | 56.0% | 61.0% | 64.8% | 61.5% | 61.6% |
| 1–2 | 28.0 | 26.0 | 21.1 | 30.8 | 25.1 |
| 3–4 | 4.0 | 4.5 | 4.2 | – | 4.2 |
| 5+ | 12.0 | 8.4 | 9.9 | 7.7 | 9.1 |
| N | (25) | (154) | (71) | (13) | (263) |

a. Some columns do not total to 100% due to rounding errors.

prise 75.8% of the total number of nominations for good judgment received by Liberals. Nor is the situation much different in the opposition parties. 46.5% of the Conservative nominations for good judgment were allocated to the party leader, house leader, and chief whip; 54.5% and 58.5% of the votes received by the Social Credit and New Democratic parties, respectively, also went to the men who held those positions. Indeed, if we combine the nominations for good judgment received by highest echelon leaders in all parties and compare them with the nominations received by all other MPs, there appears to be as high a correlation between holding a top level leadership position and being ascribed good judgment as there is between top position-holding and the ascription of influence (see table 3.6).

Nominations for good judgment (again, like those for being influential) were not randomly distributed among MPs in each provincial delegation. Nova Scotia MPs, for example, received the highest average number of good judgment nominations (see table 3.7). And, although the size of the Nova Scotia parliamentary delegation is one-sixth the size of the Quebec delegation and less than one-seventh the size of the Ontario delegation, Nova Scotia MPs also received the third largest number of the good judgment nominations. This congruence between the influence and judgment distributions of MPs led us to cross-tabulate the two distributions. Not surprisingly, there is a significant correlation (Pearson product-moment of .88) between the attribution of influence and good judgment to MPs (see table 3.8). When we computed correlations for the relationship between influence and good judgment attributions for important subgroups of MPs, we found them to be universally high as well. All were significant beyond the .01 level.

TABLE 3.6

**A COMPARISON OF GOOD JUDGMENT NOMINATIONS
AMONG HIGHEST ECHELON LEADERS AND OTHER MPs**

| Number of Nominations Received | Top Leaders | Others |
|---|---|---|
| 0 | 10.4% | 70.5% |
| 1–2 | 30.7 | 24.1 |
| 3–4 | 12.8 | 2.7 |
| 5+ | 46.1 | 2.7 |
| N | (39) | (224) |

TABLE 3.7

## MEAN NUMBER OF NOMINATIONS AND PROPORTIONS OF TOTAL NUMBER OF GOOD JUDGMENT NOMINATIONS RECEIVED BY THE MPs OF EACH PROVINCE

| Province | $\overline{X}$ Nominations | Proportion of Total Nominations |
|---|---|---|
| British Columbia | 1.2 | 7.2% |
| Alberta | 2.1 | 9.8 |
| Saskatchewan | 1.9 | 6.3 |
| Manitoba | 1.2 | 4.1 |
| Ontario | 1.2 | 27.0 |
| Quebec | 1.2 | 22.4 |
| Nova Scotia | 4.5 | 13.8 |
| New Brunswick | 1.8 | 4.6 |
| Prince Edward Island | 2.0 | 2.0 |
| Newfoundland | 1.8 | 2.8 |

As we observed in the first chapter of this book, much of the literature that chronicles the decline of parliament makes clear that the loss of status of private members and their effective exclusion from participation in the policy process has been accompanied by the increased concentration of power in the cabinet. Scholars such as Bernard Crick have argued that the process has now been extended to the cabinet itself, that power within the cabinet is so concentrated in the person of the prime minister that the label "prime ministerial" rather than "cabinet" government is a realistic description of current

TABLE 3.8

## THE RELATIONSHIP OF INFLUENCE TO GOOD JUDGMENT ASCRIPTIONS (IN PERCENT)

| Good Judgment Nominations | Influence Nominations | | | | | | |
|---|---|---|---|---|---|---|---|
| | 0 | 1–5 | 6–10 | 11–40 | 41+ | Total | (N) |
| 0 | 78.4 | 18.5 | 3.1 | — | — | 61.6 | (162) |
| 1–2 | 37.9 | 50.0 | 10.6 | — | 1.5 | 25.1 | (66) |
| 3–4 | — | 72.7 | 27.3 | — | — | 4.2 | (71) |
| 5+ | — | — | 8.3 | 41.7 | 50.0 | 9.1 | (24) |
| Total | 57.8 | 27.0 | 6.5 | 3.8 | 4.9 | | |
| (N) | (152) | (71) | (17) | (10) | (13) | | |

Note: Gamma = .88.

practice in British-model parliamentary systems.[18]  The data presented in this chapter generally support the assumption that power is unequally distributed in that it is disproportionately ascribed to the cabinet and the top leaders of the opposition parties. And good judgment, like power, also is attributed much more to the top leaders of parliament than to ordinary members. However, the data presented to this point do not provide a really precise measure of the extent of this inequality in influence and good judgment. Nor do they permit us to make precise comparisons of the extent to which influence and good judgment are concentrated among members of major subgroups other than top leaders and private members in parliament. To make these determinations, we computed a series of Gini coefficients.[19]

We find that, overall, influence is somewhat more unequally distributed among Canadian MPs than is a reputation for good judgment. But, as table 3.9 indicates, for both influence and good judgment the Ginis attain magnitudes of over .80. Influence and good judgment seem to be most equally distributed among the MPs of Prince Edward Island and among the highest echelon leaders of the parliamentary parties and most unequally distributed among the provincial delegations of Manitoba, Saskatchewan, and Quebec (see table 3.9). It should be noted, however, that some of these coefficients may be unstable because of the small size of some of the subgroups.

We may infer from the data presented in tables 3.5 through 3.9 that our influence question, although its wording differs from the wording of Eulau's question, does measure the kinds of qualities that Eulau assumed were the bases of power and authority in legislatures. The very strong correlations between the distributions of major subgroups of MPs along the two variables indicate that individuals who are attributed influence also are ascribed good judgment. To further assure the reader that the influence and good judgment questions are measuring the same qualities, in chapter 6 we will generate a series of regression and multiple discriminant function analyses in which first the influence and then the good judgment nominations are employed as dependent variables. We will demonstrate that the variables that are the best predictors of influence also are the best predictors of good judgment.

The data in tables 3.5 through 3.9, together with the responses to the question on the criteria used to select cabinet ministers, also allow us to speculate about the influence that is attributed to

TABLE 3.9

**A COMPARISON OF THE GINI COEFFICIENTS MEASURING OVERALL INEQUALITY OF ASCRIBED INFLUENCE AND GOOD JUDGMENT WITHIN SUBGROUPS OF THE CANADIAN HOUSE OF COMMONS**

| Groups | Influence | Good Judgment | N |
|---|---|---|---|
| All MPs | .876 | .836 | 263 |
| NDP | .863 | .796 | 25 |
| Liberals | .869 | .828 | 154 |
| Conservatives | .880 | .858 | 71 |
| Creditistes | .880 | .741 | 13 |
| Western | .873 | .822 | 69 |
| Ontario | .856 | .791 | 89 |
| Quebec | .904 | .890 | 73 |
| Atlantic | .811 | .787 | 32 |
| British Columbia | .705 | .678 | 23 |
| Alberta | .848 | .807 | 18 |
| Saskatchewan | .915 | .855 | 13 |
| Manitoba | .917 | .894 | 13 |
| Ontario | .856 | .791 | 89 |
| Quebec | .904 | .890 | 73 |
| Nova Scotia | .778 | .812 | 12 |
| New Brunswick | .785 | .744 | 10 |
| Prince Edward Island | .515 | .312 | 4 |
| Newfoundland | .732 | .712 | 6 |
| Liberal Cabinet | .614 | .561 | 31 |
| Other Liberals | .894 | .859 | 123 |
| Top Leaders | .600 | .576 | 39 |
| Other MPs | .861 | .829 | 224 |
| MPs elected before 1963 | .826 | .772 | 99 |
| MPs elected 1963–1967 | .871 | .859 | 59 |
| MPs elected 1968 or later | .830 | .773 | 105 |

parliamentary leaders who have achieved their positions because of factors other than personal merit. Appointments to positions of top leadership in a parliament, it seems clear, are constrained by a variety of nonmerit factors. In the Canadian House of Commons the most important of these are geographic, ethnic, and religious, all of which seem to be taken into account when appointments to the cabinet are being made.[20] Thus, a Canadian prime minister must ask himself questions such as: will the appointment of "X" gratify or alienate particular groups? To what extent can the reactions of "Y" and "Z" groups be discounted or ignored if I appoint "X"? These kinds of questions undoubtedly also are asked by the leader of the principal opposition party when he is making top-level appointments. Normally a prime minister or an opposition party leader will try to select individuals who have demonstrated—or at least have a reputation for—ability, special knowledge and skills and who can interact easily and effectively with others. Understandably, such individuals are sometimes difficult to find, particularly if the selections have to be made from a relatively small pool of candidates, as, for example, when three members of a governing party have been elected from a province that by custom is entitled to two representatives in the cabinet. Under such a condition an individual who lacks special skills, expert knowledge, or other desirable qualities may have to be appointed.[21] The observations of a minister who witnessed the formation of the cabinet of Sir Robert Borden suggest that the practice of giving cabinet appointments to individuals whose chief claim to the position seemingly was that they represented a particular territory or social group or were personal friends of a prime minister has been followed for at least three generations.

> Those who have not witnessed the making of a Government have reason to be happier than those who have. It is a thoroughly unpleasant and discreditable business in which merit is disregarded, loyal service is without value, influence is the most important factor and geography and religion are important supplementary considerations. . . . There were some broken hearts, others regarded it philosophically, but the pills were large and the swallowing was bitter.[22]

It follows, then, that when leadership appointments are made for reasons other than merit, the individuals selected very likely have difficulty generating a reputation for being influential. Relatedly, some individuals who are regarded by their parliamentary colleagues as eminently qualified to hold high office never are appointed. Since they are respected and deferred to, however, they probably have influence attributed to them.

Of course, a variety of political factors constrain leadership selection in virtually all existing parliamentary bodies. They differ only in terms of their number and their relative salience for those making the selections. It is safe to assume that the larger the number and the more important such other-than-merit factors are, the greater the number of leaders who will not be considered influential and the more likely it is that at least some members outside of the formal leadership structure will be regarded as influential. If these assumptions are valid, incumbency in a formal position of leadership cannot be considered a sufficient condition for acquiring a reputation for influence. Moreover, if one wishes to stretch the point a little, it may not even be a necessary condition. What advantages, then, do leadership positions bestow upon their incumbents? In our view, the two principal advantages are that they provide incumbents with: (a) resources; and (b) showcases to display talents and abilities. In Canada, for example, being a top leader provides a MP with frequent opportunities to speak to audiences both within and outside of parliament, to demonstrate administrative skills, and to make use of resources to assist colleagues and constituents in solving their problems. Less fortunate MPs (i.e., nonleaders) find it far more difficult to acquire a reputation for being influential. Nonetheless, some opportunities do exist—principally on the floor of the House, in committees, and through behind-the-scenes interactions with colleagues, bureaucrats and members of the public. How extensive these opportunities are, the extent to which members recognize and take advantage of them, and the degree to which they actually affect influence ascription are matters to which we will address ourselves in the remainder of this book.

## SUMMARY

In this chapter we tried to delineate the distribution of influence and of a related quality that we termed "good judgment" among Canadian MPs. We also were concerned with ascertaining the MPs perceptions of the bases of the influence they attributed to their colleagues. We found that less than one-half (42.2%) of the MPs were nominated even once. On the other hand 5% received more than 40 nominations for being influential. The Conservative parliamentary party contained the largest group of unnominated MPs, the NDP the smallest. In fact the NDP parliamentary delegation was the only one to receive a larger proportion of the total number of influence nominations made than their numbers alone warranted.

A comparison of the influence attributed to Liberal cabinet ministers and to the highest echelon leaders in the opposition parties with the influence ascribed to all other MPs indicated there was a very strong correlation between holding a top level position and being considered influential. We also compared the influence attributed to cabinet ministers and private members of the parliamentary delegations of Canada's four principal regions. The average private member from the Atlantic provinces was ascribed the greatest influence; private members from the West were the second most highly regarded group followed by private members from Ontario and Quebec. Although private members from the province of Quebec were not regarded as influential, the ministers from that province certainly were. Ministers from the Atlantic provinces were considered the second most influential group, those from Ontario the third most influential and ministers from the Western provinces the least influential.

Insofar as the basis of influence is concerned we were able to classify these in terms of five categories: (1) attributes that reflected position; (2) attributes that reflected specific knowledge and expertise; (3) attributes that reflected skillful role performance; (4) attributes that reflected valued personal characteristics; and (5) attributes that reflected status and successful interaction with significant others. With respect to particular characteristics, the one that was most frequently cited to explain influence was the occupancy of a top leadership position. The second most frequently cited characteristic was the ability to speak and debate skillfully. However, an examination of the distribution of good judgment nominations (which also were highly skewed) and of other relevant data strongly suggested that the relationships between ascribed influence, the occupancy of a top level leadership position, and skill in debate were far more complex than initially appeared. Consequently, these relationships will be explored more intensively in chapters 6 through 8.

## Chapter 4

# DIMENSIONS OF PARLIAMENTARY ACTIVITY: THE SCOPE OF FORMAL PARTICIPATION

## INTRODUCTION

There is considerable debate among parliamentary scholars about the proper function(s) of parliament. One reason for this debate is that most parliaments are engaged continuously in a variety of diverse activities that do not yield easily to classification or empirical analysis. In the first session of the 28th Parliament alone, for example, the House of Commons was convened for 198 sitting days, processed more than 211 pieces of legislation, voted on more than 80 motions, and passed more than 42 bills. Simultaneously it appointed and organized 17 standing committees, 2 special committees and a special joint committee. Together these conducted 778 full committee meetings, and 143 subcommittee meetings. The committee members listened to the testimony of more than 200 witnesses, issued 153 separate reports, considered 52 government, private, and private member public bills and ordered the printing of 811 separate issues totaling more than 30,000 pages. In addition to their committee activities, the members rose before the House to ask more than 13,000 questions and to deliver more than 5,000 speeches—the latter filling almost 1,000,000 lines in Hansard. And these were but the most visible and perhaps smallest tiles in the mosaic of activities that characterizes the Canadian legislative process. Less visible but perhaps as important as these formally prescribed activities are the myriad informal tasks that MPs perform. There are party caucus meetings to attend, constituents to meet, lobbyists to listen to, speeches to make outside of parliament, interviews to give and a constant flood of mail, telegrams, and telephone calls, all soliciting assistance or offering advice, all demanding action and requiring a commitment of the member's time and energy.

Despite the fact that parliament is an institution characterized by constant motion and activity, relatively little attention has been given to the description and explanation of this behavior. Indeed, although it is customary to include virtually all legislative research under the category of "legislative behavior," in fact very little of this research really is concerned with behavior. It tends to focus on legislative attitudes and role perceptions or on processes such as political recruitment, which presumably act as determinants of elite behavior, but which clearly are not in themselves a part of that behavior.[1] Consequently, students of legislative behavior generally, and of the behavior of Canadian MPs in particular, still lack even the most basic information concerning the scope and substance of the macrobehavior of parliament as an institution, or of the substance, extent, functional importance, or determinants of the micro-level behavior of individual MPs.[2] By way of illustration, questions such as those that follow still have not been addressed in any systematic fashion. Who participates in parliament? Who speaks before the House? What topics are addressed? Who asks what types of questions—and with what results? To what extent does the revitalized committee system provide backbench and opposition members an opportunity to influence policy? How much informal communication is there between backbench and cabinet? With what is it concerned? What results, if any, do these communications achieve? Do members who participate extensively in the work of the House have any more influence than those who are less active? If not, why then do some members participate more than do others? The present study tries to suggest answers to all of these questions, but, in this chapter we are concerned primarily with describing the scope and level of formal legislative behavior in the House of Commons.

## PARTICIPATION IN HOUSE DEBATE

We noted in chapter 1 that policy-making and policy-evaluating opportunities of individual MPs have diminished considerably in this century because of a number of procedural and environmental constraints. The Canadian House of Commons, like its British counterpart, "has largely lost the three functions for which its procedures were evolved, and to which they are relevant: the making of Ministries, the initiation of legislation shared with the cabinet, and the watchdog control of finance and administration."[3] Although the decline in backbench and opposition participation in the legislative functions of parliament is undeniable, the individual MP retains a number of formal avenues for participating in and attempting to influence government policy and decision-making. Among these are the opportunity to participate in House debates, the right to ask and receive answers to questions during question period, the opportunity (if not the obligation) to attend and participate in committee meetings, and the opportunities, whatever their significance, to introduce legislation and to participate in the division votes that finalize many of the important policy decisions ratified by parliament.

With respect to the first of these, a recent volume on the decline of western legislatures suggests that the most important function of parliamentary bodies is not the initiation or review of legislation but rather debate-talk for which parliament is named.[4] Whether or not this is the case, debate in the House is the formal activity that consumes the greatest percentage of time in any session. As we noted above, the record of debates in the first session of the 28th Parliament alone fills almost one million lines of Hansard, and, although participation in debate is restricted in a number of important ways, opportunities do exist for all MPs to take part in this activity.

The extent of these opportunities and the degree to which members avail themselves of them are well illustrated by the distributions of MPs along two measures of speaking activity for the first and second sessions of the 28th Parliament.[5] Table 4.1 reveals, although a typical MP participated in debate 19 times during the first session of parliament and 13 times in the second, delivering speeches totalling more than 2,700 lines in Hansard during Session I and 2,100 during Session II, that participation in debate during both parliamentary sessions was radically skewed toward the low end of a participation continuum. In each session the Gini coefficients of inequality for both the number of speeches and number of Hansard lines underline this fact.

The pattern of differences revealed in table 4.1 is congruent with some of our common sense notions about parliamentary participa-

TABLE 4.1

## THE DISTRIBUTION OF THE NUMBER AND LENGTH OF SPEECHES MADE IN THE HOUSE DURING THE FIRST AND SECOND SESSIONS OF THE 28TH PARLIAMENT BY LEADERSHIP STATUS

### SESSION I (N = 263)

#### All MPs

| Proportion Who Made | | Proportion Whose Speeches Ran: | |
|---|---|---|---|
| 0–5 Speeches | 37.6% | 0–500 Lines | 30.8% |
| 6–10 | 14.8 | 501–1000 | 9.9 |
| 11–20 | 18.6 | 1001–2000 | 17.1 |
| 21–30 | 8.7 | 2001–3000 | 12.5 |
| 31–40 | 6.1 | 3001–4000 | 7.2 |
| 41 or more | 14.1 | 4001 or more | 22.4 |
| $\overline{X}$ = 19.3  SD =30.3  Gini =.63 | | $\overline{X}$ =2768  SD =3662  Gini =.62 | |

#### All Leaders

| Proportion Who Made: | | Proportion Whose Speeches Ran: | |
|---|---|---|---|
| 0–5 Speeches | 20.0% | 0–500 Lines | 21.2% |
| 6–10 | 16.2 | 501–1000 | 3.8 |
| 11–20 | 18.8 | 1001–2000 | 18.8 |
| 21–30 | 15.0 | 2001–3000 | 18.8 |
| 31–40 | 5.0 | 3001–4000 | 6.2 |
| 41 or more | 20.0 | 4001 or more | 31.2 |
| $\overline{X}$ =32.2  S.D. =46.6  Gini =.60 | | $\overline{X}$ =4230  S.D. =4988  Gini =.57 | |

#### All Nonleaders

| Proportion Who Made: | | Proportion Whose Speeches Ran: | |
|---|---|---|---|
| 0–5 Speeches | 44.8% | 0–500 Lines | 35.0% |
| 6–10 | 14.2 | 501–1000 | 12.6 |
| 11–20 | 18.6 | 1001–2000 | 16.4 |
| 21–30 | 6.0 | 2001–3000 | 9.8 |
| 31–40 | 6.6 | 3001–4000 | 7.6 |
| 41 or more | 9.8 | 4001 or more | 18.6 |
| $\overline{X}$ =13.7  S.D. =16.5  Gini =.60 | | $\overline{X}$ =2129  S.D. =2675  Gini =.61 | |

tion. For example, the finding that party leaders consistently participate in House debates more than do backbench MPs is consonant
with our understanding of the roles they (leaders) play in the
Canadian parliamentary system. On a day-to-day basis, leaders are
expected to be the principal spokesmen of their parties. They also

#### Table-4.1 (continued)

#### SESSION II (N = 263)

#### All MPs

| Proportion Who Made: | | Proportion Whose Speeches Ran: | |
|---|---|---|---|
| 0–5 Speeches | 42.2% | 0–500 Lines | 31.2% |
| 6–10 | 20.2 | 501–1000 | 13.7 |
| 11–20 | 16.3 | 1001–2000 | 19.4 |
| 21–30 | 11.4 | 2001–3000 | 11.8 |
| 31–40 | 3.8 | 3001–4000 | 7.6 |
| 41 or more | 6.1 | 4001 or more | 16.3 |
| X̄ =13.0  S.D. =19.0  Gini =.60 | | X̄ =2106  S.D. =2545  Gini =.58 | |

#### All Leaders

| Proportion Who Made: | | Proportion Whose Speeches Ran: | |
|---|---|---|---|
| 0–5 Speeches | 26.2% | 0–500 Lines | 21.2% |
| 6–10 | 20.0 | 501– 000 | 8.8 |
| 11–20 | 25.0 | 1001–2000 | 26.2 |
| 21–30 | 11.2 | 2001–3000 | 12.5 |
| 31–40 | 5.0 | 3001–4000 | 8.8 |
| 41 or more | 12.5 | 4001 or more | 22.5 |
| X̄ =19.4  S.D. =27.8  Gini =.57 | | X̄ =2814  S.D. =2797  Gini =.52 | |

#### All Nonleaders

| Proportion Who Made: | | Proportion Whose Speeches Ran: | |
|---|---|---|---|
| 0–5 Speeches | 48.6% | 0–500 Lines | 35.6% |
| 6–10 | 20.2 | 501– 000 | 15.8 |
| 11–20 | 12.6 | 1001–2000 | 16.4 |
| 21–30 | 11.5 | 2001–3000 | 11.4 |
| 31–40 | 3.3 | 3001–4000 | 7.1 |
| 41 or more | 3.8 | 4001 or more | 13.7 |
| X̄ = 10.2  S.D.=12.5  Gini=.59 | | X̄=1797  S.D.=2273  Gini=.60 | |

a. Some columns do not total 100% because of rounding error.

are expected to take the lead in major debates such as those following the Throne Speech. If party leaders are cabinet members, not only is there an expectation that they will articulate their party's positions on issues, but also a constitutional obligation that they introduce and defend the policies and programs of the ministries for which they are responsible. The backbenches of both parties contain a number of would be leaders who undoubtedly would be quite willing to share with current leaders the responsibility of being party spokesmen. We assume, however, that one reason such ambitious backbenchers do not speak more frequently and at greater length is that their oratorical aspirations are dampened by party leaders. In Canada, the leaders of the Liberal party most often have been accused of "muzzling" their backbenchers. Of course, as our introductory biographical sketch of "Roger Cyr" indicates, some MPs prefer not to participate in House debates and do not have to be muzzled.

Table 4.2 presents the average number and length of speeches made by the leaders and backbenchers of each party during the first two parliamentary sessions. Again, the data are consistent with conventional wisdom. For example, conventional wisdom holds that the House "belongs" to the opposition in the sense that debate provides the opportunity for institutionalized, overt opposition to the government of the day. However, since a government must get as much of its program through parliament as it can, some constraints must be placed on individual participation. In a British-model parliamentary system the burden of not participating falls most heavily on a government's own backbenchers.

The data indicate that, as a party, the governing Liberals spoke less often than the members of the three opposition parties. In fact, opposition MPs made approximately two-thirds of the speeches and used almost two-thirds of the House's time in the first two years the 28th Parliament was in session. Another indicator of the willingness of a governing party to allow the opposition to dominate debate is that 22 of the 31 nonspeakers in Session I and 29 of the 35 nonspeakers in Session II were Liberal backbenchers. The several Liberal committee chairmen were almost as quiet as the backbenchers. Even the cabinet ministers, including the prime minister, spoke considerably less often and for much less time than the leaders of the opposition parties. The government leaders spoke, it would appear, only when it was necessary to defend their policies or to make a public record. One has the impression that they might have been willing to forego even these opportunities, if, by so doing, they could have speeded passage of their legislative proposals.

If we look at leader-follower differences in participation within each party we find that Liberal cabinet members spoke about five times as often and that each of their speeches was about four times as long as the speeches of their noncabinet colleagues in the first

## TABLE 4.2
## AVERAGE NUMBER OF SPEECHES, AVERAGE LENGTH OF SPEECHES, STANDARD DEVIATIONS AND GINI COEFFICIENTS FOR LEADERS AND NONLEADERS IN FOUR PARLIAMENTARY PARTIES

| | SESSION I | | | | | | SESSION II | | | | | |
|---|---|---|---|---|---|---|---|---|---|---|---|---|
| | $\bar{X}$ Speeches | S.D. | Gini | $\bar{X}$ Length | S.D. | Gini | $\bar{X}$ Speeches | S.D. | Gini | $\bar{X}$ Length | S.D. | Gini |
| All Liberals (N = 154) | 11.5 | 27.5 | .68 | 1362 | 1865 | .63 | 7.6 | 15.7 | .62 | 1163 | 1425 | .59 |
| Liberal Cabinet (N = 31) | 33.3 | 55.9 | .58 | 3379 | 2848 | .44 | 18.8 | 31.6 | .53 | 2608 | 2041 | .40 |
| Liberal Committee Chairmen (N = 20) | 6.7 | 7.1 | .56 | 927 | 926 | .54 | 5.8 | 7.7 | .57 | 1039 | 1120 | .55 |
| Liberal Backbenchers (N = 103) | 6.0 | 8.2 | .60 | 840 | 1103 | .62 | 4.4 | 5.2 | .57 | 750 | 904 | .60 |
| All Conservatives (N = 71) | 23.0 | 23.6 | .49 | 3595 | 3539 | .49 | 16.2 | 18.8 | .51 | 2716 | 2756 | .49 |
| Conservative Frontbench (N = 23) | 39.0 | 32.7 | .44 | 5782 | 4961 | .45 | 26.0 | 27.4 | .49 | 3821 | 3817 | .49 |
| Conservative Backbench (N = 48) | 15.4 | 12.2 | .42 | 2547 | 1915 | .42 | 11.4 | 10.1 | .44 | 2187 | 1899 | .46 |
| All NDP (N = 25) | 45.2 | 40.3 | .37 | 6923 | 5349 | .39 | 34.2 | 23.1 | .33 | 5676 | 3578 | .34 |
| NDP Leaders (N = 2) | 133.0 | 111.7 | — | 18253 | 9681 | — | 71.0 | 60.8 | — | 9642 | 4682 | — |
| NDP Backbench (N = 23) | 37.5 | 21.1 | .30 | 5938 | 3778 | .35 | 30.9 | 16.7 | .29 | 5331 | 3377 | .34 |
| All Creditistes (N = 13) | 41.7 | 32.8 | .42 | 6921 | 5840 | .45 | 79.5 | 13.6 | .38 | 3085 | 2116 | .36 |
| Creditiste Leaders (N = 3) | 84.0 | 21.6 | — | 14945 | 4079 | — | 32.0 | 14.4 | — | 5132 | 2388 | — |
| Creditiste Backbench (N = 10) | 29.0 | 23.6 | .42 | 4514 | 3725 | .43 | 15.7 | 11.6 | .38 | 2471 | 1699 | .36 |

parliamentary year. In the second year cabinet members spoke about four times as often and three times as long as other Liberal MPs. Frontbench members of the official Conservative opposition spoke approximately twice as often and twice as long as backbenchers in that party. Nor was the situation any different in the two minor parties, despite their lower Gini coefficients. The five top leaders of the NDP[6] and Social Credit parties spoke approximately three times as often and three times as long in the first session of parliament as did their party colleagues. The gap between leader-follower speaking in the two minor parties narrowed considerably in the second session, although the leaders still spoke almost twice as often and one and one-half times as long. Indeed, by themselves the five top leaders of the two minor parties made 10% of all speeches delivered during parliament's first year and 7% of all speeches made during the second. Small wonder that a number of Liberal and Conservative MPs complained of the tedium of sitting in the House hour after hour listening to debate (see chapter 2). Had these five MPs the oratorical skills of a Demosthenes, they still might have irritated their own party colleagues, let alone the members of other parties, by speaking so often and at such length (an average of over 16,000 Hansard lines in Session I and approximately 7000 lines in Session II).

The size of a parliamentary party (as well as whether or not it is in power) also appears to affect the speaking opportunities available to its members. Although the Conservatives (N = 71) made 1636 speeches totalling over 255,000 Hansard lines in the first session of parliament and 1148 speeches totalling over 192,000 lines in the second, the average Conservative spoke only 23 and 16 times and delivered speeches that averaged approximately 3600 and 2700 lines in the first and second sessions respectively. In contrast, the 13 Social Credit members spoke an average of 41 times each in the first year of parliament's existence and 19 times each during parliament's second year. Although they may not have been thanked for it by other MPs, the average Social Credit member spoke almost twice as long as the average Conservative in the first session and about 15% longer in the second session. The average NDP MP did even better, speaking twice as often and about twice as long as the average Conservative in both sessions. Thus, although the arrangements entered into by the House leaders of the four parties insure that each party receives an allocation of speech time commensurate with its numerical strength,[7] the smaller size of the two minor parties provides their members with more frequent opportunities to participate in parliamentary deliberations. A comparison of the Gini coefficients which measure the extent to which speaking time is unequally distributed among members of each of the parties reinforces this point.

## SUBSTANCE

Tables 4.3 and 4.4 suggest that a government's task of defending its policy proposals is made easier by the fact that: (a) not all of the speeches of opposition MPs are condemnatory; and (b) machinery exists to limit both the time opposition speakers will be given and the matters on which they may comment.[8] Table 4.3 presents the percentages of speeches made by each party and leadership group that may be termed: (1) supportive of the Liberal government; (2) critical of the government; and (3) more-or-less neutral. In both sessions more than 50% of the speeches were critical of the government while less than one-third (30%) in Session I and only about one-quarter in Session II may be considered supportive of government positions or policies.

Both NDP and Social Credit MPs sided more frequently with the opposition than with the government during debates, but neither party was as frequently and consistently critical of the government as was the official Conservative opposition. The Creditistes, in fact, supported government proposals in almost a quarter of their speeches and although only 15% of the speeches of NDP members could be considered pro government, they tended to take an essentially neutral posture in another 30% of their speeches. Although the backbench members of the Conservative party were almost as critical of the government as were the members of the frontbench (there was, in fact, no statistically significant difference in the respective proportions of their "antigovernment" speeches) their critical comments tended to be directed toward different targets. The members of the backbench (not all of them, to be sure) tended to criticize individual ministers whereas the most important figures on the frontbench tended to criticize broad policies and individual programs of the government. Given the very strong support the party historically has received from the province of Quebec, a substantial number of ministers in any Liberal government are of French descent. The 28th Parliament was no different from other parliaments in this respect. Thus a great number of the critical comments of Conservative backbenchers, of necessity, were directed toward French-Canadian minis-

TABLE 4.3

DISTRIBUTION OF PRO-GOVERNMENT, ANTI-GOVERNMENT AND NEUTRAL SPEECHES
MADE IN FIRST AND SECOND SESSIONS OF 28th PARLIAMENT BY MAJOR SUBGROUPS OF MPs

| | SESSION I | | | SESSION II | | |
|---|---|---|---|---|---|---|
| | Pro Govern- ment | Anti Govern- ment | Neutral | Pro Govern- ment | Anti Govern- ment | Neutral |
| All MPs | 30.5% | 51.2% | 18.3% | 26.3% | 50.7% | 23.0% |
| Liberals | 84.6 | 4.8 | 10.5 | 80.6 | 8.6 | 10.7 |
| Conservatives | 6.4 | 77.3 | 16.3 | 3.7 | 71.9 | 24.4 |
| NDP | 14.8 | 56.8 | 28.4 | 13.2 | 56.3 | 30.5 |
| Creditistes | 26.2 | 54.2 | 19.6 | 21.5 | 61.4 | 17.0 |
| All Backbenchers | 23.9 | 54.5 | 21.6 | 20.3 | 53.8 | 25.8 |
| All Leaders | 40.8 | 45.8 | 13.4 | 41.1 | 43.0 | 15.8 |
| Liberal Backbenchers | 78.3 | 11.0 | 10.7 | 75.4 | 12.4 | 12.2 |
| Liberal Leaders | 89.0 | 0.7 | 10.3 | 85.3 | 5.0 | 9.7 |
| Conservative Backbenchers | 8.0 | 73.5 | 18.5 | 5.1 | 69.6 | 25.3 |
| Conservative Leaders | 4.7 | 80.8 | 14.6 | 0.9 | 75.7 | 23.4 |

ters, a matter that escaped neither the ministers nor the public they represent.

Of course, it could be argued that if the opposition's criticism of a government's policies and programs is to be vigorous and effective in a parliament modeled on the British system, then a certain amount of it inevitably must be directed at the principal advocates of these policies and programs. It could be argued further that the members of the New Democratic and Creditiste[9] parties also criticized both the government's policies and programs and the individual ministers who were responsible for them to parliament. As Table 4.3 indicates, however, the members of the two minor parties were less critical of the government overall than were members of the Conservative party. Further, (although, unfortunately, our data do not illustrate it) the tendency toward two-tracked criticism was not as pronounced in the minor opposition parties as in the Conservative party. Moreover, since the Conservative party was larger than the other two opposition parties combined, the volume of New Democratic and Creditiste criticism was much smaller than the Conservative's. This withering criticism of Liberal governments generally and of Quebec members of those governments in particular is partially responsible for the "anti-French" label that has been applied to the Conservative party. The labeling has important political consequences that will be discussed in our concluding chapter.

The view that a major function of parliamentary debate is to provide an institutionalized opportunity for the opposition to continuously scrutinize, criticize, and publicize the shortcomings of a current government and the policies it pursues is supported by the data in table 4.3. However, since a government has the initiative in allotting the time the House will spend on considering particular issues, we may assume a government will use its initiative to try to limit both the scope and intensity of an opposition's criticism. They can do this in two ways: (1) by establishing a claim that certain policy areas, of necessity, are their special preserve; and (2) by focusing debate on subjects and in areas in which they feel least vulnerable. To illustrate the first of these strategies, we may note that defense and foreign affairs are areas that governments long have claimed as their bailiwicks.[10] With respect to the second strategy, even the most casual observer of House debates would be impressed with the frequency and the resourcefulness with which members of a government resist proposals by the opposition to suspend regularly scheduled debate in order to discuss matters of "urgent public importance," as for example, the increase in the level of unemployment during winter months.

Table 4.4, which presents all first and second session speeches classified by issue,[11] suggests that the expectation that a government will use its initiative to channel House debate into particular areas is well founded. There was not a single group in any party in either session devoting more than 6% of its speeches to defense and foreign policy. A second area that did not appear to receive much attention was labour and secondary industry. Again, only about 6% of parliamentary debate focused on labor related subjects despite the fact that the level of unemployment in Canada during this period generally was considerably higher than in the United States, Japan, or most Western European countries. Since the subject was salient and since there is no reason to assume that the members of parliament were less interested in labor and secondary industry than in other areas, we can speculate that the Liberal government felt particularly vulnerable on this group of issues and attempted, rather successfully, to restrict the volume of parliamentary attention these issues received during House debates.

With regard to the remaining issue areas, no clear pattern of dominance is apparent. In general, discussions of public finance, social welfare, legal and political issues, and primary extractive industries tended to dominate debate. In particular, all of the parties devoted considerable attention to (generally procedural) legal and political matters.[12] The NDP and Liberal parties also devoted substantial time to social welfare; the Conservatives and the NDP to primary industry-extractive issues; and the Creditistes to issues of public finance. Nevertheless, differences in these regards were minimal and suggest that all the parties devoted approximately the same amount of attention to similar issues.

## PARTICIPATION IN QUESTION PERIOD

Although formal debate consumes the largest part of the legislative calendar in the House of Commons, it is the question period (although strictly limited) that fulfills a major parliamentary function—that of theoretically providing any member of the House with the opportunity to ask the government questions on virtually any topic and giving nongovernment MPs an opportunity to participate in the affairs of parliament.[13] Given the emphasis on confrontation that is

TABLE 4.4

THE DISTRIBUTION OF SPEECHES BY PARTY AND ISSUE AREA IN SESSIONS I AND II

| | Defense & External Affairs I | Public Finance II | Social Welfare III | Legal-Political IV | Primary Industry—Extractive V | Labor & Secondary Industry VI | Internal Development VII | Miscellaneous VIII |
|---|---|---|---|---|---|---|---|---|
| **Session I** | | | | | | | | |
| All MPs | 4.5% | 14.2% | 16.1% | 20.7% | 11.6% | 5.9% | 10.0% | 16.9% |
| Liberals | 5.4 | 17.7 | 18.8 | 15.1 | 8.8 | 9.1 | 8.9 | 16.2 |
| Conservatives | 4.2 | 13.1 | 11.0 | 25.2 | 15.0 | 3.7 | 12.0 | 15.7 |
| NDP | 5.2 | 10.7 | 16.1 | 18.2 | 13.8 | 6.4 | 9.7 | 19.8 |
| Creditistes | 1.4 | 17.7 | 24.7 | 25.1 | 5.5 | 3.1 | 8.3 | 14.0 |
| All Backbenchers | 4.2 | 13.3 | 17.8 | 15.5 | 14.8 | 4.8 | 10.9 | 18.5 |
| All Leaders | 4.9 | 15.3 | 14.0 | 27.0 | 7.7 | 7.2 | 9.0 | 15.0 |
| Liberal Backbenchers | 4.5 | 14.3 | 18.8 | 12.3 | 8.8 | 6.1 | 12.9 | 22.2 |
| Liberal Leaders | 6.0 | 19.8 | 19.2 | 16.9 | 8.9 | 11.1 | 6.0 | 12.1 |
| Conservative Backbenchers | 3.4 | 13.2 | 13.8 | 17.2 | 20.2 | 1.9 | 11.8 | 18.5 |
| Conservative Leaders | 5.0 | 13.1 | 8.2 | 33.0 | 9.6 | 5.9 | 12.4 | 12.8 |
| **Session II** | | | | | | | | |
| All MPs | 4.1 | 15.3 | 13.9 | 17.0 | 20.2 | 5.2 | 10.3 | 14.0 |
| Liberals | 4.0 | 14.7 | 15.8 | 22.0 | 15.3 | 6.3 | 9.6 | 12.3 |
| Conservatives | 4.3 | 13.9 | 11.9 | 16.2 | 22.4 | 3.6 | 12.4 | 15.3 |
| NDP | 4.7 | 15.4 | 15.8 | 11.6 | 22.6 | 6.3 | 9.7 | 14.0 |
| Creditistes | 3.2 | 24.8 | 8.9 | 17.9 | 20.3 | 4.9 | 6.6 | 13.4 |
| All Backbenchers | 3.0 | 14.5 | 14.5 | 14.6 | 23.5 | 4.9 | 10.6 | 14.6 |
| All Leaders | 6.1 | 16.6 | 13.2 | 20.5 | 15.1 | 5.8 | 9.8 | 13.0 |
| Liberal Backbenchers | 1.5 | 11.9 | 16.4 | 22.9 | 14.2 | 3.8 | 11.0 | 18.4 |
| Liberal Leaders | 6.0 | 16.9 | 15.5 | 21.0 | 16.4 | 8.5 | 8.5 | 7.2 |
| Conservative Backbenchers | 3.1 | 15.1 | 13.1 | 11.9 | 27.2 | 3.4 | 11.7 | 14.6 |
| Conservative Leaders | 5.8 | 12.3 | 10.6 | 21.5 | 16.5 | 3.8 | 13.1 | 16.3 |

inherent in the procedures of British-model parliamentary systems, a reasonable expectation is that question period in Canada will be dominated by members of the opposition. The government's back-bench members, although not prohibited from asking questions, are constrained by the norm of party loyalty, by the threat—usually implicit—of party sanctions against disloyal members, and by a quite normal disinclination to attack something of which they are a part.[14] Because of this, we may assume: (a) that there will be only limited participation by government members in question period; and (b) that the questions they do ask generally will be requests for information that neither express nor imply criticism of government policy. To the extent that politically embarrassing questions are asked by governing party members, they are likely to come from backbenchers who are willing to risk being passed over for promotion to party leadership positions.

Table 4.5 presents the distribution of questions asked by noncabinet MPs. Perusal of the table indicates that MPs generally participate considerably more (by a margin greater than 2:1) in question time than they do in debate. Tables 4.6 and 4.7 present for these same members (disaggregated by party and leadership status) the mean number of questions that were asked in sessions I and II respectively and the proportion of these questions that were: (1) oral as opposed to written;[15] (2) argumentative and political as opposed to requests for information that were more or less neutral; and (3) answered as opposed to being ruled out of order or left unanswered by the government.[16] Interestingly, and seemingly contrary to many journalistic accounts of the highly charged and antigovernment atmosphere of question period, only about 20% of the questions asked in the two sessions were political and argumentative. The great majority of the combined number of oral and written questions appear to have been designed primarily to elicit information from the government.

Of course, one reason that we may have failed to find a greater proportion of politically motivated questions is that we may have defined "political" too narrowly. A question that is informational in form can have a political intent, as for example, a question ostensibly seeking information that is followed by a supplementary question which is manifestly political. In our analysis we have coded the first question informational, the second political. It could be argued that we should have classified both questions as "political." Moreover, although we included supplementary questions in our analysis, we

TABLE 4.5
THE DISTRIBUTION OF QUESTIONS ASKED BY NONCABINET MPs
DURING THE FIRST AND SECOND SESSIONS
OF THE 28th PARLIAMENT

| Session I | | Session II | |
|---|---|---|---|
| **All Noncabinet MPs** | | **All Noncabinet MPs** | |
| Proportion Who Asked: | | Proportion Who Asked: | |
| 0–5 Questions | 43.8% | 0–5 Questions | 42.9% |
| 6–15 | 13.3 | 6–15 | 17.6 |
| 16–30 | 9.0 | 16–30 | 6.4 |
| 31–50 | 5.2 | 31–50 | 8.2 |
| 51–100 | 12.8 | 51–100 | 14.2 |
| 101 or more | 15.9 | 101 or more | 10.7 |
| **Noncabinet Leaders** | | **Noncabinet Leaders** | |
| Proportion Who Asked: | | Proportion Who Asked: | |
| 0–5 Questions | 36.0% | 0–5 Questions | 40.0% |
| 6–15 | 12.0 | 6–15 | 12.0 |
| 16–30 | 6.0 | 16–30 | 2.0 |
| 31–50 | 4.0 | 31–50 | 6.0 |
| 51–100 | 10.0 | 51–100 | 22.0 |
| 101 or more | 32.0 | 101 or more | 18.0 |
| **All Nonleaders** | | **All Nonleaders** | |
| Proportion Who Asked: | | Proportion Who Asked: | |
| 0–5 Questions | 45.9% | 0–5 Questions | 43.7% |
| 6–15 | 13.7 | 6–15 | 19.1 |
| 16–30 | 10.4 | 16–30 | 7.6 |
| 31–50 | 4.9 | 31– 50 | 8.8 |
| 51–100 | 13.7 | 51–100 | 12.0 |
| 101 or more | 11.5 | 101 or more | 8.8 |

did not include attempts by MPs to comment on the answers they received from government spokesmen. Some of these comments were political. Again, an argument for their inclusion could be made. We chose not to because they were comments rather than questions. A second reason that we may have failed to find a larger proportion of political questions is that oral and written questions were not analyzed separately. If it is true that oral questions are intended to embarrass the government in a highly visible milieu, whereas written questions are less likely to injure the government politically and hence are more likely to be requests for information, we might have confirmed conventional wisdom had we treated each category separately. We cannot test this hypothesis because of the format of the data, but even if we could, it is unlikely that the outcome would have changed the results in any drastic fashion. The fact that about 70% of all questions were asked orally but that only 20.5% of all questions were political means that no more than 30% of the oral questions could have been political. Even if—assuming that our classification of political questions was unduly restrictive—the proportion of political questions was 40 or 45%, such a figure still is unexpectedly small given conventional wisdom and journalistic accounts of the question process. One possible explanation for this disparity is that conflict in parliament is dramatic, interesting, and makes the best copy. The question period itself, particularly partisan questions and the political conflict such questions generate, probably receives disproportionate attention from the media thus giving an impression of sharp interparty and interpersonal confrontations. Whatever the explanation, however, the data strongly suggest that the primary purpose for which question period is employed is to elicit information.

We recognize that MPs may be motivated to ask informational questions by considerations other than a desire for information. Well structured, substantively significant questions that reflect intelligence and industry can bring MPs to the attention of the media and the leaders of their respective parties. Favorable attention from the media may not only help a member be reelected, it may also help him become something of a national figure.[17] Whether asking the right questions also enhances a MP's reputation for influence and the closely related quality we have termed good judgment is a matter that will be considered in chapter 6. For the present it should be noted that although MPs tend to participate more in question period than in debate, closer inspection of these data reveals that the variations in participation in the question period, as in debate, are quite extreme. Whereas the mean number of questions asked in sessions I and II of this parliament approaches or exceeds 40, the median number of questions asked is 9 for each session. In other words slightly over one-half of the members of the 28th Parliament asked fewer than 10 questions in each session, whereas the remainder asked considerably more. Indeed, several members asked more than 200 questions in the first session alone and one MP asked nearly 600!

TABLE 4.6

MEAN NUMBER OF QUESTIONS ASKED AND THE DISTRIBUTION OF QUESTIONS
BY TYPE, PARTY AND RESPONSE FOR ALL NONCABINET MPs IN SESSION I

| | Mean Number of Questions | Oral | Written | Informational | Political | Out of Order | Oral Answers | Written Answers | No Answers |
|---|---|---|---|---|---|---|---|---|---|
| All MPs | 44.9 | 69.8% | 30.2% | 79.5% | 20.5% | 11.5% | 50.0% | 28.2% | 10.3% |
| Standard Deviation | (74.2) | | | | | | | | |
| Liberals | 15.6 | 53.3 | 46.7 | 86.0 | 14.0 | 3.9 | 40.2 | 47.1 | 8.8 |
| S.D. | (62.1) | | | | | | | | |
| Conservatives | 72.5 | 76.4 | 23.6 | 78.1 | 21.9 | 11.4 | 57.1 | 21.4 | 10.0 |
| S.D. | (70.6) | | | | | | | | |
| NDP | 92.7 | 80.6 | 19.4 | 80.9 | 19.1 | 10.0 | 60.5 | 17.3 | 12.3 |
| S.D. | (77.1) | | | | | | | | |
| Creditistes | 75.0 | 46.7 | 53.3 | 84.8 | 15.2 | 8.9 | 23.9 | 55.2 | 11.9 |
| S.D. | (86.7) | | | | | | | | |
| All Backbenchers | 36.0 | 65.8 | 34.2 | 80.6 | 19.4 | 10.0 | 50.0 | 30.0 | 10.0 |
| S.D. | (64.9) | | | | | | | | |
| All Noncabinet Leaders | 77.5 | 79.7 | 20.3 | 80.6 | 19.4 | 11.4 | 55.9 | 22.8 | 10.3 |
| S.D. | (96.9) | | | | | | | | |
| Liberal Backbenchers | 17.3 | 52.9 | 47.1 | 83.3 | 16.7 | 3.7 | 41.1 | 47.7 | 7.5 |
| S.D. | (67.5) | | | | | | | | |
| Liberal Noncabinet Leaders | 7.2 | 45.2 | 54.8 | 93.1 | 6.9 | 2.7 | 32.4 | 48.6 | 16.2 |
| S.D. | (18.7) | | | | | | | | |
| Conservative Backbenchers | 53.2 | 74.5 | 25.5 | 78.4 | 21.6 | 9.1 | 56.4 | 25.5 | 9.1 |
| S.D. | (50.0) | | | | | | | | |
| Conservative Frontbench Leaders | 116.7 | 86.7 | 13.3 | 76.4 | 23.6 | 12.6 | 60.5 | 14.3 | 12.6 |
| S.D. | (90.2) | | | | | | | | |
| Cabinet Replies | 86.0 | 70.1 | 29.9 | 78.9 | 21.1 | | | | |
| S.D. | (116.8) | | | | | | | | |

# TABLE 4.7
## MEAN NUMBER OF QUESTIONS ASKED AND THE DISTRIBUTION OF QUESTIONS BY TYPE, PARTY AND RESPONSE FOR ALL NONCABINET MPs IN SESSION II

| | Mean Number of Questions | Oral | Written | Informa-tional | Political | Out of Order | Oral Answers | Written Answers | No Answers |
|---|---|---|---|---|---|---|---|---|---|
| All MPs | 38.0 | 73.5% | 26.5% | 78.1% | 21.9% | 10.0% | 56.7% | 23.3% | 10.0% |
| Standard Deviation | (73.6) | | | | | | | | |
| Liberals | 14.8 | 51.2 | 48.8 | 85.4 | 14.6 | 3.9 | 46.8 | 44.1 | 5.2 |
| S.D. | (73.6) | | | | | | | | |
| Conservatives | 59.2 | 83.9 | 16.1 | 74.1 | 25.9 | 10.7 | 60.7 | 17.9 | 10.7 |
| S.D. | (60.1) | | | | | | | | |
| NDP | 91.3 | 71.7 | 28.3 | 78.4 | 21.6 | 9.0 | 55.1 | 24.4 | 11.5 |
| S.D. | (71.6) | | | | | | | | |
| Creditistes | 39.4 | 61.5 | 38.5 | 85.0 | 15.0 | 8.6 | 45.7 | 34.3 | 11.4 |
| S.D. | (29.8) | | | | | | | | |
| All Backbenchers | 33.3 | 70.0 | 30.0 | 82.1 | 17.9 | 7.7 | 53.8 | 26.9 | 11.5 |
| S.D. | (72.9) | | | | | | | | |
| All Noncabinet Leaders | 56.0 | 83.3 | 16.7 | 66.7 | 33.3 | 12.5 | 60.4 | 16.7 | 10.4 |
| S.D. | (71.1) | | | | | | | | |
| Liberal Backbenchers | 16.9 | 49.5 | 50.5 | 84.6 | 15.4 | 3.7 | 45.1 | 46.3 | 4.9 |
| S.D. | (80.7) | | | | | | | | |
| Liberal Noncabinet Leaders | 4.4 | 72.7 | 27.3 | 90.9 | 9.1 | — | 64.4 | 28.9 | 6.7 |
| S.D. | (7.9) | | | | | | | | |
| Conservative Backbenchers | 42.4 | 81.4 | 18.6 | 83.3 | 16.7 | 9.1 | 61.4 | 20.5 | 9.1 |
| S.D. | (39.4) | | | | | | | | |
| Conservative Frontbench Leaders | 96.7 | 89.4 | 10.6 | 61.9 | 38.1 | 12.0 | 60.0 | 15.0 | 13.0 |
| S.D. | (79.9) | | | | | | | | |
| Cabinet Replies | 88.6 | 79.0 | 21.0 | 85.1 | 14.9 | | | | |
| S.D. | (119.3) | | | | | | | | |

The wide disparity in the participation rates[18] can be explained in part by party and leader-follower differences. We find, for example, that the Liberals, as a party, asked substantially fewer questions than any other party and that party leaders, on the whole, asked substantially more questions than backbench MPs. Conservative party leaders, in fact, asked more than twice as many questions as their backbench colleagues. Among the Liberals, however, noncabinet leaders asked fewer questions than any other. The small absolute number of questions asked by members of the government party confirms our expectation that question period is used primarily by the opposition parties. The differences between middle-level leaders and backbenchers in the governing Liberal party may be explained by a number of factors. Middle level leaders (primarily committee chairmen) may voluntarily refrain from asking questions and from speaking frequently in the House as a matter of personal choice or style. Alternatively, given their responsibilities as leaders, they may be away from the House frequently and thus have less opportunity to speak and ask questions than do other private members. Yet another possibility is that they regard their appointment to middle level leadership positions as a first step toward ministerial office. Asking potentially embarrassing questions of current cabinet ministers or "wasting" their cabinet colleagues' time by speaking too frequently may be counter-productive to their ambitions. It may be that middle level leaders, again because of their positions, are privy to more information than backbenchers and thus do not need to ask as many questions, or it may be some combination of these and still other factors.

The Liberal party was not the only one in which there were differences in leader-follower participation rates. The relatively high standard deviations from the mean that we find for each party combined with the fact that (other than in the NDP) the mean number of questions asked by each party substantially exceeds the median number they ask, indicates that the members of the 3 parties did not take anything like equal advantage of their opportunities to ask questions of the Government. During the first session of parliament, for example, the Gini coefficient for the noncabinet members of the Liberal party was .87, for the Conservatives .52, and for the Social Credit and NDP it was .51 and .43 respectively. The Gini coefficients for the second session were similar and ranged from .38 for the NDP to .87 for the Liberals. In summary, then, although the opportunity to participate in question period theoretically is open to all MPs, the actual asking of questions tended to be confined to a small group of opposition leaders and, to a lesser extent, to the members of the NDP.

Also of interest in the data on questions are the patterns of party and leadership differences with respect to the type (i.e., oral or written) of question asked. We find in general that members of the Liberal party not only asked the fewest questions but also that the questions disproportionately were of the written variety. This probably works against the government by increasing the opportunities available to the opposition to ask oral questions. On the other hand, asking written questions permits the government's backbenchers to question their party leaders without drawing undue public attention either to themselves or to their leaders. The Social Credit members seemed almost as inclined as government backbenchers to put their questions to the government in writing and were almost as loathe as noncabinet Liberals to ask the government partisan questions. In fact, they did not ask a significantly larger percentage of political questions than the Liberal backbenchers. Given our earlier observation that the Creditistes also were the least likely to criticize the government in debate, it appears from these data that even if they were not ardent supporters of the Liberal government, Creditiste MPs certainly were not its severest critics.

More generally, the pattern of findings suggests the existence of a relationship among the types, orientations (i.e., political or informational), and dispositions (i.e., ruled our of order, answered orally, answered in writing, not answered) of questions. Overall, it appears that in both sessions there was a small positive relationship between the proportion of questions that were oral and the proportion that were partisan. There also was a relationship between the proportion of partisan questions and the proportion ruled out of order or not answered; it appears that the partisan questions were more likely to be ruled out of order or to go unanswered. Finally, it appears that the distribution of oral and written answers generally followed the disposition of questions by type so that oral answers tended to be partisan and to be ruled out of order. Written answers, like written questions, tended to be informational.

### LEGISLATIVE INITIATIVE AND REVIEW

Central to the thesis that the legislative role of parliament in complex societies is declining is a belief that the private member's role in the initiation and disposition of legislation has declined.[19] Notwithstanding the general validity of this argument, in Canada the formal trappings of the individual MP's legislative role—the mechanisms through which private member participation in public policy making is realized—have survived relatively intact over time. Two of these, debates in the House and asking oral and written questions of the government, already have been considered. MPs may also: (a) propose resolutions for debate; (b) introduce legislation in the form of a private bill or a private member's public bill (commonly called "private members' bills");[20] and (c) vote on a variety of substantive and procedural issues on which there are formal divisions.[21]

It already has been demonstrated that Canadian MPs do not participate equally in House debates and question period, the two principal vehicles for influencing the content of public policy. Students of parliament probably would argue that introducing resolutions and private members' bills and voting in divisions are not likely to have great impact on policy. These acts are largely symbolic and ritualistic. Although their principal value is to demonstrate to constituents and local party supporters that their members care about their problems and are doing something about them,[22] all of these devices could have some effect on legislative decision-making. For example, in a situation in which a government majority is very small, or during a period of minority government, the votes of individual members can take on importance. In such instances the influence of the private member increases, not because he is likely to vote against his party (although this has happened), but because a member may be absent for a critical vote or, even if present, may register his opposition to his party's position by abstaining. Moreover, even if few resolutions or private members' bills actually become law,[23] they sometimes can lead a government to adopt policies with the same intent. For this to occur, however, the proposed private members' bills and resolutions must identify and publicize important problems and their sponsors must persist in their efforts (i.e., the bills must be reintroduced in each session of parliament) to secure a second reading (agreement in principal) for their bills.

In the 28th Parliament, the conditions that enhance the importance of an individual member's vote simply were not present. The Liberal majority in parliament was large and the opposition parties not always united in their opposition. Consequently, data on members' voting for all division votes in each of the four sessions (presented in Appendix A) offer few, if any, interesting insights into the character of individual member participation in parliament's policy-making business.[24] For example, we did not find any significant party or leadership differences in the incidence of voting. Nor did we find any arresting patterns with respect to the frequency of voting across the eight substantive issue areas. In general it appears that the areas of finance and of primary industries-extractive tend to generate the highest levels of voting whereas internal development matters stimulate the least. These differences, however, are both small and inconsistent across the four sessions.

What is interesting with respect to the data on division votes is the distribution of the number of votes by issue area (see table 4.8). Because the government party takes the initiative in establishing the agenda, the issues on which parliament votes reflect a government's legislative bias. It is significant, therefore, that although the number of division votes that took place in each of the four sessions of parliament varied from 49 to 149, the distribution of these votes by issue area was relatively stable for all sessions. Legal-political, primary industry-extractive, and social welfare issues were subject to the greatest number of House votes in the 28th Parliament whereas external affairs-defense and secondary industry-labor issues were voted on least. There is, then, a strong similarity between the pattern of voting by issue area observed in these data and the pattern observed with respect to the distribution of speeches during debates on this same set of issues. Indeed, there is a Spearman rank-order correlation of .79 between the rankings of the number of speeches in the several issue areas and the number of formal divisions in each area. We interpret this correlation as empirical support for the assumption that both the focus of debate and the issues that become the subjects of formal divisions reflect, to a very substantial degree, the preferences of a governing party in a British-model parliamentary system.[25]

Although the conditions under which backbenchers could exercise some influence on government legislative proposals through participation in division votes were not present in the 28th Parliament, private members still could try to influence legislation through the introduction of debatable resolutions, private bills, and private members' bills. How effective such participation is in terms of the influence it affords the MP is a question that we address in a subsequent chapter. For now we are concerned with the questions of who participates in these activities and how frequently the opportunities to participate are used. Table 4.9 presents, for each session of

TABLE 4.8

DISTRIBUTION OF DIVISION VOTES IN THE HOUSE OF COMMONS BY
ISSUE AREAS DURING FOUR SESSIONS OF THE 28TH PARLIAMENT

| Session | Defense & External Affairs | Public Finance | Social Welfare | Legal- Political | Primary Industry— Extractive | Labor and Secondary Industry | Internal Development | Miscellaneous | N |
|---|---|---|---|---|---|---|---|---|---|
| I | 5% | 6% | 6% | 52% | 4% | — | 8% | 19% | 84 |
| II | — | — | 29 | 29 | 19 | 12% | 4 | 6 | 78 |
| III | — | 5 | 17 | 30 | 19 | 9 | 3 | 16 | 149 |
| IV | 8 | 12 | 12 | 12 | 19 | 8 | — | 28 | 49 |

parliament, the percentages of MPs introducing debatable resolutions (DRs) and the mean number of private and private members' bills (PMBs) introduced by: (a) the members as a body; and (b) the members of each of the several party and leadership groups. At most, about 17% of the noncabinet MPs introduced a debatable resolution in any session of parliament and only about a quarter of the members introduced a single PMB in any given session.[26] The average number of PMBs introduced by all MPs in any session never exceeds 1.0, and in the first session the average was considerably less. The relatively infrequent use made of the debatable resolution tactic can be explained in part by the procedural requirement that a member have no more than one DR on the Order Paper at any one time. Since debatable resolutions rarely become the topics of an actual debate (although the subjects may be introduced later by the government), they remain on the Order Paper until the session ends, thereby preventing the member from introducing additional resolutions. Insofar as differences did occur in the frequency with which particular groups of MPs introduced debatable resolutions, we find that it was the Liberal MPs, in particular, and the backbench MPs more generally, who were least likely to participate in this way. The Conservative and NDP members together with noncabinet, middle-level Liberal leaders introduced debatable resolutions most often, although the differences among the rates of introduction were not great. Nor do these differences explain why a larger proportion of the several groups did not make use of the opportunity.

There are no procedural constraints governing the introduction of PMBs yet in only one instance did the mean number of PMBs introduced by any group exceed 3.0.[27] Only NDP members introduced private member legislation with any regularity (on the average they each introduced 2.5 to 3 private members' bills per session). Although Conservative MPs ranked high with respect to the percentage of members introducing debatable resolutions, they consistently ranked near the bottom in terms of the mean number of PMB's they introduced. The Social Credit and Liberal MPs generally ranked somewhere between the NDP and Conservatives—but considerably closer to the Conservatives.[28] Noncabinet Liberal parliamentary leaders appear to have introduced more PMBs than did Liberal backbench MPs. Again, the differences observed generally are both small and inconsistent so it is difficult to ascribe significance to them.

TABLE 4.9

## PERCENTAGE OF MEMBERS INTRODUCING DEBATABLE RESOLUTIONS (DR) AND MEAN NUMBER OF PRIVATE AND PRIVATE MEMBERS' BILLS (PMB) INTRODUCED, SESSIONS I–IV

| | SESSION I | | SESSION II | | SESSION III | | SESSION IV | | N |
|---|---|---|---|---|---|---|---|---|---|
| | DR | PMB | DR | PMB | DR | PMB | DR | PMB | |
| All Noncabinet MPs | 11.6% | .65 | 9.9% | .89 | 16.7% | .93 | 5.1% | .83 | 233 |
| Standard Deviation | | (1.82) | | (3.25) | | (3.31) | | (2.06) | |
| Liberal Noncabinet MPs | 7.3 | .42 | 7.3 | .76 | 7.3 | .78 | 1.6 | .56 | 123 |
| S.D. | | (1.10) | | (3.92) | | (3.93) | | (1.42) | |
| Conservative MPs | 16.9 | .28 | 9.9 | .52 | 28.2 | .62 | 10.0 | .61 | 71 |
| S.D. | | (.68) | | (.97) | | (1.23) | | (1.12) | |
| NDP MPs | 20.0 | 2.84 | 24.0 | 2.68 | 24.0 | 2.92 | 8.0 | 3.16 | 25 |
| S.D. | | (4.17) | | (4.03) | | (4.28) | | (4.53) | |
| Creditiste MPs | 7.7 | .77 | 7.7 | .77 | 30.8 | .23 | 8.0 | .23 | 13 |
| S.D. | | (1.69) | | (1.53) | | (.50) | | (.60) | |
| All Backbench MPs | 10.9 | .58 | 9.8 | .85 | 14.7 | .93 | 5.5 | .82 | 184 |
| S.D. | | (1.84) | | (3.51) | | (3.61) | | (2.16) | |
| All Noncabinet Leaders | 14.3 | .92 | 10.2 | 1.04 | 24.5 | .92 | 4.0 | .86 | 49 |
| S.D. | | (1.74) | | (2.02) | | (1.85) | | (1.67) | |
| Liberal Backbench MPs | 4.9 | .32 | 6.9 | .71 | 5.9 | .78 | 1.0 | .50 | 101 |
| S.D. | | (.92) | | (4.20) | | (4.25) | | (1.38) | |
| Liberal Noncabinet Leaders | 19.0 | .86 | 9.5 | 1.05 | 14.3 | .76 | 4.5 | .82 | 22 |
| S.D. | | (1.68) | | (2.11) | | (1.73) | | (1.59) | |
| Conservative Backbench MPs | 20.8 | .19 | 10.4 | .54 | 27.1 | .58 | 14.6 | .62 | 48 |
| S.D. | | (.49) | | (1.03) | | (1.22) | | (1.26) | |
| Conservative Leaders | 8.7 | .48 | 8.7 | .48 | 30.4 | .70 | — | .56 | 23 |
| S.D. | | (.95) | | (.85) | | (1.29) | | (.79) | |

We can speculate, however, about the substantive and theoretical implications of the party differences observed with respect to private members' bills. The finding that the members of the more conservatively oriented parties participate infrequently in the introduction of PMBs whereas the traditionally liberal-activist party, the NDP, consistently shows the highest level (by a margin of 3:1 or 4:1) of activity in this regard, suggests an ideological difference in perspective regarding the scope of governmental activity. The more limited use by the Conservative and Social Credit members of their opportunities to initiate legislation is consistent with the conservative view that government ought not to interfere, whereas the higher level of NDP activity is consistent with the interventionist preferences of the ideological left. We may speculate further that the majority of Liberal MPs share this ideological preference for intervention but limit their opportunities to initiate legislation for cosmetic reasons (the introduction of a large number of bills by Liberal private members could be construed as an implicit criticism of the government) and because they can communicate views on desirable legislation directly to their party colleagues who are cabinet members.

## PARTICIPATION IN COMMITTEES

Committees often have been termed miniature legislatures. Insofar as they vary in size, in the resources they have available, in the frequency with which they meet, in the formal powers they possess, and in being composed of individuals who vary considerably in their abilities or willingness to perform their duties, the label of miniature legislature is a fairly accurate one.[29] The most important difference, at least for our purposes, is that many of the activities of committees either are not seen (e.g., committees may meet in executive session) or are relatively invisible. They thereby provide a setting in which noncabinet members of a governing party in a British-model parliamentary system can scrutinize proposed expenditures, and closely evaluate or even amend legislation without fear that their actions will be construed as either a criticism of cabinet policies or an indication that the governing party is disunited. This is not to suggest that cabinet ministers are unconcerned with what their noncabinet colleagues do and say in committees. They are concerned, as are the leaders of the opposition parties. Party whips—in the case of the government, parliamentary secretaries—keep relatively close watch over committee proceedings particularly when major legislation and, to a lesser extent, estimates are being considered. However, despite the concern of party leaders, committees were intended to provide an environment in which members could participate more intensively and extensively in the legislative process than they could on the floor of the House. After all, the rationale that was most frequently advanced to support the extensive procedural changes that restructured the committee system was that a strengthened and invigorated committee system not only would increase the efficiency with which parliament disposed of legislation, but also would enable private members to have a more significant impact on its content.[30] Consequently, we assumed that the members of all parties would participate more extensively in committees than they did in the House. However, since the burden of not participating in House debates falls most heavily on the members of a governing party we further assumed that the latter would compensate by participating even more in committees than would members of the opposition parties.

A second reason we expected differences in the extent and direction of individual participation in committees is that there is no limit in standing orders on the number of committees on which a member can serve. Since the total number of seats on the several committees to which each party is entitled is much greater than the number of members in each party, each member holds several committee seats. It seems reasonable, therefore, to assume that many MPs would be only nominal members and marginally active in some of the committees to which they belonged, restricting their participation largely to more prestigious committees or to committees that deal with subjects on which they hope to have some impact. Greater awareness of which committees were engaged in salient (for them) activities presumably would increase this tendency over time as would an expanded work load.

We will restate our principal assumptions in the form of specific hypotheses and test them with the following three kinds of data: (1) attendance in committees by all MPs during four parliamentary sessions; (2) the extent of actual participation in committee as measured by the number and length of speeches made in committees by 34 randomly selected private members; and (3) the relative prestige of the several standing committees derived from a variety of sources. The specific hypotheses to be tested with these data are: (a) individual member participation in committees is much more extensive than is participation in House debates; (b) participation in committees, like participation in the House, tends to be highly variable and is concentrated among relatively few individuals; (c) Liberal party MPs participate more in committee affairs than do members of opposition parties; (d) middle-level party leaders participate more in committee affairs than do backbenchers; (e) attendance and participation in committee activities decline during the lifetime of a parliament; and (f) the more prestigious the committee the higher and more stable the rate of attendance.

Table 4.10, which presents the distribution of speeches and the length of speeches made by a subsample of 34 MPs, strongly supports hypothesis "a." We may note that only in the abbreviated fourth session of parliament did the proportion of MPs making fewer than 100 committee speeches rise above 20% while in the first two sessions some 40% of these MPs made 500 or more speeches in committee. The contrast between the extent of member participation in committees and in the House is more vividly illustrated in table 4.11, which compares the ratios of the number of speeches made in committees by the 34 MPs to the number they made in the House during four sessions of parliament. In the first session the group as a whole made 22 speeches in the reconstituted (since the 1968 election) committees for each speech they made in the House. During the second parliamentary year when the committees began to operate in "high gear" and the incidence of speaking on the floor of the House fell off somewhat, the MPs made 43 speeches in committee for every speech they made in the House. In the third session their ratio of committee to House speeches declined somewhat to 29:1 and fell to 18:1 in the abbreviated fourth session. Insofar as the length of speeches is concerned, in all but the first session of parliament the speeches they delivered in committee were, on the average, somewhat longer than the speeches they delivered on the floor of the House. The finding that MPs speak much more often in committee than they do in the House but not at much greater length is a reflection, we feel, of the more relaxed and informal environmen on which committees work. Procedure in committee facilitates a flow of conversation, give-and-take. Thus members feel less constrained to make speeches and more inclined to interact.

Table 4.11 indicates that the Liberal MPs appear to have been the principal beneficiaries of the revamped committee system. Whereas the highest ratio of committee to House speaking for opposition MPs occurred in the second session when they made 22 speeches in committee for every speech they made in the House, the Liberal MPs made 149 committee speeches for every House speech during that

TABLE 4.10

# THE DISTRIBUTION OF SPEECHES AND LENGTH OF SPEECHES MADE IN STANDING COMMITTEES[a] DURING 28TH PARLIAMENT BY SUBSAMPLE OF 34 MPS[b]

## SESSION I

| Proportion of MPs Who Made: | | Proportion of MPs Whose Speeches Ran: | |
|---|---|---|---|
| 0–99 Speeches | 14.7% | 0–1000 Hansard Lines | 23.5% |
| 100–199 | 17.6 | 1001–2000 | 23.5 |
| 200–499 | 29.4 | 2001–4000 | 17.6 |
| 500 more | 38.2 | 4001 or more | 35.3 |

## SESSION II

| Proportion of MPs Who Made: | | Proportion of MPs Whose Speeches Ran: | |
|---|---|---|---|
| 0–99 Speeches | 17.6% | 0–1000 Hansard Lines | 23.5% |
| 100–199 | 17.6 | 1001–2000 | 14.7 |
| 200–477 | 20.6 | 2001–4000 | 17.6 |
| 500 or more | 44.1 | 4001 or more | 44.1 |

## SESSION III

| Proportion of MPs Who Made: | | Proportion of MPs Whose Speeches Ran: | |
|---|---|---|---|
| 0–99 Speeches | 11.8% | 0–1000 Hansard Lines | 20.5% |
| 100–199 | 14.7 | 1001–2000 | 26.5 |
| 200–499 | 44.1 | 2001–4000 | 26.5 |
| 500 or more | 29.4 | 4001 or more | 26.5 |

## SESSION IV

| Proportion of MPs Who Made: | | Proportion of MPs Whose Speeches Ran: | |
|---|---|---|---|
| 0–99 Speeches | 35.3% | 0–1000 Hansard Lines | 70.6% |
| 100–199 | 41.2 | 1001–2000 | 11.8 |
| 200–477 | 14.7 | 2001–4000 | 14.7 |
| 500 or more | 8.8 | 4001 or more | 2.9 |

a. The Committee on Miscellaneous Private Bills is not included in our analysis because of the infrequency with which it met.

Note: N = 34.

b. Columns may not add to 100% because of rounding even.

TABLE 4.11

RATIO OF STANDING COMMITTEE TO HOUSE SPEECHES MADE
BY SUBSAMPLE OF THIRTY-FOUR MPS DURING
FOUR SESSIONS OF 28TH PARLIAMENT

| | Ratio of Committee to House Speeches | | | |
|---|---|---|---|---|
| | Session I | Session II | Session III | Session IV |
| Everyone (N = 34) | 22:1 | 43:1 | 29:1 | 18:1 |
| All government members (Liberals) (N = 12) | 99:1 | 149:1 | 133:1 | 86:1 |
| All Liberal leaders (N = 3) | 61:1 | 154:1 | 204:1 | 95:1 |
| All Liberal backbenchers (N = 9) | 121:1 | 147:1 | 111:1 | 82:1 |
| All opposition MPs (N = 22) | 10:1 | 22:1 | 13:1 | 10:1 |
| All leaders (N = 8) | 19:1 | 154:1 | 40:1 | 15:1 |
| All backbenchers (N = 26) | 24:1 | 39:1 | 34:1 | 31:1 |
| All Conservatives (N = 11) | 20:1 | 35:1 | 18:1 | 20:1 |
| All NDP (N = 6) | 9:1 | 22:1 | 13:1 | 7:1 |
| All Creditistes (N = 5) | 1.6:1 | 4:1 | 5:1 | 2:1 |

session. In the first and third sessions the Liberal committee-to-House ratios were almost ten times as great as were the opposition's and even in the shortened fourth session the Liberals still made 86 committee speeches (as compared to 10 by opposition MPs) for every one of their House speeches. Moreover, it was not simply the Liberal backbenchers who, unable to speak on the House floor, [31] availed themselves of the opportunity to do so in committee. The three Liberal leaders, two of whom were committee chairmen, made even more extensive use of their opportunities than did their backbencher colleagues. On the average, the leaders made 128 speeches in committee for every speech they made in the House during the four years, and the backbenchers made 115.

Table 4.11 makes it appear that the relative rate of participation in committees by each party was inversely related to its participation in the House. However, an examination of Table 4.12 indicates this was only partially true. Table 4.12 presents the means and standard deviations for the number of speeches and the number of lines spoken in committees by the 34 MPs during the four parliamentary sessions. These data indicate that in each session the Liberal members of our subsample spoke more frequently and at greater length than did members of the opposition parties. However, the Conservatives who, as we observed earlier, had less opportunity because of the size of their party to participate in House debates than did the members of the NDP and Social Credit parties, in fact did not participate as much in committee as did members of the NDP—although they certainly participated considerably more than did the members of the Social Credit party.

The differences overall in the parliamentary participation rates between the NDP and Social Credit parties are striking. The Social Crediters participated very little in either the House or committees during the first and fourth parliamentary sessions. The NDP MPs, in contrast, participated very extensively in the House (see tables 4.2 and 4.3), and even more extensively in committees. Indeed, on the average, they managed to make 13 speeches in committee for every speech they made in the House during the four parliamentary sessions. This meant that the average NDP MP made seven times as many speeches as his counterpart in the Social Credit party during the first session of parliament. Moreover, his average speech was more than eight times as long as the average Social Crediter's speech. In the second parliamentary session the average NDP MP spoke almost nine times as often and eleven times as long as the average Social Crediter, and although the committee participation gap between the two parties narrowed during the third and fourth sessions, the NDP members still participated about five times more in committees as did the Social Crediters.

The sizes of the standard deviations from the means for both speeches and lines in table 4.12 indicate that participation in committees, as in the House generally, was skewed so that some members spoke briefly and infrequently whereas others spoke often and at great length. Among the Liberals, for example, one MP made 2,920 committee speeches during the first session of parliament alone while a colleague spoke only 36 times during that entire session. The variations in committee participation that occurred among the Liberals can be explained in part by the fact that two of them were committee chairmen and were required, because of their official status, to speak more often and at greater length than their party

## TABLE 4.12
## STANDING COMMITTEE PARTICIPATION OF SUBSAMPLE OF 34 MPS DURING FOUR PARLIAMENTARY SESSIONS

| Group | | SESSION I Speeches | SESSION I Hansard Lines | SESSION II Speeches | SESSION II Hansard Lines | SESSION III Speeches | SESSION III Hansard Lines | SESSION IV Speeches | SESSION IV Hansard Lines |
|---|---|---|---|---|---|---|---|---|---|
| Everyone | $\bar{X}$ | 571 | 3614 | 664 | 4339 | 533 | 4355 | 188 | 1098 |
| | S.D. | 657 | 3497 | 924 | 4719 | 640 | 5745 | 220 | 1070 |
| | | (N = 34) | | (N = 34) | | (N = 33) | | (N = 32) | |
| All Government Members (Lib.) | $\bar{X}$ | 973 | 5268 | 1046 | 5709 | 1036 | 5925 | 317 | 1668 |
| | S.D. | 857 | 3818 | 1327 | 5628 | 911 | 5778 | 291 | 1383 |
| | | (N = 12) | | (N = 12) | | (N = 11) | | (N = 11) | |
| All Liberal Leaders | $\bar{X}$ | 878 | 4867 | 1233 | 7617 | 1365 | 8660 | 379 | 1441 |
| | S.D. | 669 | 2161 | 417 | 3388 | 1353 | 10578 | 482 | 1809 |
| | | (N = 3) | | (N = 3) | | (N = 3) | | (N = 3) | |
| All Liberal Backbenchers | $\bar{X}$ | 1004 | 5402 | 985 | 5073 | 913 | 4901 | 295 | 1753 |
| | S.D. | 949 | 4336 | 1536 | 6234 | 772 | 3568 | 235 | 1345 |
| | | (N = 9) | | (N = 9) | | (N = 8) | | (N = 8) | |
| All Opposition MPs | $\bar{X}$ | 352 | 2712 | 454 | 3592 | 306 | 3371 | 138 | 799 |
| | S.D. | 389 | 3028 | 539 | 4093 | 239 | 5728 | 149 | 762 |
| | | (N = 22) | | (N = 22) | | (N = 22) | | (N = 21) | |
| All Leaders | $\bar{X}$ | 636 | 3759 | 933 | 6043 | 662 | 7269 | 310 | 1313 |
| | S.D. | 649 | 3400 | 770 | 5651 | 931 | 10403 | 346 | 1435 |
| | | (N = 8) | | (N = 8) | | (N = 8) | | (N = 7) | |
| All Backbenchers | $\bar{X}$ | 551 | 3569 | 580 | 3815 | 513 | 3247 | 168 | 1037 |
| | S.D. | 671 | 3592 | 965 | 4386 | 540 | 3010 | 165 | 964 |
| | | (N = 26) | | (N = 26) | | (N = 25) | | (N = 25) | |
| All Conservatives | $\bar{X}$ | 424 | 2810 | 468 | 3532 | 296 | 4172 | 177 | 945 |
| | S.D. | 471 | 3053 | 657 | 4916 | 145 | 7625 | 186 | 875 |
| | | (N = 11) | | (N = 11) | | (N = 11) | | (N = 10) | |
| All NDP | $\bar{X}$ | 462 | 4352 | 738 | 6225 | 490 | 4049 | 167 | 1082 |
| | S.D. | 287 | 3424 | 343 | 2085 | 336 | 3531 | 95 | 632 |
| | | (N = 6) | | (N = 6) | | (N = 6) | | (N = 6) | |
| All Creditistes | $\bar{X}$ | 65 | 528 | 85 | 566 | 111 | 798 | 26 | 172 |
| | S.D. | 43 | 406 | 83 | 486 | 92 | 796 | 23 | 152 |
| | | (N = 5) | | (N = 5) | | (N = 5) | | (N = 5) | |

colleagues. However, this same pattern of skewed participation also can be observed among Conservative MPs. Only in the third session of parliament was there relatively equal participation among Conservatives in terms of committee speech-making. As indicated by the magnitudes of the Gini coefficients of inequality for the length of speeches made during that parliamentary session, however, the remarks that some of the Conservative MPs made during these meetings were rather brief (see table 4.13). Parenthetically, it should be noted this generally was less true of the NDP MPs (the length of whose speeches generally were relatively equal) than of MPs in the other parties.

In addition to supporting our first four hypotheses, the data in table 4.12 also support the hypothesis that individual member participation in committee affairs decreased during the lifetime of parliament. Since the number of committee meetings that were held varied by session, a direct comparison of the mean number of speeches made in each parliamentary session would have been misleading. Thus, we standardized this figure by dividing the mean number of committee speeches made in each session by the number of meetings held during that session. This yielded a measure that reflects the number of speeches an average MP made during an average committee meeting in a particular session. In the first session this figure was .74; in the second .76. It then dropped to .55 in the third session and increased to .57 in the fourth session.

TABLE 4.13

GINI COEFFICIENTS MEASURING INEQUALITY OF PARTICIPATION IN STANDING COMMITTEES AND ON THE FLOOR OF THE HOUSE BY SUBSAMPLE OF 34 MPS

| Session: | Length of Speeches in Committees | | | | Number of Speeches in Committees | | | |
|---|---|---|---|---|---|---|---|---|
| | I | II | III | IV | I | II | III | IV |
| Everybody | .50 | .52 | .58 | .52 | .54 | .56 | .53 | .54 |
| All Liberals | .38 | .45 | .51 | .47 | .44 | .51 | .48 | .49 |
| All Liberal Leaders | .46 | .46 | .62 | .59 | .50 | .42 | .54 | .61 |
| All Liberal Backbenchers | .41 | .50 | .44 | .44 | .46 | .57 | .48 | .43 |
| All Nonliberals | .54 | .54 | .60 | .49 | .52 | .54 | .39 | .51 |
| All Nonleaders | .51 | .52 | .49 | .47 | .54 | .58 | .51 | .47 |
| All Conservatives | .50 | .56 | .60 | .42 | .50 | .54 | .26 | .48 |
| All NDP | .38 | .16 | .40 | .29 | .31 | .24 | .34 | .27 |
| All Creditistes | .38 | .43 | .48 | .40 | .32 | .44 | .41 | .42 |

The decline in individual participation in the deliberations of committees is reflected also in a decline in attendance. 68.2% of the members eligible to attend meetings in the first session of parliament, in fact, did. In the second session this figure declined to 59.8%. It remained relatively stable in the third (60%) and fourth sessions (60.8%), but there was a net decline in attendance of 7.5% from the first to the fourth session. As might be expected, the Liberal MPs attended committee meetings most faithfully, averaging 68% overall attendance during the four sessions. The NDP MPs had the second highest rate of attendance, 64%, while the level of attendance among Conservatives was only 55%. The Social Credit attendance figure, 24%, helps explain why they participated so little relative to the other parties in the actual deliberations of committees. Table 4.14, which presents attendance figures for each of the several standing committees, indicates that only three experienced a net gain in attendance: Privileges and Elections, Public Accounts, and Procedure and Organization. A fourth committee, Veterans Affairs, had the same attendance rate in the fourth session as in the first, while all other committees experienced a net decline. The most precipitous declines in member attendance took place in the National Resources and Public Works and in the Fisheries and Forestry committees.

In addition to an overall decline in the level of attendance at the meetings of most committees, the data in table 4.14 reveal three patterns. The first is one in which the attendance levels are relatively high and remain high. The fluctuations from session to session are modest so that the net change in attendance between the first and fourth sessions is negligible. This pattern characterized attendance in committees such as Finance, Trade, and Economic Affairs; Labour, Manpower and Immigration; and Veterans Affairs. A second pattern of attendance is one in which committee attendance is high in the first session but declines rather sharply and in a monotonic fashion thereafter. This second pattern characterized attendance in committees such as Fisheries and Forestry and Natural Resources and Public Works. A third pattern is one of relatively sharp fluctuations in attendance from session to session. In some committees with this pattern of attendance (e.g., Agriculture; Justice and Legal Affairs; Public Accounts) the net change between the first and fourth sessions of parliament was a modest one. In other committees of this type, however (e.g., Miscellaneous Estimates; Regional Development; and Broadcasting, Films, and Assistance to the Arts), there was a

## TABLE 4.14
## STANDING COMMITTEE ATTENDANCE DURING FOUR PARLIAMENTARY SESSIONS

| Standing Committees | Percent Attendance Session I | Percent Attendance Session II | Percent Attendance Session III | Percent Attendance Session IV | $\bar{X}$ for Parliament | Overall Attendance Rankings | Aggregate Change Sessions I–IV | Net Change Sessions I–IV |
|---|---|---|---|---|---|---|---|---|
| Transport and Communications | 78 | 77 | 69 | 65 | 72.2 | 1 | 13 | −13 |
| Agriculture | 71 | 62 | 83 | 67 | 70.7 | 2 | 46 | − 4 |
| Labour, Manpower and Immigration | 77 | 68 | 66 | 70 | 70.2 | 3 | 15 | − 7 |
| Procedure and Organization | 74 | 61 | 68 | 76 | 69.7 | 4 | 26 | + 2 |
| Veterans Affairs | 69 | 65 | 72 | 69 | 68.7 | 5 | 14 | 0 |
| Finance, Trade and Economic Affairs | 69 | 64 | 68 | 67 | 67.0 | 6 | 9 | − 2 |
| Fisheries and Forestry | 76 | 61 | 62 | 54 | 64.7 | 7 | 24 | −22 |
| Indian Affairs and Northern Development | 70 | 75 | 57 | 56 | 64.5 | 8 | 24 | −14 |
| National Resources and Public Works | 78 | 64 | 62 | 53 | 64.2 | 9 | 25 | −25 |
| Health, Welfare and Social Affairs | 72 | 59 | 60 | 64 | 63.7 | 10.5 | 18 | − 8 |
| Regional Development | 70 | 58 | 72 | 55 | 63.7 | 10.5 | 43 | −15 |
| Justice and Legal Affairs | 70 | 60 | 52 | 69 | 62.7 | 12 | 35 | − 1 |
| External Affairs and National Defence | 73 | 62 | 55 | 57 | 61.7 | 13.5 | 20 | −16 |
| Public Accounts | 61 | 67 | 55 | 64 | 61.7 | 13.5 | 27 | + 3 |
| Privileges and Elections | 58 | 57 | 59 | 67 | 60.2 | 15 | 11 | + 9 |
| Miscellaneous Estimates | 63 | 46 | 64 | 45 | 54.5 | 16 | 54 | −18 |
| Broadcasting, Films and Assistance to the Arts | 63 | 62 | 39 | 52 | 54.0 | 17 | 37 | −11 |

precipitous decline in attendance between the first and fourth sessions.

Obviously, the content of the business before a committee at any particular time will have a general effect on attendance. Attendance tends to be higher at organizational meetings than when estimates are being considered. Attendance also tends to be high—in fact, it tends to be highest—during the clause-by-clause consideration of prospective legislation. Normally attendance is not as high during an investigation, although if what is being investigated is important, it will be higher than when estimates are being considered. Beyond the general affect of the nature of the business being considered, the inferences that may be drawn from the first and second patterns of attendance seem clear. The first pattern suggests committees whose work commanded a sustained high level of member interest. We infer from the second pattern of attendance that the interest of members initially was high but for a variety of reasons (failure to take up matters of importance or concern to MPs, perhaps) it declined steadily. It is more difficult to draw any inferences from the third pattern of attendance. We might speculate, however, that it characterizes committees that deal with subject matter that is of uneven importance. Consequently, attendance tends to be episodic; it rises when subjects of major substantive importance or of particular interest to members are being considered and declines when routine or relatively uninteresting matters are before the committees.

Another hypothesis we wished to test is that committees that are not regarded as particularly prestigious will suffer sharper declines in attendance than committees that are more honored. To test this assumption, we generated a prestige index for committees, independent of attendance rates. Two distinct approaches were pursued in constructing this measure. First, because committee prestige is a subjective concept dependent upon the attitudes and perceptions of the members, we developed several indices of committee prestige that were intended to tap the relative importance that members ascribed to the several standing committees. One of the ways we did this was to ask MPs which committees they thought were most important or were of greatest interest to them. From their responses we generated a standardized measure of committee interest by dividing the number of members on each committee expressing a high level of interest in that committee by the total number of respondents holding seats on the committee. We were unable to interview all committee members, however, and since an interviewee could nominate any number of important committees (thus reducing the power of the question to discriminate between levels of interest), we constructed a second indicator of prestige based upon the frequency with which members of a committee voluntarily give up their committee seat. Following the logic implicit in existing studies of committee prestige in the U.S. Congress,[32] we reasoned that the level of turnover in committee membership in large part is a consequence of the importance that members ascribe to that committee. Unfortunately, the use of committee turnover rates as an index of committee importance in the Canadian House of Commons is complicated by the practice of party whips assigning temporary substitutes to committees. When a member cannot attend an important committee meeting, the party whip replaces the absent member with a party colleague so that party strength on the committee will be maintained. Although, in theory, such substitutions are permanent and are recorded as such, in practice, the original member usually is reassigned to the committee when he again is able to attend its meetings. The effect of this practice, therefore, is to inflate artificially the turnover rate of important committees and to make them appear to be less important than they actually are. To use turnover rates as a measure of prestige, we had to compensate for this distortion. Our method was to define as a temporary or substitute member of a committee any MP who was eligible to attend 10% or less of a committee's meetings. Change in permanent membership or real turnover then was defined as the ratio of: (a) the number of MPs eligible to attend at least 10% of the meetings of a committee minus the number of members authorized for that committee; over (b) the number of members authorized for the committee. The resulting figure represented the percentage change in the permanent membership of a committee during a particular parliamentary session.

The practice of assigning temporary replacements to committees, although complicating attempts to generate a measure of turnover, provides a third measure of committee prestige. Since substitutions on a committee usually are made only for meetings in which a committee is considering an unusually important or controversial matter, the number of short term substitutions can be interpreted as another indicator of committee importance. Accordingly, we calculated the ratio of the number of short term substitutes in a single session over the number of regular committee members.

In addition to these three measures of ascribed committee prestige, we attempted to measure committee importance by collecting data on both the number of times each committee met in each of the four sessions and the number of reports that were issued by each committee in each session. Both of these are indices of the frequency and volume of committee activity and reflect our assumption that the importance of a committee is almost always related to its work load. Of course, as in other areas of parliamentary activity, the workload of standing committees is determined in part by the actions of a government. Thus, for example, the workload of the Committee on Justice and Legal Affairs will be much heavier in a session in which the government decides to amend the Canadian Criminal Code and introduces one or more major pieces of legislation to implement the desired changes. For the same reason the work load of the Committee on Agriculture and the Committee on Defense and External Affairs will be much heavier in a session in which the government asks the former to investigate and report on pricing practices in the dairy industry and the latter to investigate and report on the effects of the unification of the armed services on military career patterns.

The workload of committees, however, also is independent of the orientations and legislative preferences of a current government. The activities of the several government departments will continue even if the cabinet does not introduce legislation that would affect them. They have ongoing policies and programs that must be funded. Consequently, all standing committees must spend a substantial part of their time considering departmental spending estimates. Committees that oversee the operations of a number of large departments will have many more estimates to consider and therefore a heavier workload than committees that do not. Similarly, the matters with which some committees deal are extremely complex and/or controversial while the subjects with which others deal are less so. The former committees generally will have heavier workloads than the latter. There may not be a one-to-one relationship between the volume of a committee workload and its importance, but in the absence of direct indicators of qualitative importance, we feel that how much a committee does can be regarded as a useful surrogate measure.

The prestige index, then, is a composite measure that reflects: (1) long and short term interests of individual members in the several committees; (2) the significance of the subject matter with which the committees deal; and (3) the collective industry and performance of members of the several committees. The prestige rankings of each committee for each of four sessions, are presented in table 4.15 together with the committee's overall rankings (an average of the four), the aggregate changes in their rankings and the net changes in their rankings between the first and fourth sessions. This table indicates that there were three committees whose prestige was high and remained high during the lifetime of the 28th Parliament: Finance, Trade and Economic Affairs; Justice and Legal Affairs; and Transport and Communications. Three other committees, External Affairs and National Defence, Agriculture, and Health, Welfare and Social Affairs also may be regarded as highly prestigious. However, the rankings of the last three committees fluctuated more over four sessions than did those of the first three. At the other end of the prestige scale were: Privileges and Elections; Broadcasting, Films and Assistance to the Arts; Regional Development; Procedure and Organization; Fisheries and Forestry; and Miscellaneous Estimates. Of these, the ranking of Privileges and Elections was consistently low. The rankings of the others fluctuated somewhat from session to session but remained low. The remaining committees may be regarded as being of middle-level prestige. The rankings of all but the Indian Affairs and Northern Development committee fluctuated over the four year period, but their overall rankings were not as high as the top prestige committees. With regard to net changes, we may note that by session four the prestige of the Labour, Manpower and Immigration, and the Miscellaneous Estimates committees had had the greatest increase, whereas the prestige of the Fisheries and Forestry committee and Health, Welfare, and Social Affairs suffered the greatest net decline during the four years.

These findings provide few surprises. Committees that regularly confront complex and controversial issues (e.g., Finance, Trade and Economic Affairs; Transport and Communications; External Affairs and National Defence) ranked high in prestige while those that ranked low are involved primarily with either procedural and technical affairs (e.g., Miscellaneous Estimates) or are concerned with other relatively low-interest matters. What is somewhat surprising is the relatively low ranking received by the Public Accounts committee, parliament's watchdog over Executive finances.[33] Also surprising is the lack of member enthusiasm for the Regional Development committee since it is concerned with resource allocation such as the approval of loans, grants and development projects. These matters are regarded as "pork" in most societies and one might assume that MPs, regardless of party, would ascribe great value to sitting on this

TABLE 4.15

## DISTRIBUTION OF PARLIAMENTARY STANDING COMMITTEES ALONG A PRESTIGE INDEX DURING FOUR PARLIAMENTARY SESSIONS

| Standing Committees | Session I Rankings | Session II Rankings | Session III Rankings | Session IV Rankings | Overall Rankings | Aggregate Change in Rankings | Net Change in Rankings |
|---|---|---|---|---|---|---|---|
| Finance, Trade and Economic Affairs | 1 | 1 | 1 | 1 | 1 | 0 | 0 |
| Transport and Communications | 2 | 3 | 3 | 4 | 2 | 2 | +2 |
| External Affairs and National Defence | 4 | 2 | 6 | 2 | 3 | 10 | +2 |
| Justice and Legal Affairs | 6 | 4 | 4 | 5 | 4 | 3 | +1 |
| Agriculture | 5 | 7 | 2 | 6 | 5 | 11 | −1 |
| Health, Welfare and Social Affairs | 3 | 6 | 7 | 8 | 6 | 5 | −5 |
| Indian Affairs and Northern Development | 8 | 8 | 9 | 7 | 7 | 3 | +1 |
| Labour, Manpower and Immigration | 12 | 10 | 8 | 3 | 8 | 9 | +9 |
| Public Accounts | 11 | 11 | 5 | 10 | 9 | 11 | +1 |
| Veterans Affairs | 7 | 9 | 12 | 11 | 10 | 6 | −4 |
| National Resources and Public Works | 10 | 5 | 13 | 12 | 11 | 14 | −2 |
| Miscellaneous Estimates | 16 | 13 | 11 | 9 | 12 | 7 | +7 |
| Procedure and Organization | 14 | 15 | 10 | 14 | 13 | 10 | 0 |
| Regional Development | 13 | 14 | 16 | 13 | 14.5 | 6 | 0 |
| Fisheries and Forestry | 9 | 16 | 14 | 17 | 14.5 | 12 | −8 |
| Broadcasting, Films and Assistance to the Arts | 15 | 12 | 15 | 15 | 16 | 6 | 0 |
| Privileges and Elections | 17 | 17 | 17 | 16 | 17 | 1 | +1 |

committee. The fact that they do not suggests either that the committee did not play an important role in allocating grants, contracts, etc.; that it primarily ratified decisions made by the minister and his advisers; that MPs had other more effective instruments for influencing assignment decisions; or some combinations of these reasons.

The ability and the willingness of a committee to deal adequately and effectively with issues that are of interest to parliamentarians may explain why the Labour, Manpower and Immigration committee's prestige rank, in contrast to that of Regional Development, rose from 12 to 10 to 8 to 3 during the four-year period. It will be recalled that our analysis of House debates indicated that relatively little time was spent discussing labor and manpower issues, although these issues were and are critically important concerns in Canada. We speculated that the reasons for this lack of public discussion included the fact that government may have felt particularly vulnerable on these issues and, feeling vulnerable, used its ability to control the content and timing of House debates to avoid public discussion. If these speculations are realistic, the data in table 4.15 suggest some additional possibilities: that the MPs were highly interested in labor and manpower issues; that the Labour committee provided them with opportunities to thoroughly discuss and do something about these and related issues; that the government was willing to permit such discussions because the forum was a relatively invisible one; that members took advantage of the opportunity; and that the rising prestige of the committee reflects the fact that under certain conditions a committee, even in a parliamentary system of the British-model, can gratify individual interests, fulfill party needs, and generate efficacious policies. If this is the case, then the reconstituted system of standing committees may have a major role to play in the Canadian parliamentary process despite the decline in attendance and participation in committee affairs revealed by our data.

Turning from the speculative to the empirical, we were able to test our hypothesis that the more prestigious a committee is the more likely its meetings are to be well attended by generating Spearman rank-order correlations between the prestige rankings of the committees and their level of attendance in each session. The results of this analysis are displayed in table 4.16 and provide at least a modicum of support for the hypothesis. Overall, the correlation between the average prestige of committees and average attendance at committee meetings was .48. Across all four sessions the correlation falls below

TABLE 4.16

**SPEARMAN CORRELATIONS BETWEEN
PRESTIGE RANKINGS AND COMMITTEE
ATTENDANCE RANKINGS OF
SEVENTEEN STANDING COMMITTEES
BY SESSION**

| | |
|---|---|
| Session I | .42 |
| Session II | .47 |
| Session III | .18 |
| Session IV | .33 |
| Total[a] | .48 |

a. Correlation between mean rankings for all four sessions.

.30 only in session three. Closer scrutiny of the data from which these correlations were derived, however, suggests that the relationship between prestige and attendance is not linear. If we divide the committees into three prestige groups—"high," "moderate," and "low"—and calculate the mean attendance figures for the committees in each group, we find the only large and consistent differences in attendance are between the low prestige committees on the one hand and the moderate and high prestige committees on the other. Differences between the moderate and high prestige committees, it should be noted, tend to be both small and statistically insignificant. Even if we refine the classification and divide the committees into quartiles, the pattern persists; the only statistically significant differences in attendance are between the lowest prestige committees and all others. In a limited sense, then, it does appear that the prestige of a committee has some bearing upon whether or not members will participate in its deliberations. MPs seem less inclined to attend meetings of the four or five standing committees that are lowest in prestige. However, attendance (although highly variable), and presumably participation, in the dozen or so other committees does not appear to be significantly related to their prestige.

In part, our inability to demonstrate a significant relationship between the 12 most prestigious committees and member attendance may stem from our use of aggregate measures. The importance attributed by members to individual committees might vary considerably, being affected by factors such as individual interest or desire to specialize. If so, a more accurate assessment of this relationship may require a more refined measure of importance that considers only the member's personal interest in a committee, irrespective of the evaluation of his colleagues. Unfortunately, the generation of such a measure must be left to future research.

## SUMMARY

We began this chapter by noting the undeniable decline in backbench and opposition participation in traditional legislative functions. There are, however, four formal avenues available to the noncabinet MP who wishes to influence government policy. One of these is participation in floor debate in the House. Our data indicate that debate in the 28th Parliament was dominated by opposition party leaders, with the members of the minor parties speaking more often and longer than Conservatives. The substance of about half of the speeches from the floor was critical of the government. The official opposition, the Conservative party, leveled the severest attacks, followed by the NDP. The Creditistes were least critical, actually supporting the government in about 25% of their speeches. The finding that several salient issue areas received very little attention in the House seemed to reflect a government's ability to control the topics and duration of debate. No significant party-issue linkages emerged.

A second method of influencing policy is participation in the question period. Conventional wisdom characterizes this part of parliament's schedule as a public forum for censuring the government but the data reveal it to be more of a mechanism by which MPs ask for and receive information. As in debate, Conservatives more often than the other two opposition parties asked questions that were critical of the Government. However, participation in question period, like that in debate, was dominated by a small group of opposition leaders (and, to a lesser extent, by members of the NDP). We found also that there was a small positive relationship among oral questions, partisan questions and questions which were ruled out of order or not answered.

In special circumstances (minimum majority government or minority government) a noncabinet MP has an opportunity to influence policy through his division vote. Although this condition did not obtain in the 28th Parliament, division vote results are of interest because they give further evidence of government's ability to select the topics parliament considers. While legal-political, primary industry-extractive, and social welfare were the subjects of most votes, external affairs-defence and secondary industry-labor, which were issue areas of high interest and government vulnerability, were subjects of the fewest division votes.

Division votes are part of a third category of opportunities members have to influence legislation. Also included were debatable resolutions, and private and private members' bills. Although party differences in the introduction of DRs and PMBs were statistically insignificant, there is a pattern in the introduction of PMBs which is of theoretical interest. Members of the Social Credit and Conservative parties were less likely to use this opportunity than were members of the NDP, possibly reflecting the differences between their laissez-faire and activist governmental postures. (Liberals who might have shared the NDP orientation may have had other, more effective ways of influencing policy since they formed the government).

Participation in committee work is the fourth formal avenue the nongovernment MP may use to try to influence policy. Our data revealed that the individual member spoke more often in committee than in House debate but not much longer. The Liberals, especially middle-level Liberal leaders, had the highest committee to debate speech ratio, followed, in order, by the NDP, Conservatives, and Creditistes. As in the House debates and question period, committee participation was variable, dominated by a few, and leaders were more active than backbenchers. Committee attendance (and presumably, participation) declined overall during the life of the parliament but three distinct attendance patterns were discernible: (1) committees where members presumably were interested in the committee's work, and remained so had high attendance levels throughout all four sessions; (2) committees where members initially may have been interested in the work but failed to maintain interest lost their early high attendance levels; and (3) committees where interesting matters may have been considered only occasionally had very uneven attendance levels.

## Chapter 5

# INFORMAL DIMENSIONS OF PARTICIPATION

## INTRODUCTION

Our discussion of behavior in the House of Commons in chapter 4 focused upon aspects that are essentially formal and explicitly provided for by parliamentary rules of procedure. Although House debates, question period, formal divisions, standing committees' deliberations, and the right to introduce public bills provide MPs with substantial opportunities to participate in parliamentary affairs, there are also a number of less visible opportunities available for them to affect public policies and to pursue the interests of individuals and groups within or outside of their constituencies. In the first chapter we suggested that as the legislative responsibilities of private members were restricted, these informal avenues became increasingly important. Their importance was enhanced also by a gradually increasing expectation by the public that the evaluation and solution of complex national and international problems should be left to a handful of parliamentary leaders and to their technical experts in the bureaucracy. Concomitant with the development of this view has come a corollary assumption that individual MPs should spend their time looking into and taking action on matters that are of concern to their individual constituents. Although legislative scholars generally agree that parliament's institutional roles and the functions of individual legislators have changed and are still changing,[1] even less systematic attention has been devoted to what we will term the "informal" dimension of parliamentary activity than to the more formal behavior considered in the last chapter. In this chapter we will delineate as best we can some of the principal components of behind-the-scenes behavior of members of the 28th Parliament. Specifically, we will be concerned with participation in party caucus, and with the extent and content of communications between private members and cabinet members, top-level civil servants, and middle-echelon leaders of the governing Liberal party. We also will describe the frequency and content of communications between MPs and members of the public.

With respect to participation in party caucuses, we assumed that caucus serves a number of purposes,[2] two of which are the formulation of party positions on broad policy and on particular pieces of legislation on the one hand, and the selection of tactics to be employed in pursuit of these positions on the other. We assumed that members of the governing party would be likely to view caucus as an opportunity to make their positions known to party colleagues who are charged with the task of formulating government policy and to learn what policies were being proposed before they were made public in the House. Members of the opposition parties, we felt, would have a somewhat different orientation to caucus. We felt they also would use the caucus to apprise party colleagues of their policy positions. Unlike their counterparts in the governing party, however, they would be making their views known to party leaders who can criticize and oppose government policy but who cannot, under normal conditions, directly affect its content. Thus opposition MPs may be less likely than government MPs to view caucus meetings as opportunities to affect the content and direction of policy. However, all MPs can use a variety of other-than-caucus opportunities (e.g., telephone conversations, office visits, discussions over meals and on social occasions) to inform cabinet ministers and their parliamentary assistants of policy preferences. Thus, a second assumption underlying our attempt to shed light on the dimensions of informal parliamentary behavior was that members of all parties would communicate with cabinet ministers and their assistants, the parliamentary secretaries. A third major aspect of informal parliamentary activity we expected to encounter was communication between MPs and the permanent heads of the several departments of government, the deputy-ministers. The bureaucracy is often the appropriate agent to help solve problems brought to the attention of an MP by individuals who have been or who may be adversely affected by the way particular laws are being administered.

A final dimension of informal activity in which we assumed all members would engage was extensive communications with both individual constituents and with organized and unorganized constituent groups. Our assumption was that MPs would receive both requests for assistance and information concerning constituents' views on policy matters. We further assumed that MPs would solicit public attitudes generally as well as "grass-roots" opinions in their districts in particular.[3]

We tested our assumptions in several ways. First, after an extended series of questions on formal parliamentary activities that included questions on interest and participation in standing committee affairs we asked each MP an open-ended question: "Are there any other ways, other than committees, that is, that individual members like yourself can influence the work of the House?" Second, because of our assumption regarding the importance of caucus we asked MPs who did not refer to caucus in their responses to the above question a second question: "And what about your party caucus, could that help?" We also used responses to two agree-disagree statements to delineate attitudes toward the functions performed by caucus.

I. The caucus promotes party cohesion in the Canadian parliamentary system in two ways. First, it permits a frank exchange of opinions that members really hold. Second, the tactics that are planned in caucus help insure smooth and coordinated performance in the House and in committees that individual members find gratifying.

II. The caucus does not give the backbench MP an opportunity to participate in party policy-making. It does, however, provide him with the regular opportunity to bring to the attention of his party colleagues any personal or constituency grievances against them.

Third, we asked each MP a series of questions about his contacts with ministers, parliamentary secretaries, and deputy-ministers.

I. Speaking of Cabinet Ministers (Deputy-Ministers, Parliamentary Secretaries) how often do you contact a minister (Deputy-Minister, Parliamentary Secretary) during an average month?

II. Which ministers (Deputy-Ministers, Parliamentary Secretaries) do you contact often—that is, the Ministers (Deputy-Ministers, Parliamentary Secretaries) of which departments?

III. Is the occasion for such contact usually constituency matters or in regard to the policies of the department(s)?

IV. How successful would you say you have been in getting what you have asked for, or getting your points across?

Fourth, we asked a series of questions regarding communications to and from constituents.

I. Do you get much mail from the people in your constituency each week?

II. What is the mail that you do get generally about?

III. Do the people in your constituency communicate with you in other ways, such as personal visits or telephoning, or sending you telegrams and so on?

IV. What are these other types of communication about usually?

V. Generally, what types of people communicate with you?

VI. And how about you? Do you try to find out how people in your constituency are thinking, especially how they feel about major issues that come before parliament?

VII. How do you go about finding out how they feel?

VIII. Which, if any, of the following do you normally consult if you want information about grass roots feelings in your district?[4]

IX. Which of these do you generally feel give you the most accurate and reliable information?

In the sections that follow we will present the responses to the questions in an effort to delineate the dimensions of informal parliamentary participation.

### FINDINGS—INFLUENCING THE WORK OF THE HOUSE

An examination of table 5.1 indicates that most of the members of each party felt that there were ways they could influence the work of the House other than by participating in committee work. Table 5.2 indicates what these are. It is interesting to note, even though a substantial part of the interview already had focused on formal activities such as House debates and the question period, that debates and question period still were cited as major vehicles for influencing the work of parliament. The members of the two minor parties were more inclined to cite such formal activities than were members of the major parties, although the differences between them were not statistically significant.

Insofar as the more informal activities are concerned, we find two statistically significant interparty differences: (1) members of the Liberal party were far more inclined than were members of the opposition to regard party caucus as a vehicle for influencing parliamentary affairs; and (2) members of the opposition parties tended to emphasize the importance of public opinion and the impact, when mobilized, that public opinion can have on parliament. These differ-

TABLE 5.1

PERCENTAGE OF MPS BY PARTY WHO PERCEIVE
OTHER THAN COMMITTEE ACTIVITIES
AS POTENTIALLY INFLUENTIAL

Are there other ways to influence House?

| Party | No | Yes |
|-------|-----|-----|
| Liberals | 15% | 85% |
| | (13) | (74) |
| Conservatives | 26% | 74% |
| | (14) | (41) |
| NDP | 39% | 61% |
| | (7) | (11) |
| Creditistes | 17% | 83% |
| | (1) | (5) |
| Total | 21% | 79% |
| | (35) | (131) |

ences seem to be consistent with our aforementioned assumption: that government and opposition would regard caucus differently as an instrument of policy influence. In mentioning an influence mechanism appropriate to its "out" position, the opposition stressed public opinion—considered a powerful force in democratic societies—and

TABLE 5.2

PERCENTAGE OF MEMBERS BY PARTY CITING VARIOUS
NONCOMMITTEE ACTIVITIES AS BEING INFLUENTIAL
IN HOUSE OF COMMONS[a]

| | Lib | Con | NDP | Cred | Total | SIG |
|---|-----|-----|-----|------|-------|-----|
| Formal Activities | | | | | | |
| 1) Question Period | 7% | 9% | 6% | — | 7% | NS |
| 2) Debate | 22 | 27 | 39 | 33% | 26 | NS |
| 3) Division Votes | 2 | 6 | 6 | 17 | 4 | NS |
| 4) Other | 2 | 2 | 11 | — | 3 | NS |
| Informal Activities | | | | | | |
| 1) Party Caucus | 51% | 16% | 11% | — | 33% | <.001 |
| 2) Knowledge of Rules | 2 | 6 | 6 | 17% | 4 | NS |
| 3) Personal Contact/ | | | | | | |
| Commun. in Cabinet | 23 | 16 | 11 | 17 | 19 | NS |
| 4) Mobilize Public Opinion | 2 | 13 | 28 | 17 | 9 | <.001 |
| 5) Work Collectively with | | | | | | |
| Others | 8 | 10 | — | — | 8 | NS |
| N | 87 | 55 | 18 | 6 | 166 | |

a. Percentages may add to more than 100% because of multiple responses.

claimed that its force could be used to induce the government to alter or to reconsider legislative proposals they regard as particularly offensive or undesirable.

The findings that Liberal members more frequently mentioned personal contacts and communications with cabinet members, but that these government-opposition differences were not statistically significant, can be regarded as supporting our assumption that all MPs, regardless of party, will employ a variety of opportunities to make their views and problems known to the cabinet. When we compared the views of leaders and followers in both the government and the opposition parties on alternative methods of exerting influence, we found that Liberal backbenchers were more inclined than either their counterparts in the opposition parties or their own leaders to mention contacts with cabinet ministers. The leaders of the opposition parties mentioned cabinet contacts more often than did their backbench colleagues and seemed to have less faith in the power of aroused public opinion (see table 5.3). Although neither of these differences was statistically significant, we can speculate that the reason backbenchers in the Liberal party cited cabinet contacts more frequently was that their membership in the governing party enabled them to take fuller advantage of these contacts. Opposition party leaders also can take advantage of contacts with cabinet members as their positions as leaders enable them to communicate as

TABLE 5.3

**PERCEPTIONS OF NONCOMMITTEE OPPORTUNITIES TO INFLUENCE PARLIAMENT HELD BY LIBERAL BACKBENCH, LIBERAL LEADERSHIP, OPPOSITION BACKBENCH AND OPPOSITION LEADERSHIP AS PERCENTAGE LISTING**

| Informal Opportunities | Lib B/B | Lib Lead | $X^2$ SIG | Opp B/B | Opp. Lead | $X^2$ SIG |
|---|---|---|---|---|---|---|
| Party Caucus | 50 | 52 | NS | 14 | 12 | NS |
| Knowledge of Rules | 4 | – | NS | 5 | 12 | NS |
| Personal Contact/ Commun. w. Cabinet | 28 | 13 | NS | 13 | 24 | NS |
| Mobilize Public Opinion | 2 | 3 | NS | 18 | 6 | NS |
| Work Collectively with Others | 9 | 6 | NS | 6 | 12 | NS |
| N | 56 | 31 | | 62 | 17 | |

status equals. Opposition backbenchers, in contrast, lack this status and thus must rely on other methods.

## PARTICIPATION IN THE CAUCUS

The importance of the party caucus is widely recognized in the literature. There is, however, considerable disagreement among scholars concerning the actual functions performed by, and the real beneficiaries of, participation in the caucus. One of the current authors, for example, concluded that: (1) caucus performed a cathartic function for members of the 25th Parliament; (2) it provided them with an opportunity to discuss parliamentary strategy and tactics; and (3) it enabled them to hammer our agreement on party policies.[6] On the other hand, Van Loon and Whittington, in their excellent textbook on Canadian politics, acknowledge what they call the traditional view that "the government MP can influence policy by presenting his critical comments and expressing his discontent (in the caucus),"[7] then proceed to discount this view asserting that:

> In an opposition party, caucus meetings can often be quite lively; since there are only a few men who are clearly recognized as party leaders, almost all MPs feel free to have their say, and consequently policy debates can become heated. In the caucus of a governing party, the situation is different. There are clearly recognized party leaders. . . . The government backbenchers have the clearly defined role of supporting the policies put forward by the leaders. The cabinet has tremendous expertise available to advise it, . . . and is more likely to listen to the experts than to its non-expert backbenchers on matters of policy. The debates may be lively, but they do not influence policy significantly.[8]

The views of J. W. Pickersgill tend to support, at least partially, Van Loon and Whittington's opinions. Pickersgill, a former Liberal cabinet minister, observed that the late and long-time Liberal prime minister, W. L. MacKenzie King, regarded the Liberal caucus as a kind of cheering section that functioned principally to sanction policies that already had been decided by the cabinet. In Pickersgill's words, King explained "the whys and wherefores of government action and suggested lines on which the government could be supported most effectively."[9] And, Liberal Mark MacGuigan, a member of the 28th Parliament, opined that, "The history of Canadian politics leaves little doubt that the Government caucus is of greater utility to the ministry than to the members, and that it is, in effect, the chief instrument of Government control of the House of Commons."[10] If the views of Van Loon and Whittington, MacGuigan and Pickersgill are descriptive of current reality, it may be that the greater enthusiasm registered by Liberal MPs for their party caucus (see table 5.2), rather than being a reflection of backbench feeling that the caucus provides them with a vehicle they can use to influence policy, instead may reflect the belief of party leaders that the caucus is the principal means by which party discipline can be achieved and cabinet control of the policy process thereby insured.

To test the possibility that Liberal leaders are more enthusiastic about caucus than their backbench colleagues we compared the responses of Liberal leaders and backbenchers to a question in which they were asked directly whether caucus could help individual MPs to influence the work of the House. Similar comparisons also were made of the responses of leaders and backbenchers in the three opposition parties to this question. These data, together with leader-follower figures on the frequency with which caucus was mentioned in replies to our open-end question on ways of influencing the House, are presented in table 5.4. We find that there is a significant difference in leader and backbencher attitudes towards the utility of caucus among Liberals, but contrary to expectations, it was the backbenchers who viewed caucus as an instrument to pursue their ends more often than the leaders claimed it served theirs. In contrast, there are no significant differences in this regard between leaders and backbenchers in the opposition parties. Nor are there statistically significant differences between leaders and followers in either the Liberal or the opposition parties with regard to their tendencies to mention caucus in their responses to the open-end question. What these data suggest is that there is rather remarkable agreement (witness the proportion who mention caucus without being cued) in the Liberal party that caucus can be an instrument that facilitates the influence of individual MPs. This view is not as widely shared by members in the opposition parties. When respondents are not cued, only a relatively small proportion of opposition members—leaders and backbenchers alike—spontaneously assert that caucus can be an instrument of influence.

It will be recalled that we also presented MPs with two "agree-disagree" statements on the functions performed by caucus and asked their views on these. The first statement asserts that caucus facilitates party cohesion in two ways: by permitting a frank exchange of

TABLE 5.4
## LEADER-BACKBENCH ATTITUDE TOWARD THE INFLUENCE
## POTENTIAL OF PARTY CAUCUS

|  | Lib B/B | Lib Lead | Opp B/B | Opp Lead |
|---|---|---|---|---|
| % Who feel Caucus Could Help Facilitate Influence | 97 | 71 | 83 | 89 |
| % Who feel Caucus Could Not Help | 3 | 29 | 17 | 11 |
|  | Sig. <.001 | | N.S. | |
| % Who Spontaneously Mentioned Caucus Could Help Influence | 50 | 52 | 14 | 12 |
|  | N.S. | | N.S. | |
| N | (56) | (31) | (62) | (17) |

opinions and by enabling caucus members to plan strategy so that their performance, as a party, on the floor of the House and in Committee will be more effectively integrated. This statement rests on data derived from the responses of members of the 25th Canadian Parliament to the open-end question: "In general, what do you discuss in caucus?" After analyzing these data, Kornberg concluded that "the caucuses of the two left-wing parties contribute to structural integration because they are primarily employed to plan and coordinate the performance of individual members. A smooth and efficient performance is likely to be rewarding to the individual; it may also increase or reinforce his attraction to party colleagues." [11] He went on to observe that although caucuses are employed in this way in the Conservative and Social Credit parties, they tend primarily to be used to vent grievances and to hammer out agreement on party policies: "In their discussions members are likely to express to one another attitudes and opinions they really hold. Such frank and accurate interpersonal communications, to the extent that they inhibit the development of excessive group normativeness, contribute to group cohesion." [12]

An inspection of the responses of current MPs to the first statement indicates that the great majority of those interviewed (83%) agreed or tended to agree that caucus does promote party cohesion in two ways. Indeed, only 5% disagreed or tended to disagree and the remaining MPs, most of whom were Liberals, generally agreed with one part of the statement but disagreed with the other. Although the evaluations of leaders and followers were similar, the Conservative and Social Credit MPs tended to be more supportive of this evaluation of caucus (92%) than were the Liberal and NDP MPs: 92% of Conservative, 86% of the Creditiste, 78% of the Liberal and 77% of NDP members agreed or tended to agree with the first statement.

The second statement asserts that caucus does not give backbench MPs an opportunity to participate in party policy-making but it does permit members to bring to the attention of party colleagues any personal or constituency problems and grievances—an opportunity that Kornberg described as the "cathartic" function of caucus. An analysis of the responses to this statement indicates that a minority of MPs (26%) agreed or tended to agree with this assessment of caucus. The majority (57%) disagreed or tended to disagree and the remaining 17% disagreed with one part of the statement but agreed with the other. Leader-follower differences were small but, again, there were some interesting interparty differences. The members of the two right-of-center parties, the Conservative and Social Credit, more often agreed (33% and 43% respectively) than did the members of the left-of-center parties (25% Liberal and 9% NDP) that caucus is not a policy-influencing mechanism but permits members to air grievances. In contrast, 82% of the NDP, 58% of the Liberals, 48% of the Conservatives, and 43% of the Social Credit disagreed or tended to disagree with this position.

We may infer from the analysis of these data that Whittington and Van Loon's assessment of the policy potential of caucus is only partially accurate. They are correct in asserting that in their respective caucuses opposition members discuss and presumably have some impact on the policies their parliamentary parties pursue. They undoubtedly also are correct in asserting that government backbenchers support policies put forward by their leaders. In this regard, Pickersgill's observations also seem to be accurate. However, we cannot infer from our data that Liberal backbenchers simply take as "given" the policies enunciated by party leaders or accept without reservation the suggestions of their leaders on how they can best support government policies. Nor can we find support for Van Loon and Whittington's position that, however lively the debate in caucus, government backbenchers do not influence the content of government policy. The majority of Liberal respondents felt that caucus does give them an opportunity to influence policy. Moreover, although caucus may facilitate party discipline and thus the government's control of the House (as Mark MacGuigan contends), it can be argued, on the basis of the responses of Mr. MacGuigan's colleagues in the Liberal party, that this discipline is voluntary and achieved as a consequence of discussion and concession and not imposed upon a passive backbench by an authoritarian group of cabinet ministers.[13] In this sense party caucus appears to perform the same function in the 28th Parliament as it did in the 25th Parliament a decade earlier.

## COMMUNICATION WITH THE CABINET, DEPUTY MINISTERS AND PARLIAMENTARY SECRETARIES

Other than participation in party caucus meetings, the informal legislative activity to which the MPs in our sample ascribed greatest value was personal contact with cabinet ministers or other ranking officials in the government. Although Liberal MPs were significantly more likely to value opportunities for communication with ministers, approximately 15% of opposition respondents, including almost a quarter of the party leaders, asserted that such communications potentially were an important source of member influence. Nor is this surprising. Given the numerous opportunities for informal contact among members of the House, there can be little doubt that if a member has a particular point of view to express, or a favor to request, he has ample opportunity to do so. As we noted earlier in this chapter, we tested our assumption that private members are able to interact with the leaders of the governing party and with high level bureaucrats by asking several questions regarding the frequency and nature of their communications with ministers, deputy-ministers and parliamentary secretaries.[14] We also asked them how successful they were in getting what they had asked for.

Excluding the cabinet members and, in the case of the third question, the parliamentary secretaries in our sample, table 5.5 presents for each party the percentage of respondents who reported making contact with ministers, deputy-ministers, and/or parliamentary secretaries "Often" or "Quite Often" in an average month. The most striking pattern in these data is the tendency for all MPs, regardless of party, to communicate more often with cabinet ministers than with either deputy-ministers or parliamentary secretaries. In part, this pattern may reflect the tendency of MPs wanting to communicate with members of the bureaucracy to "go through" the

TABLE 5.5
## PERCENTAGE OF MPS BY PARTY WHO REPORTED CON-TACTING MINISTERS, DEPUTY-MINISTERS, OR PARLIAMEN-TARY SECRETARIES OFTEN OR QUITE OFTEN

| | Ministers | Dep. Ministers | Parl. Secretaries |
|---|---|---|---|
| Liberal | 83% | 36% | 28% |
| Conservative | 71 | 46 | 12 |
| NDP | 64 | 64 | 0 |
| Creditiste | 83 | 67 | 20 |
| All MPs | 76 | 44 | 17 |
| N = | 168[a] | 165[a] | 145[b] |
| | $x^2 < .05$ | $x^2 < .01$ | $x^2 < .01$ |

a. Excludes cabinet ministers.
b. Excludes cabinet ministers and parliamentary secretaries.

responsible minister. It is not that MPs cannot contact bureaucrats directly. They can. However, comments they made during interviews with them suggest the feeling exists that most civil servants are likely to be more forthcoming—particularly with opposition members—if MPs first direct their requests to the responsible minister. The assumption is that no high level civil servant (and deputy-ministers are on the top rung of the civil service ladder) wants to be accused of making trouble for his boss, the minister, by, for example, providing information to MPs that might prove embarrassing to the minister.

Another possible explanation for the observed pattern also emerged from comments made by respondents during interviews. Some MPs felt there was much to be gained from referring a constituent's request for assistance directly to a cabinet minister. For example, a copy of a letter written to a minister and sent to a constituent can be used to impress him with the fact his MP has gone "right to the top" in his efforts to help him. The MP's letter is sent with the knowledge that one of the minister's staff will refer the matter to the appropriate civil servant. A letter then will be sent from the minister's office informing the MP of the action the minister has taken. Copies of letters to and from ministers that are forwarded to a constituent can have a salutary "multiplier" effect. MPs assume such correspondence will not always be kept confidential. It may be shown to friends, neighbors, and even coworkers to illustrate the way in which the MP "went to bat" for the constituent. On such fond hopes are plans for reelection sometimes based!

Beyond these possibilities the fact that almost twice as many members communicate frequently with ministers as with deputy-ministers, and that more than four times as many MPs communicate frequently with ministers as with parliamentary secretaries, suggests, other things being equal, that members tend to communicate most often with those in the best positions to help them realize their requests. Pursuing this line of reasoning one additional step, a reasonable hypothesis is that the higher the ascribed status of the minister, the greater the frequency of his contacts with individual members. However, a comparison of the influence ascribed to a minister by respondents with the number of times the minister is cited as being frequently contacted shows the relationship to be both statistically insignificant and in the opposite direction to that predicted (Pearson's $r = -.05$).

Perhaps the most graphic illustration of the discrepancy between influence and communication is the case of the prime minister. Although the prime minister was listed by almost 75% of our respondents as one of the ten most influential men in parliament, only one MP listed Mr. Trudeau as one of the five ministers he had occasion to contact most often. Nor is it possible to explain this disparity in terms of the possibility that most members consider the prime minister too important to approach directly. If this were the case we would expect the membership to solicit the assistance of the prime minister indirectly through such individuals as the PM's parliamentary secretary. But the data indicate that only two MPs reported having frequent contact with the parliamentary secretary to the prime minister.

A second and more plausible explanation for our failure to find the expected relationship between influence and communication is that our ceteris paribus assumption is not valid. It probably is inaccurate to assume, as the influence hypothesis implicitly does, that the general influence of a minister can be equated with his particular influence in a specific subject matter area. Although the prime minister clearly is the most influential member of parliament overall, it does not follow that he will wield the greatest influence in a particular area. The frequency with which MPs contact particular cabinet ministers then is likely to depend more upon the interests and concerns of the MPs and their constituents than upon the relative power and influence ascribed to the ministers concerned. Although our interview schedule did not include specific questions about the members' personal interests in the various departmental issue areas, D. C. Rowat reports (based upon a 1966 survey of 70 MPs) that of the 30,000 to 50,000 constituent complaints received by MPs each year, the most frequent complaints were concerned with the general topics of pensions, income tax, citizenship and immigration, health and welfare, unemployment insurance, and veterans' affairs.[15] In general, these complaints are concerned with subjects under the jurisdiction of the departments of National Health and Welfare, National Revenue, Manpower and Immigration, Labour, and Veterans Affairs. Our data indicate that the five ministers in charge of these departments constituted about 16% of the population of cabinet ministers, and received almost 30% of the nominations for the most frequently contacted ministers, but only 4% of the total influence nominations given to the cabinet (see table 5.6).

A further illustration of the relationship between member interest and frequency of communication is the correlation between individual member interest in parliamentary committees and the volume of communications with the several cabinet ministers. Although we did not ask our respondents to name the departments whose subject matter concerned them most, we did ask them to do this for the standing committees of parliament. By combining the communications nominations of ministers whose departmental concerns were encompassed by a single committee, we were able to compare member interest in these more broadly defined subject matter areas with the frequency of member contact with the appropriate ministers. The correlation (Pearson's r) between these attributes was a statistically significant .41 (p ≤ .001). Clearly, the evidence suggests that MPs communicate most frequently with the ministers whose departments' jurisdictions embrace the subject matter areas of greatest interest to them or their constituents.

Notwithstanding the tendency of MPs to communicate more with cabinet ministers than with deputy-ministers or parliamentary secretaries, it is apparent from table 5.5 that Liberal MPs relied upon such communication substantially more often than did the members of the other parties. Indeed, if we divide the parties in terms of their government-opposition status, we find a positive correlation between government party membership and the frequency of member contact with both ministers and parliamentary secretaries ($tau_b$ = .21 and .17 respectively) and a negative correlation of −.18 between government membership and communication with deputy-ministers. Though relatively small, these correlations are statistically significant (p ≤ .001)

TABLE 5.6
## A COMPARISON OF THE INFLUENCE NOMINATIONS OF CABINET MINISTERS AND THE FREQUENCY OF MEMBER COMMUNICATIONS WITH CARINET MINISTERS

|  | Number of Influence Noms. | Number of Communications |
|---|---|---|
| Prime Minister | 119 | 1 |
| Minister 1 | 79 | 30 |
| Minister 2 | 53 | 14 |
| Minister 3 | 46 | 2 |
| Minister 4 | 45 | 26 |
| Minister 5 | 42 | 21 |
| Minister 6 | 42 | 20 |
| Minister 7 | 36 | 22 |
| Minister 8 | 33 | 50 |
| Minister 9 | 26 | 19 |
| Minister 10 | 23 | 7 |
| Minister 11 | 18 | 36 |
| Minister 12 | 14 | 25 |
| Minister 13 | 9 | 4 |
| Minister 14 | 8 | 2 |
| Minister 15 | 7 | 0 |
| Minister 16 | 6 | 22 |
| Minister 17 | 6 | 44 |
| Minister 18 | 4 | 25 |
| Minister 19 | 4 | 16 |
| Minister 20 | 4 | 13 |
| Minister 21 | 3 | 8 |
| Minister 22 | 3 | 0 |
| Minister 23 | 2 | 32 |
| Minister 24 | 2 | 32 |
| Minister 25 | 1 | 7 |
| Minister 26 | 1 | 3 |
| Minister 27 | 1 | 3 |
| Minister 28 | 0 | 1 |
| Minister 29 | 0 | 25 |
| Minister 30 | 0 | 0 |

and suggest the existence of two fairly distinct patterns of emphasis in the interactions between MPs on the one hand and ministers, deputy-ministers, and parliamentary secretaries on the other. Since both cabinet members and their current assistants, the parliamentary secretaries, are appointed from among members of the governing party, other members of the party have relatively easy and continuous access to them. Whether it is because they do not have as good access to ministers and hence cannot press their points of view or their requests with quite the same frequency and vigor, or because they are unwilling to, or feel less comfortable in presenting their requests to ministers and parliamentary secretaries, or because of a combination of these reasons, opposition members more often convey their interests to and seek assistance from the professional bureaucracy. Although deputy-ministers may themselves be appointed by the governing party, and although the conventional wisdom on parliament hill is that government members are listened to somewhat more carefully than are opposition MPs, the assumption may be that deputy-ministers still are the most likely of the three sets of officials to give opposition MPs a sympathetic hearing.[16]

## THE CONTENT OF COMMUNICATIONS

Thus far in this analysis we have found: (1) that the level of informal communication in parliament is quite high; (2) that members generally communicate more frequently with ministers than with deputy ministers or parliamentary secretaries; (3) that members are particularly apt to contact ministers who have responsibility for the subject matter area of greatest interest to them (or their constituents); and (4) that in relative terms, government MPs rely more upon communication with ranking members of their party—cabinet ministers and parliamentary secretaries—while opposition members place relatively greater emphasis upon contacts with deputy-ministers. Given the increasing centralization of policy-making in the cabinet as well as the supposedly decreasing role of the backbench MP in the policy process on the one hand and the increasing importance of his role as an ombudsman on the other, we assumed that the content of communications would be heavily weighted toward constituency matters. Moreover, we assumed that content also would determine whether a communication was directed to a parliamentary leader or to a civil servant. It seemed reasonable to assume that communications with cabinet members and parliamentary secretaries more often would involve matters of policy whereas communications with top level bureaucrats, deputy-ministers, who are charged with the implementation of policies, more often would be concerned with the problems of individual constituents who had been affected by the ways specific policies were being implemented.

In order to test these hypotheses, we asked those MPs in our sample who indicated that they "often" or "quite often" contacted ministers, deputy-ministers or parliamentary secretaries whether the occasions for these contacts were usually policy matters, constituency matters or both. As is evident from their responses (see table 5.7) the great majority of communications between MPs and ministers, deputy-ministers, and parliamentary secretaries are concerned entirely, or, in great part, with constituency matters. At most, only 16% of the MPs reported that their conversations with any of the officials concerned primarily policy matters. Moreover, our assumption that the content of communications with ministers and parliamentary secretaries would tend to be policy-oriented whereas those with deputy-ministers would tend to be constituency-oriented also is confirmed. It is further apparent from the data in table 5.7 that on the whole, the content and direction of communications initiated by the members of the four parties are consistent with their representational role styles and foci. We had previously observed that the Liberals and the NDP tended to be more policy-oriented and the Conservative and Social Credit parties more constituency-oriented. The data in table 5.7 generally support this assertion by indicating that Conservative MPs were both more likely to concentrate on constituency problems in their discussions with ministers and other officials and less likely to discuss matters of public policy than the members of the other parties. In fact, whereas the communication of 61% of the Liberals and 59% of the NDP were at least occasionally concerned with policy, only about 40% of the Conservative MPs reported ever discussing policy matters with members of the cabinet.[17] Nor did the Conservatives display any greater policy interest in their contacts with deputy-ministers or parliamentary secretaries. Only 24% of the Conservatives compared to 36% of the Liberals (but only 19% of the NDP) manifested any concern with policy in their contacts with deputy-ministers. Further, only 33% of the Conservatives, as compared to 61% of the Liberals, ever discussed policy matters with parliamentary secretaries.[18] It appears from these data that the Conservative MPs may have placed greater emphasis upon communications with deputy-ministers because: (a) they felt these top level bureaucrats would be more likely to give opposition members a fair hearing; and (b) they believed their prevailing constituency concerns would be less effectively articulated by political opponents. That the NDP MPs also communicated disproportionately with deputy-ministers, despite their manifest concern with matters of public policy, suggests they may have shared the Conservatives' perceptions of the advantages of communicating with a nonpartisan set of officials.

**TABLE 5.7**

**PERCENTAGE OF MPS BY PARTY WHOSE CONTACTS WITH CABINET MINISTERS, DEPUTY-MINISTERS AND PARLIAMENTARY SECRETARIES CONCERNED PRIMARILY CONSTITUENCY MATTERS, POLICY MATTERS OR BOTH**

| | | Communication With | | | | | | | | |
|---|---|---|---|---|---|---|---|---|---|---|
| | | Cabinet | | | Deputy-Ministers | | | Parliamentary Secretaries | | |
| | | Const. | Both | Pol. | Const. | Both | Pol. | Const. | Both | Pol. |
| Lib | % | 39.2 | 47.3 | 13.5 | 64.1 | 33.3 | 2.6 | 38.9 | 44.4 | 16.7 |
| | (N) | (29) | (35) | (10) | (25) | (12) | ( 1) | ( 7) | ( 8) | ( 3) |
| Con | % | 59.6 | 36.5 | 3.8 | 75.8 | 21.2 | 3.0 | 66.7 | 16.7 | 16.7 |
| | (N) | (31) | (19) | ( 2) | (25) | ( 7) | ( 1) | ( 8) | ( 2) | ( 2) |
| NDP | % | 41.2 | 47.1 | 11.8 | 81.3 | 18.8 | 0.0 | 0.0 | 0.0 | 0.0 |
| | (N) | ( 7) | ( 8) | ( 2) | (13) | ( 3) | ( 0) | ( 0) | ( 0) | ( 0) |
| Cred | % | 16.7 | 66.7 | 16.7 | 25.0 | 50.0 | 25.0 | 0.0 | 100.0 | 0.0 |
| | (N) | ( 1) | ( 4) | ( 1) | ( 1) | ( 2) | ( 1) | ( 0) | ( 1) | ( 0) |
| Total | % | 45.6 | 44.3 | 10.1 | 69.6 | 27.1 | 3.3 | 48.4 | 35.5 | 16.1 |
| | (N) | (68) | (66) | (15) | (64) | (25) | ( 3) | (15) | (11) | ( 5) |

It must be emphasized that our observations and speculations assume the existence of a majority government. In situations in which the government holds a minority of seats, as in the recent and short-lived 29th Parliament, the frequency and policy content of communications with the cabinet, especially by members of a minority party holding a balance of power (such as the NDP in the 29th Parliament) might well increase substantially. Although our data do not permit us to test these speculations, the events of the 29th Parliament appear to support them. Not only did the Liberal government in this parliament make a number of significant policy concessions to the NDP, but when, at last, the Liberals refused to compromise further, the NDP abandoned their informal alliance with the Liberals and voted with the Conservatives to bring down the government.

### THE CONSEQUENCES OF COMMUNICATION

Before a MP petitions an official, he makes a series of assumptions (mentioned above) based on the interrelationship of his own position, the subject matter of his request and the various positions and areas of specialization of those whom he might possibly petition. In order to test the accuracy of MPs' judgments, we asked those in our sample how successful they had been in "getting what they asked for or in getting their points across" with each of three groups of officials.[19] Table 5.8 presents for each party the percentage of MPs who responded that they had been "very successful" or "quite successful" in communicating with each set of officials. Since we asked the success question only of those MPs who indicated that they "often" or "quite often" communicated with these officials, it is not surprising to find that the majority of all MPs, regardless of party, felt they usually were successful in their efforts. Only 4% of the members said they usually were "not very successful" in getting their point across with cabinet ministers while only 1% said the results of their communications with deputy-ministers had not been very successful. Indeed, even if we include the responses of MPs who indicated that their success "depended upon the subject under consideration," the number of members who felt they had not been successful ranged from 21% for communications with the cabinet to 27% for deputy-ministers and parliamentary secretaries.

TABLE 5.8

**PERCENTAGE OF MPS BY PARTY WHO SAID THEY WERE
USUALLY SUCCESSFUL OR QUITE SUCCESSFUL
IN THEIR COMMUNICATIONS WITH CABINET MINISTERS,
DEPUTY-MINISTERS AND PARLIAMENTARY SECRETARIES[a]**

|  | Cabinet Ministers | Deputy-Ministers | Parliamentary Secretaries |
|---|---|---|---|
| Liberals | 79.7% | 79.4% | 77.7% |
| Conservatives | 78.8 | 66.6 | 72.7 |
| NDP | 64.7 | 68.8 | — |
| Creditistes | 100.0 | 75.0 | — |
| Total | 78.6 | 72.8 | 73.3 |
| N | 149[a] | 130[a] | 30[b] |

a. Total excludes all cabinet ministers as well as all other MPs who indicated that they seldom or never contacted any of these officials.
b. Total excludes all cabinet ministers, parliamentary secretaries and all other MPs who indicated that they seldom or never contacted parliamentary secretaries.

   What is surprising about these data, however, is that they did not really support our expectations that perceptions of success would vary by party and with the perceived partisanship of the official being contacted. Although we did find that MPs were somewhat more sanguine about their successes with cabinet ministers, the difference between the ministers and the deputy-ministers and parliamentary secretaries in this regard were both very small (about 6%) and not nearly of sufficient magnitude to explain the differences previously observed in the frequency of member contact with the three groups of officials. As for our assumption that opposition MPs would be more likely to feel that they would be more successful communicating with deputy-ministers than with ministers or parliamentary secretaries, the data do indicate that NDP members said they were slightly more successful (69% to 65% respectively) communicating with deputy-ministers. However, this was not the case in the other opposition parties. Fully 81% of the Conservative and Social Credit opposition MPs reported being "very" or "quite successful" in their contacts with ministers compared to only 67% who said they were successful with deputy-ministers. In contrast, similar proportions of Liberals reported being successful with both cabinet ministers and with deputy-ministers and parliamentary secretaries. What these figures suggest is that the conventional wisdom regarding the tendency of bureaucrats to listen more carefully to the representations of government MPs may be well founded. Being a member of a governing party may very well provide an "edge" in dealings with public officials, even those who are overtly nonpartisan[20] (i.e., deputy-ministers). Finally, the data did support our assumption that MPs would be more likely to experience success if they approached officials about constituency rather than policy matters. A comparison of the perceived success rates of MPs who focused primarily upon constituency matters with those who concentrated upon policy concerns when they communicated with cabinet members and deputy-ministers[21] indicates that the former were about 13% more likely to be successful than the latter.

## COMMUNICATING WITH CONSTITUENTS

The responses of MPs indicate that regardless of party or leadership status, the great majority of Canadian MPs (80%) received a considerable amount of mail each week from their constituents. Moreover, approximately 92% reported they also received communications from constituents by means other than mail: 83.5% said they were telephoned; 53% said their constituents visited them either in their parliamentary offices or when they returned to their districts; and 32% said they received telegrams and night letters from constituents. The bulk of their mail (75%) was from constituents who wanted the assistance of MPs on matters such as pensions, income tax, veterans' payments, unemployment insurance payments, and passports and visas.[22] An additional 23% of their mail concerned requests for information. Generally these letters asked MPs who the appropriate officials were to whom complaints, questions, or further requests for information should be directed. In a very real sense, then, many of these "requests for information" also could be regarded as part of a MP's "case work." However, case work and individual problems were not the only topics of letters. Fully 66% of the respondents said that constituents wrote either to express their own views or to solicit MPs' views on matters ranging from moral issues such as abortion, euthanasia, and the death penalty to very mundane issues such as inflation and the level of employment. Parenthetically, it should be noted that individual requests for assistance (65%), related requests for information (12%), and observations on various policy matters (41%) also comprised communications via telephone conversations, telegrams, and personal visits.

The majority of the letters, telephone calls, telegrams, and personal visits came from those whom MPs termed either "average citizens" (61%) or a "good cross-section of the public" (33%). However, 23% of the MPs reported being contacted by interest groups and their spokesmen; 29% received communications from local political and community leaders; 12% were contacted by friends and acquaintances; 15% by business associates; and 6% by members of their constituency parties. Finally, 25% of the MPs said that many of the letters and other forms of communications they received came from "disadvantaged" individuals such as the poor, the elderly, the unemployed, or from people who apparently had tried unsuccessfully to secure the help of other officials in solving a particular problem.

As we suggested at the beginning of this chapter, communication between MPs and the public is not an asymmetrical process. Therefore, it was not surprising to find that fully 90% of the MPs said they tried to find out how people in their constituencies were thinking about current issues facing parliament. By far the largest proportion (65%) said they found out how people were thinking by "covering the riding" personally; in effect, they interviewed constituents in their homes ("door-to-door"), in shopping centers, on the streets and at social events. An additional 19% of the MPs, rather than surveying cross-sections of the populations of their constituencies, relied on "key" informants—most often, people in their constituency parties. Other survey research methods MPs used were questionnaires (37%), telephone interviews (9%), radio interviews via "hot line" shows (15%), and public meetings combined with question periods (19%). Approximately one-third (36%) of the respondents used a kind of reverse survey research technique; they prepared articles, "parliamentary reports," newsletters, and a variety of other mail-outs in which they expressed their own positions on current issues before parliament and to which they invited constituents' reactions. Finally, 7% said that by reading newspapers, editorials and letters to the editors of newspapers in their constituencies they were able to apprise themselves of constituency positions on important policy issues.

With regard to the delineation of "grass-roots" feelings (as opposed to positions on specific policy issues), the great majority of MPs said they depended either on local party leaders and workers (79%) or upon personal friends and acquaintances (76%) to tell them how people generally felt back home. Almost equal proportions said they depended on editorial opinions (55%) and on the opinions of business leaders (54%) in their districts. A somewhat smaller proportion (45%) said they tapped grass-roots feelings by contacting members of provincial legislatures and other elected public officials. 35% said they talked to trade union officials while 25% said they consulted with religious functionaries in their own and other churches. When asked which of these sources provided them with the most accurate and reliable information about grass-roots feelings, 45% said that party leaders and workers in their constituencies provided them with their most accurate and reliable information, while 33% mentioned personal friends and acquaintances. Members of provincial legislatures and other public officials were ranked as the best source of information by 14% of the respondents. Business leaders were considered the most reliable informants by 11% of the MPs, editorial opinions by 10%, trade union officials by 4%, and religious functionaries by 2%.

To recapitulate, there are a variety of ways in which MPs and members of the Canadian public communicate with one another. The two principal means are mail and personal interactions. Communications are initiated as often by the MP as by members of the public. Indeed, MPs appear to initiate contacts with their party officials and with the representatives of organized interests considerably more often than these individuals contact MPs. They use a variety of survey research techniques (principally personal interviews and questionnaires) to measure constituency attitudes on specific policy issues and they rely upon personal contacts with constituency party officials, personal friends and acquaintances, and representative members of organized interests such as business, labor and religion to inform them of the distribution of grass-roots opinions among their constituents—in the words of one MP, "to take the public's temperature." We found differences in the frequency and type of communications received by members of each of the four parties. This was also the case for the front and backbenches of the two major parties.[23] For example, Liberal party leaders reported receiving a larger volume of mail and more frequent personal visits from constituents than did their backbenchers. In the Conservative party, however, it was the backbenchers who reported receiving more mail and personal visits from constituents. Another example of these differences is that Liberal party backbenchers more frequently reported that their mail was concerned with policy matters than did their leaders whereas the opposite was true of the Conservative party (see table 5.9).

TABLE 5.9

## FREQUENCY AND TYPES OF COMMUNICATIONS FROM THE PUBLIC RECEIVED BY LIBERAL AND CONSERVATIVE LEADERS AND BACKBENCHERS[a]

|  | Liberal Leaders | Liberal Non-leaders | Conservative Leaders | Conservative Non-leaders |
|---|---|---|---|---|
| % Receiving a large volume of weekly mail | 88.6% | 76.6% | 72.2% | 76.2% |
| % Receiving other forms of communication: | 100.0 | 97.2 | 94.4 | 92.7 |
| By telephone | 77.1 | 83.1 | 87.5 | 83.8 |
| By telegram | 28.6 | 32.2 | 43.8 | 32.4 |
| Personal visits | 69.4 | 48.4 | 44.4 | 64.3 |
| Mail is concerned with requests for assistance | 69.4 | 76.6 | 77.8 | 78.6 |
| Mail is concerned with policy matters | 55.6 | 68.8 | 88.9 | 64.3 |
| Mail is concerned with requests for information | 19.4 | 21.9 | 33.3 | 23.8 |
| Other communications are concerned with requests for assistance | 66.7 | 62.5 | 66.7 | 71.4 |
| Other communications are concerned with policy | 50.0 | 43.8 | 50.0 | 38.1 |
| Other communications are concerned with requests for information | 8.3 | 12.5 | 16.7 | 14.3 |

a. Percentages add up to more than 100% because of multiple responses.

The members of the four parties and the leaders and backbenchers of the two major parties also tend to hear from different types of people. Illustrative of interparty differences is the finding that the great majority of Social Credit MPs reported the people who contacted them were: (a) disadvantaged members of the public; and (b) members of their constituency parties, whereas this was not the case for the members of the other three parties (see table 5.10). When we compared the leaders and backbenchers of the two major parties with regard to the kinds of people who communicate with them, we found that backbenchers were more likely to hear from average citizens than were their leaders. Backbenchers also were more likely to hear from disadvantaged individuals and people with problems. Party leaders more often received mail and were communicated with in other ways by local "pols" (e.g., MLA's, city councillors, and community leaders) and the representatives of interest groups. In the Conservative party none of the backbenchers reported receiving communications from business associates and only 2% said they heard from friends and acquaintances whereas some 30% of the Conservative leaders reported hearing regularly from each of these groups. An interesting although not unexpected finding was that almost twice as many of the leaders of the governing Liberal party reported receiving communications from interest group representatives as did the leaders of the Conservative opposition (see table 5.11).[24]

It will be recalled that virtually every respondent said he tried to find out how his constituents felt about important policy matters. The major interparty differences with respect to the manner in which they went about finding out was that members of the two major parties tended to rely on personal interactions with constituents generally and with key informants—in and out of their local party organizations—in particular, whereas members of the two minor parties tended to rely more on responses to mail surveys, questionnaires, newsletters, parliamentary reports, etc. (see table 5.12). Within the two major parties, the Liberal leaders relied more heavily on personal interactions with a more-or-less representative sample of constituents than on interactions with key informants whereas the

TABLE 5.10

**A COMPARISON OF THE KINDS OF PEOPLE WHO COMMUNICATE WITH MEMBERS OF THE FOUR PARLIAMENTARY PARTIES[a]**

| Who Communicates: | NDP | Liberal | Conserva-tive | Credi-tiste | All |
|---|---|---|---|---|---|
| Average citizens and cross-sections of public | 77.2% | 95.0% | 100.0% | 85.8% | 94.2% |
| Disadvantaged people and people with problems | 18.2 | 29.0 | 18.3 | 85.8 | 23.8 |
| Local political and community leaders | 27.3 | 24.0 | 35.0 | 42.9 | 28.6 |
| Interest group representatives | 22.7 | 25.0 | 18.3 | 42.9 | 23.3 |
| Business associates | 9.1 | 21.0 | 8.3 | 14.3 | 15.3 |
| Friends and acquaintances | 9.1 | 12.0 | 11.7 | 28.6 | 12.2 |
| Constituency party people | 9.1 | 8.0 | 1.7 | 71.4 | 5.8 |

a. Percentages add up to more than 100% because of multiple responses.

TABLE 5.11

## A COMPARISON OF THE KINDS OF PEOPLE WHO COMMUNICATE WITH LEADERS AND BACKBENCHERS IN LIBERAL AND CONSERVATIVE PARTIES[a]

| Who Communicates: | Liberal Leaders | Liberal Non-leaders | Conservative Leaders | Conservative Non-leaders |
|---|---|---|---|---|
| Average citizens and cross-sections of public | 88.9% | 98.5% | 94.5% | 100.0% |
| Disadvantaged people and people with problems | 25.0 | 31.3 | 11.2 | 21.5 |
| Local political and community leaders | 27.8 | 21.8 | 44.4 | 31.0 |
| Interest group representatives | 41.7 | 15.6 | 22.2 | 16.7 |
| Business associates | 22.2 | 20.3 | 27.8 | — |
| Friends and acquaintances | 11.1 | 12.5 | 33.3 | 2.4 |
| Constituency party people | 16.7 | 3.1 | 5.6 | — |

a. Percentages add up to more than 100% because of multiple responses.


TABLE 5.12

## SOURCES OF INFORMATION FOR MPS IN EACH PARTY REGARDING CONSTITUENCY OPINIONS ON MAJOR ISSUES CONSIDERED BY PARLIAMENT[a]

| Find out how constituents feel from: | NDP | Liberal | Conservative | Creditiste | All |
|---|---|---|---|---|---|
| Personal interactions with constituents | 58.0% | 78.6% | 64.3% | 16.7% | 69.3% |
| Interactions with party and other key informants in constituency | 10.5 | 20.2 | 23.3 | — | 19.4 |
| Surveys of constituency (questionnaires) | 52.6 | 33.7 | 35.7 | 50.0 | 37.1 |
| Telephone and radio surveys of constituency | 26.3 | 28.1 | 17.8 | 16.7 | 24.1 |
| Response to mailouts, newsletters, articles, parliamentary reports | 57.9 | 31.5 | 32.1 | 66.7 | 35.9 |
| Questions asked at public meetings in constituency | 5.3 | 22.5 | 19.6 | 16.7 | 19.4 |
| Constituency newspapers, editorials, and letters to the editor | 15.8 | 10.1 | 10.7 | 16.7 | 11.2 |

a. Percentages add up to more than 100% because of multiple responses.

Conservative leaders relied almost equally upon both. Regardless of party, however, leaders relied more on personal interactions with the public while backbench members resorted more frequently to survey research techniques to delineate constituency attitudes on major issues (see table 5.13).

With respect to the delineation of grass-roots constituency feelings, we found there were direct relationships between the left-right positions of the parties and the frequency with which they consulted local party leaders and workers as opposed to religious leaders in their districts. The further to the left the party, the more frequently its parliamentary members consulted with local officials and the less often the members talked to local religious functionaries. Not surprisingly, the members of the NDP were more likely to consult union officials than were the members of the other parties. Again, not surprisingly, Conservative MPs consulted more often than did other MPs with business leaders in their constituencies (see table 5.14). And, although Conservative and NDP MPs more often regarded businessmen and union officials, respectively, as reliable and accurate

TABLE 5.13

**SOURCES OF INFORMATION OF LIBERAL AND CONSERVATIVE LEADERS AND BACKBENCHERS REGARDING CONSTITUENCY OPINIONS ON MAJOR POLICY ISSUES[a]**

| Find out how constituents feel from: | Liberal Leaders | Liberal Non-leaders | Conservative Leaders | Conservative Non-leaders |
|---|---|---|---|---|
| Personal interactions with constituents | 90.4% | 54.2% | 55.6% | 68.4% |
| Interactions with party and other key informants in constituency | 38.7 | 10.4 | 44.4 | 13.1 |
| Surveys of constituency (questionnaires) | 25.8 | 37.9 | 16.7 | 44.7 |
| Telephone and radio surveys of constituency | 16.2 | 34.5 | 11.1 | 21.1 |
| Response to mailouts, newsletters, articles, parliamentary reports | 19.4 | 38.0 | 11.1 | 42.1 |
| Questions asked at public meetings in constituency | 35.5 | 15.5 | 22.2 | 18.4 |
| Constituency newspapers, editorials, and letters to the editor | 12.9 | 1.7 | — | 10.5 |

a. Percentages add up to more than 100% because of multiple responses.

## TABLE 5.14

## SOURCES THAT ARE CONSULTED BY MPS IN EACH PARTY AND BY LEADERS AND BACKBENCHERS IN LIBERAL AND CONSERVATIVE PARTIES REGARDING GRASS-ROOTS CONSTITUENCY FEELINGS[a]

| Sources most frequently consulted are: | NDP | Liberal | Conservative | Credi-tiste | All | Liberal Leaders | Liberal Non-leaders | Conservative Leaders | Conservative Non-leaders |
|---|---|---|---|---|---|---|---|---|---|
| Party leaders and workers | 94.4% | 81.6% | 74.5% | 50.0% | 79.5% | 90.0% | 77.2% | 94.4% | 64.9% |
| Friends and acquaintances | 72.2 | 77.0 | 80.0 | 50.0 | 76.5 | 93.3 | 68.4 | 94.4 | 73.0 |
| Local politicians and community leaders | 72.2 | 41.4 | 43.6 | 33.3 | 45.2 | 36.7 | 43.9 | 38.9 | 45.9 |
| Business leaders | 16.7 | 56.3 | 63.6 | 33.3 | 53.6 | 60.0 | 54.4 | 66.7 | 62.2 |
| Union leaders | 50.0 | 31.0 | 36.4 | 33.3 | 34.9 | 26.7 | 33.3 | 38.9 | 35.1 |
| Religious leaders | 5.6 | 25.3 | 29.1 | 50.0 | 25.3 | 26.7 | 24.6 | 27.8 | 29.7 |
| Editorial opinions, etc. | 55.6 | 55.2 | 52.7 | 66.7 | 54.8 | 70.0 | 47.4 | 50.0 | 54.1 |

a. Percentages add up to more than 100% because of multiple responses.

sources of information, Canadian MPs, regardless of party or leadership status, tended to regard group representatives—business, union and religious leaders—as far less reliable sources of information than the people in their local party organizations and/or their friends and acquaintances (see table 5.15).

## SUMMARY

In this chapter we have tried to delineate the nature and extent of several dimensions of informal behavior in parliament, including specifically: participation in party caucus; the extent and content of communications between private members on the one hand and cabinet members, high-level civil servants and middle-echelon leaders of the governing Liberal party on the other; and the frequency and content of communications between MPs and members of the public.

We found that the members of the Liberal party were far more inclined than members of the opposition parties to regard caucus as a vehicle that can be used to influence policy. There was a significant difference in leader and backbench attitudes among Liberal MPs, but contrary to expectation, it was the backbenchers rather than the leaders who more often viewed caucus as an instrument of influence. The majority of MPs, regardless of party, felt that the caucus promotes party cohesion and though it may also facilitate party discipline, we argued that this discipline is voluntary and is a consequence of give-and-take discussion and negotiation between party leaders and backbenchers.

An analysis of the frequency of communications between private members and cabinet members revealed that fully 75% of the members had frequent contact with one or more ministers in an average month. Although, in absolute terms, all the parties placed a greater emphasis on cabinet contacts than upon contacts with either deputy-ministers or parliamentary secretaries, in relative terms, the members of the opposition parties tended to emphasize contacts with deputy-ministers while Liberal MPs communicated more often with cabinet members and parliamentary secretaries. There was no relationship between the influence ascribed to a cabinet minister and the number of communications directed to him. Rather, we found that the frequency with which MPs contacted particular ministers depended upon their personal interests and the particularistic concerns of their constituencies.

## TABLE 5.15

### SOURCES OF MOST ACCURATE AND RELIABLE INFORMATION REGARDING CONSTITUENCY GRASS-ROOTS FEELINGS BY PARTY AND BY FRONTBENCH-BACKBENCH STATUS IN LIBERAL AND CONSERVATIVE PARTIES[a]

| Most accurate and reliable information sources are: | NDP | Liberal | Conservative | Creditiste | All | Liberal Leaders | Liberal Non-leaders | Conservative Leaders | Conservative Non-leaders |
|---|---|---|---|---|---|---|---|---|---|
| Party leaders and workers | 68.4% | 48.2% | 37.0% | 20.0% | 45.3% | 51.7% | 46.3% | 33.3% | 38.9% |
| Friends and acquaintances | 47.4 | 25.3 | 40.7 | 20.0 | 32.9 | 37.9 | 18.5 | 38.9 | 41.5 |
| Local politicians and community leaders | 26.3 | 9.6 | 14.8 | 20.0 | 13.7 | 3.4 | 13.0 | 22.2 | 11.1 |
| Business leaders | 10.5 | 8.4 | 14.8 | — | 10.6 | 6.9 | 9.3 | 11.1 | 16.7 |
| Union leaders | 10.5 | 2.4 | 5.6 | 20.0 | 4.3 | — | 3.7 | 5.6 | 5.6 |
| Religious leaders | — | 1.2 | 1.9 | — | 1.9 | — | 1.9 | — | 2.8 |
| Editorial opinions, etc. | 15.8 | 8.4 | 11.1 | — | 9.9 | 3.4 | 11.1 | 11.1 | 11.1 |

a. Percentages add up to more than 100% because of multiple responses.

We found the great majority of communication between MPs, deputy-ministers, and parliamentary secretaries were concerned entirely or in great part with constituency matters. At most, only 16% of the MPs reported that their conversations with or letters to any of these officials primarily were concerned with policy matters. Nonetheless, the content of communications did vary by party, with Liberal and NDP MPs tending more often to broach policy matters whereas the communications of Conservative and Social Credit MPs were constituency related. The majority of MPs, again, regardless of party, felt they usually were successful in getting their points across to cabinet ministers and other officials. Although they were somewhat more sanguine about their success with cabinet members, the differences in success rates with ministers as opposed to other officials were not statistically significant.

The responses of MPs indicated that 80% received a considerable amount of mail each week from their constituents; that 83.5% received frequent telephone calls; that 53% were visited either in their parliamentary offices or when they returned to their districts; and that 32% also received telegrams and night letters. The bulk of the communications they received came from constituents who wanted the assistance of MPs on matters such as pensions, veterans' payments and so forth. A somewhat smaller proportion wanted to express their views on public policy or elicit the policy positions of their MPs. The remaining communications tended to be requests for information. Communication between MPs and the members of the public is not asymmetrical; nine out of ten MPs said they try to find out how people feel about important matters that come before parliament and how they feel generally—a process usually described as tapping grass-roots feelings. They used a variety of survey research techniques and personal contacts with both a more-or-less representative sample of constituents and with key informants to inform themselves of constituents' positions on current policy issues. In contrast, they relied primarily upon officials in their local constituency parties and upon friends and acquaintances to delineate grassroots constituency feelings. Although substantial proportions of MPs, regardless of party or status, consulted members of interest groups to apprise themselves of constituency feelings, they felt these informants were not as reliable and did not reflect opinions as accurately as did either colleagues in their local party organizations or their personal friends and acquaintances.

*Chapter 6*

## THE CORRELATES OF INFLUENCE

### MEASURES AND METHODS

In chapter 3 we noted that influence and what we term good judgment depend substantially on the holding of a formal position of leadership. Cabinet officials and top leaders in the opposition parties were ascribed far more influence and good judgment than were rank and file MPs. Moreover, when we asked MPs why the individuals whom they had nominated were influential, they frequently made reference to the formal positions of leadership these men held as well as to a variety of personal qualities. Some of these qualities, such as decency and humanity, are highly subjective and it is extremely difficult to measure their impact. Qualities related to a member's performance in parliament, however, can be measured, albeit indirectly. Consequently, in chapters 4 and 5 we examined a number of formal and informal activities of members such as the distribution of speeches made and questions asked in the House, attendance and participation in the activities of standing committees, and frequency of communications with cabinet ministers and highest level members of the bureaucracy—activities that can be thought of as indicators, however crude, of parliamentary performance. In the present chapter we shall try to assess the relative importance of both positional and performance variables on the distribution of influence and good judgment nominations. More specifically, we will enter the variables that are indicators of formal position and effective performance in regression equations to determine: (a) which are the best predictors of variations in influence and good judgment; and (b) what proportion of the variance can be explained with the use of these variables. Since, however, the results of a regression analysis can be distorted by a J-curve distribution of the dependent variable (as is the case with the distribution of nominations for influence and good judgment), we also will use a multiple discriminant function analysis and attempt, by triangulation, to answer the two questions. Parenthetically, if we find that the variables which explain variations in influence also explain variations in good judgment, we will be even more confident that we have measured those qualities that Heinz Eulau assumed were the bases of influence in a legislative body. We then will feel free to dispense with the good judgment variable and focus on the influence variable for additional analyses and explanation.

In both the regressions and the multiple discriminant analyses the performance variables that generally are employed as predictors are: the number of speeches and questions asked on the floor of the House; the number of bills and debatable resolutions[1] introduced by each member; the frequency with which members attend meetings of standing committees; and the frequency of their communications with cabinet members, highest level bureaucrats (deputy-ministers) and their constituents.[2] The level of committee attendance is employed as a surrogate for participation in committee activities since we have participation data for a subsample of 34 randomly selected members only. (In a separate analysis we will use the number of speeches made in committees by this group as an explanatory variable to try to improve our ability to predict influence and good judgment.) In addition to performance variables, we generally will use the following positional variables as predictors: cabinet, party leadership (including House leaders), frontbench in the Conservative party, and committee chairmanships.

As was indicated, these variables were set into regression equations[3] to determine which were the best predictors of ascribed influence and good judgment. Not only were separate regressions generated for all MPs, all backbenchers, and for the members of each party, we also performed analyses for groups such as the cabinet, backbenchers within the Conservative and the Liberal parties, all opposition MPs, all party leaders, and all Atlantic, Western, Quebec, and Ontario MPs. As is known, the stepwise technique forces all independent variables to enter the regression equation according to the order in which they increase the variance explained in the dependent variable. The resulting equation provides the best fit of the observations at maximum cost (i.e., the loss of one degree of freedom for each independent variable included). We will label this conventional technique "I" in the tables in this chapter. Because of the cost involved in method "I" we also will employ a regression technique "II," that allows only those variables to enter the analysis and to be included in the final equation that add significantly to the explanation of the variance in the dependent variable. This technique gives the best fit at minimal costs (i.e., one degree of freedom is lost only for those variables that provide significant increments in the variance explained). Although technique "II" usually will not explain as much of the variance as will "I," the strongest relationships are not obscured and the significance of their "F" ratios is not diminished because variables that are not significant do not have to be controlled.

Multiple discriminant function analysis,[4] the other multivariate technique that we employ, is similar to regression in that it permits an evaluation of the relative power of a number of predictor variables to best discriminate between two or more groups that are defined a priori. Like regression, the multiple discriminant technique operates in a stepwise fashion. The independent variable that best discriminates between (or among) the members of the different groups is considered first. Then, controlling for this first variable and for its intercorrelation with all other variables in the analysis, the technique proceeds by selecting the independent variables that contribute the most additional information about the groups. Although multiple discriminant analysis suffers from the handicap of being unfamiliar to social scientists, the advantage it has over regression is that it dispenses with the assumption of linearity. In practical terms this means that discriminant procedures are able to identify significant independent variables that may remain undetected in regression, because they are related to the dependent variable only over a part of their range. Thus, discriminant analysis is capable of identifying independent variables that discriminate between low and medium influence or medium and high influence, as well as those that discriminate among all three. However, discriminant analysis tends to be most successful in classifying members of categoric groups at the extremes of a continuum and is less successful in predicting membership in categories or subgroups in between. The latter is an important feature of this technique and should be borne in mind when interpreting the results of the multiple discriminant analysis reported in this and in succeeding chapters.

In the discriminant function analyses that follow we have some-what arbitrarily defined three groups of MPs by trichotomizing the population of MPs on a "none" (0), "some" (1–5), and "consider-able" (6+) vote basis for influence and a 0, 1–2, 3+ vote basis (i.e., "none," "some," and "considerable") for good judgment. Separate analyses were performed for each of the groups for which we ran regressions. As will become apparent, the results that were obtained by using the regression and the discriminant function analytic tech-niques were similar.

## FINDINGS

Table 6.1 presents the results derived from a regression analysis of the factors influencing the ascription of influence and good judgment to MPs as a group. The top half of the table is concerned with the explanation of influence, the bottom half with good judgment. Column 1 presents the zero-order correlations between the indepen-dent and dependent variables. The second column presents the un-standardized regression coefficients ("B") that provide a rough measure of the impact each independent variable has on the total number of influence or good judgment nominations each person receives. These permit us to compare the impact that particular variables have on the overall groups. The third column presents the standardized Beta weights (Beta) that reflect the predictive power of each variable within a group. Columns 2 and 3, it should be noted, present the results that are produced by conventional stepwise re-gression—what we term method "I." Column 4 ("$R^2$") presents the proportion of variance explained by the predictor variables, while columns 5 and 6 present the values of the unstandardized and standardized coefficient (Bs and Betas) of only those variables that are significant predictors of variance in the presence of all other variables (i.e., the results obtained by employing regression method "II").

An inspection of table 6.1 indicates that there are positive zero-order relationships between ascribed influence and seven of our predictor variables. Of these, one performance variable (the number of speeches made and the questions asked and answered in the House) and two position variables (cabinet and party leader status) clearly are related most strongly to variations in influence. However, these are themselves interrelated: cabinet members speak in the House more often than those not in cabinet (r = .14), and party

TABLE 6.1

ZERO-ORDER CORRELATIONS, BETA WEIGHTS AND PROPORTION OF
VARIANCE EXPLAINED BY VARIABLES RELATED TO NUMBER OF IN-
FLUENCE AND GOOD JUDGMENT NOMINATIONS RECEIVED BY ALL MPS

| Variables | Zero-Order r | B(I) | Beta(I) | $R^2$ | B(II) | Beta(II) |
|---|---|---|---|---|---|---|
| Influence Nominations | | | | | | |
| House Speeches/Questions | .58 | 5.09 | .40 | .33 | 5.13 | .40 |
| Cabinet Position | .39 | 16.24 | .36 | .43 | 15.36 | .34 |
| Party Leader | .50 | 30.78 | .36 | .54 | 30.09 | .36 |
| Committee Attendance | −.03 | 4.19 | .06 | .55 | | |
| Conservative Frontbench | .06 | 3.38 | .06 | .55 | | |
| Frequency of Cabinet Communications | .07 | .77 | .06 | .56 | | |
| Frequency of Bureaucratic Communications | .06 | .62 | .06 | .56 | | |
| Frequency of Constituency Communications | −.02 | −2.27 | −.06 | .56 | | |
| Committee Chairman | −.01 | 2.14 | .04 | .56 | | |
| Number of Bills/Resolutions Introduced | .12 | − .09 | .00 | .56 | | |
| Good Judgment Nominations | | | | | | |
| House Speeches/Questions | .53 | 1.18 | .34 | .28 | 1.26 | .36 |
| Party Leader | .49 | 8.61 | .38 | .38 | 8.16 | .36 |
| Cabinet Position | .34 | 4.07 | .33 | .47 | 3.62 | .29 |
| Conservative Frontbench | .11 | 1.62 | .11 | .48 | | |
| Frequency of Bureaucratic Communications | .09 | .24 | .09 | .49 | | |
| Committee Attendance | −.03 | .95 | .05 | .49 | | |
| Frequency of Constituency Communications | −.02 | − .35 | −.04 | .49 | | |
| Number of Bills/Resolutions Introduced | .07 | − .15 | −.03 | .49 | | |
| Frequency of Cabinet Communications | −.02 | − .11 | −.03 | .49 | | |
| Committee Chairman | −.03 | .24 | .02 | .49 | | |

leaders (r = .36) are even more active speakers in the House than are
ministers. Moreover, there also is a correlation (r = .14) between
frequency of speaking and being a frontbencher in the Conservative
party. The activity variables are also interrelated. There is a correlation of −.13 between speaking frequently and attending committee
meetings frequently, indicating that ministers and party leaders who
speak frequently in the House do not participate in the activities of

the several standing committees. Happily, one benefit that derives from using the "II" technique in regression analysis is that the effect of multicollinearity among independent variables tends to be vitiated. Also, when all predictors in an equation are considered simultaneously and the covariance among them is taken into account, as is the case in this technique, variables that initially may appear significant or trivial in univariate comparisons can change. Thus, table 6.1 indicates that when their multicollinearity and covariance are taken into account, there are only three significant predictors of influence; frequency of speaking, being a cabinet member, and holding a party leadership position. The remaining variables explain only an additional 2% of the variance. The standardized Betas suggest the two position variables do not have as great an impact on the number of influence nominations an individual receives as does the speeches variable, which is notable because the strength of the position variables in part is a statistical artifact reflecting the fact that they are binary variables (a person either holds a particular position or he does not), whereas the speeches variable has many more than two values. If we consider only position variables, however, we observe that being a party leader has a greater impact on the number of influence nominations MPs as a group receive than does being a cabinet minister. This also is the case with regard to good judgment nominations (see table 6.1).

In chapter 3 we reported that holding a formal position of leadership was the reason most frequently cited by MPs to explain the influence (and good judgment) nominations they made. Chapter 3 also indicated (and table 6.1 of the present chapter reaffirms) that among holders of positions of leadership, the level of the office has an important effect on how much influence and good judgment are ascribed to those who hold them. However, effective role performance also affects influence ascription; individual qualities that reflect effective role performance were cited frequently by MPs to explain the nominations they made. Since frequency of speaking in the House has been assumed to be an appropriate surrogate measure of effective performance and since we know that party leaders and cabinet ministers speak more frequently in the House than do committee chairmen[5] the questions arise: are cabinet ministers[6] and party leaders more often ascribed influence and good judgment because they hold higher status positions than committee chairmen or because they speak in the House more frequently (and presumably more effectively) than do committee chairmen? One would expect both factors to contribute to influence and good judgment and table 6.2 confirms this common sense expectation. There is a stronger association between top leadership status and influence and good judgment than between committee chairmanship status and these qualities. However, the only variable that remains statistically significant when both regression methods are employed is frequency of speaking and asking or answering questions in the House. By itself this variable explains 56% of the variations in influence nominations and 48% of the attributions of good judgment.

Also of interest in table 6.2 are the relatively strong negative Betas for influence and good judgment attributions on the one hand and frequency of communication with constituents on the other. We may infer from this finding that among MPs who hold formal positions of leadership one does not acquire a reputation for being influential or possessing good judgment by communicating frequently with one's constituency. Nor for that matter does one acquire a reputation for influence by introducing private members' bills and debatable resolutions, or for good judgment by communicating frequently with members of the cabinet. A simultaneous inspection of the data in tables 6.2 and 6.3 suggests that although communicating frequently with constituents is negatively associated with influence among cabinet ministers and party leaders, such communications seem to have no impact on the influence and good judgment that are attributed to MPs who do not hold top echelon positions. Conversely, the reader also may infer that communicating frequently with members of the bureaucracy enhances the influence of party leaders[7] but not of other MPs. Indeed, for every unit of increase in the frequency of bureaucratic communications on the part of party leaders there is a four unit increase in the number of influence nominations they receive. This is not the case for nonleaders (see table 6.3).

The variables that had the strongest impact on members who were neither cabinet ministers nor party leaders were: (1) speaking frequently in the House; and (2) being a frontbench member of the Conservative party. For this group of private members, holding a committee chairmanship also was positively associated with a reputation for being influential and having good judgment, although the variable did not remain statistically significant when regression method "II" was employed.

The reader also will observe from table 6.3 that we were not able to explain a very substantial proportion of the variance either in influence or good judgment when the variables "party leaders" and

TABLE 6.2

**ZERO-ORDER CORRELATIONS, BETA WEIGHTS AND PROPORTION OF VARIANCE EXPLAINED BY VARIABLES RELATED TO NUMBER OF INFLUENCE AND GOOD JUDGMENT NOMINATIONS RECEIVED BY ALL HOLDERS OF FORMAL LEADERSHIP POSITIONS**

| Variables | Zero-Order r | B(I) | Beta(I) | $R^2$ | B(II) | Beta(II) |
|---|---|---|---|---|---|---|
| Influence Nominations | | | | | | |
| House Speeches/ Questions | .75 | 10.67 | .62 | .56 | 12.93 | .74 |
| Bureaucratic Communications | .29 | 4.00 | .22 | .59 | | |
| Committee Chairman | −.38 | −.04 | .00 | .65 | | |
| Frequency of Constituency Communications | −.28 | −12.92 | −.25 | .65 | | |
| Bills/Resolutions | .16 | − 2.19 | −.08 | .65 | | |
| Committee Attendance | −.12 | 11.64 | −.10 | .66 | | |
| Party Leader | .46 | 18.33 | .24 | .66 | | |
| Cabinet Position | .18 | 16.36 | .32 | .67 | | |
| Cabinet Communications | .10 | − 0.77 | −.02 | .67 | | |
| Good Judgment Nominations | | | | | | |
| House Speeches/ Questions | .69 | 2.49 | .55 | .48 | 3.16 | .69 |
| Committee Chairman | −.39 | − .20 | .01 | .51 | | |
| Bureaucratic Communications | .18 | .80 | .17 | .53 | | |
| Party Leader | .47 | 5.32 | .27 | .55 | | |
| Frequency of Constituency Communications | −.21 | −1.95 | −.13 | .56 | | |
| Bills/Resolutions | .10 | .00 | −.08 | .56 | | |
| Cabinet Communications | −.01 | − .89 | −.11 | .56 | | |
| Cabinet Position | .15 | 3.87 | .29 | .56 | | |
| Committee Attendance | −.18 | 1.57 | .05 | .57 | | |

"cabinet" were not included among the predictors in the regression equations. In searching for a possible third powerful predictor, we turn our attention to committee activity. Until now we have employed frequency of committee attendance as a surrogate for actual participation and although this variable generally was positively associated with influence and good judgment, it did not remain in the regression equations when method "II" was used (i.e., when only those variables that maintained statistical significance in the presence of all other variables were permitted to remain in the equation).

TABLE 6.3
ZERO-ORDER CORRELATIONS, BETA WEIGHTS AND PROPORTIONS
OF VARIANCE EXPLAINED BY VARIABLES RELATED TO NUMBER OF
INFLUENCE AND GOOD JUDGMENT NOMINATIONS RECEIVED BY ALL
PRIVATE MEMBERS NOT CABINET OR PARTY LEADERS

| Variable | Zero-Order r | B(I) | Beta(I) | $R^2$ | B(II) | Beta(II) |
|---|---|---|---|---|---|---|
| Influence Nominations | | | | | | |
| House Speeches/ Questions | .42 | 2.02 | .38 | .18 | 1.90 | .35 |
| Conservative Frontbench | .39 | 5.85 | .32 | .27 | 5.72 | .31 |
| Cabinet Communications | .06 | .42 | .09 | .28 | | |
| Committee Chairman | .02 | 1.36 | .08 | .29 | | |
| Bureaucratic Communications | −.03 | −.20 | −.06 | .29 | | |
| Committee Attendance | −.04 | .43 | .02 | .29 | | |
| Frequency of Constit- uency Communications | .04 | .00 | .00 | .29 | | |
| Bills/Resolutions | .00 | −.01 | .00 | .29 | | |
| Good Judgment Nominations | | | | | | |
| Frontbench | .39 | 2.16 | .32 | .15 | 2.16 | .32 |
| House Speeches/ Questions | .34 | .51 | .26 | .21 | .51 | .26 |
| Bureaucratic Communications | .08 | .06 | .05 | .22 | | |
| Bills/Resolutions | −.04 | −.10 | −.04 | .22 | | |
| Cabinet Communications | −.07 | −.07 | −.04 | .22 | | |
| Committee Chairman | −.03 | .20 | .03 | .22 | | |
| Committee Attendance | −.02 | .14 | .02 | .22 | | |
| Frequency of Constit- uency Communications | .00 | .04 | .01 | .22 | | |

When separate regression analyses were conducted for the subsample of 34 private members for whom we have committee participation data, and the effects of both frequency of committee attendance and frequency of participation in committee affairs were considered simultaneously, we found that participation was a significant predictor of the influence ascribed to private members whereas attendance was not (see table 6.4). Indeed, frequency of participation explained almost 25% (r = .49) of the variation in the numbers of influence nominations they received and increased the total explained variation in influence ($R^2$) from 32% to 50%. It seems reasonable to assume, given this finding, that if we had had data on differences in committee participation rates for all members, our ability to explain variations in influence among private members would have been substantially enhanced.

Membership on the Conservative frontbench and speaking frequently in the House[8] were the only other variables that were significant predictors of influence and good judgment among the members of the 34 member subsample. Conventional stepwise regression indicated that communicating frequently with constituents, with members of the bureaucracy, and holding a committee chairmanship were negatively associated with the reputation for having good judgment. The first two of these variables, together with the frequent introduction of private members' bills and debatable resolu-

TABLE 6.4

ZERO-ORDER CORRELATIONS, BETA WEIGHTS AND PROPORTION OF VARIANCE EXPLAINED BY VARIABLES RELATED TO NUMBER OF INFLUENCE AND GOOD JUDGMENT NOMINATIONS RECEIVED BY SPECIAL SUBSAMPLE OF 34 MPS

| Variable | Zero-Order r | B(I) | Beta(I) | $R^2$ | B(II) | Beta(II) |
|---|---|---|---|---|---|---|
| Influence Nominations | | | | | | |
| Frontbench | .57 | 8.44 | .50 | .32 | 8.54 | .51 |
| Committee Speeches | .49 | .04 | .30 | .50 | .04 | .37 |
| House Speeches/Questions | .32 | 1.57 | .29 | .54 | 1.12 | .21 |
| Frequency of Constit- | | | | | | |
| uency Communications | −.02 | −2.26 | −.18 | .56 | | |
| Cabinet Communications | .19 | .57 | .14 | .57 | | |
| Bills/Resolutions | −.15 | − .96 | −.10 | .58 | | |
| Committee Chairman | .06 | 1.15 | .06 | .59 | | |
| Bureaucratic | | | | | | |
| Communications | .00 | − .06 | −.02 | .59 | | |
| Committee Attendance | .09 | .07 | .00 | .59 | | |
| | | | | | | |
| Good Judgment | | | | | | |
| Nominations | | | | | | |
| Frontbench | .56 | 2.70 | .54 | .31 | 2.73 | .55 |
| House Speeches/Questions | .32 | .50 | .31 | .40 | .48 | .30 |
| Cabinet Communications | .16 | .26 | .21 | .44 | | |
| Frequency of Constit- | | | | | | |
| uency Communications | −.02 | −.57 | −.15 | .46 | | |
| Committee Attendance | .00 | .65 | .09 | .46 | | |
| Committee Chairman | −.15 | −.52 | −.09 | .47 | | |
| Bureaucratic | | | | | | |
| Communications | −.04 | −.03 | −.04 | .47 | | |
| Committee Speeches | .25 | .00 | .03 | .47 | | |
| Bills/Resolutions | −.06 | .01 | .00 | .47 | | |

tions, also were negatively associated with a reputation for being influential. In fact, the constituency communications variable barely missed attaining statistical significance when we employed regression method "II." This impression that frequent communication with constituencies had a negative effect was strengthened when we compared the correlates associated with the influence of MPs from each of the four principal geographic regions (see table 6.5). In fact, it was positively associated with influence only among Western MPs. In contrast, among Quebec MPs every unit of increase in constituency communications was associated with a loss of more than three influence nominations.

Two of the principal benefits that derive from the use of regression techniques are well illustrated in table 6.5. The first, which we mentioned in our discussion of table 6.1, is that variables which appear important or trivial when univariate associations are examined can gain or lose significance when multivariate comparisons are made. For example, two performance variables, frequency of committee attendance and frequency of introducing bills and debatable resolutions, have very low zero-order correlations with influence among Atlantic MPs. Moreover, the zero-order relationships between influence on the one hand and the number of bills and resolutions introduced on the other is negative. When these relationships are set into a regression equation, however, not only do both their magnitudes increase substantially, but also the direction of the relationship between bill introduction and the number of influence nominations received by Atlantic MPs becomes positive. Conversely, an examination of the data for Western MPs indicates that a number of predictor variables that have fairly strong zero-order associations with influence become relatively trivial when they are entered in a regression analysis. The regressions for the Western MPs indicate that only three variables (holding a party leadership position, being a frontbencher in the Conservative party, and speaking frequently in the House) explain significant variations in influence and good judgment. A second benefit of regression is that it enables us to compare the impact of particular variables on different subgroups of MPs. Thus, by way of illustration, the unstandardized coefficients (B) reveal that frequency of speaking in the House has a far greater impact on the influence attributed to Quebec members than it has on the influence of members of the other three regional delegations. Again, frequent attendance at committees has a very strong positive effect on the number of influence nominations received by MPs from the Atlantic

TABLE 6.5

**ZERO-ORDER CORRELATIONS, BETA WEIGHTS AND PROPORTION OF VARIANCE EXPLAINED BY VARIABLES RELATED TO NUMBER OF INFLUENCE AND GOOD JUDGMENT NOMINATIONS RECEIVED BY MPS FROM FOUR REGIONS**

### ATLANTIC MPs

| Variable | Zero-Order r | B(I) | Beta(I) | $R^2$ | B(III) | Beta(II) |
|---|---|---|---|---|---|---|
| Influence Nominations | | | | | | |
| Party Leader | .85 | 74.8 | 1.06 | .73 | 60.37 | .85 |
| Bureaucratic Communications | −.27 | −6.73 | −.53 | .80 | −3.40 | −.26 |
| House Speeches/Questions | .47 | −1.03 | −.06 | .83 | | |
| Committee Attendance | .03 | 32.06 | .34 | .85 | | |
| Bills/Resolutions | −.09 | 21.23 | .51 | .89 | | |
| Frontbench | .06 | 11.20 | .25 | .92 | | |
| Cabinet Communications | .02 | 2.96 | .17 | .93 | | |
| Cabinet Position | .34 | −8.32 | −.14 | .94 | | |
| Committee Chairman | .02 | 5.64 | .06 | .95 | | |
| Frequency of Constituency Communications | −.26 | −.25 | −.01 | .95 | | |

### QUEBEC MPs

| Variable | Zero-Order r | B(I) | Beta(I) | $R^2$ | B(III) | Beta(II) |
|---|---|---|---|---|---|---|
| Influence Nominations | | | | | | |
| House Speeches/Questions | .73 | 16.30 | .96 | .53 | 15.41 | .91 |
| Cabinet Position | .67 | 22.95 | .41 | .71 | 24.99 | .45 |
| Committee Attendance | −.06 | 36.26 | .48 | .82 | 32.04 | .48 |
| Bills/Resolutions | .14 | −6.04 | −.15 | .87 | −7.43 | −.19 |
| Cabinet Communications | .02 | −5.72 | −.36 | .89 | −5.42 | −.34 |
| Bureaucratic Communications | −.22 | −3.07 | −.25 | .92 | −2.71 | −.22 |
| Frontbench | −.06 | −25.25 | −.27 | .96 | −23.47 | −.26 |
| Frequency of Constituency Communications | −.15 | −3.43 | −.15 | .97 | | |
| Party Leader | .14 | −12.07 | −.10 | .97 | | |
| Committee Chairman | −.10 | 1.29 | .02 | .97 | | |

*( continued on overleaf )*

**TABLE 6.5** ( *continued* )

### ATLANTIC MPs

| Variable | Zero-Order r | B(I) | Beta(I) | R² | B(III) | Beta(II) |
|---|---|---|---|---|---|---|
| Good Judgment Nominations | | | | | | |
| Party Leader | .82 | 27.10 | 1.06 | .67 | 20.97 | .82 |
| Bureaucratic Communications | .25 | 2.07 | .45 | .74 | 1.15 | .25 |
| Frontbench | .08 | 4.14 | .26 | .77 | | |
| Committee Chairman | .15 | 6.26 | .18 | .80 | | |
| Bills/Resolutions | -.16 | 6.30 | .42 | .81 | | |
| Committee Attendance | .02 | 8.76 | .26 | .83 | | |
| Cabinet Position | 20 | -5.45 | -.26 | .86 | | |
| Cabinet Communications | 03 | -.67 | -.11 | .87 | | |
| House Speeches/Questions | 41 | -.56 | -.08 | .87 | | |
| Frequency of Constituency Communications | -.27 | -.28 | -.05 | .87 | | |

### ONTARIO MPs

| Variable | Zero-Order r | B(I) | Beta(I) | R² | B(III) | Beta(II) |
|---|---|---|---|---|---|---|
| Influence Nominations | | | | | | |
| Party Leader | .49 | 33.56 | .47 | .24 | 37.96 | .46 |
| Cabinet Position | .43 | 11.74 | .37 | .44 | 12.11 | .38 |
| House Speeches/Questions | .46 | 3.29 | .27 | .52 | 3.49 | .29 |
| Bills/Resolutions | .19 | .99 | .11 | .54 | | |

### QUEBEC MPs

| Variable | Zero-Order r | B(I) | Beta(I) | R² | B(III) | Beta(II) |
|---|---|---|---|---|---|---|
| Good Judgment Nominations | | | | | | |
| House Speeches/Questions | .71 | 2.53 | .73 | .50 | 2.57 | .74 |
| Cabinet | .64 | 5.44 | .48 | .68 | 4.86 | .43 |
| Committee Attendance | -.06 | 4.21 | .30 | .78 | 4.99 | .36 |
| Bills/Resolutions | .17 | -1.38 | -.17 | .80 | | |
| Cabinet Communications | .34 | -.64 | -.20 | .83 | | |
| Frequency of Constituency Communications | .18 | .67 | .18 | .84 | | |
| Bureaucratic Communications | -.15 | -.78 | -.11 | .85 | | |
| Party Leader | .08 | -2.78 | -.12 | .85 | | |
| Committee Chairman | -.11 | -.43 | -.03 | .85 | | |
| Frontbench | -.07 | .53 | .02 | .85 | | |

### ALL WESTERN MPs

| Variable | Zero-Order r | B(I) | Beta(I) | R² | B(III) | Beta(II) |
|---|---|---|---|---|---|---|
| Influence Nominations | | | | | | |
| Party Leader | .77 | 42.26 | .55 | .60 | 47.34 | .62 |
| House Speeches/Questions | .67 | 2.88 | .31 | .67 | 2.69 | .29 |
| Frontbench | .22 | 9.71 | .22 | .72 | 9.68 | .29 |
| Committee Chairman | .31 | 5.96 | .11 | .73 | | .23 |

| | | | | | |
|---|---|---|---|---|---|
| Bureaucratic Communications | | | | | |
| Committee Chairman | .09 | .31 | .04 | .54 | |
| Frontbench | −.07 | 1.04 | .03 | .54 | |
| Committee Attendance | −.03 | −1.42 | −.02 | .54 | |
| Frequency of Constituency Communications | −.08 | −1.49 | −.02 | .54 | |
| | .11 | −.41 | −.02 | .54 | |
| Cabinet Communications | −.08 | .01 | .00 | .54 | |

**Good Judgment Nominations**

| | | | | | | |
|---|---|---|---|---|---|---|
| Cabinet Position | .45 | 3.54 | .40 | .20 | 4.07 | .46 |
| Cabinet Communications | −.40 | −.90 | −.35 | .36 | −.94 | −.36 |
| Party Leader | .30 | 5.36 | .28 | .44 | 5.60 | .29 |
| Bureaucratic Communications | .24 | .28 | .15 | .48 | | |
| House Speeches/Questions | .35 | .42 | .13 | .50 | | |
| Bills/Resolutions | .15 | .28 | .12 | .51 | | |
| Committee Attendance | .02 | .92 | .05 | .51 | | |
| Committee Chairmen | −.13 | −.33 | −.04 | .51 | | |
| Frequency of Constituency Communications | .01 | .33 | .04 | .51 | | |
| Frontbench | .01 | .54 | .03 | .51 | | |

| | | | | | |
|---|---|---|---|---|---|
| Cabinet Position | .00 | 3.62 | .08 | .74 | |
| Cabinet Communications | .16 | .70 | .06 | .74 | |
| Bureaucratic Communications | .20 | .58 | .06 | .74 | |
| Bills/Resolutions | .22 | .85 | .04 | .75 | |
| Committee Attendance | −.03 | 2.52 | −.04 | .75 | |
| Frequency of Constituency Communications | .03 | .70 | .02 | .75 | |

**Good Judgment Nominations**

| | | | | | | |
|---|---|---|---|---|---|---|
| Party Leader | .70 | 12.14 | .53 | .48 | 12.10 | .53 |
| House Speeches/Questions | .64 | .85 | .31 | .57 | .85 | .31 |
| Frontbench | .24 | 2.97 | .23 | .62 | 3.04 | .24 |
| Cabinet Position | .09 | 2.10 | .17 | .65 | | |
| Bureaucratic Communications | .20 | .24 | .09 | .66 | | |
| Committee Attendance | −.09 | −1.27 | −.06 | .66 | | |
| Cabinet Communications | .14 | .21 | .06 | .66 | | |
| Bills/Resolutions | .08 | −.20 | −.03 | .66 | | |
| Committee Chairman | .14 | −.16 | −.01 | .66 | | |
| Frequency of Constituency Communications | −.01 | .02 | .00 | .66 | | |

and Quebec delegations, a more modest but still positive impact on the influence of Western MPs, and a fairly strong negative impact on the influence that is attributed to Ontario MPs.

Turning to the correlates of good judgment, an inspection of the unstandardized Bs reveals that being a member of the cabinet is positively associated with a reputation for having good judgment among Quebec, Ontario and Western MPs whereas it has a strong negative impact on the good judgment attributed to MPs from the Atlantic provinces. Indeed, one might infer from an examination of these unstandardized regression coefficients for Atlantic MPs that being a party leader or a frontbench member of the Conservative party or a committee chairman are statuses that enhance a reputation for good judgment, whereas being a cabinet minister has the opposite effect. Of course, this is not the case, or, more correctly, this is not the inference to be drawn from the data. Rather, party leaders, frontbench Conservatives, and Liberal committee chairmen who represented Atlantic constituencies were ascribed good judgment more often than were Liberal cabinet ministers from this region. Further, good judgment was more often ascribed to Conservative frontbenchers who represented Western and Atlantic constituencies than to frontbench Conservatives from Quebec and Ontario. Frequent attendance at committees also seemed to contribute to the good judgment reputations of Quebec and Atlantic MPs. It apparently had little impact on the reputations of Ontario members, and it was fairly strongly and negatively associated with the good judgment ascribed to MPs from the West.

Three other aspects in table 6.5 merit comment. The first is the negative association between cabinet membership and a reputation for influence among Atlantic MPs. It was not surprising, given the relatively small number of influence nominations received by the average Western cabinet minister, that "cabinet" was not a significant predictor of either influence or of good judgment among Western MPs. Somewhat more surprising, given the considerable influence and good judgment attributed to Atlantic cabinet ministers (see chapter 3, tables 3.5 and 3.10), is the finding that membership in the cabinet was not a significant predictor of influence or good judgment in this group either. The reason for this is largely statistical and stems from the relatively high multicollinearity of several of the independent variables. It is not that the three ministers representing the Atlantic provinces lacked influence. Two of the three were regarded as very influential. But the data suggest that their influence rested on their extensive participation in parliamentary debate and question period and on their introduction of government bills. (The third minister participated less often in debate and introduced little of the government's programs.) The Atlantic provinces' delegation also included two top party leaders who were in frequent communication with deputy-ministers. Consequently, there was little variance left in the influence and good judgment to be explained by the cabinet variable after the prior variables were controlled.

The second point which merits attention is the degree of usefulness of the ten variables in explaining the variation in the numbers of influence and good judgment nominations received by MPs from the four regions. For the Quebec MPs we find that virtually all of the positional and performance variables were significantly related to the number of influence nominations they received. Among Atlantic MPs only one positional variable, party leadership, and one performance variable, frequency of communication with top echelon bureaucrats, were significant predictors of influence when regression method "II" was employed. However, the effect of party leadership on influence was an exceedingly strong one; by itself it explained 73% of the variation in the number of influence nominations received by Atlantic MPs. Because so many of the independent variables were significantly correlated with influence among Quebec MPs and since party leadership had such a strong impact on the influence of Atlantic MPs we were able to explain virtually all the variance in the dependent variable for these two subgroups (97% and 95% respectively). Among Western MPs, two positional variables (party leadership and frontbench membership in the Conservative party) and one performance variable (frequency of speaking in the House) were the only statistically significant predictors of influence. The party leadership variable together with cabinet membership and frequency of speaking in the House helped explain the influence ascribed to Ontario MPs. However, although the association between party leadership and influence accounted for 60% of the variance in the influence ascribed Western MPs, it explained only 24% for Ontario MPs. Consequently, the ten variable set of predictors explained 75% of the variations in influence among Western MPs but only 54% of the variance among Ontario MPs.

The number of variables that are significant predictors of good judgment and the strength of their associations also account for the fact that we are able to explain a larger proportion of the variance in the number of good judgment nominations received by Atlantic and

Quebec as opposed to Western and Ontario members. Thus, for example, one position variable, party leadership, explained 67% of the variance in the good judgment nominations of Atlantic MPs while one performance variable, frequency of House speaking, explained 50% of the variance for Quebec MPs. Two other variables increased the proportion of explained variance to 78% for the Quebec MPs and to 77% for the Atlantic provinces MPs. In contrast, the best predictor of the variance in good judgment nominations received by Ontario MPs, cabinet membership, explained only 20%. Two other variables (party leadership and frequency of communication with members of the cabinet) raised this to 44% and seven other variables increased this figure to 51%. Among Western MPs party leadership was a powerful predictor of good judgment and explained fully 48% of the variations in the number of their nominations. Frequency of speaking in the House and frontbench membership in the Conservative party raised the proportion of explained variance for Western MPs to 62% but the other seven variables increased this figure to only 66%.

Finally, the pattern of positive and negative relationships among the independent and dependent variables, the third point worthy of note, suggested party-related effects were present in the data. The introduction of bills and debatable resolutions was negatively associated with the influence attributed to Quebec MPs but positively associated with the influence ascribed to Atlantic province MPs. The Quebec delegation largely was made up of backbench members of the governing Liberal party from whom the frequent introduction of bills and debatable resolutions might be regarded unfavorably. In a sense, their introduction could be construed as implicit condemnation of the government for its failure to deal with the matters in question. The Atlantic parliamentary delegation, however, included a substantial proportion of Conservative MPs—members of the official opposition. Engaging in activities that are critical of the government is appropriate for members of an opposition party; indeed, they are expected.

When we compared the correlates associated with influence and good judgment among government and opposition MPs we found there were indeed some interesting differences. Speaking frequently in the House contributed much more to a reputation for influence among governing than opposition MPs and communicating frequently with constituents reduced the influence of government MPs more than it did the opposition. Moreover, communicating frequently with cabinet ministers had a strong negative effect on both the influence and the good judgment attributed to governing MPs, whereas it was modestly but still positively associated with the dependent variables among opposition MPs. Interestingly, however, the introduction of bills and debatable resolutions (which we assumed would not contribute much to the influence and good judgment of governing MPs) was positively associated with influence among the governing Liberals but negatively related to the influence of opposition MPs (see table 6.6). However, when we removed cabinet members, the house leader, and party whips from the population of governing MPs and examined the correlates of influence of Liberal backbenchers, we found that frequent introduction of bills and resolutions was negatively associated with both influence and good judgment—as were frequent communications with the cabinet and with top echelon members of the bureaucracy (see table 6.7). These negatively signed Bs in the regression of Liberal backbenchers suggest that the formal and informal behavior of government backbenchers in a British-model parliamentary system must take place within certain vaguely defined but still understandable limits. We may speculate that it is appropriate for a government backbencher to contact a cabinet minister periodically over a policy matter or to discuss with him a constituent's problem; that it is all right for him to contact a deputy-minister occasionally when he needs the assistance of the bureaucracy; and that it even is all right to introduce a private members' bill once in a while or a debatable resolution, about which the member feels strongly. It seems reasonable to assume that such actions not only are considered appropriate but, in fact, are encouraged by cabinet members and by senior party colleagues, for they are consistent with a model of the backbencher as a socially concerned, hard working, and responsible member of parliament.

It may not be all right, however, for a government backbencher to do these things too often, for too frequent contacts with cabinet colleagues and high echelon bureaucrats and too many private bills and resolutions introduced into the House may seem to be irresponsible. It is likely that an offending member who crosses the line that separates appropriate and responsible from inappropriate and frivolous behavior is told in a nice way, usually by the party whip, that he is becoming something of a pest and an embarrassment to his party colleagues in the government; that he might more appropriately concern himself with doing the "homework" required to speak effectively in the House—when he is called upon—and attending and

# TABLE 6.6

## ZERO-ORDER CORRELATIONS, BETA WEIGHTS AND PROPORTION OF VARIANCE EXPLAINED BY VARIABLES RELATED TO NUMBER OF INFLUENCE AND GOOD JUDGMENT NOMINATIONS RECEIVED BY GOVERNMENT AND OPPOSITION MPS

### GOVERNMENT MPs

| Variables | Zero-Order r | B(I) | Beta(I) | $R^2$ | B(II) | Beta(II) |
|---|---|---|---|---|---|---|
| **Influence Nominations** | | | | | | |
| House Speeches/Questions | .70 | 10.91 | .61 | .49 | 10.74 | .60 |
| Cabinet Communications | -.12 | -3.14 | -.22 | .55 | -3.36 | -.24 |
| Cabinet Position | .55 | 8.61 | .24 | .60 | 9.45 | .26 |
| Party Leader | .18 | 16.29 | .13 | .62 | | |
| Frequency of Constituency Communications | -.05 | -2.22 | -.09 | .62 | | |
| Bills/Resolutions | .15 | .49 | .03 | .52 | | |
| Bureaucratic Communications | -.10 | .32 | .03 | .62 | | |
| Committee Chairman | -.08 | -.58 | -.01 | .62 | | |
| Committee Attendance | -.06 | 3.56 | .00 | .62 | | |
| **Good Judgment Nominations** | | | | | | |
| House Speeches/Questions | .64 | 2.53 | .59 | .42 | 2.58 | .60 |
| Cabinet Communications | .35 | -1.52 | -.44 | .63 | -1.50 | -.44 |
| Cabinet Position | .55 | 2.48 | .28 | .70 | 2.56 | .29 |
| Bureaucratic Communications | .04 | .34 | .15 | .72 | .40 | .17 |
| Party Leader | .22 | 3.91 | .13 | .74 | 3.99 | .13 |
| Committee Chairmen | -.14 | -.80 | -.08 | .74 | | |
| Committee Attendance | .02 | 1.63 | .09 | .75 | | |
| Bills/Resolutions | .15 | .22 | .06 | .75 | | |
| Frequency of Constituency Communications | -.03 | .28 | .04 | .75 | | |

### OPPOSITION MPs

| Variables | Zero-Order r | B(I) | Beta(I) | $R^2$ | B(II) | Beta(II) |
|---|---|---|---|---|---|---|
| **Influence Nominations** | | | | | | |
| Party Leader | .77 | 42.04 | .65 | .59 | 42.60 | .66 |
| House Speeches/Questions | .60 | 3.08 | .26 | .65 | 3.07 | .26 |
| Frontbench | .09 | 5.96 | .15 | .68 | 6.44 | .16 |
| Bureaucratic Communications | .08 | .57 | .05 | .69 | | |
| Bills/Resolutions | .07 | -1.64 | -.06 | .69 | | |
| Committee Chairman | .15 | .62 | .05 | .70 | | |
| Committee Attendance | .05 | 3.22 | .05 | .70 | | |
| Frequency of Constituency Communications | -.05 | -.92 | -.01 | .70 | | |
| **Good Judgment Nominations** | | | | | | |
| Party Leader | .65 | 10.75 | .54 | .42 | 10.87 | .55 |
| House Speeches/Questions | .52 | .92 | .26 | .47 | .86 | .24 |
| Frontbench | .13 | 2.06 | .17 | .51 | 2.32 | .19 |
| Bills/Resolutions | -.05 | -1.26 | -.16 | .53 | | |
| Bureaucratic Communications | -.09 | .22 | .07 | .55 | | |
| Frequency of Constituency Communications | -.05 | .35 | .04 | .55 | | |
| Cabinet Communications | .13 | .15 | .03 | .55 | | |
| Committee Attendance | .05 | .56 | .03 | .55 | | |

TABLE 6.7

ZERO-ORDER CORRELATIONS, BETA WEIGHTS AND PROPORTION
OF VARIANCE EXPLAINED BY VARIABLES RELATED TO
NUMBER OF INFLUENCE AND GOOD JUDGMENT NOMINATIONS
RECEIVED BY LIBERAL BACKBENCHERS ONLY

| Variable | Zero-order r | B(I) | Beta(I) | $R^2$ | B(II) | Beta(II) |
|---|---|---|---|---|---|---|
| Influence Nominations | | | | | | |
| House Speeches/Questions | .35 | 1.31 | .41 | .12 | 1.36 | .43 |
| Cabinet Communications | −.22 | −.44 | −.33 | .22 | −.44 | −.32 |
| Committee Attendance | .16 | 1.12 | .15 | .24 | | |
| Bureaucratic Communications | −.12 | −.09 | −.09 | .25 | | |
| Frequency of Constituency Communications | .01 | .37 | .10 | .25 | | |
| Bills/Resolutions | .07 | −.06 | −.04 | .25 | | |
| | | | | | | |
| Good Judgment Nominations | | | | | | |
| Cabinet Communications | −.38 | −.46 | −.41 | .15 | −.42 | −.38 |
| House Speeches/Questions | .06 | .41 | .16 | .17 | | |
| Committee Attendance | .14 | .76 | .12 | .19 | | |
| Bills/Resolutions | −.05 | −.04 | −.04 | .19 | | |
| Bureaucratic Communications | .06 | −.02 | −.02 | .19 | | |
| Frequency of Constituency Communications | −.15 | −.05 | −.01 | .19 | | |

participating in the standing committees of which he is a member.
(Note the positively signed Bs between speeches, committee attendance, and influence and good judgment.) He probably will be
reminded that the standing committee system was strengthened and
restructured to give members such as himself a larger and more
effective role in the conduct of parliamentary affairs.[9] Most government backbenchers will modify their behavior after receiving such a
message. Others, for a variety of reasons, will not, but they also will
not have good judgment ascribed to them, nor, apparently, will they
be considered influential. What our tables do not tell us is precisely
how many communications with ministers and deputy-ministers are
too many and under what conditions (when six telephone calls to
one cabinet minister are acceptable and two phone calls to another
minister are unacceptable) they detract from rather than enhance a
government backbencher's reputation for possessing influence and
good judgment.

Our tables also do not tell us why more influence and good
judgment are not ascribed to opposition MPs who communicate

frequently with constituents and with cabinet members and high echelon bureaucrats on behalf of constituents. We already have demonstrated that the majority of opposition members, like those in the governing Liberal party, engaged in these kinds of activities. Moreover, we also have shown that a majority of the MPs—again regardless of party affiliation—felt they had been successful in their efforts on behalf of constituents. Thus we may infer that the political leaders of the government and top level bureaucrats facilitate efforts by all MPs to assist constituents with their problems because they believe these activities are legitimate and that in carrying them out MPs perform a very important political function. Why then, we must ask, does not status, and hence influence, accrue to members of parliament who perform these tasks most energetically? Moreover, since they do not contribute to a member's reputation for being influential, while participating in House and committee debate does, why do not more MPs eschew the former for the latter?

One reason that MPs do not participate more in House debate is that the government places constraints upon its backbenchers, assuming this expedites the passage of its program through the House. A second reason is that the leaders of the opposition parties are recognized by the speaker far more often than are opposition backbenchers. Since each of the parties is allotted only its "fair share" (see note 7, chapter 4) of debate time one effect of this practice is to limit the amount of time available to opposition backbenchers.

With regard to the large number of MPs who perform what we have termed delegate-servant functions (i.e., ascertaining constituents' views and performing services for them), our feeling is that most MPs find this orientation a congenial one. Our belief is strengthened by the knowledge that the only specific expectations many MPs had for the positions they assumed were that they would be "representatives" and "ombudsmen." They come to parliament expecting to perform delegate-servant functions and their initial expectations undoubtedly are reinforced by post-election socialization by party leaders and parliamentary old hands.[10] They probably learn, for example, that the public expects them to run errands and that their reelection, in part at least, depends upon how successful they are at this task. They also may learn that it is difficult to represent their districts unless they know what the people in them are thinking, so they probably are encouraged to apprise themselves of constituents' opinions. Yet another thing they may learn is that party leaders expect to take the lead in discussing the great issues of the day, and that their principal tasks, at least initially, are to observe and support their leaders. (We also know from recurring complaints voiced by backbenchers that a shortage of time and personal staff makes it difficult for them to do the homework required to participate knowledgeably and effectively in House debates on major policy issues.) Accordingly, personal expectations for the position of member of parliament, post-election socialization and empirical experiences combine to structure their participation in delegate-servant directions. These tasks come to feel natural. They also come to be taken for granted—despite the fact that one's colleagues really do not know whether they are being performed effectively. After all, delegate-servant tasks are carried out largely behind the scenes. In contrast, one participates in House debates in full view of one's colleagues. Thus, effective performance can be more readily assessed. Moreover, since the opportunity to participate in House debate is relatively restricted, the activity is not simply taken for granted.

An analogy can be made between formal and informal parliamentary participation and the attribution of influence to MPs on the one hand and university research and teaching activities and the ascription of influence to professors on the other. Effective teaching, at least in United States and Canadian universities, generally is taken for granted. The implicit assumption is that anyone can teach and, therefore, that all professors are good teachers. The assumption is rarely, if ever, tested, however, since professors seldom observe their colleagues in teaching situations. In contrast, no assumption is made either that anyone can conduct research or that all professors are good researchers. Since meritorious research cannot be taken for granted a premium is placed on visible examples of high quality research (i.e., that which merits publication). Initial appointments to university positions, subsequent promotion to tenure, not to mention status and influence within one's own department and discipline, are based almost entirely upon a professor's record of scholarly achievement rather than on his teaching ability. If one substitutes informal parliamentary activities (such as communicating with cabinet members and bureaucrats on behalf of constituents) for teaching and formal participation in House debates for scholarly research, perhaps one can better understand why even MPs who are most energetic in performing the former tasks seemingly have little or no influence ascribed to them for their efforts. Although some readers may feel that the analogy we have drawn between two types of parliamentary and university activities and the ascription of influence to members of these institutions is not entirely appropriate,[11] we believe it does enhance understanding and merits consideration. In the concluding chapter we again will discuss the relationship or, more accurately, the lack of a relationship between the performance of delegate-servant functions and influence.

## MULTIPLE DISCRIMINANT FUNCTION ANALYSIS

Given the skewed distributions of the two dependent variables, we relied upon triangulation to delineate the position and performance variables that were significantly correlated with variations in the levels of influence and good judgment. The multiple discriminant function technique was used to check the results of the regression analyses. Our decision not to report the results in detail was strongly influenced by the fact that although the specific variables that were significant in each analysis sometimes differed, the results generated by both techniques were essentially similar. The principal differences were that "cabinet communications" and "bureaucratic communications" attained statistical significance or came close to attaining significance a number of times in the regression but not in the discriminant function analyses, whereas "committee chairmen" attained or came close to attaining statistical significance a number of times in the multiple discriminant function analyses but not in the regressions (see tables 6.8 and 6.9). The fact that there were some variations among specific significant indicators is not surprising given that: (a) in order to be used in the discriminant function analyses the dependent variables had to be converted from variables to attributes (i.e., the number of nominations for each MP had to be trichotomized on a "none," "some," and "many" vote basis); and (b) the two techniques treat the assignment of interaction effects differently. What is important in our view is the extent to which both statistical techniques corroborated the subjective assessment by MPs of the basis of influence in the Canadian parliamentary system. The occupancy of high-level leadership positions and effective role performance predicted influence and the closely-related quality we termed "good judgment." With respect to performance, speaking frequently in the House emerged as the single best predictor of both influence and good judgment. The fact that a second dimension of formal activity, participation in the affairs of standing committees, emerged as another important predictor of influence among the 34 MPs for whom we have relevant data, strongly suggests that the principal

## TABLE 6.8
## A COMPARISON OF SIGNIFICANT PREDICTORS OF INFLUENCE NOMINATIONS GENERATED BY REGRESSION AND MULTIPLE DISCRIMINANT ANALYSIS

| Group | Significant Predictors | |
|---|---|---|
| | Using Regression | Using Discriminant Function |
| MPs | House speeches,[a] cabinet position, party leadership position | Cabinet position, House speeches, party leadership position, frontbench position, committee attendance |
| Formal Leaders | House speeches | House speeches, cabinet position |
| Private Members (Other Than Party Leader and Cabinet Member) | House speeches, frontbench position | House speeches, frontbench position, committee attendance, committee chairman |
| 34 MP Subsample | Frontbench position, committee speeches, House speeches | Committee speeches, frontbench position |
| Atlantic MPs | Party leadership position, bureaucratic communications | House speeches |
| Quebec MPs | House speeches, cabinet position, committee attendance, bills and resolutions, cabinet communications, bureaucratic communications, frontbench position | House speeches, cabinet position, party leadership position, committee attendance |
| Ontario MPs | Party Leadership position, cabinet position, House speeches | Party leadership position, House speeches, cabinet position, committee chairman |
| Western MPs | Party leadership position, House speeches, frontbench position | House speeches, party leadership position, bureaucratic communications |
| Opposition MPs | Party leadership position, House speeches, frontbench position | House speeches, party leadership position, frontbench position |
| Liberal MPs | House speeches, cabinet communications, cabinet position | Cabinet position, House speeches, committee chairman |
| Liberal Backbenchers Only | House speeches, cabinet communications | House speeches, committee attendance |

a. Throughout this table "House speeches" denotes the frequency of speech and questions, or in the case of cabinet ministers, speeches and replies to questions.

measure of a member of parliament remains his ability to participate in the "talking" that historically has been the raison d'etre of parliaments. It seems to matter very little whether the individual being judged is a cabinet minister or a backbencher, a newly-elected or a veteran member, a member of a governing or of an opposition party, or a representative of one region as opposed to another. The more frequently he speaks the greater will be the influence and good judgment ascribed to him. Since, regardless of whether regression or a multiple discriminant multivariate mode of analysis is employed, the positional and performance variables that explain variations in influence almost always also explain variations in good judgment, and because we clearly have demonstrated (chapter 3) that the influence and good judgment measures are very strongly correlated, we will restrict our focus in the remainder of this book to the incremental measure of the influence ascribed to MPs.

Both the multiple discriminant and the regression analyses enable us to explain a substantial proportion of the overall differences in the number of nominations for influence received by MPs. In the case of discriminant function analysis, the predictor variables were used to assign individual cases to one of the three categories of the dependent variable. The proportion of cases that were correctly grouped, are analogous to the proportion of variance explained by a regression analysis. As may be seen from an inspection of table 6.10, when discriminant function analyses were used, the predictor variables were best able to group MPs who received no influence nominations (e.g., backbench Liberal MPs who did not speak frequently in the House or participate extensively in committee affairs). On the average we were able to correctly group approximately 80% of such individuals. The discriminant function analysis also was able to group about two thirds of the MPs who received a "considerable" number of nominations, as, for example, cabinet ministers from Quebec and top echelon party leaders from all other regions who spoke frequently in the House and who frequently communicated with highest echelon civil servants. However, we only were able to group about one third of the MPs who received "some" influence nominations (e.g., Liberal MPs who participate extensively in committee work but who do not introduce a large number of PMBs and/or who do not communicate frequently with ministers and high level bureaucrats).

There are a number of methodological reasons why the ten predictor variables were relatively unsuccessful in correctly grouping MPs in the middle category of the dependent variable. Two may be particu-

TABLE 6.9

**A COMPARISON OF SIGNIFICANT PREDICTORS OF GOOD JUDGMENT NOMINATIONS GENERATED BY REGRESSION AND MULTIPLE DISCRIMINANT ANALYSIS**

| Group | Significant Predictors | |
|---|---|---|
| | Using Regression | Using Discriminant Function |
| All MPs | House speeches, party leadership position, cabinet position | Cabinet position, party leadership position, frontbench position, House speeches |
| Formal Leaders | House speeches | House speeches, cabinet position |
| Private Members (Other Than Party Leader and Cabinet Member) | Frontbench position, House speeches | House speeches, frontbench position |
| 34 MP Subsample | Frontbench position, House speeches | House speeches, frontbench position |
| Atlantic MPs | Party leadership position, bureaucratic communications | House speeches, party leadership position, committee attendance |
| Quebec MPs | House speeches, cabinet position, committee attendance | House speeches, cabinet position, party leadership position |
| Ontario MPs | Cabinet position, cabinet communications, party leadership position | Cabinet position, party leadership position, frontbench position |
| Western MPs | Party leadership position, House speeches, frontbench position | House speeches, frontbench position, bureaucratic communications |
| Opposition MPs | Party leadership position, House speeches, frontbench position | Party leadership position, House speeches, frontbench position |
| Liberal MPs | House speeches, cabinet communications, cabinet position, bureaucratic communications, party leadership position | Cabinet position, House speeches, party leadership position |
| Liberal Backbenchers | Cabinet communications | No significant predictors (cabinet communications and bureaucratic communications two strongest predictors) |

TABLE 6.10

PROPORTION OF MPS WHO RECEIVE "NONE" "SOME" AND
"CONSIDERABLE" NOMINATIONS FOR INFLUENCE AND
GOOD JUDGMENT THAT ARE CORRECTLY GROUPED BY
MULTIPLE DISCRIMINANT ANALYSIS

| Group | Attribute Being Explained | Percent Correctly Grouped[a] of: | | | |
| --- | --- | --- | --- | --- | --- |
| | | None | Some | Many | All |
| All MPs | Influence | 73.4 | 35.2 | 75.0 | 65.0 |
| | Good Judgment | 85.1 | 18.2 | 80.0 | 67.7 |
| All Private Members Other than Cabinet and Party Leaders | Influence | 70.4 | 48.3 | 52.9 | 63.2 |
| | Good Judgment | 77.9 | 23.6 | 66.6 | 64.1 |
| All Formal Leaders | Influence | 80.0 | 18.5 | 60.6 | 51.2 |
| | Good Judgment | 68.9 | 60.0 | 54.8 | 61.2 |
| 34 MP Subsample | Influence | 66.6 | 58.3 | 50.0 | 61.7 |
| | Good Judgment | 72.7 | 55.5 | 66.6 | 67.6 |
| Atlantic MPs | Influence | 86.6 | 37.5 | 44.4 | 62.5 |
| | Good Judgment | 82.3 | 14.3 | 87.5 | 65.7 |
| Quebec MPs | Influence | 91.6 | 26.6 | 90.0 | 78.0 |
| | Good Judgment | 88.6 | 28.5 | 100.0 | 78.0 |
| Ontario MPs | Influence | 89.7 | 31.0 | 63.6 | 67.4 |
| | Good Judgment | 100.0 | 11.1 | 81.8 | 70.7 |
| Western MPs | Influence | 85.0 | 31.5 | 90.0 | 71.0 |
| | Good Judgment | 90.2 | 16.6 | 80.0 | 69.5 |
| All Opposition MPs | Influence | 67.6 | 43.4 | 61.1 | 61.4 |
| | Good Judgment | 73.5 | 42.3 | 66.6 | 65.1 |
| Liberal MPs | Influence | 85.7 | 29.1 | 81.8 | 67.5 |
| | Good Judgment | 94.8 | 0.0 | 90.0 | 70.8 |
| Liberal Backbench | Influence | 68.4 | 29.6 | 50.0 | 57.8 |
| | Good Judgment[b] | | | | |

a. Because we divided influence and good judgment nominations into three groups (i.e., none, some, and many) we would expect to correctly group 33% of the respondents in each group and 33% of All MPs simply by chance.
b. None of the position or speech variables achieved statistical significance as a predictor of good judgment.

larly important. A majority of the predictor variables employed in the discriminant analysis were dichotomous variables whereas the dependent variable was trichotomous. Had we simply dichotomized the dependent variable into, let us say, those MPs who received 0–2 votes (on the assumption that MPs who received one or two votes were almost randomly selected by the nominators) and those who received three or more nominations, we would have substantially improved our ability to group MPs correctly. Second, although some of the predictor variables discriminated admirably among the three groups (e.g., frequency of speeches by MPs in the House and in committees), and others discriminated the "none" and "some" groups from the "considerable" (e.g., number of bills and resolutions introduced in the House) very few discriminated the middle from the two polar groups.

In addition to methodological factors, we found, through a cursory inspection of other variables in the data set, that there were very few that clearly differentiated MPs in the middle category of influence from MPs in the two end groups (see Appendix B). At times we found a monotonic progression in the values of the variables that distinguished the three groups of MPs. For example, we found that MPs in the middle category were better educated and were derived from higher socioeconomic origins than MPs who received no influence nominations, but they were not as well educated nor did they derive from social origins as high as the MPs who received a considerable number of such votes. However, such differences did not occur with great frequency. At other times, the values of variables for MPs who received some and a considerable number of votes were relatively similar and differed from those who received no votes while for the values of still other variables, the opposite was true. These patterns suggested there were empirical as well as statistical reasons why the middle group of MPs could not be clearly distinguished. They lead us to ask: what does it mean for some MPs to secure 1–5 votes in a situation in which the majority receives no recognition and a few receive a great deal of recognition? Our feeling is that such individuals may not be sufficiently visible to their vote-giving colleagues to create a consensus that they either deserve or do not deserve recognition. We may speculate that one reason for this is that every parliament has a very substantial group of "comers," so many, in fact, that vote-givers find it difficult to distinguish those who really merit recognition for being influential. A second reason may be that, although they may have the qualities that merit recognition, for a variety of reasons (e.g., short parliamentary tenure, middle-level leadership positions) they may not have had the opportunity to demonstrate to other than a small group (e.g., colleagues on a standing committee) that they deserve a vote for influence. If and when they get the opportunity to display their talents fairly frequently to a wider audience of parliamentary colleagues (the average committee, after all, is comprised of approximately 20 members) they also may receive more votes.

In addition to these low profile MPs, there is a second group who might occupy this middle range—those who are competent, hard-working and "solid" but not outstanding performers, the kind who may make excellent assistant whips or deputy chairmen of the caucuses but who normally are not considered for positions such as cabinet minister or house leader. MPs who fall into this category probably are House veterans who, over a period of time, have earned the respect and affection of colleagues—a small number of whom may have been impressed sufficiently with their "solidity" to vote for them.

## SUMMARY

In this chapter we have examined the relationships among several positional and performance variables on the one hand and the ascription of influence and good judgment on the other. We found that positional variables are strongly related to receiving votes for being influential and possessing good judgment; the higher the level of the position, the more votes one receives. When we control for position, we find that the frequency with which position-holders speak and ask or answer questions in the House distinguishes those who receive many nominations from those who do not. However, holding a high level position and participating frequently in House debates are not synonyms of influence. If they were, all, or at least most, cabinet ministers would be highly influential, which is not the case. Other variables affect the level of influence ascribed to cabinet members and to top leaders in the opposition party. By way of illustration, the influence of cabinet ministers seemingly is enhanced if they frequently introduce government programs into the House, while the influence of opposition leaders who communicate frequently with highest echelon bureaucrats seems to be greater than that of those who do not.

The two dependent variables were not normally distributed. Consequently, we used a second multivariate technique, multiple discriminant function analysis, to check the results obtained by using regression. Happily, they were relatively similar. Both techniques, regression and multiple discriminant analysis, enabled us to identify the positional and behavioral attributes of MPs who either have a considerable amount of influence or no influence. We were less successful in delineating the attributes of individuals who received some, but not many, influence nominations. We speculated that the latter have some of the qualities and attributes of people who are widely recognized as influential. However, they may not have enough, or enough of their colleagues may not know that they have them, for there to be wide agreement that they deserve recognition. Despite our difficulty in identifying individuals who have some but not a great deal of influence, the analyses did suggest that government members who held committee chairmanships and/or spoke fairly frequently in the House and who also were extensively engaged in committee work but who did not introduce too many bills and resolutions and who also did not communicate too frequently with cabinet ministers and high level bureaucrats were ascribed some influence. In the opposition parties, a position on the frontbench, fairly frequent participation in House debates and question period and extensive participation in the work of the House's standing committees distinguish MPs who are ascribed some influence from those who are not. (A more complete list of the attributes of those with "some" and also "no" and "considerable" influence may be found in Appendix B).

Since the analyses revealed that the relatively crude indicators of performance and position that we used did explain a substantial proportion of the variations in the number of influence and good judgment nominations MPs received, in the next chapter we shall try to delineate the factors that explain variations in the levels of individual participation in some of the more formal aspects of parliamentary activity. In chapter 8 we will try to explain why some MPs occupy leadership positions while others do not.

## Chapter 7

# THE CORRELATES OF PARTICIPATION

## INTRODUCTION

The acquisition of a reputation for being influential is principally dependent upon holding a position of parliamentary or party leadership and participating in certain formal activities of the House. In the next chapter we will focus on the acquisition of leadership positions. This chapter tries to delineate some of the significant correlates of formal participation in: (1) House debates and question period; (2) the introduction of private members' bills and debatable resolutions; and (3) the deliberations of standing committees. These may help explain why some MPs participate extensively in parliament's formal affairs while others do not. We should be able to ascertain with greater certainty whether differences in participation are functions of certain characteristics of the legislative environment or of the attributes of individual members. It may also be the case that differences in participation are rooted in MPs political recruitment experiences, their reactions to their first political activity, perhaps even in the politicizing experiences of their childhoods. Whatever the case, the analyses in this chapter should shed considerable light on these and a number of related questions.

## MOTIVATION DETERMINANTS OF PARTICIPATION

To engage in political activity an individual must have both the desire and the opportunity to participate.[1] With respect to parliament, the motivation to participate probably is more important than, and certainly antecedent to, the opportunity to participate. This is not to say that relative opportunity does not affect participation rates. It does. We already have noted that over the years a series of procedural changes has eroded both the time and instances available for private members to participate in parliamentary affairs. We also discussed the strong informal pressures on a government's back-benchers to restrict participation in House debates and question period. Certain other activities restrict all MPs, regardless of party. However, it can be argued that the reformed committee system has actually increased the opportunities for effective backbench partici-pation and it therefore seems reasonable to assume that variations in individual participation, in part, are a function of differences in MPs' motivations.

The assumption that the study of motivation is critical for under-standing elite behavior is neither new nor controversial. As the author of a recent book on French Deputies points out, "numerous other scholars have independently come to the same conclusion: active political participation must be explained by internal motivat-ing forces."[2] In one of the earliest attempts to measure systemati-cally the motivations of political elites, Wahlke, Eulau, Buchanan and Ferguson argued persuasively for the conceptualization of motiva-tions in terms of individual role perceptions.[3] More recently, the framework they developed has been applied to such diverse legisla-tive settings as the U.S. Congress, the Chilean Senate, and the Canadian House of Commons.[4] On the other hand, several other scholars have critized the role approach as being too restricted. Barber, for example, makes this argument and offers instead the some-what broader personality concepts of individual character and style.[5] Building upon Barber's earlier motivation typology of Connecticut state legislators,[6] James Payne and Oliver Woshinsky have developed what they call an incentive theory of elite behavior that focuses upon the motives impelling the individual to become involved in politics,[7] whereas others, such as Joseph Schlesinger, advocate the conceptual-ization of motivations in terms of individual political ambitions.[8]

Rather than joining this debate (all of these approaches have demonstrated an ability to explain significant aspects of elite behav-ior) or attempting to specify a priori which of these approaches or motivational constructs best explains MP participation in parliament, we have attempted to construct several measures of elite motivations derived from (or at least consistent with) each of these theories. In all we generated 22 motivational indicators. These include: eight

variables that tap member role perceptions;[9] five variables that tap
the respondents' ambitions for higher public or parliamentary office;
four measures of the incentives MPs cite for seeking a seat in
parliament, and five variables that delineate the member's general
orientation toward politics and toward his position as MP. The latter
category includes a measure of the member's political ideology, two
variables that measure his satisfaction or dissatisfaction with the
work of a MP, and three variables that relate to his sense of personal
and institutional efficacy and/or effectiveness. These variables were
included in the analysis because of our belief that individuals who
have had a negative reaction to House work, or who are skeptical,
even cynical, about the effectiveness of the role they play in parliament, or of the role that parliament as an institution plays in society,
will be less motivated to participate in parliamentary activities than
will individuals with more positive orientations.

## THE EFFECTS OF MOTIVATION

Table 7.1 presents the results of regression analyses of the motivational determinants of: (1) speaking and asking questions in the
House, labeled "debate" in the tables; (2) introducing legislation and
debatable resolutions, an activity we label "legislation"; and (3)
speaking in committees by the subsample of 34 MPs, labeled "committees."[10]  The first column in this and the four succeeding tables
presents the zero-order Pearson correlations (r) between the independent variables and the dependent participation variables. Column 2
reports the unstandardized regression coefficients (B) for the variables that are statistically significant predictors of participation (a
technique we labeled method "II" in the preceding chapter) whereas
column 3 presents the standardized regression coefficients (Beta) for
the statistically significant predictors of participation. The figures at
the bottom of column 1 in these tables are coefficients of multiple
determination ($R^2$) and indicate the proportion of total variance in
the participation variable that is explained by the motivation variables in the analysis. Since both the "debate" and "legislation"
variables are factor score variables and hence are normally distributed, and since we have complete committee participation data
only for a subsample of 34 MPs, we have not buttressed these
regression analyses with discriminant function analyses as we do in
chapters 6 and 8.

Inspection of the zero-order correlations and of the coefficients of multiple determination in table 7.1 indicates that motivations are important determinants of parliamentary participation.[11] Inspection suggests, as well, some tentative generalizations regarding the relative importance of the several conceptualizations of motivation discussed above. First, although the multiple correlations in these tables clearly demonstrate that we are not able to predict participation from motivation as well as we were able to predict influence from participation, we can explain between 7% and 46% of the variance in each of the three participation measures. More importantly, our ability to explain participation is greatest for the two types of participation—speaking and asking questions in the House and speaking in committee—that we found were the strongest predictors of individual influence in parliament. The set of motivation variables explains more than 20% of the variation in House debate and almost 50% of the variation in committee participation—figures that compare favorably with the results obtained in similar studies of other elite populations in Canada and elsewhere.

Second, it is apparent from the zero-order correlations (r) that the relative importance of the subsets of motivation variables (and thus of the motivation theories they represent) varies according to the type of participation in question. Generally, the role perception and political ambition variables (particularly the latter) are the best predictors of debate in the House. The ambition variables alone explain more than 15% of the variation in this dependent variable. The political orientation variables, in contrast, are the strongest of the significant correlates of committee participation, and the personal ideology variable is the single best predictor of whether MPs introduce bills and debatable resolutions in the House. Although there also is some support for the incentive theory in these data—the directions of the incentive-participation relationships conform quite well to Woshinsky's hypothesis that policy-motivated legislators will be more active in the legislative process than those motivated by a sense of civic duty or by external pressure—none of the incentive relationships is statistically significant[12] and none approaches the sizes of the relationships between the participation variables on the one hand and the ambition, orientation, or even the role perception categories on the other.

The differences in the relative importance of the various motivation variables for the three forms of participation suggest that what

**TABLE 7.1**

**CURRENT ATTITUDINAL AND MOTIVATIONAL DETERMINANTS OF MP PARTICIPATION IN DEBATE AND QUESTION PERIOD (DEBATE), THE INTRODUCTION OF BILLS AND DEBATABLE RESOLUTIONS (LEGISLATION) AND COMMITTEE DEBATE (COMMITTEE)**

| Variable | Debate | | | Legislation | | | Committee | | |
|---|---|---|---|---|---|---|---|---|---|
| | r | B | Beta | r | B | Beta | r | B | Beta |
| Incentives for Becoming MPs | | | | | | | | | |
| Civic Duty Incentives | -.08 | | | -.05 | | | -.09 | | |
| Ideological/Issue Incentives | .07 | | | .08 | | | .13 | | |
| Cites Personal Satisfaction Incentives for Remaining a MP | -.03 | | | .01 | | | .16 | | |
| Pressure from Others | -.04 | | | -.04 | | | .00 | | |
| Role Perceptions and Conflicts | | | | | | | | | |
| Delegate-Servant Role Style | -.12[a] | | | -.05 | | | -.26 | | |
| Perceives Self as Expert in Substantive Area | -.17[a] | | | .02 | | | .16 | | |
| Conflicts with Constituents | .03 | | | .10 | | | -.06 | | |
| Conflict with Party In Parliament | -.09 | | | -.02 | | | -.10 | | |
| Conflict with Party In Riding | -.04 | | | .08 | | | -.18 | | |
| Conflict with Party In Province | -.07 | | | -.01 | | | .06 | | |
| Conflict with Interest Groups | .16[a] | | | .13[a] | | | .17 | | |
| Total # of Conflicts | -.02 | | | .03 | | | -.02 | | |

| | | | | | | |
|---|---|---|---|---|---|---|
| **Ambition and Achievement** | | | | | | |
| Perceives Parliament as a Career | .22[b] | | | .15[a] | .00 | |
| Expects to be a Cabinet Minister | .35[c] | .35 | .35 | -.02 | .06 | |
| Aspires to Hold other PUblic Office | .05 | | | .09 | -.05 | |
| #of Accomplishments Cited | .17[a] | | | .01 | -.02 | |
| Cites Policy Rather Than Service Accomp. | .10 | | | .12[a] | .14 | |
| **Orientation to Politics** | | | | | | |
| Likes being a MP | .12[a] | | | -.05 | .18 | |
| Perceived Efficacy of Individual MP | .10 | | | .03 | .38[a] | |
| Decline of Traditional Functions of Parliament | .14[a] | | | .01 | -.47[b] | -.31 |
| Perceives Alternative Functions for Parliament | -.09 | | | -.01 | -.29[a] | -.47 |
| Personal Ideology (Left-Right) | .07 | .24 | .24 | .24[c] | .12 | |
| R² Stepwise Method (I) | .22 | | | .07 | .46 | |
| R² Significant Predictors Method (II) | .12 | | | .06 | .22 | |

a. Significant .05 level.  b. Significant .01 level.  c. Significant .001 level.

we are observing in these data are the activities of three different types of MPs. The first of these types includes MPs who direct their principal efforts to speaking and asking questions on the House floor. Their motivational profiles suggest they are "professionals" or members of what might be termed a House of Commons "establishment." Somewhat like the members of the Senate establishment in the United States,[13] they tend disproportionately to define their political goals and aspirations in terms of a parliamentary career or higher parliamentary office. They are ambitious for a seat in the cabinet but display little or no interest in seeking political positions outside of parliament. These "insiders" are convinced that they have been able to accomplish their goals and they ascribe considerable importance to the norm of specialization. At least they believe they are expert in some area of House activity. In brief, the MPs who dominate debate in the House appear to be parliamentary professionals, men who run parliament and for whom parliament is the highest political calling.

Although this discussion is predicated on our interpretation of the significant univariate relationships in column 1 of table 7.1, inspection of the unstandardized regression coefficients (B) and the standardization Beta weights (Beta) in the table tends to confirm this interpretation. It also makes clear that the ambition to become a cabinet minister is the single most important determinant of participation in debate. In fact, this measure of ambition accounts for almost 15% of the variation in speaking activity and when employed as a control, eliminates all other motivational variables in the equation. Moreover, when we replicated the regressions in table 7.1 for six party and leadership subgroups[14] (data not shown) we found that ambition for a cabinet post was a significant determinant of participation in House debate for all but one group.[15] No other measure of motivation enters the equations as often. In fact, only the parliamentary career variable, another measure of ambition, enters more than once (in the Liberal party equation and the equation for the parliamentary leaders).

In contrast to the insider who participates extensively in House debates are the MPs who introduce the greatest number of private members' bills and debatable resolutions. We shall call them legislative "gadflies." Their most distinctive feature is their liberal ideology, the only significant predictor of propensity to introduce legislation in the whole set of motivational variables. The gadflies share the insiders' desire to make parliament a career, but they either are not ambitious for ministerial posts or they are pessimistic regarding the prospects of obtaining them. They appear to define their worth in terms of their policy accomplishments. Given the cluster of zero-order relationships, the significance of ideology as a predictor variable, and the fact that NDP backbenchers, committee chairmen to a lesser extent, and Liberal backbenchers disproportionately introduce private members' bills and debatable resolutions, we may infer that the gadfly group is predominately made up of backbenchers in these two parties.

More striking than the differences observed in the motivational profiles of MPs who monopolize debate and those who dominate the introduction of private member legislation, are the differences we find in the motivational attributes of the insiders and gadflies on the one hand and the committee activists on the other. First, and most important, the committee activists appear to be amateurs rather than parliamentary professionals. Not only are they pessimistic about their prospects of becoming cabinet ministers, they also fail to manifest any ambition to make parliament a career. Nor, for that matter, do committee activists aspire to political offices outside of parliament. Nonetheless, it would be inaccurate to characterize committee activists as MPs who have decided to "drop out" of politics. They are not individuals who are bored and frustrated with the inefficiency of parliament and their own lack of influence. More than any other group of MPs, the committee activists are convinced of the importance of the individual MP. They reject out of hand the suggestion that parliament has abdicated its role as legislative initiator and executive overseer, even as they reject the less controversial assertion that the function of parliament has evolved from making legislation to setting national priorities and informing public opinion. Since we know that participation in the affairs of parliament's standing committees does contribute to the influence ascribed MPs, the optimism displayed by committee activists may not simply be misplaced sound and fury. It may derive instead from a quite normal tendency to exaggerate the importance of a subsystem in which they are able to occupy center stage.

## THE EFFECTS OF POLITICAL ENVIRONMENT

Unlike Athena, who sprang fully grown from the brow of Zeus, political elites are not born with a complete range of attitudes and motivations that subsequently determine the nature of their political activities. Motivations are but a link in the long, complex, and still poorly understood chain of circumstances and events that lead from the cradle to whatever political roles individuals assume. Behavior probably also is influenced by the political environment, its effects mediated through the intervening effects of motivations.[16] It seems likely that such aspects of the political environment as the level of constituency interparty electoral competition, the nature of the constituency's composition, the member's length of service in parliament and his sensitivity to and awareness of the informal rules and sanctions that regulate behavior in parliament will be some of the factors that influence substantially both a member's political attitudes and motivations and his participation in various aspects of parliamentary life.

In order to test this assumption we employed a number of variables indicative of several aspects of a MP's environment. These included the level of interparty electoral competition in his constituency, the level of voter turnout in his constituency, the level of urbanization of his constituency, the member's age when he entered parliament, his length of parliamentary service, and his awareness of various informal rules-of-the-game in parliament and of the sanctions that are available to enforce them. As in our analysis of motivations, we regressed these 13 indicators of current political environment on each of the three measures of parliamentary participation. The resulting simple correlations, unstandardized regression coefficients, standardized coefficients, and coefficients of multiple determination for the debate, legislation, and committee activity equations are displayed in table 7.2.

Consistent with our expectation that the current political environment is one step removed from behavior and affects participation through the intervening influence of motivations, a comparison of the variations in participation explained by motivational and political environment factors suggests that political environment does not predict participation as strongly as does motivation (see table 7.1). Although both sets of independent variables predict variations in the introduction of legislation equally well (or equally poorly as seems to be more the case), the political environment succeeds in explaining only about two thirds as much of the variation in debate participation as is explained by motivations, and less than half as much of the variation in committee participation. In absolute terms, however, the political environment indicators do account for a substantial percentage of the variance in all three participation variables. Like the motivational variables, the categories in which environmental vari-

TABLE 7.2

## CURRENT POLITICAL SITUATIONAL AND ENVIRONMENTAL DETER-MINANTS OF MP PARTICIPATION IN DEBATE AND QUESTION PERIOD (DEBATE), THE INTRODUCTION OF BILLS AND DEBATABLE RESOLU-TIONS (LEGISLATION) AND COMMITTEE DEBATE (COMMITTEE)

| Variable | Debate | | | Legislation | | | Committee | | |
|---|---|---|---|---|---|---|---|---|---|
| | r | B | Beta | r | B | Beta | r | B | Beta |
| Age at Entry Into Parliament | .02 | | | −.06 | | | −.01 | | |
| # Years of Parliamentary Experience | .23[c] | .04 | .20 | .02 | | | .09 | | |
| Represents Urban Constituency | −.09 | | | .22[b] | .005 | .22 | .13 | | |
| Constituency Turnout 1968 | .03 | | | .02 | | | .05 | | |
| Constituency Competition 1968 | .04 | | | −.09 | | | −.12 | | |
| Constituency Competition First Election to Parliament | .08 | | | −.04 | | | .04 | | |
| # of Political Rules Cited | −.04 | | | −.06 | | | −.08 | | |
| # of Organizational Rules Cited | .13[a] | | | −.01 | | | −.02 | | |
| # of Social Rules Cited | .02 | | | .08 | | | −.16 | | |
| # of Political Sanctions Cited | .14[a] | | | .00 | | | −.29[a] | | |
| # of Organizational Sanctions Cited | .29[b] | .74 | .24 | .03 | | | −.38[a] | −.38 | −.38 |
| # of Social Sanctions Cited | −.08 | | | −.14[a] | | | .14 | | |
| Aware of Informal Sanctions | −.04 | | | .04 | | | −.06 | | |
| R² by Stepwise Method (I) | .15 | | | .08 | | | .21 | | |
| R² by Significant Predictors Method (II) | .11 | | | .05 | | | .15 | | |

a. Significant .05 level.

b. Significant .01 level.

c. Significant .001 level.

ables had the most explanatory power were debate and committee—
areas that, in turn, help explain the degree of influence ascribed to
individual MPs.

As revealing as these multiple correlations are, it is the simple
zero-order relationships in the tables that best illustrate the nature
and extent of the political environment's impact upon member
participation. Perhaps the most interesting inference to be drawn
from these relationships is that the relative electoral competitiveness
of their constituencies has very little effect on the three dimensions
of parliamentary participation. The only significant relationship between constituency factors and participation is the correlation between the level of constituency urbanization and the frequency with
which the members introduce debatable resolutions and private
member legislation. The urbanization measure alone accounts for
almost two-thirds of the variance the 13 variable set is able to
explain.

The observation that the initiation of legislation is characteristic of
MPs from highly urbanized constituencies lends an interesting perspective to our earlier observation that in motivational terms these
same individuals are best described as legislative gadflies. Since these
individuals are disproportionately Liberal and NDP backbenchers
who tend to be ideological liberals, we might speculate that the urban
constituency organizations of the two parties are more likely than
rural organizations to nominate candidates who are left-of-center.
Alternatively, ideological liberals may feel they have a better chance
of being nominated and elected in urban constituencies than they
have in rural areas. Whatever the reason, it would appear that when
they are elected they tend to be impatient with the traditional
workings of parliament and with the roles ascribed to private members and so pursue alternatives to them. However, the gadfly orientation to parliament usually is not one that generates influence (the
reader will recall the weak and generally negative correlations between the frequency of introduction of PMBs and DRs and ascribed
influence).[17]

The data in table 7.2 also help illuminate the profiles of MPs who
participate extensively in House debates as opposed to those who are
particularly active in committees. Consistent with our speculation
that MPs who dominate debate in the House are parliamentary
professionals, the size of the correlation between parliamentary seniority and debate indicates that not only do the parliamentary

insiders more frequently aspire to a career in parliament, but they also already have served in parliament for a longer period.

Moreover, inspection of the relationships between the several independent variables and both debate and committee activities reveals that in addition to being significantly more sensitive to the existence of organizational rules in parliament than either the gad-flies or amateur committee activists, the insiders also manifest a significantly greater awareness of the informal organizational and political sanctions that help enforce those rules. The committee activist, in contrast, is far less aware of organizational and political sanctions in the House than is either other group. To the extent that knowledge of the rules of the parliamentary game and of their related sanctions reflects a MP's political sophistication, these data support our assumptions that insiders are individuals with political "savvy" whereas committee activists are politically naive. The gad-flies, it would appear, fall somewhere between. In light of our earlier assumption that gadflies share the professionalism and career orienta-tions of the insiders, a reasonable speculation is that gadflies' com-parative insensitivity to these norms is less a product of unawareness than it is a decision to ignore them and to accept the resulting sanctions. Finally, inspection of the regression coefficients in table 7.2 together with a second set of coefficients (not shown) generated by replicating these regression analyses for six party and leadership subgroups, reinforces both the importance of constituency urbaniza-tion as a predictor of legislative initiative and of parliamentary tenure and knowledge of institutional norms as determinants of participa-tion in House debate.[18]

## THE EFFECTS OF RECRUITMENT AND EARLY LIFE POLITICAL SOCIALIZATION

Previous investigations of the relationship between elite recruit-ment and early life socialization experiences on the one hand and elite behavior on the other suggest that events prior to entry into parliament may affect individual behavior within parliament. In particular, the relatively limited body of research on the early life socialization experiences of future political elites as well as the extensive study of the early political socialization experiences of mass publics have reported a strong, positive association between the level of politicization of the individual's early environment and the extent of his subsequent participation in all aspects of political life.[19] With respect to the impact of political recruitment experiences, students of the recruitment process are almost unanimous in the belief that recruitment and early political career experiences may have a significant effect both upon the individual's later orientations to and his level of activity in an elected office.[20] In order to determine the extent to which their socialization and recruitment experiences influenced the parliamentary behavior of MPs we ran two regression analyses on each of the three participation variables. As independent variables in the first analysis, we employed 14 measures of the individual's recruitment experiences and motivations for first becoming a candidate. In the second, we used 7 measures of the level of politicization of the respondent's childhood environment. Tables 7.3 and 7.4 present the results.

It is obvious that the data provide little support for the proposition that early life socialization and recruitment experiences substantially affect later life elite political behavior. Inspection of the multiple correlations in tables 7.3 and 7.4 reveals not only that these two sets of variables explain less of the variation in the initiation of legislation than do the motivation and current political environment variable sets, but also that they account for only 6 or 7 percent of the variation in debate activity as well. Only one socialization variable and one recruitment variable are significantly correlated with debate activity. When we repeated these regressions for the six party and leadership subgroups even these marginal relationships disappeared for three of the recruitment and four of the socialization subgroups. Interestingly, although the recruitment and socialization variables show no appreciable relationship to debate or legislation initiation, they appear to have a marked impact upon committee participation. The recruitment variables account for 62% and the socialization variables for 37% of the variance in committee participation. Closer scrutiny of the socialization and recruitment variables that are significantly related to committee activity, however, reveals a largely serendipitous pattern of relationships. The data indicate, for example, that although the committee activists are not appreciably different from other MPs in terms of their recruitment experiences, they are significantly different from other MPs in terms of the kinds of motivations that prompted them to run for office in the first place. But the nature of these differences is puzzling. The committee activists less often report being motivated to seek office because of a need to promote a particular political philosophy or because of a dislike for an opposition party. Instead they claim to be motivated

TABLE 7.3

**POLITICAL RECRUITMENT, CAREER, AND EARLY POLITICAL MOTIVA-
TION DETERMINANTS OF MP PARTICIPATION IN DEBATE AND QUES-
TION PERIOD (DEBATE), THE INTRODUCTION OF BILLS AND DEBATABLE
RESOLUTIONS (LEGISLATION) AND COMMITTEE DEBATE (COMMITTEE)**

| Variable | Debate | | | Legislation | | | Committee | | |
|---|---|---|---|---|---|---|---|---|---|
| | r | B | Beta | r | B | Beta | r | B | Beta |
| (Recruitment Experience) | | | | | | | | | |
| Experienced Difficulty in Receiving Parlia. Nomin. | −.11 | | | .05 | | | .08 | | |
| Prior Public Office-Holder | −.05 | | | −.07 | | | −.18 | | |
| Level of Pre-Parliamentary Party Activity | .07 | | | .05 | | | .03 | | |
| Self-Motivated (vs. Recruited) | .04 | | | .09 | | | −.17 | | |
| Previous Unsuccessful Candidacies for Public Office | −.13[a] | .17 | .13 | .11 | | | −.01 | | |
| (Reasons for First Political Candidacy) | | | | | | | | | |
| Appeal of Party | −.04 | | | .00 | | | .28 | | |
| Pressure from Others | .08 | | | −.02 | | | −.10 | | |
| Dislike of Party In Power | .02 | | | .01 | | | −.29[a] | | |
| Cites Ideological Motives for Becoming Candidate | .02 | | | .02 | | | −.29[a] | .29 | .29 |
| Civic Duty | .05 | | | −.03 | | | −.08 | | |
| (Reasons for Getting Into Politics) | | | | | | | | | |
| Pressure from Others | −.08 | | | −.07 | | | .26 | | |
| Improve Local/Provincial Government | .04 | | | .01 | | | −.20 | | |
| Improve Federal Government | .00 | | | .12 | | | .22 | | |
| Personal Satisfaction and Gain | −.02 | | | −.04 | | | .22 | | |
| R² by Stepwise Method (I) | .06 | | | .06 | | | .62 | | |
| R² by Significant Predictors Method (II) | .02 | | | None | | | .08 | | |

a. Significant .05 level.

by a positive assessment of the principles for which their own party
stands. It is not at all apparent, however, what it means to be
motivated by principles but not philosophy, or to be motivated by a
positive assessment of one's own party without simultaneously view-
ing competing parties from a negative perspective.

TABLE 7.4

**EARLY POLITICAL SOCIALIZATION DETERMINANTS OF MP PARTICIPATION IN DEBATE AND QUESTION PERIOD (DEBATE), THE INTRODUCTION OF BILLS AND DEBATABLE RESOLUTIONS (LEGISLATION) AND COMMITTEE DEBATE (COMMITTEE)**

| Variable | Debate | | | Legislation | | | Committee | | |
|---|---|---|---|---|---|---|---|---|---|
| | r | B | Beta | r | B | Beta | r | B | Beta |
| Political Environment of Childhood | −.08 | | | −.14[a] | −.15 | −.14 | −.42[a] | −.24 | −.42 |
| Positive Reaction to first Political Event | .05 | | | −.10 | | | −.14 | | |
| # of Changes in Party ID during Life | .06 | | | .05 | | | −.02 | | |
| Belong to High School or College Political Clubs | −.10 | | | .09 | | | −.25 | | |
| Level of Peer Group Political Interest | .10 | | | −.02 | | | −.09 | | |
| $\bar{X}$ Early Ages of Political Socialization | −.08 | | | −.02 | | | −.29[a] | | |
| Early Life Importance of Politics | .15[a] | .20 | .15 | −.10 | | | −.03 | | |
| $R^2$ by Stepwise Method (I) | .07 | | | .04 | | | .37 | | |
| $R^2$ by Significant Predictors Method (II) | .02 | | | .02 | | | .17 | | |

a. Significant .05 level.

Moreover, and even more perplexing, the correlations in table 7.4 suggest that the committee activists were reared in substantially less politicized environments than other MPs, yet they became aware of and interested in politics and first identified with a political party at a substantially earlier age. According to socialization theory and more than two decades of empirical research, the ages of first political awareness, interest, and party identification are inversely related to, if not actually determined by, the politicization level of the individual's early life environment. Thus, if the early life environments of the committee activists were less politicized than most MPs they ought to have developed an initial interest in politics at a later age than the others.

Although we cannot document our suspicions with the data at hand, a reasonable assumption is that these apparent inconsistencies in the data are simply a further manifestation of the committee activist's relative lack of political sophistication compared to his colleagues in parliament. The reader may recall from chapter 2 that in comparison to the public as a whole and especially to local political party elites in Canada, the MPs in our study reported unusually high ages of first partisan identification and political interest. We attempted to explain this phenomenon in terms of the extraordinary political sophistication of the MPs which led them to interpert party identification and political interest as active commitments to party and politics and not simply as affective attachments to labels. If this interpretation is valid, then the apparent discrepancy in the relationship between age of awareness and level of politicization within the group of MPs may simply be a function of the committee activists' less rigorous interpretation of the meaning of political interest and party identification. We might speculate still further that the contradictory recruitment motivations expressed by the committee activists also may be a function of their naivete and of their confusion concerning the meaning of such terms as philosophy, principles, and the like. If so, then the differences, at least in the nature of the recruitment motivations of committee activists and other MPs, may be essentially semantic.

## THE EFFECTS OF SOCIAL BACKGROUND

Despite the importance we have ascribed to motivations as determinants of elite behavior, and to the socialization and recruitment processes and the current political environment as determinants of both motivations and behavior, these relationships have not benefited from as much research and scholarly attention as those between social backgrounds and elite behavior. Apart from the fact that social background data are readily available and easily acquired, social scientists assumed that social backgrounds reflect and significantly affect the nature of elite socialization and recruitment and the formation of elite attitudes and behavior. Donald Matthews perhaps best articulates this assumption when he argues that, "if we are to understand their (U.S. Senators') behavior we must know who they are; the kinds of experiences they have had; the skills, group loyalties, and prejudices they bring with them into the Senate cham-

ber."[21]   Although  Edinger  and  Searing[22]   more  recently  have
demonstrated that the link between background and attitudes cannot
be assumed, their data and the data from a vast array of other social
background studies of elite populations convince us that certain social
background characteristics of elites do reflect significant aspects of
their environment and do anticipate certain of their political attitudes and behavior.

To take advantage of the explanatory power the social background
data  might  provide  concerning  the  parliamentary  behavior  of
Canadian  MPs,  we  initially  constructed  28  indicators  of  the
ethnic, religious, educational, occupational and social status backgrounds of the 189 MPs in our study and employed them as independent variables in a series of regression analyses of the three parliamentary participation variables. The results of these analyses are
displayed in table 7.5.

Most striking of the observations to be made on the basis of these
data is that despite both the imprecision of social background concepts as indicators of elite experiences and attitudes and the fact that
social background experiences are presumed to influence behavior
only  indirectly,  no  other  set  of  variables  in  this  study  predicts
parliamentary participation as well. Inspection of the coefficients of
multiple-determination in table 7.5 reveals not only that these social
background data account for fully 55% of the variation in committee
activity (compare this with the 46% explained by motivations and
the 21% explained by the current political environment), but also
that the social background variables explain 11% of the variation in
the initiation of legislation and 26% of the variation in debate. In
contrast, none of the other variables sets considered thus far account
for more than 8% of the variation in legislation activity or 22% of the
variation in debate.

Important as these social background indicators are in the aggregate, certain subsets of these variables demonstrate particularly
strong relationships with each of the participation variables. The set
of ethnic origin and place-of-birth variables, for example, together
with quality of education, religious affiliation, and current age are
considerably better predictors of debate activity than of the tendency to introduce legislation or engage in committee activities.
Similarly, growing up in a large urban center and being relatively low
on the SES ladder are attributes that are strongly associated with
committee activism. Focusing upon these differences, it is possible to
elaborate  still  further  upon  the  profiles  of  MPs  who  engage

TABLE 7.5

## SOCIAL BACKGROUND DETERMINANTS OF MP PARTICIPATION IN DEBATE AND QUESTION PERIOD (DEBATE), THE INTRODUCTION OF BILLS AND DEBATABLE RESOLUTIONS (LEGISLATION) AND COMMITTEE DEBATE (COMMITTEE)

| Variable | Debate | | | Legislation | | | Committee | | |
|---|---|---|---|---|---|---|---|---|---|
| | r | B | Beta | r | B | Beta | r | B | Beta |
| Born in Quebec | -.20[b] | | | -.06 | | | -.08 | | |
| Born in Ontario | -.11 | | | .09 | | | .05 | | |
| Born in Atlantic Provinces | .03 | | | -.04 | | | -.12 | | |
| Born in Western Provinces | .14[a] | | | -.01 | | | .15 | | |
| Born in Canada | -.21[b] | -.90 | -.22 | -.02 | | | .01 | | |
| Catholic | -.22[b] | -.51 | -.24 | -.05 | | | -.18 | | |
| Protestant | .12 | | | -.03 | | | .04 | | |
| Jewish | .10 | | | .07 | | | .22 | | |
| Other Religions | .05 | | | -.04 | | | .02 | | |
| Professional | -.01 | | | -.01 | | | .04 | | |
| Prestige of College | -.18[b] | | | .05 | | | -.13 | | |
| Has College Degree | .14[a] | | | .08 | | | .00 | | |
| # Years of Schooling | .05 | | | .04 | | | .10 | | |
| SES at Initial Election to Parliament | -.01 | | | -.01 | | | -.27[a] | 113.97[c] | -.56 |
| # of Club Memberships | -.02 | | | -.18[a] | -.08 | -.18 | .12 | | |
| Business Club Memberships | -.08 | | | -.10 | | | .16 | | |
| Social Club Memberships | .11 | | | -.11 | | | -.17 | | |
| Civic Club Memberships | -.04 | | | -.04 | | | .24 | | |
| Religious Club Memberships | -.04 | | | -.11 | | | -.06 | | |

(continued on overleaf)

**TABLE 7.5** *continued*

| Variable | Debate | | | Legislation | | | Committee | | |
|---|---|---|---|---|---|---|---|---|---|
| | r | B | Beta | r | B | Beta | r | B | Beta |
| Holds Office in Clubs | -.06 | | | -.03 | | | -.15 | 1087.[c] | .36 |
| Current Age | .15[a] | | | -.03 | | | .02 | | |
| Reared Large Urban Center | .01 | | | .08 | | | .26 | 2480.[c] | .40 |
| Parents' SES | .00 | | | -.04 | | | .18 | | |
| # of Years MP has lived in Constituency | -.05 | | | -.07 | | | -.16 | | |
| Anglo-Celtic or N. European Ethnic Origins | .11 | | | -.01 | | | -.01 | | |
| East or South European Ancestry | .02 | | | -.03 | | | .00 | | |
| French or French-Canadian Ancestry | -.20[b] | | | -.12[a] | -.27 | -.11 | -.12 | | |
| Parents Born in Canada | -.19[b] | | | -.07 | | | .03 | | |
| R² by Stepwise Method (I) | .26 | | | .11 | | | .55 | | |
| R² by Significant Predictors Method (II) | .10 | | | .06 | | | .34 | | |

a. Significant .05 level.
b. Significant .01 level.
c. Other things being equal, the magnitude of the unstandardized regression coefficients (B's) varies directly with the size of the unit of measure. Thus, the unusually large B's for MP participation in Committee debate result from the measurement of this variable as the *number of lines* spoken in committee. Unlike Debate and Legislation factor score variables, both of which range approximately from -1.0 to +1.0, the Committee participation variable ranges from 0 to more than 4,000. The size of the unit of measure does *not* influence the standardized regression coefficient (Beta).

disproportionately in House debate, the introduction of private bills and resolutions, and committee deliberations. Inspection of the significant correlates of debate suggests that in addition to their careerist orientations, leadership ambitions, political sophistication, and seniority, MPs who dominate participation in debate also are more likely to have been born to parents of other than Canadian or French-Canadian extraction. That these MPs are of non-French and non-Catholic backgrounds together with our previous observation that insiders are to be found disproportionately in the Liberal leadership cohort suggests that the other-than-Quebec wing of the Liberal party tends to carry the ball during debate in the House.

Consonant with our earlier observation that those who participate most in House debates have enjoyed longer tenure in parliament, the data indicate that parliamentary insiders, on the average, are somewhat older than their colleagues, and are more likely to have a college education, although they tend to be graduates of less prestigious institutions than other MPs with a college degree.

Unfortunately, the data do not reveal as much about the backgrounds of the committee activists and gadflies. Consistent, nonetheless, with their relative lack of political sophistication, we find that the committee activists enjoyed less prestigious occupations at the time they entered parliament than did other MPs. However, the committee activists may not have experienced the same degree of upward social mobility as some of their other colleagues in parliament; their fathers' SES levels, on the average, were slightly higher than those of the other MPs.

Committee activists also are characterized by having been born and reared in more urban communities and by multiple memberships in civic clubs. Although the relationship is not statistically significant, the observation that these MPs are "joiners" suggests, in addition to their other traits, that the committee activists may be somewhat more gregarious than other MPs, or at least are more convinced of the value of small group activity. If so, then this may be another reason for their involvement in committee work. It may be that committee activists express themselves more fully in committees because they feel comfortable in the small group setting which committees presumably provide.

Indeed, the relatively strong sociability of the amateur committee activist appears to be a major difference between him and the legislative gadfly. Unlike the committee activist, the MP who concentrates upon introducing legislation belongs to significantly fewer social, profes-

sional and civic clubs and organizations. If this relative lack of memberships reflects his lack of sociability, or of sense of small group
efficacy, it is possible that he has chosen to participate in parliament
through the introduction of largely symbolic legislation because he
feels excluded from effective participation in debate and feels "out
of water" in the small group setting of committees. Alternatively, he
may have a kind of "lone wolf" image of himself. He may see himself
as a person who stands apart from the group, who goes his own way,
does his own thing, and glories in the fact that he does.

All of this discussion, of course, is highly speculative and based
upon analyses of the MPs as a group. Because of the possibility of
significant party or leadership differences in the pattern of relationships displayed in table 7.5, we also analyzed the social backgrounds
of the six party and leadership subgroups. Happily, these analyses
tended to confirm patterns observed previously. Particularly interesting was the finding (anticipated in chapter 2) that among the Conservative MPs social status best predicted debate participation (Beta =
.32). Supportive also of our speculation that participation in debate
among Liberals is dominated by the English-speaking element of the
party (in spite of the fact that the prime minister and several of the
most important cabinet MPs are of French-Canadian origin), we
found that Liberal MPs of French-Canadian origin participated significantly less in debate than did other members of the party (Beta =
−.21).

## SUMMARY

In this chapter we examined the relationships between MPs' participation levels in debate and question period, in legislative initiation,
and in committee activities on one hand, and characteristics of their
environment and personal attributes on the other, in order to determine why some MPs participate extensively in parliamentary affairs
while others do not. Table 7.6 provides a convenient summary of our
findings.

Analysis of the zero-order Pearson correlations, the unstandardized regression coefficients and the standardized Beta weights yielded
three participation profiles (see table 7.6). Those who dominate
debate in the House we labeled "insiders," MPs who define their
political goals in terms of a parliamentary career and hope for a
cabinet seat. They seem to come disproportionately from the Liberal
and Conservative leadership groups, have been in parliament rather

## TABLE 7.6
## SUMMARY CHARACTERISTICS OF PARTICIPANTS IN DEBATE AND QUESTION PERIOD, THE INTRODUCTION OF BILLS AND RESOLUTIONS AND COMMITTEE DEBATE

| Attributes | Participants in Debate and Question Period | Participants in the Introduction of Bills and Resolutions | Participants in Committee Debate |
|---|---|---|---|
| **Attitudes and Motivations Variables** | | | |
| Perceives parliament as a career | yes | yes | no |
| Expects to be a cabinet minister | yes | no | no |
| Aspires to hold other public office | no | no | no |
| Perceives self as expert in substantive area | yes | mixed | yes |
| Personal ideology | middle of the road | very liberal | somewhat liberal |
| Believes that parliament's traditional functions have declined | yes | uncertain | no |
| Perceived efficacy of individual MP | very slightly | uncertain | very strongly |
| Likes being a MP | yes | yes and no | yes |
| Oriented to delegate-servant role style | somewhat less than average | about average | much less than average |
| **Current Political Situational Variables** | | | |
| # years of parliamentary experience | much longer than average | average | slightly longer than average |

*(continued on overleaf)*

TABLE 7.6 (*continued*)

| Attributes | Participants in Debate and Question Period | Participants in the Introduction of Bills and Resolutions | Participants in Committee Debate |
|---|---|---|---|
| Type of constituency | less urban than average | much more urban than average | slightly more urban than average |
| Sensitivity to informal rules and sanctions | much more than average | about average | much less than average |
| **Political Recruitment Variables** | | | |
| Experienced difficulty in receiving parliamentary nomination | slightly more than average | slightly more than average | average |
| **Political Socialization Variables** | | | |
| Politicized environment and early importance of politics | more than average | slightly less than average | much less than average |
| **Social Background Variables** | | | |
| Ethnicity | other than French-Canadian stock | other than French-Canadian stock | nothing distinctive |
| Religion | strongly other than Catholic | nothing distinctive | slightly other than Catholic |
| Personal socioeconomic status when entering parliament | above average | about average | less than average |
| # of club memberships | average | slightly less than average | more than average |
| Current age | slightly older than average | average | average |
| Education | better than average | average | average |
| Party | Liberal leaders and Conservative front-benchers Minor party leaders | NDP and Liberal backbenchers and committee chairmen | Liberal backbenchers, some NDP |

longer than others, tend to be non-French, non-Catholic, somewhat older, and are convinced they have been able to accomplish many of their goals in parliament. These attributes, as well as the fact that they believe themselves to be personally expert in some area of House activity, led us to characterize these MPs as parliamentary professionals.

MPs who introduce the largest number of private members' bills and debatable resolutions we called legislative "gadflies." These MPs have a very strong liberal ideological orientation. They share the insiders' desire to make parliament a career but do not seem ambitious for ministerial status. This group, which seems to be most concerned with policy accomplishments, is composed primarily of Liberal and NDP backbenchers who represent urban constituencies.

Those MPs who are most active in committee share very few characteristics with the other two groups. They appear to be amateurs, do not seem to want to have a career in parliament or in any other political office. They reject the assertion that the role of the individual MP has diminished and are much less aware than the gadflies or insiders of informal behavior norms and the sanctions which enforce them.

*Chapter 8*

# THE CORRELATES OF POSITION

In his study of the 25th Parliament, Allan Kornberg observed that the Canadian House of Commons was a particularly appropriate parliamentary body for testing the Michelian theory of oligarchy because we "will not be loading the dice against the theory because of a structural factor, the seniority system."[1] He went on to observe that in the American Congress the

> operation of a seniority system assures that the reins of power will be held by those individuals whose primary claim to leadership is that they have the longest period of continuous service on a legislative committee. Thus the ability to choose leaders freely is largely circumscribed. But it is precisely this ability to choose, to screen, to include and exclude, that is intrinsic to elitist theory since this is the means by which leaders insure their own positions as well as the social homogeneity of the leadership group.[2]

His comparison of 39 parliamentary leaders of all parties and 126 other MPs indicated that the social and political backgrounds of the leadership group differed significantly. For example, the panel of leaders tended to derive from higher status backgrounds; they were better educated; they more often were brought up in large metropolitan areas; they were reared in more politicized familial environments; and they tended more often than did nonleaders to be businessmen or members of a profession at the time of their election to parliament. And, despite the fact that electoral success and parliamentary longevity are not the sine qua non for occupying a position of leadership in the Canadian parliamentary system, the cohort of leaders had enjoyed substantially longer tenure as MPs, a consequence and also a reflection of the fact that the level of inter-party

[ 256 ]

competition in their constituencies was substantially lower than in the constituencies represented by nonleaders. He also found that in certain important respects the leaders were not significantly different. For example, the ethnic and religious affiliations were similar and both groups tended to be distributed relatively similarly along a "French-Canadian Cultural Index."

Since Kornberg was undertaking a limited test of the Michelian theory, he focused only on a small number of variables. In this chapter we will extend his comparisons in three ways. First, we not only will compare the social and political backgrounds of leaders and nonleaders in the four parties, but we also will try to determine whether the recruitment experiences, motivations, and the current attitudes and perspectives of the two groups systematically differ. Second, we will make the same comparisons between the Liberal cabinet and Conservative frontbenchers[3] to determine whether the pathways that led to a leadership position in one party were the same as those that led to leadership in another. This is a matter of considerable theoretical importance to Canadian scholars. For example, John Meisel, although acknowledging that parliamentary party leaders constitute a very homogeneous elite in many respects, nonetheless argued that even the leaders of supposed look-alike parties, such as the Liberal and Conservative, differ in a number of subtle and not so subtle ways.[4] These differences are important because they affect and have been affected by both a party's "style" and policy preferences[5] over the years. Finally, we will make these comparisons among three groups of members in the governing party: (1) those who make it to the "top" of the party, the members of the cabinet; (2) those who achieve middle-level leadership positions, in this instance the chairmen of the several standing committees; and (3) those who occupy no formal positions of leadership. If there are few differences between the first two groups, we may assume, ceteris paribus, that the middle-level leaders are part of a pool from which Liberal top leaders are drawn. Eventually at least some of them will succeed to cabinet positions. If, however, there are substantial differences in the backgrounds and the current statuses of top and middle-level leaders, and if the committee chairmen cannot be clearly distinguished from backbenchers, then we may infer that a large group of the members of the governing Liberal party are destined to be hewers of wood and drawers of parliamentary water for a small group of more favored colleagues. It may be that in any governing party, despite the relative homogeneity of the social and political backgrounds and the current statuses of MPs, and despite the theoretical equality of status of MPs qua MPs, a small group may well be "more equal" than their other colleagues. John Porter has argued that this certainly has been the case in Canada. He attributes it to the fact that both Liberal and Conservative prime ministers, but particularly Liberal leaders, have gone "outside" parliament to recruit cabinet ministers. Most often these men have been coopted provincial party leaders and members of the corporate and bureaucratic elites.[6]

In the correlational analyses that are generated to test these expectations, we generally will remark on only those zero-order relationships that are statistically significant or come close to being significant. Initially, group differences will be reported in percentage terms. All of the independent variables then will be entered into a series of multiple discriminant function analyses to distinguish between or among two or more groups. Although the multiple discriminant technique is particularly suited for use in multivariate analyses with nominal dependent variables, we again will rely on triangulation for confirmation; the results obtained by discriminant function analysis will be compared with those generated by regression techniques. If they generally are similar, we can be relatively confident that the observed differences between specific groups further illuminate the relationship between leadership positions and the possession of influence in Canada's 28th Parliament.

## FINDINGS

As was the case in 1962, there were significant differences in social and political backgrounds between those who occupy formal positions of leadership[7] in the Canadian House of Commons and those who do not. Moreover, these differences generally were congruent with the patterns observed earlier. As a group the top leaders of all four parliamentary parties derived from significantly higher socioeconomic backgrounds than did nonleaders and were substantially better educated. On the average, leaders of the four parties had completed 18 years of formal schooling as compared to 15.5 years completed by nonleaders. Fully 92.9% of the leaders as opposed to 67.7% of the nonleaders had at least one university degree. Leaders also tended to have been reared in metropolitan areas more frequently than nonleaders (51.9% and 29.8% respectively). At the time of their election to parliament, 51.8% of the leaders (as opposed to 24.8% of the nonleaders) were lawyers and the mean SES scores of the leaders were significantly higher than were those of nonleaders (74.7 vs. 67.1). As was the case in 1962, however, there were no statistically significant differences in the ethnic origins and religious affiliations of leaders and nonleaders.

Insofar as political backgrounds and early life politicization were concerned, the leaders tended to report significantly lower average ages of initial political awareness, first political interest and first psychological identification with a political party. They also tended to have been reared in more politicized families, and to have ascribed more importance to politics during adolescence and early childhood than nonleaders. There were, however, relatively few differences between leaders and nonleaders in the circumstances surrounding their recruitment into politics and public affairs. Indeed, the only statistically significant ones were that: (1) the leaders had been more active in their respective party organizations prior to their election to parliament; (2) they had less often been unsuccessful candidates for public office; and (3) before becoming parliamentary candidates the leaders had not held a public office as often as had nonleaders. Leaders and nonleaders also tended to cite relatively similar motives for initially becoming active in politics, for first becoming a candidate for any kind of public office, and for becoming a candidate for a parliamentary position. The only significant motivational differences were that the leadership group more frequently cited the "challenge of office" as a reason for becoming candidates for parliament whereas nonleaders more often cited "good government" reasons for initially becoming involved in public affairs.

With respect to what might be termed "current attitudes and motivations," the party leaders were more likely to feel they were experts in some area of parliamentary activity; they were less likely to prefer the "delegate-servant" representational role style; and they were more likely than those not in the leadership group to view being a MP as a career. Another significant difference was the greater awareness and sensitivity of leaders to the informal behavioral norms of parliament. They also were more aware of the sanctions available for use against those who break the rules. Finally, leaders had a longer period of tenure in parliament (10.9 years vs. 7.9 years) although they tended to be somewhat younger.[8] In part (as was suggested of the 1962 leadership group), their longer tenure was due to the fact that leaders disproportionately represented less politically competitive urban constituencies.

The leadership group for whom the above comparisons were made included holders of leadership positions in all four parties. However, as we observed at the beginning of this chapter, it has been argued that there may be as many or more differences between the leaders of opposing parties, or between the leaders and followers within a particular party, as there are between leaders and followers generally. Moreover, the attributes in terms of which leaders and followers in one party differ may not be the same as those on which they differ in another party. We shall test these assumptions by looking at leaders and nonleaders in the governing Liberal party and in the official opposition, the Conservative party.

## LEADERSHIP DIFFERENCES IN THE LIBERAL PARTY

The cabinet Liberals, more than their party colleagues, tend to have been recruited from the ranks of what we have called the inner club of parliament. For example, they are more often better educated. In fact, all of the cabinet MPs in our data set (and over 90% of all the men who served in the cabinet of the 28th Parliament) had at least one university degree whereas only about two-thirds of their Liberal colleagues were as highly educated. Cabinet ministers also were significantly more likely than other Liberals to have been reared in a highly urban environment (72% of the ministers as opposed to 46% of other Liberals)—a characteristic not included in our profile of parliamentary insiders largely because of the offsetting small town origins of frontbench Conservative MPs, the other major group comprising the inner club.

Although we noted previously that differences in political backgrounds are not related in a statistically significantly fashion to differences in parliamentary participation, we did find statistically significant political socialization differences between Liberal leaders and nonleaders. On the average, cabinet members became aware of the world of politics more than three years earlier, and became interested in politics almost four years earlier than their noncabinet, Liberal colleagues. Cabinet members also more often reported that: (a) their parents were strongly interested in politics; (b) their friends in high school and college were strongly interested in politics; and (c) they were active in political clubs and organizations in high school and as undergraduates. These differences are reflected in the cabinet ministers' significantly higher scores on the aggregate political environment factor. (Liberal cabinet members average .41 on this factor scale compared to an average score of −.16 for their party colleagues.)

If Liberal cabinet members were more precocious politically than other Liberals, one might assume they continued to display this trait in their early political careers and were more often than other Liberals (what Eldersveld[9] has termed) political "self-starters." Happily, an inspection of the differences in the recruitment and political career experiences of cabinet and non-cabinet Liberals confirms this assumption. In addition to being more active in the Liberal party organization before becoming MPs (47% of the Cabinet but only 20% of the other Liberals had held two or more party offices by the time they became MPs) two thirds of the members of cabinet as opposed to 35% of their colleagues volunteered their services to the party rather than waiting to be recruited. On the other hand, almost twice as many noncabinet as cabinet Liberals ran for a public office prior to becoming candidates for parliament, a finding that may explain why noncabinet Liberals also had a significantly higher rate of unsuccessful public office candidacies. Their lack of public office experience also may help explain why cabinet members more often reported being motivated to become parliamentary candidates by the "challenge of the office" (94% vs. 52%).

The fact that they were less involved in social organizations outside of parliament than were other Liberals and that they were more aware of and sensitive to the informal behavioral norms of parliament and the sanctions that support those norms places cabinet ministers still more firmly in the insider category. Cabinet members were less likely to find the "delegate-servant" role style congenial and they were less likely to perceive parliament as performing other than its "traditional" functions. Further, they were more likely to feel they were experts in some aspect of parliament's work; they were more likely to view the position of MP as affording an opportunity for a career; and, although on the average they were approximately two years younger than noncabinet colleagues, they nonetheless had enjoyed approximately two more years of parliamentary tenure—again, in great part, because they represented constituencies that were less competitive than the constituencies represented by other Liberals. In summary, the data suggest that cabinet members are a distinguishable group. They differ from noncabinet Liberals not only in terms of their preparliamentary backgrounds, but also in their current statuses and perspectives. All of these differences clearly imply that cabinet ministers were members of what we have termed the inner club of parliament. Indeed, their membership in that group may very well have been one of the reasons they were appointed to cabinet.

Our feeling that cabinet ministers constitute a distinct and distinguishable group is further reinforced by introducing standing committee chairmen into our comparisons between cabinet ministers and Liberal backbenchers. These 3-way comparisons revealed a number of relatively narrow differences between the committee chairmen and the backbenchers (e.g., in the average ages at which they experienced important politically socializing events, the level of their peer groups' interest in politics, in their perceptions of conflict with important groups, their perceptions of what they have accomplished as MPs, their awareness of rules of the game, and the extent of their parliamentary experience). The comparisons also indicated that along some variables there were monotonic orderings in which the cabinet members were on one end, the backbenchers on the other, and the committee chairmen somewhere in between (e.g., in their average ages, the levels of their educations, their ethnic origins, the proportion that were reared in metropolitan regions, their motivations for becoming candidates, and perceptions of expertise). Again, however, the differences between the committee chairmen and the backbenchers were rarely substantial.

Two important inferences may be drawn from the patterns of these differences and similarities. The first is that apart from general similarities in the recruitment experience of cabinet and noncabinet Liberal MPs, the cabinet members constitute a distinct group who stand in a hierarchical relationship to their noncabinet colleagues. Kornberg, Falcone, and Mishler, after comparing a cross-section of Canadian public with private members and cabinet ministers during the period 1867–1968, observed that "cabinet members may be considered an elite among elites in that they stand in approximately the same relationship to backbenchers as do the latter to the general public."[10] The analyses we have just conducted strongly suggest this situation did not change in the 28th Parliament. A second inference is that the position of chairman of a standing committee is a not very satisfactory consolation prize[11] awarded to certain backbenchers who will not become ministers. As was noted above, on a number of variables committee chairmen occupied an intermediate position between cabinet ministers and backbenchers, suggesting some selection on the part of those assigning MPs to the position (the "consolation" factor). However, on most variables for which comparisons can be made[12] committee chairmen were not significantly different from backbenchers indicating that the position is not an important stepping stone in the parliamentary career, one which the most able MPs occupy before moving on to the cabinet.

But what of the position of parliamentary secretary? Some might argue that in a parliamentary system of the British model, this position rather than the position of committee chairman is used to groom future ministers. There are two reasons why such an argument, although possible, is not very persuasive. First, a substantial proportion of the MPs who were committee chairmen at the time these interviews were taken (and with whom we compared the cabinet ministers) either already had been parliamentary secretaries or became parliamentary secretaries by the time parliament was dissolved in 1972. Thus, it is highly unlikely that we would have found either relatively few differences between the ministers and their secretaries on the one hand or very marked differences between the secretaries and backbench Liberals on the other. Second, it is difficult to argue that a parliamentary secretaryship is an important stepping stone in a parliamentary career given Prime Minister Trudeau's practice of replacing, en masse, one cohort of parliamentary secretaries with another in virtually every parliamentary session. Critics of this practice have complained (and their objections never have been vigorously denied) that by so doing Mr. Trudeau has debased the position. They claim that the benefits deriving from being named a parliamentary secretary largely are financial, a fairly significant albeit temporary increase in salary. There are almost no career advantages, they argue. Moreover, even before Mr. Trudeau began the practice of rotating Liberal MPs in and out of the position, critics such as John Porter had claimed that the parliamentary secretaryship was not an important stage in the parliamentary career. His data indicated that from the time the position was created (1943) until 1960 "more people reached cabinet positions without the experience than with it."[13]

Indeed, he argues that there is no political career, per se, in Canada. He contends that if there were,

a person following a model political career would probably begin with some activity as a member of a political party and gradually proceed through a series of stages, as candidate, as a member of Parliament, as party official, as a party leader of junior status, as a person with an increasing power role within the party, and eventually as front bench material to alternate between government and opposition. Such career stages, it could be argued, are consistent with the parliamentary form of government. There would be in this model a kind of apprenticeship system from which existing leaders would recruit their party's crown princes. In the process the politician would increasingly become a public figure with a following in the party and in the country, who would articulate for the society particular values and goals. The political leadership role would call for certain skills in persuasion and in the management of party and of Parliament. Like all skills, political ones require training and experience within the political system, whatever personality qualities, such as strength of will, that a person may have and that make him a good leader.[14]

Careers of this kind have not been possible in Canada, he believes, because of the practice of Liberal prime ministers, beginning with Wilfred Laurier in 1896, of coopting provincial politicians, corporate lawyers and high echelon bureaucrats for cabinet posts. Except for the provincial party leaders, these men had virtually no political experience. The practice has been for the prime minister either to recruit these individuals by promising them cabinet posts or to actually name them to the cabinet. There is no evidence to suggest that the former really required much coaxing but in either case they were placed in constituencies from which they could be elected to parliament. (It should be noted, however, that individuals who were "parachuted" into constituencies in this manner often faced intra-party contests for their nominations.)

The most enthusiastic practitioner, the late W. L. Mackenzie King, rationalized his actions in terms of the necessity for representing significant societal interests in the cabinet. "Apparently," Porter observes, "the significant interests as perceived by the prime minister were not reflected in those elected to the House of Commons." [15] Even if they were, Porter contends the "representation of interests" argument still would not hold water, for beyond the representation of ethnic and religious interests "sectional and interest divisions are analytically more difficult to support, simply because within a differentiated society the range is infinite."[16] Moreover, "all the significant differentiations in Canadian society seem to be represented by lawyers and businessmen with university degrees. Their social homogeneity in terms of education and occupation far outweigh any heterogeneity in terms of regionalism, religion, or other interests." [17]

Nor will Porter accept the claim that prime ministers are forced to go outside parliament to find cabinet ministers because a vicissitudinous electorate deprives them of backbench talent before it has had a chance to mature. According to Porter, there is a "vicious circle" operating in the argument that prime ministers must coopt outsiders to "strengthen" the government because the practice prevents already-elected members from acquiring the stature, the political experience, and the national visibility which not only would make them cabinet material, but also would help insure that they were reelected.

He acknowledges that the Conservatives, when in office, have not coopted outsiders for cabinet positions as frequently as have the Liberals, but they have not ignored the tactic either. The practice of coopting outsiders into the cabinet has serious consequences. The principal ones, according to Porter, are that the status of bureaucrat vis-a-vis MP and the role of bureaucrat as policy initiator are enhanced, the level of public support for parliament as an institution is eroded, and the political system becomes depoliticized so that it is "strong in administration but weak in creativity."[18]

Although the contention of Van Loon and Whittington (and the supporting sources they cite) that parliament's role in the policy process is largely a "refining" one offers at least oblique support for Porter's charge, and although the Canadian public appears to have somewhat ambivalent attitudes toward parliament as an institution and toward individual MPs,[19] it is rather difficult to evaluate his "consequences" arguments as some of the same claims have been made for countries (e.g., Great Britain) in which the coopting of cabinet ministers is not widespread.[20] Let us instead consider some of his specific assertions regarding the absence of the parliamentary career per se. Porter's data make clear that Canadian prime ministers at times have appointed individuals to the cabinet who have had very little or no previous parliamentary experience. Indeed, in this regard, four of the last five prime ministers may be said to have been coopted (King and Pearson from the bureaucracy, St. Laurent from corporate law and Trudeau from the university). Only Mr. Diefenbaker, the former Conservative leader, had had long seasoning as an MP before becoming prime minister. Further, a comparative study by Joseph Schlesinger of cabinet appointments in Canada (1921–1957), Australia (1946–1957), Great Britain (1922–1960), and France (1947–1958) indicates that a substantially higher proportion (28.7%) of members with a year or less of parliamentary experience were appointed to the cabinet in Canada than in Australia (6%), Great Britain (4.1%) or France (15.7%). However, Schlesinger's data make clear that there is a considerable difference between Liberals and Conservatives in this regard. For example, the modal (36.2%) Conservative group of ministers had had five to nine years of parliamentary experience at the time of appointment whereas the modal (36.4%) Liberal group had had one year or less before becoming ministers. [21] In effect, Schlesinger's study suggests that in comparison to members of three other parliamentary systems, Canadian MPs either have "made it" to the cabinet relatively early in their parliamentary lifetimes or they have not made it at all.

Porter's observation that the different interests that are supposedly represented in the Canadian cabinet seem "to be represented by lawyers and businessmen with university degrees" is supported by both the current data and by the findings of studies that have examined the composition of cabinets over time.[22] Moreover, the present and previously reported research also support his contention that over time the preparliamentary public office-holding experience of cabinet ministers has declined. Indeed, their lack of such experience is one of the factors that best distinguishes the current group of cabinet ministers from their parliamentary party colleagues. However, Porter is not correct in asserting that Liberal cabinets have been composed disproportionately of men who have been apolitical, since the data from our current study indicate that cabinet ministers do have histories of long service in their party organizations—significantly longer, in fact, than their party colleagues who are not in the cabinet.

On balance, then, if a parliamentary career is conceived as the totality of member experiences within a parliamentary structure with the prospect of continuous, predictable, upward movement through a hierarchy of positions, then clearly relatively few of the current group of Liberal cabinet ministers had had much in the way of a career. Indeed, the parliamentary careers of a majority of them may well have begun only after their appointment to cabinet. They may have moved, for example, from a junior ministerial position (e.g., Minister Without Portfolio) to an intermediate appointment (e.g., Minister of Northern Affairs) to a senior position (e.g., External Affairs or Finance).

Their enjoyment of the model career posited by John Porter seems to have been confined largely to activities in the Liberal party organization outside parliament. As was indicated above, cabinet ministers had significantly more service in their party organizations than had their nonparty colleagues. A number of ministers had begun their party work in para-party groups such as university and Young Liberal Clubs. As holders of high level offices in these organizations they were able at regional and national party conventions to rub shoulders with men who then were in the cabinet and in the highest level positions of the regular party organization. They continued to be active in highly visible party activities such as "thinkers' conferences" after leaving the university and establishing themselves in professions or in the business world. During interviews they reported being "encouraged" to seek a parliamentary nomination by the former Liberal prime minister, the late Lester B. Pearson, or some of his closest associates in the cabinet or the national Liberal organization. We may assume that individuals who were well enough acquainted with a former prime minister to be encouraged by him to become parliamentary candidates experienced little difficulty in moving into the cohort of insiders after their election. It is from the ranks of the insiders that ministers are disproportionately drawn. Of course, there are exceptions to this generalization. Mr. O'Dare, the subject of an introductory vignette, was one. However, the preparliamentary experience of his cabinet colleague with whom he shared an office when both were freshmen MPs was fairly typical of Liberal cabinet ministers. Parenthetically, O'Dare's complaint about his former officemate and current cabinet colleague ("They already were talking about him as a future Prime Minister although we were in opposition at the time and he had yet to demonstrate that he could do anything but dance well") provides an interesting footnote to Porter's claim regarding cooptive tendencies in the Liberal party.

## LEADERSHIP DIFFERENCES WITHIN THE CONSERVATIVE PARTY

If the Liberal party recruits its upper echelon leaders from a group of Liberal MPs whose backgrounds and attitudes suggest they are part of an inner parliamentary club, we may ask whether Conservative leaders also can be regarded as parliamentary insiders. Since many of the differences we observed between Liberal leaders and nonleaders also obtain between Conservative leaders and nonleaders, we suggest they can. For example, Conservative frontbenchers derived from markedly higher socioeconomic backgrounds than their backbench colleagues. They tended to be better educated and their educations were more cosmopolitan in the sense that they more often attended schools outside the provinces in which they were reared. In addition, they were more frequently professionals and businessmen at the time they became candidates for a public office.

They also differed significantly in their ethnic and religious origins from backbenchers, tending more often to be Protestants and to derive from Anglo-Celtic and Northern European backgrounds. (Although Liberal cabinet ministers also were more often Protestants who derived from Anglo-Celtic ethnic origins, the zero-order relationships between these variables and cabinet/noncabinet status were not statistically significant.)

Conservative frontbenchers, like Liberal cabinet members and the "typical" parliamentary insider, also derived from more politicized backgrounds than their backbench colleagues. On the average, the Conservative leaders initially identified with their party 3.7 years earlier and first became interested in politics almost five years earlier than did the backbenchers. The leaders' parents also tended to be more politically active than the parents of backbenchers when these members were growing up; politics tended to be more important for them during the preadult stage of life; and they more frequently belonged to political clubs. In addition, their friends were more frequently interested and involved in politics than was the case with backbenchers and so forth.

With regard to recruitment experience (and unlike the Liberal cabinet members), Conservative frontbenchers more often were recruited into the political system and were less often self-starters than were backbenchers. Like cabinet ministers, Conservative leaders more frequently had backgrounds of service in their party organizations and they less frequently had been unsuccessful candidates for an elected public office before becoming a MP. Moreover, none of the Conservative frontbench members had tried unsuccessfully to secure a parliamentary nomination whereas 14% of the backbenchers had. When the frontbenchers did become candidates, they more often were motivated by ideological considerations and by the challenge of office and less often by good government considerations. Further, less than half of the Conservative frontbench had any intraparty competition at the time of nomination while over two-thirds of the backbenchers had had to run in intraparty contests to become the party's candidate.

Finally (and again consistent with the expectation that Conservative frontbenchers are selected from the ranks of an inner club) we find they were more aware of both rules of the game and sanctions in parliament than were their backbench colleagues. They were more "policy-oriented" and did not find the delegate-servant representational role style as appealing as did backbenchers. They also were more inclined to regard being a MP as a career.

## DIFFERENCES BETWEEN COHORTS OF LEADERS IN THE LIBERAL AND CONSERVATIVE PARTIES

It would appear that in many respects Conservative frontbenchers were drawn from the same population as are Liberal cabinet ministers. There were, however, a number of differences between the two groups that are worth noting. The Conservative frontbenchers, on the average, were more than eight years older than the Liberal ministers, and they tended as well to be small town rather than big city boys (approximately three-fourths of the cabinet ministers grew up in large cities whereas some 70% of the Conservative frontbenchers grew up in small towns). In addition, they tended to be more native Canadian, more Protestant, and more frequently derived from Anglo-Celtic and Northern European stock. They were less frequently university graduates, and those who were graduates tended to have received their undergraduate degrees from provincial universities whereas almost one-fourth of the cabinet had been undergraduates at Canada's "big three" universities—Toronto, McGill, and Queen's. Further, although both groups were reared in politicized environments, the environments in which cabinet ministers grew up were somewhat more politicized.

Conservative frontbenchers became active in party organizations approximately four years earlier than did cabinet ministers; their motives for becoming active differed from those of cabinet ministers; and they seemingly had far less difficulty securing the nominations of their party. In fact, a perusal of the responses of Conservative frontbenchers to the battery of questions on recruitment suggests that many of them had had to be coaxed to become candidates and they agreed only reluctantly out of a spirit of something akin to noblesse oblige. The Liberal cabinet members, in contrast, gave the appearance of being aggressive go-getting types who were motivated by the appeal of their party's programs and policies and by their dislike of the Conservative party's policies and leaders. One gets the impression they required little, if any, urging to become their party's candidates. Yet another difference between the two groups was that the Liberals tended to attribute their nominations to the hard work of friends and colleagues in their party organizations whereas the

Conservatives ascribed their selections as candidates to their personal statuses and social backgrounds.

Currently, the cabinet ministers represent more urban and less politically competitive constituencies and they have resided in them approximately nine fewer years than the Conservatives. They also are far less involved in social organizations outside of parliament. Cabinet ministers are more likely to perceive parliament as offering them a career, and they tend more to see themselves as experts in a particular area. We regard this as a particularly interesting finding since, although both groups had enjoyed a longer period of tenure than their backbench colleagues, the Conservatives, on the average, had had 16.2 years of parliamentary experience whereas the Liberal cabinet ministers had had only 8.5 years.

On a more impressionistic level,[23] we may note that the Conservative frontbenchers (a number of whom had held cabinet positions during the period, 1957–1963, when John Diefenbaker was prime minister) projected an image of being relaxed, easygoing, and confident men who seemed to regard parliament as a very good men's club. They simply took for granted their right to lead the club. The Liberal leaders, in contrast, gave the impression of being a far less relaxed, more energetic group of men for whom parliament was a very serious business and they were orderly and quite systematic in the way in which they conducted it. They were equally as confident as the Conservatives that they had a right to head the business, but their confidence appeared to rest on the belief that they had earned the right because of what they did rather than who they were.

In an interesting and perceptive essay, Canadian party scholar John Meisel[24] has argued that although the leaders of both the Liberal and Conservative parliamentary parties have been a part of a political elite that is homogeneous with respect to its socioeconomic origins, each party's cadre of leaders has tended to become increasingly different in terms of perspectives, values, and even life styles since the 1930s. Very briefly, he observes that the Liberal party has been fortunate to have had "lively, continuous, and close contacts"[25] with the worlds of business, the bureaucracy, and the university. The individuals whom the party has recruited or (more frequently) who have been attracted to the party (i.e., self-starters) have tended disproportionately to be drawn from these three circles. Thus, for more than a generation Liberal party leaders have tended to be part of an urban, highly educated and successful, professional-managerial elite which prizes and rewards competence, predictability, responsibility, and efficiency. It is an elite that has been receptive to moderate social change, but change that is planned and directed by experts. Thus, Liberal leaders have had an affinity for administrators and a talent for administration in part because "parties with long governmental records and expectations of continued success . . . accumulate more managerial and power-seeking candidates than those likely to remain out of office."[26] Meisel goes on to argue that the differences between the Liberal and Conservative leadership cohorts extend to "persistent and patterned differences in values and tastes when it comes to aesthetics, literature, preferred ways of spending one's leisure and so on."[27] If a label can be attached to each group, then the Liberal leaders can be regarded as possessing "elite" tastes, the Conservatives "public" tastes. He recognizes that elite and public-oriented leaders are ideal types; that even if they existed, some would be found in each party. However, "it is a question of more-or-less. The Liberals, although harboring their share of yahoos, simply had a large enough concentration of elite-taste leaders to affect their party's style. The Conservatives did not."[28] Meisel admits his impressions are just impressions but they reinforce our own and add another and interesting perspective from which to view the findings we have reported above. We will pursue and try to shed more light on interparty leadership differences in the next chapter and in the concluding chapter and suggest some consequences they have had for the functioning of the Canadian parliamentary system.

## MULTIVARIATE ANALYSES

To recapitulate, not only do parliamentary leaders differ in a variety of ways from their colleagues who hold no leadership positions, but the leadership cadres of the two major parties also differ from one another in terms of backgrounds, current situations, attitudes, and perspectives. The problem is to determine in which ways they differ most. As we indicated in chapter 6, one of the benefits of using multivariate analytic techniques is that they enable an investigator to consider simultaneously the relative effects of several predictor variables. In this instance we want to select the variables that best discriminate: (a) all parliamentary leaders from nonleaders; (b) Liberal cabinet ministers from other Liberals; (c) Liberal cabinet members from Liberal committee chairmen and from Liberal backbenchers; (d) Conservative frontbenchers from Conservative back-benchers; and (e) Conservative frontbenchers from Liberal cabinet ministers. For this purpose we used a series of multiple regression analyses (for all but the Liberal cabinet-committee chairman-back-bench groups) in a manner consistent with our analyses in chapter 7. Through triangulation—by comparing the significant predictors identified by the discriminant function and regression analyses—we hoped to answer the questions posed at the beginning of this chapter.[29] Both the multiple discriminant and regression analyses were conducted in a stepwise fashion and only those independent variables that attained statistical significance beyond the conventional .05 level were permitted to enter and remain in equations.

In both the regression and discriminant function analyses we grouped the independent variables into the five attitudinal and environmental categories of the framework developed in the previous chapter. These categories were selected, it may be remembered, to encompass major segments of the life experiences and attitudes of MPs. Included were "social background," "early life socialization," "recruitment," "current political environment," and "current motivations and political attitudes." Within the social background category are variables such as the MPs' religious affiliations, the national origins and socioeconomic status of their parents, their own ethnic origins, the relative urbanism of their places of birth, their education levels, and their occupations and social statuses at the time they entered parliament. In the early life socialization category we included a factor score measuring the politicization of the MPs' early life environments, a factor score measuring the importance ascribed to politics during high school and college, a summary measure of the age at which MPs became aware of politics, initially identified with a political party, and became interested in politics as well as several measures of their school friends' interest in politics, the MPs' membership in political clubs, and the numbers of times they switched party affiliations—seven variables in all. There are fourteen variables in the recruitment and political career category, including variables that were concerned with the MPs' motives for getting into politics or running for office, whether the MPs had held public office before running for parliament, to what extent, if any, they were involved in party work before becoming candidates for parliament, and whether they had ever been unsuccessful in a bid for elected public office. In the current political environment category, we included twenty-one variables; multiple indicators of MPs' awareness of or sensitivity to the informal rules and sanctions of parliament, a measure of their length of service in parliament, and several measures of the levels of urbanization and electoral competition in their constituencies. Finally, in the current attitudes and motivations category, we used eight measures of the MPs' role perceptions and perceptions of role conflicts, five indicators of their political ambitions or feelings of accomplishment, four measures of the incentives they mention for becoming MPs, and six measures of their orientation toward politics in general and parliament in particular—a total of twenty-three attitudinal and motivational variables.

Table 8.1 presents the results we obtained by using the two techniques. Even a cursory inspection reveals that the same variables tend to be significant correlates of leadership regardless of the technique being used. With regard to the ability of the several categories of attitudinal and background variables to explain the differences observed, both the regression and discriminant function analyses indicated that "current situational" variables and, particularly, "attitudes and motivations" best explained differences between parliamentary leaders and nonleaders. Social background variables were somewhat less powerful predictors and political socialization and political recruitment variables seemed to be the least important determinants of who moves to the front and who remains on the backbenches. In the next chapter we will see how well these several categories of variables are able to explain variations in ascribed influence.

## SUMMARY

We began this chapter intending to answer questions about whether the social and political backgrounds, the recruitment experiences, and the current statuses and motivations of parliamentary leaders systematically differ from those of nonleaders. Our analyses suggest that they do.

Another question we tried to address was whether there were systematic differences between top leaders, secondary leaders, and backbenchers in a governing party. We concluded that the differences between a cabinet on the one hand and all other members of a governing party on the other were more significant and probably more meaningful than were those between a governing party's cadre

TABLE 8.1

## A COMPARISON OF SIGNIFICANT DETERMINANTS OF PARLIAMENTARY LEADERSHIP OBTAINED BY USING MULTIPLE DISCRIMINANT AND REGRESSION ANALYSES

|  | Using Multiple Discriminant Analysis | Using Regression Analysis |
|---|---|---|
| **Leaders vs. Nonleaders** | | |
| Social Background Variables | # years of schooling<br>Reared in large urban center<br>Anglo-Celtic and Northern<br>  European ethnic origins<br>% who were lawyers | # years of schooling<br>Reared in large urban center<br>Anglo-Celtic and Northern<br>  European ethnic origins |
| Political Socialization<br>  Variables | $\overline{X}$ early ages of political<br>  socialization | $\overline{X}$ early ages of political<br>  socialization |
| Political Recruitment<br>  Variables | Prior public office-holder<br>Cites ideological motives<br>  for becoming candidate | Prior public office-holder |
| Current Political Situational<br>  Variables | # of years parliamentary<br>  experience<br>Cites organizational rules<br>Represents urban constit-<br>  uency | # of years parliamentary<br>  experience<br>Cites organizational rules<br>Represents urban constit-<br>  uency |
| Attitude and Motivation<br>  Variables | Perceives self as expert in<br>  substantive area<br>Cites personal satisfaction<br>  incentive for remaining<br>  a MP<br>Dislikes delegate-servant<br>  role style<br>Likes being a MP | Perceives self as expert in<br>  substantive area<br>Cites personal satisfaction<br>  incentive for remaining<br>  a MP<br>Dislikes delegate-servant<br>  role style |
| **Liberal Cabinet vs. Other Liberals** | | |
| Social Background Variables | # Years of schooling<br># of club memberships | # Years of schooling<br># of club memberships |
| Political Socialization Variables | $\overline{X}$ early ages of political<br>  socialization | $\overline{X}$ early ages of political<br>  socialization |
| Political Recruitment Variables | None | None |
| Current Political Situational<br>  Variables | Aware of informal sanctions<br>Aware of rules of game | Aware of informal sanctions<br>Aware of rules of game |
| Attitude and Motivation<br>  Variables | Feels parliament is a<br>  career<br>Dislikes delegate-servant<br>  role<br>—<br>Perceives himself as expert<br>  in substantive area<br>Likes being a MP | Feels parliament is a<br>  career<br>—<br>Perceives alternative functions<br>  for parliament<br>Perceives himself as expert<br>  in substantive area<br>Likes being a MP |
| **Liberal Cabinet vs. Standing Committee<br>Chairmen vs. Backbenchers** | | |
| Social Background Variables | # of years of schooling | Not Conducted |
| Political Socialization<br>  Variables | Political environment of<br>  childhood | Not Conducted |
| Political Recruitment<br>  Variables | None | Not Conducted |

Table 8.1 (continued)

| | Using Multiple Discriminant Analysis | Using Regression Analysis |
|---|---|---|
| Current Political Situational Variables | Represents urban constituency Aware of informal sanctions | Not Conducted |
| Attitude and Motivation Variables | Perceives parliament as a career Perceives himself as expert in substantive area | Not Conducted |
| **Conservative Frontbench vs. Backbench** | | |
| Social Background Variables | Has college degree Current age Parents' SES "Other" than Protestant religious denominations | Has college degree Current age Parents' SES |
| Political Socialization Variables | $\overline{X}$ early ages of political socialization Level of peer group political interest | $\overline{X}$ early ages of political socialization Prior importance of politics |
| Political Recruitment Variables | Level of pre-parliamentary party activity | Level of pre-parliamentary party activity |
| Current Political Situational Variables | # of years of parliamentary experience Cites organizational rules Aware of rules of game | # of years of parliamentary experience Cites organizational rules Aware of rules of game (borderline) |
| Attitude and Motivation Variables | Expects to be a cabinet minister Dislikes delegate-servant role style | Dislikes delegate-servant role style |
| **Liberal Cabinet vs. Conservative Frontbench** | | |
| Social Background Variables | # of club memberships Current age Born in Quebec | # of club memberships Current age Born in Quebec |
| Political Socialization Variables | Political environment of childhood | Political environment of childhood |
| Political Recruitment Variables | Experienced difficulty in receiving parliamentary nomination | Experienced difficulty in receiving parliamentary nomination |
| Current Political Situational Variables | # of years of parliamentary experience Cites organizational sanctions | # of years of parliamentary experience Cites organizational sanctions |
| Attitude and Motivation Variables | Perceives parliament as a career Perceives himself as expert in substantive area # of accomplishments cited | Perceives parliament as a career Perceives himself as expert in substantive area # of accomplishments cited |

of secondary leaders and its backbenchers. More specifically, it did not appear that the position of committee chairman was being used to groom future cabinet ministers.

The last question we attempted to answer was whether there were

Liberal and opposition Conservative party to suggest that those who made it to the top of the former were not the same kind of individuals as those who made it to the top of the latter party. Our data suggest that Liberal leaders differ in various subtle and not so subtle ways from their Conservative counterparts, findings that are consonant with the impressions of Canadian party scholar John Meisel.

## Chapter 9

# MODELS OF INFLUENCE IN THE CANADIAN HOUSE OF COMMONS

## INTRODUCTION

Central to our discussion of the determinants of influence in the Canadian House of Commons has been the explicit assumption that influence in a parliamentary system derives from a complex chain of attributes and experiences that evolve during the life of the MP, beginning perhaps even as far back as his social origins or first political consciousness. In the introduction to this volume, we presented a diagram of this process. We hypothesized that parliamentary influence is a function of two conditions, participation in parliament and holding a formal position in that body. Participation and position, in turn, are conceptualized as direct products of individual attitudes and motives (with opportunity fulfilling a gatekeeper function), and indirect consequences of factors in the current political environment and of the individual's social background and political socialization and recruitment experiences. Subsequent chapters were devoted to the elaboration and validation of this general causal sequence. We operationalized and described the structure of influence and participation in parliament and thereafter examined the associations between influence, participation and position on the one hand, and a variety of social, psychological, and behavioral variables on the other.

Although necessary, these univariate descriptions of the data and multivariate correlational analyses cannot, by themselves, validate the direct and indirect pathways among and between the components of the conceptual framework developed in the introduction.

Consequently, the central concern of this chapter is the application of multivariate techniques of causal inference and path analyses in a systematic empirical test of the framework. First, we will employ conventional Simon-Blalock techniques of causal inference to test and revise the empirical structure of the model for the members of parliament as a whole and for specific parliamentary groups. Then we will use path analysis techniques to assess the relative strengths of the various pathways to influence incorporated in the model in order to enhance our understanding of the determinants of influence. Before turning to these substantive concerns, however, a brief explanation of our methodology is in order.

## A NOTE ON METHODOLOGY

Although, by now, the use of causal models in social science research is almost commonplace, considerable controversy and discussion continue with respect to the most appropriate techniques for their construction. In particular, the literature concerning asymmetric or recursive models continues to labor the differences between: (a) Simon-Blalock procedures for testing the tenability of the linkages specified in a model; and (b) path analysis or dependence analysis techniques for assessing the magnitudes of these linkages. As often is the case in such controversies, however, discussions of the differences in these approaches tend to overlook the fact that path analysis and Simon-Blalock techniques are complementary. Indeed, properly viewed, the Simon-Blalock approach is only a special case of more general path analytic procedures[1] —a special case whose idiosyncratic properties provide valuable information concerning the validity of model linkages not necessarily apparent from path analysis.

For our purpose, the most important difference between these approaches is the use of correlation coefficients in the Simon-Blalock approach and the use of regression coefficients (standardized or unstandardized) in path analysis. Although the numerators of these coefficients are identical, their denominators are not. Thus, while the correlation and regression coefficients reach zero simultaneously,[2] they approach zero at different rates. The practical consequence of this is that the slope of the regression equation may persist largely intact, though the identical correlation coefficient has been reduced to near zero. To the extent that one is working with "accepted theory" and can be relatively confident that the linkages specified are empirically valid this difference does not pose a problem. But where theory is scarce, the regression coefficient may estimate a slope for a linkage that for all practical purposes is nonexistent. In light of these differences Blalock concludes that:

> The method of path coefficients appears to be primarily useful in situations where practically all of the variation in a given dependent variable can be associated with all other variables in a system. It also seems to be most appropriate where theory has been well developed and where it is merely necessary to estimate the magnitudes of empirical constants.[3]

Since there is no well developed theory of the determinants of parliamentary influence, and because the residual or unexplained variance in some of our dependent variables is substantial, prudence dictates that we first use the Simon-Blalock procedure to validate the hypothesized linkages in our model. We then will use the path analytic technique to estimate the strengths of the linkages that survive validation.

## MODELS OF PARLIAMENTARY INFLUENCE

A necessary first step is the specification and measurement of both the model's components and the links by which the concepts are related. Previous chapters contain detailed descriptions of how we performed these initial operations. Indeed, with regard to the operationalization and measurement of concepts, we may have, in a sense, overperformed. Since it is not feasible to specify, much less test, the myriad possible linkages either between or among the multiple indicators of the eight concepts included in the schematic framework,[4] we have had to simplify the operational model by selecting a single indicator to represent each of its conceptual components. In some cases the selection of a representative variable was obvious. For example, the factor index of participation in House debate and question period was an obvious representative indicator of the participation concept because of the primary importance of these activities in parliament. The selection of representative indicators of other concepts, however, proved more difficult. Lacking theoretical reasons for selecting a single indicator to represent most of the concepts, we proceded empirically and selected the variable from each category that achieved the highest average correlations with the final dependent variables in the model (i.e., influence, participation, and position). Since the selection of representative indicators was subgroup specific, the variables included in our analyses vary slightly from one model to another[5] (see table 9.1).

One other adjustment was required to transform the conceptual framework into an operational model. Consistent with our hypothesis that participation in parliament is both a principal pathway to achieving a leadership position in parliament (debate activity gives the aspiring leader visibility and is, in itself, a valuable leadership skill) and an important responsibility of the individual who is promoted to a position of leadership, the framework posits a reciprocal linkage between parliamentary position and participation. However, the need to specify only recursive linkages in ordinary least squares analyses, together with the lack of instrumental variables (i.e., additional exogeneous variables that would permit us to estimate the independent effects of the interdependent endogenous variables) led us to specify a one-way linkage from participation to position. Our decision to do so rested largely on the empirical observation that we are able to predict participation using other variables in the model better than we are able to predict position. Figure 9.1 presents the resulting operational model of the determinants of individual influence in the House of Commons.

The second stage in the construction of a causal model is validation, or the assessment of the degree to which the properties and behavior of the model conform to "reality" (i.e., the data). Several validation techniques have been suggested in the literature[6] but

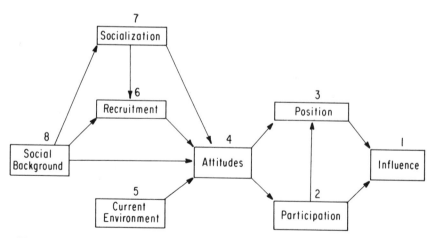

FGIURE 9.1. HYPOTHESIZED GENERAL MODEL OF INFLUENCE AMONG CANADIAN MPs

TABLE 9.1
## VARIABLES USED TO OPERATIONALIZE AND MEASURE CONCEPTS INCLUDED IN EXPLANATORY MODEL OF INFLUENCE IN THE CANADIAN HOUSE OF COMMONS

| Concept | For All MPs | For Liberals | For Conservatives |
|---|---|---|---|
| | Operational Variable | Operational Variable | Operational Variable |
| Social Background | College Education | College Education | Own SES |
| Political Socialization | SAGE[a] | SAGE | SAGE |
| Political Recruitment | PARAC[b] | PARAC | PARAC |
| Attitudes and Motivations | Perceptions of Expertise | Perceptions of Expertise | Perceptions of Representational Role Style |
| Current Political Environment | Number of Years of Parliamentary Experience | Knowledge of Organizational Rules of the Game | Number of Years of Parliamentary Experience |
| Position | Holds Formal Position in Parliament (Cabinet) or Party | Holds Formal Position in Parliament (Cabinet) or Party | Holds Formal Position of Leadership in Party |
| Participation | Extent of Participation in House Debate and Question Period | Extent of Participation in House Debate and Question Period | Extent of Participation in House Debate and Question Period |
| Influence | Number of Nominations Received for Being One of Ten Most Influential MPs | Number of Nominations Received for Being One of Ten Most Influential MPs | Number of Nominations Received for Being One of Ten Most Influential MPs |

a. Factor score of ages of first awareness of politics, first political interest, and first partisan identification.

b. Factor score of extent of pre-parliamentary activity in party organization.

Naylor's multistage strategy, in our view, is the most appropriate. There are three stages in this process: (1) preliminary validation by inspecting the logical tenability of the theoretical propositions embodied in the model; (2) validation of the hypothesized linkages in the model by means of statistical tests of significance; and (3) validation by testing the predictive accuracy of the model.

With respect to the first of these, we already have defended the theoretical properties of the model (see the introduction and chapter 7). Although the assessment of "face-validity" largely is subjective, we may note that the model is consistent with our understanding of current theory on the attitudes and behavior of legislative elites with the two exceptions noted above (i.e., the specification of an asymmetrical linkage between participation and position and the omission from the model of several potentially important variables for the sake of statistical parsimony). The practical consequences of these departures from theory, however, should not prove critical. At worst, they may result in some underestimation of the variance we can explain in the participation variable and in certain of the variables that appear earlier in the model where the most general and underspecified concepts are located.

The second validation procedure, validation of the hypothesized relationships by means of statistical tests of significance, closely corresponds to the Simon-Blalock technique for testing the tenability of hypothesized linkages in causal models. As Blalock has shown, when certain assumptions are met,[7] the structure of a causal model can be reproduced as a series of mathematical predictions concerning the equality or inequality of the zero- and higher order partial correlations between appropriate variables in the model. For the model in figure 9.1, the appropriate predictions are listed in the left-most column of table 9.2. Since there are twenty-eight of these predictions, we will not attempt to justify or explain each one individually. The reader should note, however, that wherever the model posits an arrow between two variables, we predict that the partial correlation will persist even when we control for all intervening or mutually antecedent variables (i.e., $r_{xy} \cdot {}_{abc} \ldots i \neq o$). Wherever an arrow is missing from the model (e.g., between attitudes and influence) the prediction is that the partial correlation controlling for the intervening or mutually antecedent variable (in this case, position and participation) will vanish or at least diminish to near zero (i.e., $r_{xy} \cdot {}_{abc} \ldots i \cong o$). Table 9.2 presents the empirically derived coefficients corresponding to each of these predictions for all

## TABLE 9.2
## PREDICTED AND ACTUAL CORRELATIONS IN THE INITIAL INFLUENCE MODEL FOR ALL MPS AND FOR LIBERAL AND CONSERVATIVE MPS

| Predicted | Actual Results All MPs | Actual Results Liberal MPs | Actual Results Conservative MPs |
|---|---|---|---|
| **Included Linkages** | | | |
| 1) $r_{12\cdot3}\neq0$ | .46 | .34 | .68 |
| 2) $r_{13\cdot2}\neq0$ | .42 | .50 | .34 |
| 3) $r_{23\cdot4}\neq0$ | .17 | .33 | .30 |
| 4) $r_{24}\neq0$ | .16 | .22 | −.20 |
| 5) $r_{34\cdot2}\neq0$ | .16 | .20 | −.39 |
| 6) $r_{45}\neq0$ | .18 | .22 | −.15 |
| 7) $r_{46\cdot8}\neq0$ | .20 | .25 | $-.08^a$ |
| 8) $r_{47\cdot8}\neq0$ | −.27 | −.28 | .18 |
| 9) $r_{48\cdot67}\neq0$ | .20 | .19 | −.31 |
| 10) $r_{67\cdot8}\neq0$ | −.25 | −.28 | −.18 |
| 11) $r_{68\cdot7}\neq0$ | $.02^a$ | $.08^a$ | .34 |
| 12) $r_{78}\neq0$ | −.17 | $-.10^a$ | $.00^a$ |
| (Mean) | (.22) | (.25) | (.26) |
| (#Wrong) | (1) | (2) | (2) |
| **Omitted Linkages** | | | |
| 13) $r_{14\cdot23}=0$ | .02 | .05 | .08 |
| 14) $r_{15\cdot23}=0$ | .08 | $-.27^a$ | .02 |
| 15) $r_{16\cdot23}=0$ | −.08 | −.05 | −.05 |
| 16) $r_{17\cdot23}=0$ | $.18^a$ | $.14^a$ | −.01 |
| 17) $r_{18\cdot23}=0$ | −.01 | .05 | −.03 |
| 18) $r_{25\cdot4}=0$ | $.20^a$ | $.15^a$ | $.24^a$ |
| 19) $r_{26\cdot4}=0$ | .04 | −.09 | $.21^a$ |
| 20) $r_{27\cdot4}=0$ | −.04 | −.06 | $-.22^a$ |
| 21) $r_{28\cdot4}=0$ | $.11^a$ | $.16^a$ | $.28^a$ |
| 22) $r_{35\cdot4}=0$ | $.22^a$ | $.14^a$ | $.45^a$ |
| 23) $r_{36\cdot4}=0$ | $.17^a$ | $.12^a$ | $.38^a$ |
| 24) $r_{37\cdot4}=0$ | $-.24^a$ | $-.17^a$ | $-.35^a$ |
| 25) $r_{38\cdot4}=0$ | $.21^a$ | $.20^a$ | .06 |
| 26) $r_{56}=0$ | .03 | .05 | $.21^a$ |
| 27) $r_{57}=0$ | −.03 | −.10 | $-.24^a$ |
| 28) $r_{58}=0$ | −.02 | −.06 | .00 |
| (Mean) | (.10) | (.12) | (.18) |
| (#Wrong) | (7) | (8) | (9) |

a. Indicates error in prediction.

Key:
1) Influence
2) Parliamentary Participation in Debate
3) Parliamentary Position
4) Perceptions of Expertise—Role Style
5) Organizational Rules—Years in Parliament
6) Prior Party Activity
7) Ages of Socialization
8) College Education—Own SES

MPs, and for the members of the Liberal and Progressive-Conservative parliamentary parties respectively. We did not attempt to assess the validity of individual models for the NDP and Social Credit party subgroups because of their small sizes.[8]

Turning to the coefficients in table 9.2, it is apparent that although the data for "All MPs" do not perfectly "fit" the model, there is sufficient congruence to support the overall validity of the model's basic structure. Of the twelve direct linkages incorporated in the model and represented by the predictions in the upper half of table 9.2, only one, the linkage between social background and recruitment, fails to achieve a correlation greater than .10 when the appropriate variables are controlled. Social background, it appears, does not directly determine the nature of the recruitment experience, although it clearly influences this process indirectly through the intervening effect of political socialization. The average (mean) absolute magnitude of these twelve correlations is .22—not overwhelming but, clearly, substantially greater than zero.

Somewhat less support exists for our omission of certain linkages from the model for all MPs. Particularly suspect in this regard is our assumption (represented by predictions 18 through 25) that social background, recruitment, and political socialization experiences, together with current environmental variables, influence participation and position in parliament *only indirectly* through the intervening effects of individual attitudes and motivations. Although the average correlation of the linkages excluded from the model is only .10, the magnitudes of seven of the linkages are greater than .10. In other words, even with attitudes and motivations controlled, both an MP's level of educational attainment and the length of his parliamentary experience exercise a direct effect upon the extent to which he participates in parliamentary debate. Moreover, his level of education, the extent of his preparliamentary activity in a party organization, and the length of his parliamentary experience directly determine whether or not he will secure a leadership position. Indeed, if we revise the model by linking the latter three variables with position, we find that the initially hypothesized link between attitudes and motivations on the one hand and position on the other hand is spurious ($r_{34} \cdot {}_{255678} = .01$). Put another way, attitudes and motivations do influence position but only indirectly through the intervening effect of participation.

More disturbing than the observation that both position and

participation are directly related to factors such as education, preparliamentary party activity, and length of parliamentary tenure (or the finding that the hypothesized relationships between attitudes and motivations and position is spurious) is the finding that when the effects of both participation and position are controlled (prediction 16) the political socialization variable still exerts a direct and fairly substantial impact upon the influence ascribed to an MP ($r_{17} \cdot {}_{23} =$ .18). In contrast to the findings of previous studies on the effects of political socialization experiences on adult political behavior, moreover, we find that MPs who became aware of politics, identified with a political party, and became interested in politics later in life are more likely to be ascribed influence than those who experienced these events at an earlier age.

What has happened, we believe, is that the introduction of statistical controls for position and, particularly, for participation in debate and question period, have effectively restricted the variation in influence to MPs who participate largely in committee work and/or the introduction of private bills and resolutions. Since, in comparison to other MPs, committee activists tend to be relatively unsophisticated politically, and since they also tend to have been socialized politically at a later age (see chapter 7), the positive partial correlation between political socialization and influence may represent the unmeasured effect of participation in committees. If this speculation is correct, we should find that the introduction of committee activity as a control variable will severely attenuate the partial correlation. Happily this proves to be the case; the resulting partial correlation between political socialization and influence for the 34 MPs for whom committee data is available erodes to −.01.

The discrepancies between the data and the hypothesized linkages that we found in table 9.2 enabled us to revise the model for all MPs. We deleted the linkages between social background and recruitment and between attitudes and position, and we added links from political socialization to position and influence, from recruitment to position, from social background to position and participation, and from current environment to participation and position. We generated a new set of predictions that are consistent with this revised model and tested their validity by comparing them with the data. The results, displayed in table 9.3, indicate we have a much better fit between the revised model and the data. The average correlation for the 17 links included in the revised model is .22. In contrast, none of

TABLE 9.3

## PREDICTED AND ACTUAL CORRELATIONS IN THE REVISED INFLUENCE MODELS FOR ALL MPS

### Included Linkages

| Predicted | Actual | Predicted | Actual |
|---|---|---|---|
| 1) $r_{12\cdot3}\neq0$ | .46 | 10) $r_{37\cdot468}\neq0$ | −.23 |
| 2) $r_{13\cdot27}\neq0$ | .51 | 11) $r_{38\cdot47}\neq0$ | .21 |
| 3) $r_{17\cdot23}\neq0$ | .18 | 12) $r_{45}\neq0$ | .18 |
| 4) $r_{23\cdot458}\neq0$ | .17 | 13) $r_{46\cdot7}\neq0$ | .12 |
| 5) $r_{24\cdot58}\neq0$ | .11 | 14) $r_{47\cdot68}\neq0$ | −.19 |
| 6) $r_{25\cdot4}\neq0$ | .20 | 15) $r_{48\cdot7}\neq0$ | .20 |
| 7) $r_{28\cdot4}\neq0$ | .11 | 16) $r_{67}\neq0$ | −.27 |
| 8) $r_{35\cdot42}\neq0$ | .24 | 17) $r_{78}\neq0$ | −.17 |
| 9) $r_{36\cdot47}\neq0$ | .26 | | |

### Omitted Linkages

| Predicted | Actual | Predicted | Actual |
|---|---|---|---|
| 18) $r_{14\cdot237}=0$ | .06 | 24) $r_{24\cdot25678}=0$ | .01 |
| 19) $r_{15\cdot23}=0$ | .08 | 25) $r_{56}=0$ | .03 |
| 20) $r_{16\cdot23}=0$ | −.08 | 26) $r_{57}=0$ | −.03 |
| 21) $r_{18\cdot237}=0$ | .01 | 27) $r_{58}=0$ | −.02 |
| 22) $r_{26\cdot4}=0$ | .04 | 28) $r_{68\cdot7}=0$ | .01 |
| 23) $r_{27\cdot4}=0$ | −.04 | | |

Note: Avg. Included Linkage = .22; Avg. Omitted Linkage = .04.

Key

| | |
|---|---|
| 1) Influence | 5) Years In Parliament |
| 2) Participation in Debate | 6) Prior Party Activism |
| 3) Parliamentary Position | 7) Ages of Socialization |
| 4) Perceptions of Expertise | 8) College Education |

the 11 linkages excluded from the model has correlations as large as .10, and their average magnitude is only .04.[9]

## VALIDATING SUBGROUP MODELS

Since different causal processes might have been operating within different subgroups of MPs,[10] we replicated the validation procedure for the members of the governing Liberal party and for the official opposition, the Progressive-Conservatives. The models hypothesized for the two parties are identical in structure to the model that we initially proposed for all MPs. Hence, the predictions that are generated are identical to those listed in table 9.2. The reader will recall, however, that although the concepts contained in the model are similar, the variables that we selected to represent these concepts differed somewhat for the Liberals and Conservatives. Specifically, level of education is used to represent social background in the Liberal model but respondents' SES scores represent this concept in the Conservative model. Similarly, the attitudes-motivation concept is represented by perceptions of expertise in the Liberal model and by representational role perceptions in the Conservative model. Finally, the concept we term current political environment is represented in the Liberal model by a knowledge of rules of the game (i.e., organizational norms) whereas in the Conservative model it is represented by the length of parliamentary experience. The columns labeled "Liberal" and "Conservative" in table 9.2 indicate that the initial fit between data and predictions is not quite as good for either the Liberals or the Conservatives as it is for all MPs. Among the Liberals, for example there is no strong link between social background and recruitment ($r68.7 = .08$), nor between social background and political socialization. (The latter difference, however, can be partially explained by the relative homogeneity of social backgrounds of Liberal MPs.)

More serious are the discrepancies observed between predictions and data for links that were not supposed to exist. As was the case with all MPs, the data for the Liberals do not support our initial hypothesis that the social backgrounds, the political socialization and recruitment experiences and the current environment are linked only indirectly to parliamentary position and participation. Again, as with the model for all MPs, there is a fairly substantial positive relationship between a Liberal MP's influence and the age at which he was socialized politically. Moreover, we find that even when debate participation and parliamentary position are controlled, the current environment variable exercises a direct and independent, although negative, effect upon the influence ascribed to Liberal MPs. Again, however, the substantial negative partial correlation between current environment (represented by awareness of organizational norms) and influence erodes to a statistically insignificant and positive .12 when we control for committee activity for those Liberals for whom such data are available.

A revised Liberal model that takes into account the discrepancies between the data and the initial predictions is presented in table 9.4.

Although several of the predictions in the revised model are border-line (note the magnitudes of the correlations between political social-ization and social background, between current environment and socialization and between recruitment and participation), not one is contradicted by the data. The average magnitude of the links in the revised model is .24 whereas links excluded from the model have an acceptable average strength of only .07.

It is apparent from an inspection of the column in table 9.2 labeled "Conservatives," that again a number of our initial predic-tions do not fit very well with the data. In fact, although the average

TABLE 9.4

**PREDICTED AND ACTUAL CORRELATIONS IN THE REVISED INFLUENCE MODEL FOR LIBERAL MPS**

| Included Linkages | | | |
|---|---|---|---|
| Predicted | Actual | Predicted | Actual |
| 1) $r_{12 \cdot 3} \neq 0$ | .34 | 10) $r_{36 \cdot 7} \neq 0$ | .17 |
| 2) $r_{13 \cdot 257} \neq 0$ | .58 | 11) $r_{37 \cdot 6} \neq 0$ | −.20 |
| 3) $r_{15 \cdot 23} \neq 0$ | −.17 | 12) $r_{38 \cdot 2} \neq 0$ | .18 |
| 4) $r_{17 \cdot 23} \neq 0$ | .14 | 13) $r_{45} \neq 0$ | .22 |
| 5) $r_{23 \cdot 58} \neq 0$ | .30 | 14) $r_{46 \cdot 7} \neq 0$ | .19 |
| 6) $r_{24 \cdot 58} \neq 0$ | .15 | 15) $r_{47 \cdot 6} \neq 0$ | −.24 |
| 7) $r_{25 \cdot 4} \neq 0$ | .15 | 16) $r_{48} \neq 0$ | .21 |
| 8) $r_{28 \cdot 4} \neq 0$ | .20 | 17) $r_{67} \neq 0$ | −.28 |
| 9) $r_{35 \cdot 2} \neq 0$ | .13 | | |

| Omitted Linkages | | | |
|---|---|---|---|
| Predicted | Actual | Predicted | Actual |
| 18) $r_{14 \cdot 2} = 0$ | .06 | 24) $r_{56} = 0$ | .05 |
| 19) $r_{16 \cdot 23} = 0$ | −.05 | 25) $r_{57} = 0$ | .10 |
| 20) $r_{18 \cdot 23} = 0$ | .05 | 26) $r_{58} = 0$ | −.06 |
| 21) $r_{26 \cdot 4} = 0$ | −.09 | 27) $r_{68} = 0$ | .08 |
| 22) $r_{27 \cdot 4} = 0$ | .07 | 28) $r_{78} = 0$ | −.10 |
| 23) $r_{34 \cdot 25678} = 0$ | .08 | | |

Avg. Included Linkage = .24; Avg. Omitted Linkage = .07.

Key:
1) Influence
2) Participation in Debate
3) Parliamentary Position
4) Perceptions of Expertise
5) Knowledge of Organi-
   zation Rules
6) Prior Party Activity
7) Ages of Socialization
8) College Education

correlation for the 12 hypothesized links is .26, the average correlation for the links that are not supposed to exist was not appreciably smaller (r = .18). However, the errors in the Conservative model are almost identical to the errors that we made initially in constructing the other two: seven of the eleven erroneous predictions derive from our notion that social background, political socialization, and current political environment variables are indirectly linked to participation and position. Thus the hypothesized direct link between attitudes-motivations and participation proved spurious when we introduced controls for social background, political socialization and current environment variables ($r24 \cdot 578 = -.05$). The other errors in the initial Conservative model include a specification of a linkage, when none exists, between social background and political socialization and a failure to specify links that do exist between the political socialization and recruitment variables and the current environment (measured among Conservatives by length of parliamentary tenure). These errors were corrected in the revised model displayed in table 9.5.[11] As with the revised models for all MPs and Liberals there is a reasonably good fit between the revised predictions and the data for the Conservatives. The value of the average absolute correlation of the links included in the revised model is greater than .26; that of the linkages omitted is less than .05.

Having satisfied ourselves with the face validity of the theoretical properties of the model of individual influence, and having tested, revised and validated the model structures, the final step in the validation process is an assessment of the extent to which the revised models account for the observed variations in their respective endogenous variables. The squared multiple correlations are displayed in table 9.6. The models correctly predict 4 to 14% of the variation in the MPs' socialization and recruitment experiences; between 15 and 21% of the variance in their attitudes and motivations; 10% of the variation in current environmental factors (in the Conservative model); 8 to 23% of MP participation in House debates; 23 to 48% of the variance in parliamentary position; and 45 to 60% of the observed variation in individual ascribed influence.

Our inability to explain a higher percentage of the variation in parliamentary participation probably stems from our previously mentioned decision to specify (for methodological reasons) a unidirectional arrow from participation to position, as well as from our inability, other than for the special subsample of 34 MPs, to measure directly the extent of individual opportunities to participate in

## TABLE 9.5
## PREDICTED AND ACTUAL CORRELATIONS IN THE REVISED INFLUENCE MODEL FOR CONSERVATIVE MPS

| Linkages Included | | | |
|---|---|---|---|
| Predicted | Actual | Predicted | Actual |
| 1) $r_{12\cdot3}\neq0$ | .68 | 10) $r_{37\cdot2456}\neq0$ | −.25 |
| 2) $r_{13\cdot2}\neq0$ | .34 | 11) $r_{38\cdot246}\neq0$ | −.13 |
| 3) $r_{23\cdot578}\neq0$ | .23 | 12) $r_{45.7}\neq0$ | −.12 |
| 4) $r_{25\cdot7}\neq0$ | .26 | 13) $r_{47\cdot5}\neq0$ | −.12 |
| 5) $r_{27\cdot5}\neq0$ | −.19 | 14) $r_{48\cdot5}\neq0$ | −.12 |
| 6) $r_{28\cdot5}\neq0$ | .32 | 15) $r_{56\cdot7}\neq0$ | .18 |
| 7) $r_{34\cdot578}\neq0$ | −.37 | 16) $r_{57\cdot6}\neq0$ | −.21 |
| 8) $r_{35\cdot2467}\neq0$ | .35 | 17) $r_{67}\neq0$ | −.14 |
| 9) $r_{36\cdot578}\neq0$ | .31 | 18) $r_{68}\neq0$ | .33 |

| Linkages Omitted | | | |
|---|---|---|---|
| Predicted | Actual | Predicted | Actual |
| 19) $r_{14\cdot23}=0$ | .08 | 24) $r_{24\cdot578}=0$ | −.05 |
| 20) $r_{15\cdot23}=0$ | .02 | 25) $r_{26\cdot578}=0$ | .04 |
| 21) $r_{16\cdot23}=0$ | −.05 | 26) $r_{46\cdot578}=0$ | .03 |
| 22) $r_{17\cdot23}=0$ | −.01 | 27) $r_{58\cdot6}=0$ | −.07 |
| 23) $r_{18\cdot23}=0$ | −.03 | 28) $r_{78}=0$ | −.08 |

Avg. Included Linkage = .27; Avg. Omitted Linkage = .05.

Key:
1) Influence
2) Participation in Debate
3) Parliamentary Position
4) Representational Role
   Style
5) Years in Parliament
6) Prior Party Activity
7) Ages of Socialization
8) Own Socioeconomic
   Status

committee activities. However, since these models were designed to explain individual ascribed influence, the fact that we succeeded in predicting up to 60% of the variance in the final dependent variable is important. This level of prediction compares favorably with results achieved by other microanalytic models of elite political behavior reported in the literature.

## A PATH ANALYSIS OF INDIVIDUAL INFLUENCE

Simon-Blalock procedures test for the existence or absence of hypothesized linkages in models but they do not provide information on their strengths. Nor do they tell us anything about the relative strengths of the simple and compound paths between the seven exogenous and intermediate endogenous variables and individual influence. This additional information is provided by path analysis. Because the three models generated in the preceding section of this chapter have recursive structures, it can be demonstrated that the estimation of their path coefficients is identical to ordinary least squares analysis or multiple regression.[12] Thus, we were able to calculate the magnitudes of the path coefficients for each of the revised models of influence by regressing all of the exogenous and antecedent endogenous variables in the model upon each of the endogenous variables to which they are directly related. Figures 9.2 through 9.4 illustrate the structures of the revised models of influence for all MPs, Liberal MPs and Conservative MPs and present the path coefficients (standardized regression coefficients) for each of the linkages.[13]

Path coefficients, however, reflect only the direct and immediate effects of one variable upon another. In order to assess both indirect and spurious effects of correlations between pairs of related variables, we followed convention and measured each indirect path as the "product of the elementary path coefficients associated with the individual steps in its respective pathway."[14] In figure 9.2, for example, the indirect path between participation and ascribed influ-

TABLE 9.6

**PERCENTAGE OF VARIANCE ($R^2$) IN EACH
ENDOGENOUS VARIABLE EXPLAINED BY ALL
DIRECTLY DETERMINANT EXOGENOUS AND
ANTECENDENT ENDOGENOUS VARIABLES IN THE
THREE INFLUENCE MODELS**

| Endogenous Variable | All MPs | Liberals | Conservatives |
|---|---|---|---|
| Influence | 42% | 48% | 59% |
| Position | 23 | 23 | 48 |
| Participation | 8 | 12 | 23 |
| Attitudes-Motivation | 15 | 21 | 14 |
| Current Environment | (Exogenous) | (Exogenous) | 10 |
| Recruitment | 6 | 7 | 14 |
| Socialization | 4 | (Exogenous) | (Exogenous) |
| Social Background | (Exogenous) | (Exogenous) | (Exogenous) |

ence is measured as the product of the path coefficients for the step from participation to position and the step from position to ascribed influence (.12 X .47 = .056 or .06). Had there been more than one indirect path between these variables, the total indirect effects of participation on attributed influence would have been the sum of all individual indirect paths. In a similar manner, the total spurious relationship between two variables was defined and measured as the sum of the products of the path coefficients for all direct and indirect paths to these variables from any mutually antecedent determinants in the model. For the participation-influence linkage in figure 9.2 there are four such paths: one from the current environment variable and three that originate with the social background variable (two of which can be traced through the socialization and recruitment variables). The total spurious correlation between influence and participation, thus, is (.20 X .28 X .47) + (.13 X .21 X .47) + (.13 X −.17 X .17) + (.13 X −.17 X −.25 X .14 X .47) = .036 or .04.

Proceeding in this way for each of the revised models, we calculated the direct, indirect, and spurious effects of all seven exogenous and intermediate endogenous variables úpon individual attributed influence. These data, together with data on the total causal effect (direct + indirect), total predicted relationship (direct effects + indirect effects + spurious correlation), and total observed relationship (actual correlation) of each variable with individual influence are reported in table 9.7. The total predicted and observed correlations reported in columns 5 and 6 of this table serve primarily as a further

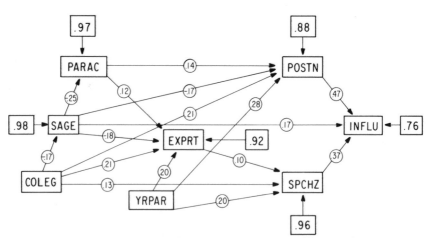

FIGURE 9.2. REVISED PATH MODEL OF THE PROCESS THROUGH WHICH CANADIAN MPs ACQUIRE A REPUTATION FOR BEING INFLUENTIAL

TABLE 9.7

COMPARISONS OF THE PREDICTED DIRECT, INDIRECT, NET,
SPURIOUS AND TOTAL EFFECTS OF EACH OF THE SEVEN
EXOGENOUS AND ANTECEDENT ENDOGENOUS VARIABLES ON
INDIVIDUAL INFLUENCE IN THE THREE MODELS

| | Direct Effect | Indirect Effect | Net Causal Effect | Spurious Effect | Total Relationship | |
| | | | | | Predicted | Observed |
|---|---|---|---|---|---|---|
| All MPs | | | | | | |
| Position | .47 | — | .47 | .03 | .50 | .51 |
| Participation | .37 | .06 | .43 | .04 | .47 | .46 |
| Expertise (Attitudes-Motivations) | — | .04 | .04 | .11 | .15 | .13 |
| Years in Parliament (Current Environment) | — | .23 | .23 | — | .23 | .22 |
| Party Activity (Recruitment) | — | .07 | .07 | −.02 | .05 | .02 |
| Political Socialization | .17 | −.11 | .06 | −.03 | .03 | −.01 |
| Education (Social Background) | — | .15 | .15 | — | .15 | .15 |
| Liberal MPs | | | | | | |
| Position | .54 | — | .54 | .05 | .59 | .58 |
| Participation | .32 | .15 | .47 | −.01 | .46 | .45 |
| Expertise (Attitudes-Motivations) | — | .07 | .07 | .01 | .08 | .15 |
| Organizational Rules (Current Environment) | −.21 | .16 | −.05 | — | −.05 | −.06 |
| Party Activity (Recruitment) | — | .07 | .07 | −.04 | .03 | −.05 |
| Political Socialization | .22 | −.11 | .11 | — | .11 | .07 |
| Education (Social Background) | — | .19 | .19 | — | .19 | .14 |
| Conservative MPs | | | | | | |
| Position | .25 | — | .25 | .16 | .41 | .48 |
| Participation | .63 | .03 | .66 | .04 | .70 | .72 |
| Representational Role Style Perceptions (Attitudes-Motivations) | — | −.08 | −.08 | −.12 | −.20 | −.19 |
| Years in Parliament (Current Environment) | — | .23 | .23 | .04 | .27 | .29 |
| Party Activity (Recruitment) | — | .09 | .09 | .11 | .20 | .21 |
| Political Socialization | — | −.23 | −.23 | — | −.23 | −.25 |
| Own Socioeconomic Status (Social Background) | — | .26 | .26 | — | .26 | .23 |

test of the empirical validity of the three revised models. Although several deviations as large as .08 may be observed between a few of these coefficients, the mean absolute difference between the predicted and observed correlations ranges from a maximum of .04 for the Liberal party subgroup to a minimum of .02 for all MPs.

Assuming that the revised models are empirically valid, a comparison of their structures, together with an examination of the path data in table 9.7 reveals a basic similarity in these models. Because we began with identical models for all MPs and for the members of the two major parties, and made only minor revisions in their structures, a high degree of similarity was inevitable. What is impressive, however, is that the similarities occur with respect to the most fundamental properties of the initial model and, therefore, support the basic theoretical premises with which this inquiry began. For example, although we have noted discrepancies in each model with respect to the persistence of direct linkages between the several background variables and both parliamentary position and participation, the path coefficient data in table 9.7 support the more fundamental assumptions of the primacy of position and participation as direct determinants of ascribed influence, and of the secondary but still significant effects of the social background and political socialization variables as indirect determinants of ascribed influence. The primacy hypothesis is verified by our finding that parliamentary position and participation, although they are not simply surrogate measures of individual ascribed influence, are its strongest direct determinants in all three revised models. In the All MPs model the direct effects of position and participation not only exceed those of the third direct determinant of attributed influence, political socialization, by a margin of more than two to one, but even including the indirect effects of these variables, the total impact of position and participation is almost double that of any other variable in the model. An almost identical pattern of effects can be observed in the Liberal model.

In the Conservative model the direct effect of participation on attributed influence clearly is great. Indeed, it is almost as great as the combined direct and indirect effects of current environmental factors and of the earlier political socialization and political background characteristics. However, the direct effect of position on the influence attributed to Conservative MPs is approximately equaled by the indirect effects, respectively, of their social backgrounds, the ages at which they were socialized politically and the lengths of their parliamentary experience. The indirect effects of these three variables, and of recruitment, on the influence attributed to MPs, regardless of party, is worth noting. Although the importance of these four variables varies in each model, on the average, the current environment factor generally has the most substantial indirect effect on influence. Social background and political socialization variables are next in importance, whereas the variable that represents political recruitment generally has the least overall effect on variations in the influence attributed to MPs.

That the recruitment variable has less impact on ascribed influence, despite the fact that from the perspective of time it stands closer to influence than do either social background or political socialization factors, may be explained, in part, by the data on spurious effects. The recruitment variable occupies an intervening position between attributed influence on the one hand and the social background and socialization variables on the other. It thus transmits the effects of these earlier variables as frequently as it exerts an independent effect of its own. In other words, because it is an intervening variable whose effects on attributed influence are partially additive, approximately 40% of the observed relationship between recruitment and influence is spurious and reflects the earlier effects of social background and/or socialization upon both the recruitment process and individual influence in parliament.

In describing the similarities in these models and explaining the support they provide for our theory of individual influence, no mention has been made of the role played by attitudes and motivations despite the importance previously ascribed to this concept. We had hypothesized that the earlier components of the models (e.g., social background) would influence participation and position only indirectly through the intervening effects of attitudes and motivations. In the process of validating the models, we found that this assumption was not supported by the data. The data in table 9.7, however, permit us to carry the analysis somewhat further. In general the data indicate that attitudes-motivations have no direct effect on ascribed influence whatever and that the average magnitude of their indirect effects is only .06.

The weakness of the attitudes-motivations variable can be attributed (even more than is the case with the political recruitment variable) to the intermediate position it occupies between social background and political socialization, on the one hand, and participation, position, and ascribed influence on the other. Inspection of the relationship between attitudes-motivations and attributed influence reveals that, on the average, about half of the observed relationship between the variables is spurious and can be attributed to the antecedent effects of other variables. Rather than being either an additive or an intervening cause of influence, attitudes-motivations and ascribed influence are both products of essentially identical determinant processes but otherwise are only marginally related.[15]

In general, analysis of the structural similarities among the three models confirms our expectations regarding the process through which individuals develop a reputation for influence. Specifically, it indicates that influential MPs typically derive from upper or upper-middle class environments in which they are exposed to a large number of politicizing stimuli. Partly as a consequence, the well educated future MPs find themselves attracted rather early in their adult lives to party work and by the prospect of holding high level public office. Once they become MPs, they learn the norms of the parliamentary game and develop reputations as frequent and effective participants in debate—qualities that begin to distinguish them. These distinctions, combined with increasing seniority, lead to their recruitment to positions of leadership in their parties. Their positions, as we indicated in chapter 3, provide them with showcases from which they can display their talents and thereby further become identified as influentials.

Notwithstanding this general pattern, a number of intriguing differences may be observed between the Liberal and Conservative models. The most apparent of these differences lies in the variables that we employed as operational measures of identical concepts: social background, current political environment and motivations and attitudes. Since we selected variables that were most strongly correlated with other data in each party's model as operational indices of these concepts, the differences observed reflect, we believe, real differences in the pathways to influence in the two parties.[16]

The inclusion of the expertise, knowledge of organizational norms, and higher education variables in the Liberal model and the representational role styles, parliamentary tenure, and socioeconomic status variables in the Conservative model reinforces our belief that Liberal MPs tend to acquire influence because of "what they are and do" (in particular, because of their political sophistication and personal skills) whereas Conservative MPs acquire influence because of "who they are" (i.e., their personal prestige, parliamentary longevity, and their agreement with the attitudes and values of current party leaders.

The differences between the Liberal and Conservative parties, however, were not limited to the variables employed to represent concepts in their models. They extended to the path structures as well. Inspection of the relative strengths of the various direct determinants of influence brings to light, for example, that although the position and participation variables consistently are the strongest direct determinants of influence in both major parties, the relative effects of these variables are reversed. In the Liberal model (figure 9.3) the direct effect of position on influence is almost double that of participation whereas in the Conservative model participation has more than two and one-half times the impact on influence that position has. There are, however, two plausible explanations that tend to strengthen our argument that Liberals earn the influence ascribed to them whereas Conservatives inherit it with their leadership positions. First, as is evident in figure 9.3, "other" factors (i.e., ethnicity, religion, and province represented) being equal, leadership positions in the Liberal party tend to go to individuals who either have performed in a superior fashion or from whom superior performance is expected. Participation in debate, a superior education, knowledge of organizational rules, and early life political socialization are the most important determinants of influence among Liberals. Other than the last, these variables may be said to reflect individual achievement and political skill and sophistication. Moreover, although perceptions of being expert do not directly determine whether one acquires a position of leadership in the Liberal party, they do have an indirect effect in the sense that they affect participation which, in turn, affects leadership selection. Within the Conservative party the principal determinants of leadership are parliamentary

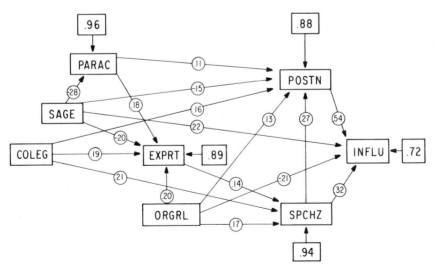

FIGURE 9.3. REVISED PATH MODEL OF THE PROCESS THROUGH WHICH LIBERAL PARTY MPs ACQUIRE A REPUTATION FOR BEING INFLUENTIAL

longevity, long service to the party before entering parliament and representational role perceptions. Although one could argue that long service in the party organization in the electorate contributes to an individual's political sophistication and that one's ability to survive periodic national elections reflects political skill, it seems to us these variables are qualitatively different from those determining leadership selection in the Liberal party.

A second and more obvious explanation of the greater importance of position in the Liberal model is that the Liberals were the governing party when this study was conducted. Not only were they the governing party for the period 1968–1972, they have been the governing party for most of this century. In fact it would not be stretching a point too much to describe the Liberals as Canada's "in party" and the Conservatives as Canada's "out party." Accordingly, the greater importance of position in the Liberal model may simply reflect the greater prestige (and thus influence) that naturally accrues to those who hold cabinet portfolios in a party that is almost perpetually in power as compared to those who are on the frontbench of a party that is almost always in opposition. Implicit in this assumption, of course, is the suggestion that should the Conservatives replace the Liberals as the governing party, the importance of the position variable as a predictor of influence might diminish among Liberal MPs and increase among Conservatives. Verification of this possibility necessarily must await a future study in which the Conservatives form the government. If valid, however, it would help explain the somewhat anomalous finding that the mere occupancy of a leadership position is exceedingly important in the Liberal party, in which influence appears to be dependent upon effective performance or the promise thereof.[17]

As we will argue in the next chapter, virtually all of the data we have acquired, even the difference in the number of direct determinants of influence in the models, point to the importance of achievement in the Liberal party and of ascription in the Conservative party. By way of illustration, in both models parliamentary position and participation are directly linked to influence, but in the Liberal model, early life socialization and current political environment also are directly linked to influence. The theoretical significance of this lies in the fact that it demonstrates the importance of the intervening effects of committee participation on influence ascribed to Liberals and also reaffirms our earlier observation that Liberal (and NDP) backbenchers place great importance on participating in committees whereas Conservative backbenchers are relatively indifferent to them.[18]

With respect to the effect of committee participation on the distribution of ascribed influence in the Liberal party, the data suggest that extensive activity in committee may very well be an alternative means of acquiring at least a moderate amount of power. It may be a particularly important vehicle because it enables MPs who lack some of the credentials of "insiders" (e.g., early political socialization, political acumen, and sophistication) to have influence. Insiders, as we tried to demonstrate in chapters 7 and 8, tend to monopolize cabinet and other top level leadership positions and also to dominate debate in the House. Although committee activity is not as important a means of acquiring a position and a reputation for influence as is activity in the House, it is an avenue that seems to be open to Liberals but not Conservatives. (Note the differences between figures 9.3 and 9.4). Given this pattern, why is the distribution of influence only slightly more concentrated in the Conservative party (Gini = .88) than in the Liberal party (Gini = .86)? Our view is that the oligarchic distribution of influence in the Liberal party (in spite of its greater number of avenues to influence), is a product of the very large number of influence nominations given to certain Liberal cabinet ministers qua cabinet ministers. One might speculate that if the Liberals were to be defeated and go into opposition, the influence attributed to some of these ministers would be considerably diminished whereas the influence attributed to Liberal private members either would remain unchanged or increase slightly. If there were a corollary increase in the influence of certain Conservative frontbenchers-turned-cabinet ministers (assuming the Conservatives would form the government), the distribution of influence in the Conservative party would be even more concentrated than it is currently whereas influence in the Liberal party would diffuse.

To recapitulate, a high level of participation—but informed participation based upon expert knowledge—appears to be a key to acquiring not only a reputation for influence but also, ceteris paribus, a position of leadership in the Liberal party. And, understandably so: among individuals who bring to parliament backgrounds of professional and managerial skills resting upon extensive and intensive educations (note the high proportion of graduate/professional degrees among Liberal MPs), informed participation is likely to be valued very highly.

If a high level of informed, even expert, activity[19] provides the

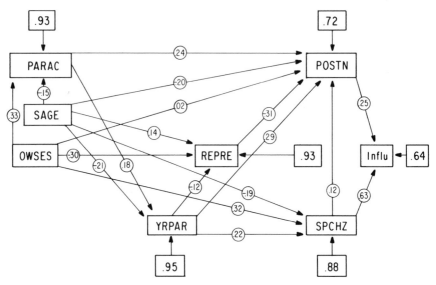

**FIGURE 9.4. REVISED PATH MODEL OF THE PROCESS THROUGH WHICH CON-
SERVATIVE MPs ACQUIRE A REPUTATION FOR BEING INFLUENTIAL**

most important explanation of how a reputation for influence and a
leadership position are acquired by Liberal MPs, social background
provides the key to understanding how these values are acquired by
Conservative MPs. Conservatives, we have argued, acquire positions
of leadership because of who they are, because of what they
believe, because of long service in their party organizations outside of
parliament and because of their extended tenures as members of
parliament. In other words they acquire positions of parliamentary
leadership primarily because they are influentials or "Notables"
when they enter parliament and because they are able to survive the
vicissitudes of two or more national elections. Having acquired a
position of leadership they participate extensively in House debate
and in question period because it is incumbent upon them as leaders
to do so. Leadership in the party carries with it the obligation to
participate in the same way that their sociopolitical background
carries with it the obligation to stand for a parliamentary seat. (The
best illustration of the importance of social background among
Conservatives is the fact that despite its location in the influence
model, the total impact of this variable upon influence is second only
to that of participation in debate.[20] ) In our view, the relationship
between participation and ascribed influence may be thought of as
being reciprocal among Conservatives; the extent of their participa-

tion in the House may be as much a product of their presumed influence as its determinant. It will be recalled that in the introduction of this book we suggested that the relationship between parliamentary participation on the one hand and parliamentary influence on the other might be reciprocal. The analyses we have conducted in this chapter indicate that for Conservative MPs this may indeed be the case. Although the paucity of purely exogenous instrumental variables prevents us from constructing the kind of nonrecursive model of ascribed influence that could test this hypothesis directly, future investigators might be well advised to conduct such a test.

## SUMMARY

We began this chapter by describing and comparing the Simon-Blalock and path analytic techniques that were employed to transform the conceptual framework presented in the introduction into an operational model whose theoretical and empirical validity could be tested. We constructed and validated three models of the process through which MPs acquire a reputation for influence—one for all MPs, a second for all members of the governing Liberal party and a third for the members of the official opposition, the Progressive-Conservative parliamentary party.

Since it was impossible to test the myriad possible linkages either between or among the multiple indicators of the eight concepts included in the conceptual framework, we had to select a single indicator to represent each of the conceptual components in an operational model. We proceeded empirically and chose variables that attained the highest average correlations with the final dependent variables in the model. Because the selection of representative indicators was subgroup specific, the variables differed slightly from one model to the next.

After we had satisfied ourselves of the face validity of the theoretical properties of each model, and after testing, revising, and validating the revised model structures, we calculated the percentage of variance in each endogenous variable that was explained by the associated exogenous and antecedent endogenous variables. The models correctly predicted 4 to 14% of the variations in MPs' socialization and recruitment experiences; they accounted for between 15 and 21% of the variance in their attitudes and motivations; for 8 to 23% of their participation in House debates; for 23 to 48% of the variance in parliamentary positions; and for 45 to 60% of the variations in MPs ascribed influence. We also were able to assess the direct, indirect, and spurious effects of each variable in the models. Parliamentary positions and participation in House debates were the most important direct determinants of ascribed influence. Current environmental factors generally have the most substantial indirect effects on influence, whereas a large proportion of the observed relationship between recruitment experiences and ascribed influence and between attitudes-motivations and influence is spurious.

Analysis of the structural similarities among the three models indicated that influential MPs typically derived from upper or upper-middle class environments in which they were exposed to a large number of politicizing stimuli. Partly as a consequence, the well educated future influentials found themselves attracted rather early in life to party organization work and by the prospect of holding high-level public office. Once elected to parliament, they became politically sophisticated and acquired reputations for being politically skilled and effective participants in debate. These tendencies, combined with increasing seniority, led to acquisition of leadership positions which provided them with the showcases they required for displaying their talents and thereby further enhanced their reputations as influentials.

Despite this general pattern, there were a number of intriguing differences between the Liberal and Conservative pathways to influence. "Proper" social background appeared to be especially important for acquiring influence in the Conservative parliamentary party and for acquiring a position of party leadership. We felt the relationship between participation and influence is best thought of as being reciprocal among Conservatives. The extent of their participation may be as much a product of their influence as its determinant. In contrast to the noblesse oblige style of the Conservatives, the Liberals appeared to ascribe great value to expertise, achievement, and a high level of informed activity. The basis of their influence thus may be said to derive from "what they are" which is a consequence of "what they do" rather than, as in the case of the Conservatives, "who they are."

*Chapter* 10

CONCLUSIONS

In the concluding chapter of his book, *Comparative Legislatures,* Jean Blondel insists that before we can assess the future and relative importance of legislatures in the political system, we need systematic studies of what it is that legislatures actually do. "What is required is a serious study of the various activities, a concern for the problems raised by detailed pressures, and an examination of the content of activities on the floor, and in committees, in most of the countries."[1] We have tried to provide such an examination for the Canadian House of Commons within a conceptual framework that focuses on the impact of antecedent variables such as social background and recruitment upon individual participation in parliamentary affairs, the acquisition of a leadership position and the development of a reputation for being influential. Following an overview of parliament's development we introduced many of the explanatory variables that were subsequently employed in the several multivariate analyses. This survey of variables also provided us with sociopolitical portraits of the members of the four parliamentary parties. In the next chapter we focused on the distribution of our key dependent variable, ascribed influence (and a related quality we termed good judgement) among MPs. We also were concerned with ascertaining MPs' perceptions of the bases of influence they attributed to their colleagues. We found that the characteristics they most frequently cited to explain influence were the ability to participate effectively in parliament's affairs and the occupancy of a leadership position. Consequently, in chapters 4 and 5 we took a critical look at member participation in the several activities in which parliament engages.

We presented factual information on matters such as the number of days the 28th Parliament sat during the period 1968–1972; the number of government, private, and private members' bills and debatable resolutions of which it disposed; the number of Orders in Council it promulgated; the number of times members rose to speak and question cabinet members in debate. We also pointed out that the House organized 18 standing and two special committees that held thousands of committee and subcommittee meetings in which the testimony of countless witnesses was heard and, as a consequence of which, hundreds of reports of findings and actions were issued. This was but the tip and most visible part of the parliamentary iceberg. Members also attended one or more meetings of their party caucuses each week, made thousands of contacts with cabinet ministers and members of the bureaucracy on behalf of constituents, received and replied to hundreds of thousands of letters, telephone calls, and other forms of communication from constituents, listened to the pleadings and the information provided by representatives of interest groups, attended innumerable meetings of their constituency party organizations, and made thousands of speeches to service and civic clubs throughout the country. We demonstrated that although these activities, in the aggregate, were massive, they also were highly skewed so that some MPs worked disproportionately hard and long, some worked less hard and others seemingly worked little or not at all.

In chapter 6 we focused on the manner in which formal and informal participation, holding a formal position of leadership and being ascribed influence were interrelated. Since the analyses revealed that even relatively crude indicators of participation and position explained a substantial proportion of the variations in the number of influence nominations MPs received, in chapter 7 we tried to delineate the factors that explain variations in the levels of individual participation. Chapter 8 considered the question of why some MPs become leaders of parliament while others do not. Our analyses of the correlates of leadership indicated that the social and political backgrounds, the recruitment experiences, and the current statuses and motivations of parliament's leaders differed systematically and significantly from those of nonleaders. But we also found that there were enough significant differences between the leaders of the governing Liberal and the opposition Conservative party to suggest that those who made it to the top of the former were not the same kind of individuals as those who made it to the top of the latter party. We examined this suggestion in more detail in chapter 9. We constructed and validated three models of the process through which MPs acquire a reputation for influence—one for all MPs, one for the governing Liberal party, and one for the opposition Conservatives. We found that high social status and background were important explanatory factors for the Conservatives. Indeed, it appeared that they acquired both positions of leadership and whatever influence was attributed to them largely because of "who they are." In contrast, members of the Liberal party seemingly acquired positions of leadership and reputations for being influential because of "what they do."

Until now we have confined ourselves to analyzing data and describing and explaining our findings. In this concluding chapter we will stand back a bit and try to assess what impact some of our principal findings have and may continue to have on the activities of parliament as an institution. The distinction between formally recognized activities and their consequences is sometimes captured in the distinction between manifest and latent functions. Our concern is not with trying to identify latent functions but simply to assess the implications some of our findings have for the understanding of what MPs do and are likely to do and how their actions will affect what parliament does.

Turning first to the individual MP, a potentially significant finding is that the reformed committee system may well lead to a fairly dramatic change in the pattern of individual participation in parliamentary affairs in the future. It seems reasonable to assume that a greater number of private members may spend more time and intellectual effort participating in the work of the committees than in either House debates or constituency service and information exchange. The fact that even in the final abbreviated session of the 28th Parliament—a session in which MPs, regardless of party, were at least as concerned with mending political fences because of an imminent election as with evaluating public policies and considering government spending—MPs made an average of 18 speeches in committee for every speech they made on the floor of the House strongly suggests the direction their efforts are taking. A number of conditions, however, must exist if this trend is to accelerate. First, members must come to believe that their efforts in committee can have an impact on the substance of public policy and the allocation of resources to public needs. Second, they must feel they have become experts in particular areas since feelings of expertise are psychically gratifying and encourage still greater efforts to become expert. Third, their committee work must earn the approval of peers in their own and other parliamentary parties. Fourth, they must feel that committee work increases their personal status and influence in parliament as well as in their parties and also increases the likelihood that they will acquire formal positions of leadership.

Some of our data strongly suggest that the first condition already is being met. The attitudes of a majority of MPs toward committees were quite positive; 45% felt that the principal function of committees was to help private members participate more fully and effectively in the affairs of parliament and an additional 37% felt committees enable MPs to affect either the direction of public policy generally or the content of specific pieces of legislation. From an empirical perspective we may infer from the sharp rise in the prestige rankings of the Miscellaneous Estimates and the Labour, Manpower and Immigration Committees that many MPs believed these committees did provide them with an opportunity to affect resource allocation and the programs of a major department of government—an opportunity that debate in the House did not always provide.[2] The data imply that the second condition is also beginning to be met. Fully 72% of the MPs we interviewed felt they were becoming expert in a particular area. Of these, 43% said they were developing their expertise because of their work in committee. On the other hand, we cannot infer from the data that a high level of committee activity already has earned MPs the approval of parliamentary peers. As was indicated in chapter 6, participation in committee was not significantly correlated with a reputation for good judgment. It was, however, strongly and significantly correlated with a reputation for possessing influence in parliament, accounting for 18% of the variations in influence attributed to the 34 private members in our special subsample. Indeed, the Liberal MP influence model (see chapter 9) suggests that extensive (and presumably effective) participation in committee affairs may well provide one means by which private members can acquire a reputation for possessing at least a moderate amount of influence in parliament. Although the small size of the New Democratic parliamentary party discouraged us from modeling its influence process, our feeling, based upon an inspection of the data, is that this also may be the case in the NDP.

Favorable attitudes toward committees as well as participation in them varied substantially by party. 41% of the Liberal, 46% of the NDP, but only 28% of the Conservatives and 14% of the Creditiste MPs felt the restructured committee system would enable private members to affect the content and direction of public policy. These attitudinal differences[3] were manifested quite clearly in behavior. The average Conservative's and Creditiste's attendance at committee meetings during the four parliamentary sessions lagged behind the attendance of their counterparts in the other two parties. In addition, Liberal and NDP members tended to speak considerably more often and longer than did Conservative and Creditiste MPs.

In part, the failure of Conservative and Creditiste MPs to take greater advantage of the opportunities to participate in committee is rooted in their perceptions of the proper function of parliament in the Canadian political system  They, more than the NDP, and certainly more than the Liberals, tend to view parliament's role principally as one of agenda-setting and of establishing national priorities.[4] These functions, they believe, can best be carried out in the highly visible House chamber rather than in relatively invisible committees. What they do in the House is more likely to be reported and commented upon by the ever-present members of the parliamentary press gallery. In fact, a recurring complaint during interviews (even with the strongest supporters of the restructured committee system) was that their efforts went largely unnoticed by the public because members of the press rarely were present at committee meetings. They also may feel that acting in the more visible arena of the House floor makes the public more familiar with their names and increases their chances of being reelected.

Yet another reason for the less favorable attitudes of Conservative MPs toward committees may lie in the Conservative party's status as a kind of perpetual opposition. The last time a Conservative government was in office was during the period 1957–1963 and this had come only after a 22-year period in opposition. We can speculate that members of a party which has held the reins of power for only relatively brief and widely separated intervals during the past half century might tend to view parliament's functions in the political system and their own role in parliament quite differently from members of a party that has exercised almost continuous hegemony over national affairs. For example, the leaders of a party that is almost constantly "Her Majesty's Opposition" might have little interest in "refining" (and improving) legislation they have not proposed. They might be less inclined, despite significantly longer parliamentary tenure than the leaders of the government, to view themselves as experts. They might more often view their membership in parliament as a kind of protracted but still temporary sojourn rather than as a career. And they might also less often "point with pride" to what they have accomplished during the course of their parliamentary careers. Instead, their overriding concern might be the desire to gain power; the principal concern of their backbench colleagues might be simply to survive politically.

If these assumptions are realistic, then the Conservative frontbenchers' concerns with agenda-setting in a highly visible forum and their backbenchers' preoccupation with tapping grass roots feelings and errand-running on behalf of constituents (whose gratitude might extent to voting for them in the next election) is understandable. Parenthetically, one also can understand why the members of a parliamentary party which almost always has been the government[5] would have very favorable attitudes toward committees. The leaders would view committees as properly performing the nuts and bolts tasks, sharing, as they seem to, the view of U.S. school children reported by Fred Greenstein,[6] that legislators are the executive's "little helpers." This would permit leaders to get on with the job of determining broader policy. Moreover, good committee work also might be regarded by them as a "quality control" mechanism, that in working over the details of specific pieces of legislation members of the several committees would improve that legislation. From the perspective of would-be leaders of such a party (currently occupying positions on the backbench) effective committee work would be a way of bringing themselves to the favorable attention of the cabinet whose ranks they hope to join. Even for those backbenchers without cabinet aspirations committee work can, and does, provide a raison d'etre for being a backbencher in a governing party (see table 7.6).

A second potentially significant finding is that constituency service and the solicitation of grass-roots opinion, although they may improve one's chances of being reelected, and may make one better informed about public opinion, do not enhance one's reputation for being influential. In fact, among Liberals, both excessive communications with cabinet members and increased communications with constituents were associated with a significant loss of influence. Among opposition MPs, communication with constituents also was associated with some loss of influence, but cabinet and bureaucratic communications were slightly but positively associated with influence.

It is ironic that the members of a governing party, who have the best access to ministers and who probably have the best chance of having their requests of ministers and high level bureaucrats favorably heard, also tend to suffer a loss in influence if they take too frequent advantage of their favored status. Opposition MPs, even if they do not suffer any loss of influence because of their activities in these areas, certainly do not receive much credit for them. Why then, do MPs continue to tap grass roots feelings and run errands on behalf of constituents? They do so, in our view because they believe—and postelection socialization by party elders reinforces that belief—that they are supposed to do these things. It will be recalled (see chapter 2) that before their election most members had only vague expectations for the position of MP. To the extent that their expectations were concrete they were structured in terms of being "representatives" and "ombudsmen." It seems reasonable to assume that party leaders believe in, and old hands on the backbench tacitly accept, a division of labor in which the former take the lead in representing the party in the House and the latter assume the initiative in the behind-the-scenes tasks of serving the public and keeping their ears to the ground. They let each cohort of newcomers know in a variety of subtle and not so subtle ways that a very important part of their job is to tap grass roots opinions and do favors for constituents. These tasks are generally rationalized in terms of necessity (e.g., "even statesmen need to be reelected and for that you have to look after your district"). But many parliamentary newcomers need little convincing. They probably feel that the association between doing things for their constituents and having their constituents vote for them is self evident. Moreover, interviews with members of both the 25th and 28th Parliaments reveal that most MPs enjoy helping constituents with problems. They find it gratifying to be of service and to know what their constituents are thinking about since many believe themselves to be insulated from the attitudes and opinions in their respective constituencies by the environment of a national capital. Moreover, since the probability of most Conservative backbenchers becoming cabinet ministers is rather remote, and since they either are not anxious and/or are not encouraged to participate extensively in committees, constituency service may be the most (indeed, the only) meaningful and personally gratifying career option open to them.

However, delineating constituents' attitudes accurately and answering their requests for assistance is both time-consuming and demanding of individual energies. Thus, MPs in Canada and in other democratic societies have been asking for "staff" to assist them in the performance of these tasks. If our data are valid, and Canadian MPs really do not derive influence from communicating with constituents and answering their requests for assistance, we predict that the pressure upon party leaders, particularly the cabinet, to provide more staff will continue because such assistance would free MPs, who really want to be influential, to direct more of their time to participation in those House and committee activities from which influence is derived.

Another finding with potential significance is that many members fit the profiles of three types of participants in the formal activities of parliament whom we have labeled "insiders," "gadflies," and "committee activists." Somewhat different clusters of attributes distinguish each type of participant. The insiders tend to be: English-speaking and Protestant; very well educated; socialized politically early in life; of high socioeconomic status at the time they became candidates for parliament; politically sophisticated veterans of parliament; expert in some area of parliament's work; and desirous of a career in parliament and of membership in the cabinet rather than a political or public office outside of parliament. They tend to dominate debate in the House. In a word they are the "pros" of parliament. The gadflies share many of the attributes of insiders. They are distinguished from the latter primarily by their liberal ideological orientations, by their representation of metropolitan constituencies and by their pessimistic assessment of their chances for becoming cabinet ministers. Gadflies tend to make extensive use of opportunities to introduce private members' bills and debatable resolutions. The distinguishing characteristics of committee activists are their relative lack of political sophistication, their lack of desire for a parliamentary career or a cabinet post and their feelings of expertise and personal efficacy.

We just suggested that given certain conditions, the number of MPs whom we have labeled committee activists is likely to increase substantially in future parliaments.[7] The pool of insiders who dominate House debate is not likely to increase much in the future, however. The need of a government to have a reasonably large proportion of its program passed by parliament within a finite period requires that limits be placed on individual participation in House debates. Although we have noted that the constraints upon participation fall most heavily on a government's backbenchers, opposition MPs are not immune, as witness their traditional resistance to procedural changes that governments have from time to time proposed to limit debate opportunities. There are additional constraints on backbenchers because of the tendency of leaders of the three opposition parties to use so much of the debate time allocated to their parties (see chapter 4).

That the status quo may be under pressure, however, is reflected in a suggestion by 16% of the opposition members and 48% of the Liberals (in response to an open-ended question) that additional limits on the length of individual speeches would enhance the ability of more private members to participate in parliament's work. Four factors help explain this change in attitude. First, many government (and some opposition) backbenchers are impatient with the speech-making of the opposition party leaders. It is not so much the frequency as the seeming interminable length of their speeches that they find so annoying. Second, there may be growing acceptance of the fact that additional constraints upon the length of individual participation in the House are necessary if situation-specific legislation is to become law in time to have some effect on the problem. Third, there may be growing disenchantment over the efficacy of House participation; the individual member may be coming to feel, given the manner in which it currently is structured, that participation in House debate does not really allow him input into the policy process. Fourth, and relatedly, a substantial number of private members may be becoming optimistic about the possibilities that committees offer those wanting to affect the policy process. Their optimism may be reflected in the suggestion by 33% of the opposition members and 21% of the Liberals that an even stronger committee system would enhance the ability of private members to participate effectively in parliament's work.[8]

The number of gadflies, like the number of insiders, also is likely to remain relatively small in future parliaments. It will be recalled that in chapter 4 we made a point of the fact that private members do not seem to take full advantage of the opportunities available to them to introduce private members' bills and debatable resolutions. The reticence of the government's backbenchers in this regard is understandable. Criticism, however, is a major dimension of the opposition role. Part of the reason, we believe, opposition members do not make more extensive use of these opportunities is simply that they lack the time and/or expertise to do so. (A frequent criticism of private members' bills, it should be noted, is that they are hurriedly and poorly drafted.) More important, however, is that opposition members feel that the introduction of this type of legislation is largely futile.[9] Barely a handful of such bills have become law in the past decade (although occasionally the government may adopt one and make it part of a subsequent legislative program). It thus requires a special kind of MP to persist in his efforts at legislative initiation. He must be an ideologue, have an extremely strong ego and a feeling that what he is proposing is worth a continuous struggle against probably insurmountable odds.[10] In the case of a member of the governing party, he may have to forego the possibility of becoming a cabinet minister. Because of these attributes, the gadfly probably will never be found in great numbers in any parliamentary system.

Another significant, although not unexpected finding is that insiders tend to monopolize highest level positions in the parliamentary parties. In the Liberal party, insiders appeared to be "achievers" whereas Conservative insiders appeared to be selected on the basis of who they are and how long they have been around parliament. Some Conservative MPs resent the practice of giving leadership positions to Canadian equivalents of British "country squires" and American "good old boys" and this may help explain the periodic palace revolts (the latest against the most recent leader, Mr. Robert Stanfield) that occur in the Conservative parliamentary party.[11] However, it would appear that only a few felt really strongly about the practice; most seemed to regard it as perfectly proper. It does, however, have consequences for the operation of the system and it is to these consequences that we now direct our attention.

In chapter 3, we demonstrated that the Creditiste and Conservative MPs taken as a group were ascribed less influence than the Liberals and NDP taken as a group. Since differences in committee participation (with the Liberals and NDP participating more) discriminate very well between these two groups it seems reasonable to suggest that should the Conservatives and Creditistes increase their efforts in committee, the influence gap might narrow. Some of the characteristics of the four parties, however, lead us to suspect that their respective orientations toward committee vs. House participation are fairly stable. It seems unlikely, therefore, that the Creditiste and Conservative members will reorder their priorities to pursue greater parliamentary influence through greater committee participation. Let us examine some of the characteristics of the four parties that reinforce our impressions.

It is fair to say that over the years, the Liberals usually have been regarded, and have regarded themselves, as good managers and administrators,[12] while NDP MPs have seen their party as parliament's most dedicated, hard working and socially conscious party. Indeed, if the remark attributed most frequently to the late Liberal prime minister, Louis St. Laurent, is not apochryphal, even Liberals believe that the New Democratic parliamentary party has acted as both their own and parliament's conscience.

Although the Liberals generally have benefited from their image of being a managerial party, their consistent effort to streamline parliament's procedures has caused the party to be labeled arrogant, officious, and contemptuous of parliament. Former Conservative leader John Diefenbaker was able, in 1957, to parlay this dimension of their image into an upset electoral victory, while Prime Minister Trudeau's widely reported remark that the members of the 28th Parliament were a bunch of nobodies may very well have cost him dearly in the election of 1972.[13] The Liberal attempts to conduct the nation's affairs in a brisk, businesslike way also may have earned the party a reputation for "muzzling" its backbenchers, particularly those from Quebec. Since the party historically has relied upon these same members to insure passage of its legislative programs and to maintain it in national office, this supposed muzzling has caused considerable resentment. Our data indicate: (1) that as a group Quebec MPs spoke less in the House and had less influence attributed to them than any other provincial contingent; (2) there were disproportionately fewer Quebec MPs in the insider group; and (3) their English-speaking colleagues tended to explain the very substantial influence of certain Quebec cabinet ministers in terms of who they are and whom they know rather than in terms of their abilities as parliamentarians. This information offers at least some support for the contention that since 1960 many of the brightest French-Canadians have chosen to enter and remain in provincial politics, supposedly leaving national politics to second-raters.

As for the NDP members of parliament, we already have noted that as a party they participate very heavily in all aspects of parliament's work and that as a party they are accorded a disproportionate amount of influence. Indeed, they even participate heavily in the initiation of private members' bills—an activity, it will be recalled, that does not generate much influence. Here, however, the NDP may be playing to a wider audience than parliamentary colleagues. They may believe that their public image as parliament's conscience will be enhanced by reports of their efforts to direct parliament's attention to important social problems.[14] We may speculate that the party must take advantage of this and every other opportunity that parliament provides for them to project a favorable image, as it labors under the burden of being a third party in an institution with features that are conducive to the perpetuation of a two-party system. Since it is unlikely, to say the least, that the party will win a national election in the near future, a vote for an NDP parliamentary candidate can be regarded as a wasted vote. This wasted vote theme consistently has been invoked by Liberal and Conservative candidates and their supporters during national campaigns. Consequently, the NDP must convince the public that a vote for its candidates is not wasted, and that the public not only will benefit from having a strong NDP parliamentary delegation but, indeed, that a strong NDP presence in parliament is a virtual sine qua non for its effective operation.

The Social Credit (Creditiste) party has been less successful in convincing the public that a vote for their political candidates is not a wasted vote and that the presence of a strong Social Credit party is a sine qua non for parliament's effective functioning. Its parliamentary delegation usually has been smaller and much more regional than the NDP. From 1935 to 1962 it managed to elect candidates only in Alberta and British Columbia. In the 1962 and 1963 elections this group was joined by a block from the small towns and rural regions of Quebec. Unfortunately for the party, the bond of Gallic and Catholic neopopulism with stolid, conservative, Protestant fundamentalism did not endure. The next two years witnessed the defection of a number of Social Credit MPs (including the party's then national leader, Robert N. Thompson) to the Conservative and Liberal benches. In addition to regionalism, its seeming single-issue orientation has hurt the Social Credit-Creditiste party. Again, unfortunately for the party, its proposed solutions to monetary problems have never gained wide popularity. Since the arrival on the parliamentary scene of Mr. Real Caouette the party has come to be regarded as a one-man show. So closely is the Creditiste party associated with the personality of its charismatic leader that even MPs have only a vague image of its positions on major policy issues.[15] Although the data (see chapter 4) indicate that the Creditistes speak on a wide range of issues (and not simply on monetary matters) and although participation is not as limited to a relatively few party members as it is in the Liberal or Conservative parties, the scope of their participation tends to be concentrated almost entirely on speaking and asking questions of ministers during House debates. (The Creditistes, it will be recalled, were absent from approximately two-thirds of the meetings of the several standing committees of the 28th Parliament.) The content of some of what they say in the House is not critical of the government (a finding that also may help explain why the positions of the party on major policy issues are not clear). The fact that they are not critical tends to support conventional Ottawa wisdom that the Credistes' principal concern is to maintain a current government in office. If this requires that criticism be muted or that a minority government be supported on key votes, this is not too high a price to pay, in the view of the Creditistes, to avoid an election which might result in the loss of precious parliamentary seats. In the 28th Parliament, the party contained a number of forceful, even eloquent, speakers. However, they spoke only in French and frequently engaged in protracted wrangling with the Speaker over his supposed bias toward them. Although such tactics may have contributed to an image of being the defender of French-Canadian culture generally and of the French-Canadian "little man" in particular, they did little, if anything, to enhance the influence of individual Creditiste members within parliament. Nor, we may speculate, do they contribute much to the party's collective reputation of being a force to be taken seriously in the operation of the parliamentary system.

If a fault of the Creditistes is that they do not oppose enough, then the Conservative's fault may be that they oppose too much. The data indicate their comments in the House during debate were far more critical of the government than were those of either Creditiste or NDP MPs. The data also indicate that Conservative MPs generally, and Conservative insiders in particular, tended to reject other than a "traditional" role for parliament. Here we must digress briefly from our discussion about the Conservative party and note that a part of the traditional view of parliament is that the principal function of an opposition party is to oppose and the function of its leaders it to lead this opposition. Also a part of this tradition is that the House of Commons is the arena in which national priorities are debated and a national agenda is set. As John Mackintosh has noted, a basic tenet of the traditional view of parliament is that those leaders who argue their positions on the great issues of the day most cogently, forcefully, and eloquently carry the day—or at least persuade a majority of the electorate that their positions are worth supporting on election day. The Conservatives whom we studied, especially Conservative insiders, certainly shared this view of parliament's traditional functions but it also was shared, more-or-less, by the members (especially the leaders) of all parties.

Interestingly, members of all parties (again, including the leadership) also more-or-less share what Mackintosh termed an "alternative" or "modern" view of parliament: that finding solutions to great issues ought to be left largely to the government and its technical experts in the bureaucracy; MPs should concern themselves with local (i.e., constituency) problems and needs; and MPs should help right any wrongs done particular citizens by a government and bureaucracy applying universalistic standards to the solution of national problems (i.e., they ought to be ombudsmen and case workers). That MPs subscribe to elements of both theories is indicated by the popularity of the "politico" role orientation.

It is also indicated by the finding that although leaders do lead—in each party they dominate debate—they also actively communicate with different groups in the public and assist individuals and groups. We suggest that if they had their "druthers," they would prefer not to spend their time tapping grass-roots opinions and servicing constituents' requests. Indeed, an antipathy toward the "delegate-servant" role orientation is one of the factors that significantly discriminates leaders from nonleaders. But since party leaders, no less than their followers, believe it is necessary to engage in delegate-servant kinds of activities—they believe the public expects them and that reelection, in part, is contingent upon them—they try, through a variety of methods, to get their party colleagues who are backbenchers to bear a disproportionate share of this burden. Indeed, it can be argued that in a very real sense Canadian party leaders have succeeded in turning their backbench colleagues into the functional equivalent of a staff that apprises them of public opinion and also handles much of the case work. This kind of division of labor, although we believe it exists in all four parties, is most characteristic of the Liberals and Conservatives. But it is a division of labor that tends to be increasingly resented by Liberal backbenchers since the burden of not participating in House debates has fallen most heavily on them. There has been less resentment among Conservative backbenchers for a variety of reasons and an examination of these leads us back to our discussion of that party.

As we pointed out in chapter 2 and as was noted in a study a decade earlier, many Conservative backbenchers tend to find the delegate-servant role orientation a fairly congenial one. They like tapping grass-roots feelings and helping constituents with problems, and not simply because they feel these activities contribute to their reelection. In addition, the average Conservative backbencher, although he does not have as much opportunity to participate in House debate as his counterparts in the New Democratic and Creditiste parties, has more of a chance than the average Liberal backbencher. Moreover, he enjoys the participatory role in the House that his leaders seem to have allocated to him. Although the figures in tables 4.3, 4.6 and 4.7 do not reveal it, even a cursory perusal of Hansard will indicate that there seem to be two tiers of Conservative participation in House debate. The Conservative frontbenchers generally, although certainly not always, take the high road; they discuss the issues. The backbenchers, generally, although again, not always, criticize individual cabinet ministers.

Although one of the most frequently cited rules of the game is "don't bring personalities into debate," opposition criticism of public policy in a British-model parliamentary system almost inevitably extends to the individual ministers who are the defenders if not the actual architects of that policy. And, since many of the most prominent ministers (not to mention three prime ministers) in Liberal governments have been French-Canadians, the effect of these attacks over time has been to make Conservative backbenchers appear to be, at best, anti-French or (if one chooses to be less charitable) ethnic and religious bigots.[16] The impression that Conservatives are bigots is sharpened by the media which tends to exaggerate these exchanges. Acrimonious tirades in which a French-Canadian prime minister asks a Conservative backbencher to perform a physically impossible act[17] make nationwide news, whereas an often-repeated statement by the Conservative party leader criticizing the government for not adopting a policy of indexing wages and salaries in the face of continuing inflation does not.

Since the pattern of Conservative participation in parliament contributes to the party's image of being hostile to French-Canadians, it practically insures that a large block of parliamentary seats in Quebec will fall to the Liberal and Creditiste parties at election time. Moreover, it gives the public an impression (at least when Mr. Robert Stanfield was the Conservative national leader) that the leader of the party cannot control a substantial portion of his backbench. The public is treated to the spectacle of Messrs. Stanfield, Fairweather, Macquarrie, and other "responsible" Conservative leaders traversing the country making very positive or at least very conciliatory statements about French-Canadian values and wooing major Quebec provincial political figures at the same time that members of their parliamentary party are attacking French-Canadian members of parliament and French-Canadian aspirations.

The impressions conveyed by Conservative backbenchers (frequently labeled "yahoos" and "cowboys" by their critics) probably reflect unfavorably on the party's general competence. When these are combined with the aforementioned tendency to allocate leadership positions on the basis of ascriptive criteria, the result is a party that does not appear to be as capable of governing as the seemingly perennially governing Liberals. In this regard it is interesting to recall that shortly after our interviews were completed and the word began to spread that a national election was imminent, one of the favorite games of the political columnists covering parliament was to speculate about which members of the Conservative party, in the event of a Conservative victory, might become cabinet ministers. Almost all such speculations concluded that, unfortunately, there was very little "cabinet timber" in either the Conservative front or backbenches.[18]

Let us now consider the implications of the finding that more than any of the other groups of opposition members, the insiders on the Conservative frontbench feel that a major function of parliament is to set a national agenda by means of House debates on national policies. Ceteris paribus, this attitude works for the government and against the opposition. Our content analysis of House debates strongly suggests that the Liberal government, through its ability to control to a large extent the substance and the time allocated to the debate of particular issues, is able to channel debate and direct it to areas in which it feels least vulnerable. The government, and not the opposition (despite even the most strenuous efforts) has the last word on what parliament's agenda will be. Moreover, because of the government's status as the government, cabinet members can and do set parliament's agenda outside of the House. They frequently make major policy statements to the public, particularly via television, before these are ever announced in the House.

Happily for the Conservative opposition and for Canadian parliamentary government, other factors are not always equal. We do not find all the heavyweights seated on the government benches and all the lightweights seated in opposition. A governing party, regardless of the size of its majority, cannot completely control the substance and timing of debates. Moreover, it hesitates to invoke procedures to limit debate lest it be accused, as it surely will, of stifling free speech and acting undemocratically. This is a charge to which the Liberal government, like all governments in countries that value free speech, is very sensitive. Finally, opposition party leaders in Canada also have access to the media and they use it to suggest alternative policies to those proposed by the government. Nonetheless, the fact remains that in the business of debating national goals and establishing national priorities, the government has a distinct edge over the opposition. That the Conservative opposition seems loathe to take the steps necessary to reduce this disadvantage by, for example, shifting some of its energies to an arena where controls by the government currently are less formidable, suggests, at least in the short run, that Conservative prospects for a return to power in Canada are bleak. Whether their longer-run prospects will be equally bleak may well depend upon their ability to recognize, and their willingness to pursue, new avenues to power and influence in parliament.

## PARTICIPATION IN DIVISION VOTES

The following tables present the percentages of MPs by party and leadership status who participated (i.e., were present and voted) in division votes (and in division votes categorized by subject matter) during each of the four sessions of the 28th Parliament. The eight coding categories and the issues they include are as follows:

(1) Defense and External Affairs—issues relating to defense, foreign policy and external affairs, questions of sovereignty, and veterans affairs.

(2) Public Finance—issues encompassed by the jurisdiction of the Treasury Board, Ministry of Finance, and Ministry of National Revenue, including the budget, the economy, taxation issues, questions concerning the Price and Income Commission or concerning banking.

(3) Social Welfare—issues pertaining to national health and welfare policy, housing problems, consumer and corporate affairs, poverty, medical care, social security, food and drugs, etc.

(4) Legal-Political—issues related to either internal parliamentary procedures or to national law and justice including questions pertaining to elections, constituency boundaries, parliamentary reforms, the Constitution, Justice Ministry or the Solicitor General.

(5) Primary Industry-Extractive—issues related to industries directly involved in the exploitation and conservation of natural resources including agriculture, fisheries, forestry, mining, the environment, pollution abatement, national parks and energy.

(6) Labor and Secondary Industry—issues concerned with labor, manpower and immigration, industry, trade, commerce, science and technology.

(7) Internal Development—issues relating to regional economic development, urban affairs, public works, transportation, communications, etc.

(8) Miscellaneous—a variety of disparate issues including such symbolic issues as bilingualism and the language bill, and such other topics as Expo 70, tourism, rainmaking, etc.

## TABLE A.1
## PARTICIPATION IN DIVISION VOTES
## SESSION I

| Group | | Issue Area I | Issue Area II | Issue Area III | Issue Area IV | Issue Area V | Issue Area VI[a] | Issue Area VII | Issue Area VIII | All Area Votes |
|---|---|---|---|---|---|---|---|---|---|---|
| All MPs | X̄ | 67.1 | 66.7 | 59.8 | 63.6 | 71.2 | 0 | 59.1 | 72.9 | 65.4 |
| | SD | (39.2) | (33.5) | (28.2) | (22.5) | (36.2) | | (33.0) | (26.3) | (20.8) |
| Liberal MPs | X̄ | 73.7 | 71.1 | 61.2 | 66.1 | 75.2 | 0 | 59.8 | 78.0 | 68.5 |
| | SD | (37.0) | (31.9) | (27.5) | (21.1) | (34.0) | | (33.3) | (24.7) | (19.5) |
| Conservative MPs | X̄ | 58.8 | 61.1 | 59.7 | 59.2 | 66.7 | 0 | 59.8 | 66.0 | 60.9 |
| | SD | (40.3) | (33.1) | (26.3) | (21.7) | (37.4) | | (31.5) | (25.8) | (19.0) |
| NDP MPs | X̄ | 67.0 | 52.8 | 56.8 | 62.5 | 60.0 | 0 | 58.3 | 68.5 | 62.5 |
| | SD | (40.0) | (37.4) | (32.5) | (29.8) | (43.0) | | (35.5) | (30.3) | (28.6) |
| Cred. MPs | X̄ | 40.4 | 76.9 | 56.9 | 67.5 | 74.4 | 0 | 57.1 | 63.5 | 64.7 |
| | SD | (38.9) | (34.5) | (35.4) | (19.7) | (33.8) | | (31.4) | (21.5) | (15.4) |
| Backbench MPs | X̄ | 66.0 | 63.9 | 58.2 | 62.4 | 70.1 | 0 | 58.2 | 72.6 | 64.3 |
| | SD | (39.0) | (34.1) | (28.0) | (22.9) | (37.0) | | (32.4) | (27.2) | (21.3) |
| All Leaders | X̄ | 69.6 | 73.2 | 63.5 | 66.5 | 73.8 | 0 | 61.1 | 73.7 | 68.0 |
| | SD | (39.8) | (31.4) | (28.6) | (21.6) | (34.5) | | (34.3) | (24.2) | (19.3) |
| Liberal backbench | X̄ | 71.8 | 69.6 | 58.4 | 64.1 | 75.5 | 0 | 58.8 | 77.9 | 67.1 |
| | SD | (38.5) | (32.2) | (28.0) | (22.6) | (34.1) | | (33.2) | (26.9) | (21.2) |
| Liberal Leaders | X̄ | 77.5 | 74.0 | 66.8 | 70.0 | 74.7 | 0 | 61.7 | 78.2 | 71.5 |
| | SD | (34.0) | (31.4) | (25.7) | (17.2) | (34.0) | | (33.8) | (19.5) | (15.3) |
| Conservative Backbench | X̄ | 58.3 | 55.8 | 60.0 | 59.3 | 61.8 | 0 | 57.4 | 63.4 | 59.8 |
| | SD | (38.0) | (33.3) | (25.1) | (20.5) | (37.7) | | (30.7) | (25.9) | (18.1) |
| Conservative Leaders | X̄ | 59.8 | 72.2 | 59.1 | 58.8 | 76.8 | 0 | 64.6 | 71.5 | 63.2 |
| | SD | (45.7) | (30.6) | (29.2) | (24.4) | (35.4) | | (33.3) | (25.3) | (21.1) |
| Issues Votes as % of all Votes | | 4.8 | 6.0 | 6.0 | 52.3 | 3.6 | 0 | 8.3 | 19.0 | 100.0 |

a. Category contains fewer than three votes.

## TABLE A.2
## PARTICIPATION IN DIVISION VOTES
## SESSION II

| Group | | Issue Area I[a] | Issue Area II[a] | Issue Area III | Issue Area IV | Issue Area V | Issue Area VI | Issue Area VII | Issue Area VIII | All Area Votes |
|---|---|---|---|---|---|---|---|---|---|---|
| All MPs | X̄ | 0 | 0 | 54.5 | 61.0 | 63.6 | 61.3 | 60.8 | 56.7 | 59.5 |
| | SD | | | (21.6) | (22.6) | (28.5) | (27.4) | (36.4) | (34.8) | (19.0) |
| Liberal MPs | X̄ | 0 | 0 | 56.1 | 62.7 | 64.1 | 63.5 | 63.6 | 62.2 | 61.4 |
| | SD | | | (21.4) | (21.1) | (28.6) | (27.6) | (36.1) | (34.3) | (18.1) |
| Conservative MPs | X̄ | 0 | 0 | 52.0 | 57.0 | 64.2 | 56.3 | 59.2 | 56.1 | 57.0 |
| | SD | | | (21.0) | (22.3) | (26.8) | (26.5) | (35.3) | (32.7) | (18.0) |
| NDP MPs | X̄ | 0 | 0 | 57.3 | 65.6 | 62.6 | 66.2 | 54.7 | 32.8 | 60.5 |
| | SD | | | (24.2) | (27.7) | (31.3) | (29.1) | (40.7) | (32.1) | (24.5) |
| Cred. MPs | X̄ | 0 | 0 | 48.6 | 58.7 | 61.5 | 59.0 | 53.8 | 46.2 | 55.5 |
| | SD | | | (17.2) | (24.7) | (30.9) | (21.9) | (37.4) | (35.9) | (16.9) |
| Backbench MPs | X̄ | 0 | 0 | 54.7 | 61.1 | 62.5 | 61.4 | 61.2 | 55.4 | 59.4 |
| | SD | | | (22.1) | (23.2) | (29.4) | (28.5) | (36.3) | (35.4) | (19.9) |
| All Leaders | X̄ | 0 | 0 | 53.9 | 60.9 | 65.9 | 61.3 | 59.9 | 59.7 | 60.0 |
| | SD | | | (20.5) | (21.4) | (26.4) | (25.0) | (36.7) | (33.2) | (17.0) |
| Liberal Backbench | X̄ | 0 | 0 | 56.3 | 62.3 | 61.3 | 61.7 | 65.0 | 63.3 | 60.7 |
| | SD | | | (23.9) | (22.8) | (30.3) | (30.1) | (35.2) | (34.9) | (20.7) |
| Liberal Leaders | X̄ | 0 | 0 | 55.5 | 63.5 | 69.9 | 67.1 | 60.7 | 60.0 | 62.7 |
| | SD | | | (15.2) | (17.3) | (23.9) | (21.3) | (37.9) | (33.3) | (11.3) |
| Conservative Backbench | X̄ | 0 | 0 | 51.8 | 57.3 | 64.3 | 58.1 | 58.3 | 51.7 | 56.8 |
| | SD | | | (19.2) | (22.9) | (28.5) | (27.2) | (36.1) | (33.0) | (17.7) |
| Conservative Leaders | X̄ | 0 | 0 | 52.4 | 56.5 | 64.0 | 52.7 | 60.9 | 65.2 | 57.4 |
| | SD | | | (24.8) | (21.5) | (23.4) | (25.1) | (34.3) | (30.9) | (19.0) |
| Issue Votes as % of All Votes | | 0 | 0 | 29.3 | 29.3 | 18.7 | 12.0 | 4.0 | 6.7 | 100.0 |

a. Category contains fewer than three votes.

**TABLE A.3**

**PARTICIPATION IN DIVISION VOTES**

**SESSION III**

| Group | | Issue Area I[a] | Issue Area II | Issue Area III | Issue Area IV | Issue Area V | Issue Area VI | Issue Area VII | Issue Area VIII | All Area Votes |
|---|---|---|---|---|---|---|---|---|---|---|
| All MPs | X̄ | 0 | 67.8 | 66.0 | 65.0 | 58.7 | 49.9 | 42.5 | 65.3 | 62.2 |
| | SD | | (23.6) | (25.3) | (18.7) | (27.0) | (33.5) | (28.7) | (22.5) | (18.0) |
| Liberal MPs | X̄ | 0 | 72.0 | 69.1 | 66.6 | 64.3 | 50.3 | 47.1 | 68.6 | 65.3 |
| | SD | | (22.1) | (23.3) | (19.1) | (27.1) | (33.4) | (29.2) | (22.5) | (18.1) |
| Conservative MPs | X̄ | 0 | 58.8 | 63.6 | 63.1 | 52.3 | 50.6 | 34.4 | 64.2 | 59.1 |
| | SD | | (23.8) | (25.4) | (15.9) | (25.6) | (33.9) | (26.7) | (19.3) | (14.7) |
| NDP MPs | X̄ | 0 | 72.5 | 66.1 | 62.5 | 52.4 | 49.8 | 40.8 | 57.2 | 59.1 |
| | SD | | (22.5) | (30.8) | (20.0) | (24.8) | (34.9) | (28.6) | (24.3) | (19.7) |
| Cred. MPs | X̄ | 0 | 65.4 | 45.5 | 64.6 | 45.6 | 42.6 | 38.5 | 51.3 | 52.2 |
| | SD | | (23.5) | (21.4) | (17.5) | (21.3) | (29.1) | (23.8) | (21.1) | (15.5) |
| Backbench MPs | X̄ | 0 | 68.5 | 66.6 | 65.2 | 60.2 | 50.3 | 42.4 | 64.4 | 62.5 |
| | SD | | (23.4) | (25.8) | (18.7) | (25.7) | (33.9) | (28.1) | (22.9) | (17.8) |
| All Leaders | X̄ | 0 | 66.1 | 64.6 | 64.4 | 55.1 | 49.1 | 42.8 | 67.1 | 61.3 |
| | SD | | (24.0) | (24.2) | (18.8) | (29.7) | (32.7) | (30.2) | (21.7) | (18.4) |
| Liberal Backbench | X̄ | 0 | 72.5 | 69.1 | 66.2 | 64.1 | 50.6 | 46.9 | 67.7 | 65.0 |
| | SD | | (22.7) | (24.8) | (20.9) | (27.8) | (34.3) | (29.0) | (24.0) | (19.8) |
| Liberal Leaders | X̄ | 0 | 70.7 | 73.3 | 67.4 | 64.6 | 49.5 | 47.6 | 70.4 | 65.8 |
| | SD | | (20.9) | (20.2) | (15.2) | (25.7) | (31.8) | (29.9) | (19.3) | (14.3) |
| Conservative Backbench | X̄ | 0 | 58.3 | 65.2 | 63.8 | 58.5 | 51.1 | 33.3 | 64.1 | 60.7 |
| | SD | | (23.8) | (25.6) | (14.7) | (22.4) | (33.6) | (26.2) | (19.0) | (13.1) |
| Conservative Leaders | X̄ | 0 | 59.8 | 60.2 | 61.7 | 39.3 | 49.5 | 36.5 | 64.5 | 55.8 |
| | SD | | (24.1) | (25.0) | (18.4) | (27.4) | (35.4) | (28.1) | (20.4) | (17.4) |
| Issue Votes as % of All Votes | | 0 | 5.4 | 17.0 | 29.3 | 19.7 | 8.9 | 3.4 | 16.3 | 100.0 |

a. Category contains fewer than three votes

**TABLE A.4**
**PARTICIPATION IN DIVISION VOTES**
**SESSION IV**

| Group | | Issue Area I | Issue Area II | Issue Area III | Issue Area IV | Issue Area V | Issue Area VI | Issue Area VII[a] | Issue Area VIII | All Area Votes |
|---|---|---|---|---|---|---|---|---|---|---|
| All MPs | X̄ | 64.4 | 68.8 | 62.0 | 55.3 | 65.4 | 59.6 | 0 | 66.3 | 63.9 |
| | SD | (38.4) | (30.6) | (28.8) | (27.4) | (31.6) | (40.6) | | (24.1) | (22.4) |
| Liberal MPs | X̄ | 70.6 | 72.9 | 62.7 | 57.3 | 68.0 | 65.8 | 0 | 70.0 | 67.3 |
| | SD | (37.2) | (30.1) | (28.8) | (27.6) | (31.4) | (39.1) | | (25.4) | (22.9) |
| Conservative MPs | X̄ | 52.1 | 59.2 | 58.9 | 50.5 | 59.2 | 45.8 | 0 | 59.3 | 56.4 |
| | SD | (37.7) | (30.1) | (27.3) | (25.4) | (31.0) | (42.3) | | (21.3) | (20.1) |
| NDP MPs | X̄ | 71.0 | 76.0 | 69.3 | 66.0 | 75.1 | 69.0 | 0 | 75.1 | 72.6 |
| | SD | (35.9) | (27.3) | (30.3) | (28.3) | (32.4) | (37.7) | | (15.3) | (18.3) |
| Cred. MPs | X̄ | 55.8 | 65.4 | 59.0 | 41.0 | 57.3 | 48.1 | 0 | 52.7 | 54.8 |
| | SD | (43.5) | (30.8) | (30.1) | (24.2) | (26.8) | (36.0) | | (12.5) | (17.7) |
| Backbench MPs | X̄ | 66.4 | 69.2 | 63.4 | 54.8 | 67.0 | 58.3 | 0 | 66.2 | 64.4 |
| | SD | (37.4) | (31.2) | (29.2) | (27.6) | (32.6) | (41.0) | | (23.0) | (22.2) |
| All Leaders | X̄ | 59.8 | 67.7 | 58.6 | 56.3 | 61.7 | 62.7 | 0 | 66.6 | 62.8 |
| | SD | (40.5) | (29.2) | (27.7) | (27.1) | (29.2) | (39.8) | | (26.6) | (23.3) |
| Liberal Backbench | X̄ | 73.3 | 73.5 | 63.7 | 56.9 | 68.4 | 64.7 | 0 | 68.4 | 63.7 |
| | SD | (35.2) | (31.3) | (29.6) | (27.7) | (32.9) | (39.7) | | (26.4) | (23.4) |
| Liberal Leaders | X̄ | 65.0 | 71.7 | 60.7 | 58.3 | 67.1 | 68.0 | 0 | 73.2 | 67.5 |
| | SD | (40.7) | (27.6) | (27.3) | (27.6) | (28.4) | (38.1) | | (23.1) | (21.8) |
| Conservative Backbench | X̄ | 54.7 | 59.0 | 59.7 | 49.0 | 63.0 | 42.2 | 0 | 60.7 | 57.4 |
| | SD | (38.8) | (31.7) | (28.5) | (26.9) | (32.5) | (42.6) | | (17.8) | (20.7) |
| Conservative Leaders | X̄ | 46.7 | 59.4 | 57.2 | 53.6 | 51.2 | 53.3 | 0 | 56.2 | 54.5 |
| | SD | (35.6) | (27.0) | (25.0) | (21.9) | (26.5) | (41.5) | | (27.6) | (19.0) |
| Issue Votes as % of All Votes | | 8.3 | 12.5 | 12.5 | 12.5 | 18.8 | 8.3 | 0 | 27.1 | 100.0 |

a. Category contains fewer than three votes

# STATISTICAL PROFILES OF MPs WITH VARYING INFLUENCE

| Characteristics | MPs With: | No Influence | Some Influence | Considerable Influence | All MPs |
|---|---|---|---|---|---|
| I. Social Background Characteristics | | | | | |
| Percent Born in Quebec | | 21 | 17 | 18 | 19 |
| Percent Born in Ontario | | 32 | 29 | 25 | 30 |
| Percent Born in Atlantic Provinces | | 09 | 17 | 21 | 13 |
| Percent Born in Western Provinces | | 33 | 27 | 25 | 30 |
| Percent Catholic | | 40 | 39 | 29 | 38 |
| Percent Protestant | | 48 | 46 | 60 | 49 |
| Percent Jewish | | 03 | 02 | 07 | 03 |
| Percent with Law Degree | | 22 | 37 | 61 | 33 |
| Percent with Any Professional Degree | | 42 | 46 | 68 | 47 |
| Percent College Graduates | | 71 | 73 | 96 | 75 |
| Mean Number of Years of Formal Education | | 15.9 | 16.1 | 18.0 | 16.2 |
| Mean SES of MPs Occupation | | 65.7 | 72.1 | 77.1 | 69.4 |
| Mean Number of Club Memberships | | 3.4 | 3.5 | 3.7 | 3.5 |
| Mean SES of Father's Primary Occupation | | 41.0 | 48.3 | 51.2 | 44.7 |
| Mean Number of Years Residence in Constituency | | 37.3 | 29.6 | 31.6 | 34.3 |
| Percent of Northern European Descent | | 46 | 54 | 61 | 51 |
| Percent of Eastern or Southern European Descent | | 10 | 09 | 04 | 08 |
| Percent of French or French-Canadian Descent | | 22 | 20 | 14 | 21 |

*( continued on overleaf )*

**APPENDIX B** (continued )

| Characteristics | MPs With: | No Influence | Some Influence | Considerable Influence | All MPs |
|---|---|---|---|---|---|
| II. Early Life Political Socialization, Political Recruitment and Political Career Characteristics | | | | | |
| Mean Politicization of Childhood Score | | .07 | .05 | .45 | .11 |
| Percent Who Belonged to Political Clubs in High School or College | | 44 | 42 | 54 | 45 |
| Mean Age of First Political Awareness, Interest, and Party Identification | | 16.7 | 16.5 | 16.2 | 16.6 |
| Mean Importance of Politics During Childhood Score | | −.02 | .02 | .14 | .01 |
| Mean Peer Group Political Interest Score | | 1.8 | 1.6 | 1.9 | 1.8 |
| Mean "Difficulty Getting Party Nomination" Score | | .03 | .09 | −.20 | .02 |
| Mean Prior "Public Office Holder" Score | | .16 | −.13 | −.31 | .00 |
| Mean Prior "Party Activity" Score | | .02 | −.06 | .02 | .00 |
| Mean "Political Self-Motivation" Score | | −.03 | −.01 | .09 | .00 |
| Mean "Prior Unsuccessful Candidacies" Score | | .06 | −.06 | −.09 | .00 |

III. Current Situation and Political
Environment Characteristics

| | | | | |
|---|---|---|---|---|
| Mean Age of MP at Entry Into Parliament | 41.3 | 41.5 | 39.8 | 41.4 |
| Mean Years of Parliamentary Service | 7.9 | 9.2 | 11.1 | 8.8 |
| Percent from Urban Constituency | 52 | 64 | 71 | 58 |
| Mean Number of Rules-of-the-Game Cited | 3.5 | 3.7 | 3.8 | 3.6 |
| Percent Citing Sanctions Reinforcing Rules | 76 | 90 | 92 | 83 |
| Percent With Winning Margins of less than 5% In 1968 | 79 | 64 | 54 | 71 |
| Percent With Margin of Less than 5% in First Election to Parliament | 93 | 100 | 95 | 96 |

( continued on overleaf )

**APPENDIX B** (*continued*)

| Characteristics | MPs With: | No Influence | Some Influence | Considerable Influence | All MPs |
|---|---|---|---|---|---|
| **IV. Political Attitudes and Motivations Characteristics** | | | | | |
| Mean Delegate-Servant Role Score | | .15 | −.08 | −.48 | .00 |
| Percent Who Perceive Self as Expert in Substantive Area | | 67 | 77 | 88 | 73 |
| Percent Who Perceive Role Conflicts With Constituents | | 28 | 29 | 40 | 30 |
| Percent Who Perceive Role Conflicts With Party in Parliament | | 47 | 57 | 59 | 52 |
| Percent Who Perceive Role Conflicts With Party in Riding | | 17 | 22 | 12 | 17 |
| Percent Who Perceive Role Conflicts With Provincial Party | | 28 | 35 | 44 | 32 |
| Percent Who Perceive Role Conflicts With Interest Groups | | 45 | 35 | 50 | 43 |
| Percent Who Are Ambitious for Other Public Office | | 55 | 46 | 41 | 51 |
| Mean Parliamentary Efficacy Score | | −.04 | .04 | .09 | .00 |
| Mean Ideology Score (5 = liberal; 1 = conservative) | | 2.6 | 2.7 | 2.9 | 2.7 |
| Perceives a Decline in the Traditional Functions of Parliament ($\bar{X}$ Score) | | −.05 | −.02 | .17 | −.01 |
| Optimistic About Becoming a Cabinet Minister[a] ($\bar{X}$ Score, 1 = Low, 3 = High) | | 2.7 | 3.0 | 3.6 | 2.9 |

a. Excludes current cabinet ministers.

## VARIABLE AND INDEX CONSTRUCTION

This appendix describes the composition and construction of the variables and aggregate indices employed as measures of the concepts which comprised the model of parliamentary influence.

### I. INDIVIDUAL INFLUENCE

See chapter 3 for description and explanation of the variables selected as measures of individual influence.

### II. PARLIAMENTARY PARTICIPATION

A total of eleven indicators of both formal and informal participation in parliament (described at greater length in chapters 4 and 5) were entered into a principal components factor analysis, using a varimax rotation. This procedure yielded three interpretable factors with eigenvalues greater than 1.0. Individual scores on each of these three dimensions were calculated by multiplying the respondent's standardized scores on each item by the item's loading on the factor and then summing the weighted scores for all items. The items loading on each factor and the interpretation of the rotated factors were as follows:

(1) Participation in Debate and Question Period
  (a) Total length of all House speeches (Hansard Lines)                 .93
  (b) Total number of all House speeches                                 .81
  (c) Total number of questions asked or answered during question
      period                                                             .59

(2) Introduction of Bills and Debatable Resolutions
  (a) Total number of government bills and private members' bills intro-
      duced                                                              .74
  (b) Total number of debatable resolutions introduced                   .53

(3) Committee Activity (Not used in analyses)
  (a) Percent attendance at committee meetings for which MP was
      eligible                                                           .56
  (b) "Has your own work on committees led you to suggest policy
      additions or changes in any area?"                                 .52

(4) Items Not Loading on Any Factor
  (a) "How often do you contact cabinet ministers in an average
      month?" (Average correlation with 10 participation variables)      .05
  (b) "How often do you contact deputy-ministers in an average
      month?" (Average correlation with 10 participation variables)      .06
  (c) "And what about your party caucus, does that help individual
      members like yourself influence the work of the House?"            .06

(5) Committee Debate

A fourth measure of parliamentary participation (the total number of speeches each member made in all committee debates) was generated for the 34 MPs whose committee activities were investigated. It was omitted from the factor analysis of participation variables because of the small number of cases for which these data were available.

## III. PARLIAMENTARY LEADERSHIP POSITIONS

Seven parliamentary leadership positions were identified and included in various phases of the analysis. These were: (1) cabinet ministers; (2) speaker; (3) House leaders for all four parties; (4) standing committee chairmen; (5) chief party whip of each party; (6) opposition leader of each of the three opposition parties; and (7) Conservative frontbench. The Conservative frontbench was defined as all past (still in parliament) and present House leaders, opposition leaders, party whips, and cabinet ministers in addition to those members who had been identified by the national press as possible cabinet ministers if the Conservatives formed a government.

A composite leadership variable also was constructed in which leaders were defined as all MPs who were cabinet ministers, party leaders, House leaders and members of the Conservative frontbench. Further descriptions of these measures are presented in chapters 3 and 6.

## IV. CURRENT ATTITUDES AND MOTIVATIONS

A. Incentives for Becoming a MP.

Four incentive measures were constructed from the responses to the question, "Can you recall why you agreed to make the race for a parliamentary seat?" The measures constructed and the response categories included in each measure were as follows:

1. Civic Duty Incentives
   (a) Improve government
   (b) Play a role in national decision making
   (c) Render service to country and constituents
   (d) Insure an electoral contest and provide competition
   (e) Interest in specific issues

2. Party Ideology or Issue Incentives
   (a) Commitment to party goals and philosophy
   (b) Concern for local party
   (c) Dislike of program of party then in power

3. Personal Satisfaction Incentives
   (a) Challenge of public office/Desire to try something new
   (b) Desire for political power, influence, or prestige

4. Pressure from Others
   (a) Party
   (b) Family

(c) Friends
(d) Business associates
(e) Unspecified others

B. Role Perceptions and Conflicts

The analyses in chapters 7–9 include eight measures of MP's role perceptions, self-perceived expertise, and perceived conflicts with other actors in the legislative system.

1. Representational Role Style

Twelve items measuring representational style and focus were entered into a principal components factor analysis producing four factors with eigenvalues greater than 1.0. (For a further discussion of the factor analysis of representational roles see chapter 2.) These varimax rotated factors included three minor factors (accounting for less than 25% of the total explained variation in these data) which we identified as a Burkean Style/National Focus dimension, a Politico dimension and a third dimension. The fourth and strongest factor (explaining more than 40% of the total explained variance in the data) was identified as a summary style-and-focus dimension. The delegate-constituency items loaded negatively; and, consistent with the assumption that Politicos vacillate between the two more clearly defined roles, the Politico items load very close to zero. Because of its content and relative strength, the summary factor is the only dimension used in the analyses. The twelve items that comprise it and their loadings are listed below:

(a) "The job of a MP entails being a sounding board for constituency opinion and then acting on it. I always attempt to find out what my constituents feel and make my decisions accordingly."  .53
(b) "My first duty is to my constituency; they are the ones who elected me."  .76
(c) "Let's face it. Insofar as people care about parliament, what they care about is what you as a MP can do for them in the way of services and favours; not what comes before parliament in the way of issues and legislation."  .30
(d) "I am not at all certain that doing favours, running errands, or serving your constituents, call it whatever you wish, really helps get you elected. I am certain that *not doing these things* when asked will assure that you don't get elected."  .15
(e) "The most important part of a MP's job—that is if he is interested in coming back to parliament—is to go to bat for his constituents in their dealings with government, which usually means the civil service. Even statesmen have to be reelected and for that you have to look after your constituents."  .54
(f) "I can't see why there is any incompatibility between serving your constituency and the nation. I was elected to serve my country, but this is not and has never been inconsistent with serving my constituency and its people."  .02
(g) "My job as a MP entails fighting for what I think is right. It also entails being a representative of the people in my constituency. I accept the fact that I have to deal with their problems but I also have to fight for the integrity of parliament and for a program of legislation that is in the national interest."  .08

(h) "Even if a MP wanted to find out what his constituents felt about a major public issue, it would be impossible. The majority of people don't know. They don't have any information on these things. The rest, or most of the rest, simply don't care."    −.14

(i) "An MP seldom has to sound out his constituents because he thinks so much like them that he knows how they would react to almost any proposal."    .01

(j) "My primary responsibility is to the nation as a whole, I am elected to serve the country."    −.59

(k) "My primary responsibility as an MP is to do as good a job as I can for the country—to act according to my conscience. The alternative is to toady to voters."    −.20

(l) "If anyone tells you he makes his decisions here in parliament on the basis of what his constituents want, assuming he knew what they want, he is either kidding your or himself."    −.50

2. Perceived Expertise

"Is there any particular area of work in the House that you feel you have becoming expert in?" (Record yes/no and all elaborations of "yes" answers.)

3. Conflicts with Constituents

"Do you feel there are differences between what you want to accomplish and what your constituents want?" (Record yes/no and all elaborations of "yes" answers.)

4. Conflicts with Party in Parliament

"Do you feel there are differences between what you want to accomplish and what your party colleagues in the House want?" (Record yes/no and all elaborations of "yes" answers.)

5. Conflicts with Party in Riding

"Do you feel there are any differences between what you want to accomplish and what your local party people want?" (Record yes/no and all elaborations of "yes" answers.)

6. Conflicts with Party in Province and Nation

"Do you feel there are any differences between what you want to accomplish and what your provincial/national party wants?" (Record yes/no and all elaborations of "yes" answers.)

7. Conflicts with Interest Groups

Do you feel there are any differences between what you want to accomplish and what important groups in your riding or province want? (Record yes/no and all elaborations of "yes" answers.)

8. Total Number of Conflicts

This variable was coded as the total number of "yes" answers to questions 3–7 above.

C. Ambitions and Achievements

Five variables were constructed from the interviews as measures of the respondents' political and parliamentary ambitions and their perceptions of their personal achievements as Members of Parliament.

1. Views Parliament as a Career

"Do you expect to make a career out of parliament?" (yes, no)

2. Optimistic about Becoming Cabinet Minister

"If your party won the next national election and you are reelected, what would you say your chances are of becoming a member of the Cabinet?" (Excellent, Very Good, Good, Not So Good, Poor, No Chance Whatsoever)

3. Aspires to Hold Other Public Office

"Are there any other public offices, elected or appointed, that you would like to hold sometime in the future?" (Record yes/no and, if "yes," what are these.)

4. Number of Accomplishments in Parliament

"Apart from looking after your constituents, what are the most important things you have tried to accomplish as a MP?" (Record.) This variable was coded as the total number of accomplishments (regardless of type) cited by the respondent.

5. Cites Policy rather than Service Accomplishments

Although the question in number 4 above specifically excepts constituency service accomplishments, a number of MPs cited them. Therefore, we constructed a second "accomplishment" variable by recording whether the accomplishments cited were focused primarily on policy, constituency service, or both about equally. Respondents who listed primarily policy accomplishments or both policy and service accomplishments were coded 1; respondents citing primarily service accomplishments were coded 0.

D. General Orientation to Politics

Five variables were constructed from the interview data to indicate the respondents' generalized orientations toward, affect for, and perceptions of parliament and its proper role.

1. Likes Being a MP

"Of all the things you did during that first year [in parliament] which did you find most gratifying?" (Record fully.) For this variable we used the total number of activities which respondent cited.

2. Perceived Efficacy of Individual MP

Four Likert-type agree/disagree items relating to the MP's perceptions of individual influence in the House of Commons were included in a principal components factor analysis producing a single factor with an eigenvalue greater than 1.0 which explained 48% of the total variation in these four items. Individual factor scores were calculated by multiplying a respondent's standardized score on an item by that item's factor loading and then summing the individual weighted scores for all items. The items employed in the factor analysis and their loadings on the "Perceived Efficacy" factor are as follows:

(a) "With the progressive exclusion of the average MP from any meaningful participation in the policy-initiation and the policy-evaluation process, his role in parliament has been reduced either to intermittently attacking or to defending policies that have been predetermined by party leaders."                    −.73

(b) "The average MP today, regardless of party, is bored, restive and frustrated. MPs, again regardless of party, want a committee system in which they can work that really is capable of effectively scrutinizing, investigating and criticizing the working of the government and its administrative bureaucracy."      −.60

(c) "The caucus does not give the backbench MP an opportunity to participate in party policy-making. It does, however, provide him with a regular opportunity to bring to the attention of his party colleagues any personal or constituency grievances against them."  −.70

(d) "When you first come to Ottawa you have all sorts of great ideas about what should be done. Then reality sets in. There is nothing, absolutely nothing, an individual MP can do about getting his ideas accepted in the form of legislation unless he's a member of cabinet."      −.74

3.  Personal Ideology (Left-Right)

Respondents were asked to locate their responses to these questions along three 9-point issue scales which were arranged so the most liberal (Left) responses received the highest score and the most conservative responses received the lowest score. We summed the responses to these three questions and then reduced the resulting 25 point scale (3–27) to a five point scale. The issues and issue scales used were as follows (in all cases, Left=9, Middle=5, Right=1):

(a) "How big a part should the federal government take in improving welfare benefits like health insurance, pension payments and that kind of thing?" (Government Should Take a Bigger Part / Government's Part Just About Right / Government Should Take Less of a Part)

(b) "The power of the federal government vis-a-vis the provinces?" (Provincial Governments Too Powerful / Federal and Provincial Powers Are Just Right / Federal Government Too Powerful)

(c) "The closeness of Canada's relations with communist countries?" (Expand Relations with Communist Countries / Relations Are Just About Right / Reduce Relations with Communist Countries)

Two additional variables were generated from a principal components factor analysis of six items pertaining to the respondents' perceptions of the functions of parliament in Canadian society. Two factors were produced with eigenvalues greater than 1.0 which together accounted for 55% of the total variation in the six items. The factors were rotated using varimax criteria and weighted factor scores were calculated for each respondent. The interpretation of the two factors and the items loading on each are as follows:

4.  Decline of Traditional Functions of Parliament

(a) "Parliament's legislative function in the sense of conceiving, amending, rejecting and accepting bills is far less important today than is its job of serving as a communications link between the Government and the public."      .49

(b) "Parliament today is neither actively involved in the policy process nor does it effectively oversee the bureaucracy although these are supposed to be its two principal functions."      .66

(c) "The decline in the power and authority of parliament with respect to the formulation of public policy is one of the most striking developments in Canadian government in the 20th Century. Parliament today is impotent. It has been stripped of any real function in the policy-making process and retains only the symbolic vestiges of its former powers." .69

5. Advocates Alternative Parliamentary Functions
   (d) "There is a role for contemporary parliament to play, a very vital role. The House must equip itself to do two things: to study, first, the conditions from which the need for legislation emerges; second, it must follow through the consequences of legislation. Put another way, the House must concern itself with the formulation of policy at the pre-legislative stage and the scrutiny of policy at the post-legislative stage." .66
   (e) "Parliament historically has served a vital function in Canadian society as the institution most responsible for promoting the economic development and modernization of this nation." .47
   (f) "Parliament is primarily a device for mobilizing and organizing consent for public policy decisions rather than a device for opposing and unmaking governments." .52

## V. CURRENT POLITICAL BACKGROUND AND ENVIRONMENT

A. Parliamentary Background Variables

1. Age at Entry into Parliament
   This variable was coded as the MP's age at the time of his first entry into parliament even if his service in parliament has not been continuous.

2. Number of years in Parliament
   This variable was coded as the total number of years that the MP had served in the House of Commons up to the beginning of the third session of the 28th Parliament, when we began our interviews.

B. Constituency Composition Variables

1. Urbanization of Constituency
   Percent urban population in 1968, the year the members of the 28th Parliament were elected.

2. Constituency Turnout 1968
   Percentage turnout of eligible voters, by constituency, in the 1968 federal elections.

3. Constituency Competition 1968
   Percentage differences in the votes received by the winning and second place candidates in the 1968 federal elections.

4. Constituency Competition, First Election to Parliament
   Percentage differences in the votes received by the winning and second place candidates in the MP's first successful campaign for a seat in parliament.

C. Knowledge of Parliament's Rules of the Game

Three variables which measure the respondents' awareness of informal rules of the game in parliament (described at length in chapter 2) were constructed from the respondents' answers to the following question: "Moving on now to the time when you were actually elected to parliament, we have been told that every legislature has its unofficial rules of the game, certain things members must do and certain things they must not do if they want the respect and cooperation of their legislative colleagues. What are some of these rules that a member must observe if he wants to have the respect and cooperation of his colleagues?" (Record fully.) The variables constructed from the responses to this question are as follows:

1.  Number of Political Rules Cited
    This variable was coded as the total number of rules cited by the respondent which applied to behavior either within or outside of parliament and whose functions are clearly political (e.g., "Maintain party solidarity," "Do not break party ranks," "No personal attacks on other members," "Attend party caucus," "Do your share of assignments").

2.  Number of Social Rules Cited
    This variable was coded as the total number of rules cited by the respondent which applied to behavior either within or outside of parliament and whose purpose is to regulate the members' social relationships (e.g., "Extend the proper courtesies during debate," "Be friendly and courteous, and respect other members in your relationships outside the House").

3.  Number of Organizational Rules Cited
    This variable was coded as the total number of rules cited by the respondent which applied to behavior either within or outside of parliament whose purpose is to expedite organizational efficiency (e.g., "Don't speak too often or long," "Do your proper share of the work," "Observe the rules of debate").

D. Parliamentary Sanctions

Members indicating an awareness of one or more rules of the game were asked, "I imagine that things could be made rather difficult for anyone who didn't observe these rules." Respondents who agreed with this statement were asked, "Can you give me some examples of these things?" Four variables were constructed from the members' responses.

1.  Knows Any Sanctions
    This is a dichotomous variable indicating whether or not the respondent cited at least one sanction that might be employed to regulate MP behavior either within or outside of parliament.

2.  Number of Political Sanctions cited
    This variable is the total number of primarily political sanctions cited (e.g., "Sanctions by the party," "Being refused renomination by constituency party").

3.  Number of Social Sanctions Cited
    This variable is the total number of largely social sanctions cited (e.g., social ostracism).

4.  Number of Organizational Sanctions Cited
    This variable is the total number of sanctions cited which resulted primarily in the denial of organizational privileges (e.g., "Nonrecognition by the speaker").

## VI. POLITICAL RECRUITMENT, CAREER, AND EARLY POLITICAL MOTIVATIONS

A. Political Recruitment and Career Variables

Five factors with eigenvalues greater than 1.0 were produced by a principal components factor analysis of eleven items pertaining to political recruitment and career experiences. Together these factors explained 77% of the total variation in the eleven items. The factors were rotated according to varimax criteria, and individual factor scores were computed. The rotated factors and the items loading on each of them are listed below:

1. Experienced Difficulty Securing Nominations
   (a) Was there any opposition to the respondent's first nomination for public office? .53
   (b) When respondent was first nominated for a seat in parliament did he face competition for the nomination? .78
   (c) Degree of competition experienced in contest for first nomination to parliament. 1.0

2. Prior Service as a Public Office Holder
   (d) "Had you ever been elected to a public office before becoming a candidate for a parliamentary seat?" .94
   (e) Respondent indicates that he served as an elected member of a provincial or local legislative body prior to becoming a candidate for parliament. .88

3. Prior Service in the Party Organization
   (f) "Were you already an active party worker at the time you first became a candidate for [first office] in [date]?" .88
   (g) "Speaking of parties, have you ever held a formal party office in a riding, at the provincial level, or at the national level?" .79

4. Self-Motivated vs. Recruited for Public Service
   (h) Did respondent volunteer or was he recruited by the party to run for office in his first campaign for any public office? .65
   (i) Did respondent volunteer or was he recruited by the party to run initially for a seat in parliament? .64

5. Previous Unsuccessful Candidacies for Public Office
   (j) "Had you ever been a candidate for public office even before you were successfully elected to [first office] in [date]?" .77
   (k) "Thinking now of how you were nominated for a parliamentary seat, had you ever tried to secure a nomination for a parliamentary seat before but were unsuccessful?" .28

B. Motivations for First Political Candidacies

Five measures of motivations for first becoming a candidate for any public office in Canada were constructed from the answers to the question, "Can you recall how it was that you first became a candidate for [Repeat the name of the first office for which respondent was a candidate and give the date]?" The motivation-related responses were divided into the following five categories which were derived from an analysis of the inter-item correlations. Since respondents were free to cite more than one motivation, the variables are not mutually exclusive.

1. Generalized Appeal of Party
   (a) Platforms and policies
   (b) Leaders
   (c) Party membership characteristics
   (d) Other candidates

2. Generalized Pressure From Others
   (a) Family
   (b) Employer
   (c) Civic and fraternal groups
   (d) Close friends

3. Dislike of Party in Power
   (a) Platform and policies
   (b) Leaders

4. General Philosophy or Ideology
   (a) General personal philosophy
   (b) Desire was stimulated by education, reading, etc.
   (c) Desire to become involved in certain issues

5. Civic Duty—Improve Government
   (a) Civic responsibility
   (b) Desire to improve government

C. Motives for Initial Political Involvement

"Legislators in this country and in other Western democracies have given a variety of reasons to explain why they became active in politics initially. What are the most important reasons you had for getting involved in politics?"

Four variables were constructed based upon an inspection of the inter-item correlations. These variables and the responses are listed below. Multiple responses were permitted so that some respondents are coded as possessing multiple motivations.

1. Pressure From Others
   (a) Friends
   (b) Civic and professional groups
   (c) Family
   (d) Employers or co-workers

2. Improve Local/Provincial Government
   (a) Local government
   (b) Provincial government

3. Improve Federal Government
   (a) Federal government
   (b) Government at all levels

4. Personal Satisfaction and Gain
   (a) Personal satisfaction, exhilaration, enjoyment
   (b) Launch a political career
   (c) Desire for power, prestige
   (d) Improve business contacts

## VII. POLITICAL SOCIALIZATION

Seven variables were constructed as measures of MPs' early life political socialization experiences.

1. Politicization of the Childhood Environment
    Seven variables reflecting the number of politicizing stimuli perceived by the MP during childhood were entered into a principal components factor analysis. A single factor with an eigenvalue greater than 1.0, which explained 58% of the total variation in these items, was extracted and weighted factor scores were generated. The variables employed in this analysis and their loadings on the politicization factor were as follows:
    (a) Parental partisan homogeneity (an index of the MP's perception of the similarity of his parents' national party affiliations).                     .69
    (b) Parental political activity (an index of the combined political activities and political interest of the MP's parents as recalled by the MP).                     .71
    (c) "As a child in grade school or earlier, did you know personally any people who then held public office?"                     .75
    (d) "During this same period of your life, were any of the people on this list (list includes family, friends, neighbors, clergy, doctors, school teachers, etc.) that you might have been close to active in politics or public affairs?" Variable coded as total number of people mentioned.                     .79
    (e) Relationship between respondent and people active in politics. This variable also was based upon the responses to the question (d) above. The variable was coded as the closeness of the relationship between the respondent and those politically active people he knew as a child.                     .83
    (f) "During this same period of your life, were any of the people on this same list that you might have been close to inactive but very interested in politics or public affairs?" Variable coded as total number of people mentioned.                     .68

2. Positive Reaction to First Political Event
    "Now would you go back as far as you can remember and tell me two things. What is the first aspect of politics or public affairs (e.g., an election outcome, a political issue, a party nominee, a party leader, the structure of government) that you were aware of?" Interviewers were instructed to probe for the circumstances surrounding this first political experience and to record, among other things, the respondent's recollection of his reaction (positive, negative, or neutral) to this experience.

3. Number of Changes in Party Identification
    Following a question concerning the age at which the respondent first identified with a political party, we asked, "Between that first identification with the (name) party and the time you first became a candidate for parliament, did you identify in this way with another party?" We then recorded any changes in identification and asked those indicating a change, "Did this ever happen again?" This variable was coded as the total number of reported changes in the respondent's party identification up to his entry into parliament.

4.  Belonged to High School or University Political Clubs
    "When you were growing up, did you belong to any political groups or organizations in school—that is, while you were in high school [and if appropriate] and in university?" (Record yes/no.)

5.  School Friends' Interest in Politics
    "And how about your friends? Were most of them interested in politics, were some of them interested, or were most not interested?"

6.  Average Age of Major Socialization Experiences
    This variable was coded as the mean age at which the respondent first identified with a political party, first became interested in politics, and first became aware of politics.

7.  Early Life Importance of Politics
    Three measures of the importance of politics to the respondent during his early life were entered into a principal components factor analysis. A single factor emerged with an eigenvalue greater than 1.0. The variables included and their loadings on this factor are as follows:
    (a)  "Now, let's consider the whole period from when you first became aware of politics until you first became active in politics. In general, how closely did you follow politics and public affairs during this period? Did you follow them very closely, somewhat closely, or very little or not at all?"                                    .62
    (b)  "How well informed would you say you were compared to most people your age during this same period? Were you more informed than the average, about average, or less informed than the average?"                                                                      .67
    (c)  "How important were such matters to you during that same period? That is, if you followed politics and public affairs closely, would it have mattered to you if you couldn't have? Or, if you hardly followed them at all, did you have any strong feelings that you would have wanted to do so?"                                          .55

## VIII.  SOCIAL BACKGROUND

The bases of the twenty-eight social background variables employed in this study, in most instances, are obvious, and do not require lengthy explanation. The religious variables are simply dichotomous variables reflecting the religious preference of the MP as indicated in his brief autobiographical sketch in *Canada's 28th Parliament*. The region of birth and parents' ethnic background variables also are recorded as a series of dichotomous variables constructed from three questions in the interview schedule eliciting the respondent's province of birth, the national background of his father's and mother's family.

Education is measured by four variables: (1) whether or not the MP graduated from college; (2) whether the MP graduated from one of the higher prestige universities (McGill University, Queen's University, and the University of Toronto for the English Canadians and the Université de Laval, Loyola, Université de Montreal, and Université de Sherbrooke for the French Canadians); (3) the total number of years of formal schooling; and (4) whether the respondent received a professional degree (law, medicine, etc.). These data were generated from the members' autobiographical sketches and were supplemented and cross checked by data generated in the interview.

Father's SES and the respondent's SES at the time of his initial election to parliament are recorded as Duncan SES scores (the method of computing these scores is described in *Occupations and Social Status,* Albert J. Reiss, Jr., et al., N.Y.: The Free Press, 1961). These scores are based upon the respondent's report of his father's usual occupation while the respondent was growing up and the respondent's reported occupation when he first was elected to parliament.

The measure of the size of the MP's place of birth was constructed from the answers to a question which concerned whether the respondent was reared in a large city, small town or on a farm. The measure of the length of time the member has resided in the constituency he represents also was constructed from a question in the interview.

Finally, the club membership variables are measured as the number of clubs (coded by purpose—religious, social, professional, civic) to which the MP reported belonging in the autobiographical sketches and our interviews.

INTERVIEW SCHEDULE

**EARLY LIFE SOCIALIZATION**

I would like to begin by asking you to recall some of the events of your early childhood and school life that are concerned with politics.

1. Now, would you go back as far as you can remember, to tell me two things. What is the first aspect of politics or public affairs (e.g., an election outcome, a political issue, a party nominee, a party leader, the structure of governments) that you were aware of? (Probe for the *one* political event, issue, or person respondent can remember as being first aware of.) And how old were you at that time?

1-a) Would it be fair to say that this is when you *first* became aware of politics and public affairs? YES NO

1-b) (If "NO" ask:) Well, how old were you when you first became aware of politics?

1-c) What was the event you were aware of then? (Correct question 1.)

1-d) With whom did you live throughout most of your late childhood and adolescence—I mean about ten to seventeen? Did you live with both your parents, one parent only, step parents, foster parents, or whom?

| | |
|---|---|
| Both Parents | Guardian or foster couple |
| Father only | Guardian or foster father |
| Mother only | Guardian or foster mother |
| Father + Step Mother | Institutional |
| Mother + Step Father | Other |

2. At the time you first became aware of politics can you remember which, if any, political party your father/mother preferred?

| | | | NDP | Other | | Not | Can't | Don't |
|---|---|---|---|---|---|---|---|---|
| SC | Con. | Lib. | (CCF) | (Specify) | None | living | recall | know |
| F. | | | | | | | | |
| M. | | | | | | | | |

2-a) Did you father/mother prefer the _____ (repeat appropriate name) party in both national and provincial politics?

| | YES | NO | Can't recall | N.A. |
|---|---|---|---|---|
| Father | | | | |
| Mother | | | | |

2-b) (If "NO" ask:)
Well, which party did your mother/father prefer at the national level?

| | | | NDP | Other | Not | Can't | Don't |
|---|---|---|---|---|---|---|---|
| SC | Con. | Lib. | (CCF) | (Specify) | living | recall | know |
| F. | | | | | | | |
| M. | | | | | | | |

And which party did your mother/father prefer at the provincial level?

| | SC | Con. | Lib. | NDP (CCF) | Other (Specify) | None | Not living | Can't recall | Don't know |
|---|---|---|---|---|---|---|---|---|---|
| F. | | | | | | | | | |
| M. | | | | | | | | | |

3. During this same period of time would you say your father's/mother's interest in politics was:

| | Very strong | Quite strong | Not very strong | Weak | No interest at all | N.A. | Can't remember |
|---|---|---|---|---|---|---|---|
| F. | | | | | | | |
| M. | | | | | | | |

3-a) (If interest of parents "VERY STRONG" or "QUITE STRONG" or "NOT VERY STRONG" ask:)
Where there discussions about politics in your home?
YES   NO   D.K.   N.A.

3-b) (If "YES":) Would you say there was:
A great deal of discussion
Some discussion
Not much discussion

3-c) (If "VERY STRONG," "QUITE STRONG" or "NOT VERY STRONG" ask:)
Was mother/father every active in politics during this time?

       YES   NO   D.K.   N.A.

F.
M.

3-d) If "YES" to 'c' and not otherwise indicated ask:)
Did your father/mother:

| | Hold elected public office | Hold appointed public office | Candidate public office | Hold party office | Campaign for party | Speak informally for party | Other |
|---|---|---|---|---|---|---|---|
| F. | | | | | | | |
| M. | | | | | | | |

4. As a child in grade school or earlier, did you know personally any people who then held a public office (elected or appointed)?
YES   NO   Can't recall   Don't know

5. (Hand respondent list A) During this same period of your life, were any of the people on this list that you might have been close to:

| | Active in politics and public affairs | Inactive, but very interested in politics and public affairs |
|---|---|---|
| Brother(s) and/or sister(s) | | |
| More distant relatives | | |
| Family friends | | |
| Schoolmates | | |
| Neighbors | | |
| Neighborhood merchants | | |

Family doctor, dentist, laywer, etc.
School teacher
Youth group leader
Other (Specify)
None of them
Don't remember

6.    Thinking back now, how did you first become interested in politics? (Probe for age, event, and circumstances surrounding first interest.)

6-a) Between the time that you first became interested in politics and the time you actually became actively involved in politics, would you say interest in politics:
1. initially was quite high and generally remained high
2. initialy was quite high but declined somewhat
3. initially was quite high but fluctuated considerably
4. initially was low but rose steadily
5. initially was low and remained generally low
6. initialy was low but fluctuated over this time

6-b) (If 2, 3, 4 or 6, ask:)
Is there any one incident during which your interests may have changed that particularly stands out in your memory?
YES    NO    D.K.    N.A.

6-c) (If "YES" ask:)
What was that? (Probe for events, processes and agents involved.)


## QUESTIONS ON PARTY IDENTIFICATION

7.    I would like to ask you a few questions about how you became attached to a particular party.

7-a) When did you first begin to identify with a political party—that is, a party you felt sympathetic, close and loyal to?

7-b) (Ask for *first* party identification and for each *change*—if there are changes.)
(Hand respondent list B) Which, if any, of the things on this list were important factors in a) the development of your sympathies for the _____ party at age _____; b) the change of your sympathies from the _____ party at age _____ to the _____ party?

|  | First identification | First change | Second change | Third change | Fourth change | Fifth change |
|---|---|---|---|---|---|---|
| (Record age) Materials used for courses |  |  |  |  |  |  |
| Teachers, regardless of whether you had them in class |  |  |  |  |  |  |

School friends and other
 schoolmates
Immediate family members
 and other close relatives
Friends, acquaintances, and
 neighbours
Work experiences, supervisors,
 co-workers
Religious activities and
 functionaries
Recreational activities,
 club and fraternal acti-
 vities, hobbies, etc.
Examples set by public
 figures
Important events that may
 have occurred
Other

7-c) And were your parents also supporting that party at the time?
   YES NO D.K. N.A. Can't remember
 F.
 M.

7-d) Between that first identification with ____ party and the time you first became a candidate for parliament, did you ever identify in this way with another party? YES NO N.A. Don't recall

7-e) (If "Yes," to 'd' record 1) Name of party; ____ and 2) Date of identification ____.)
(Hand respondent list B and ask:) Which, if any, of the things on this list were important factors in changing your sympathies and identification with ____ party to the ____ party at age ____?

7-f) Did this ever happen again? YES NO Can't Recall N.A.
(If "YES," record age and party and repeat format of handing respondent list B.)

7-g) (If "NO" to 'f', i.e., no other changes in identities, ask:)
Well when did you begin to identify again with (his current) party? (Record age ____ and hand respondent list B and repeat list B question.)

7-h) (If respondent says "NO" to 'd', i.e., he has never identified with a party other than his current one ask:) "I suppose over the years there must have been times when you felt especially close and loyal to the ____ party and others when you felt much less close. Or did your feelings in this regard remain about the same over the years?"
 Felt close. Felt distant. Felt the same.

8. When you were growing up, did you belong to any political groups or organizations in school—that is, while you were in high school (and if appropriate) in university?
High School YES NO D.K. N.A.
University

9.  Did you belong to any political groups or organizations outside the school? YES   NO   D.K.   N.A.

10. And how about your friends? Were most of them interested in politics, were some of them interested, or were most not interested?   Most interested   Some interested   Most not interested   D.K.   N.A.

11. Now, let's consider the whole period from when you first became aware of politics until you first became active in politics. In general, how closely did you follow politics and public affairs during this period? Did you follow them very closely, somewhat closely, or very little or not at all?
Very closely   Somewhat closely   Very little or not at all   Won't say   Don't recall

12. How well informed would you say you were compared to most people your age during this same period? Were you more informed than the average, about average, or less informed than the average?
More than average   About average   Less than average   Won't say   Don't recall

13. How important were such matters to you during that same period? That is, if you followed politics and public affairs closely, would it have mattered to you if you couldn't have? Or, if you hardly followed them at all, do you have any strong feelings that you would have wanted to do so?   Mattered, would have wanted to   Didn't matter, didn't want to   Don't know   Don't recall

14. Of all the experiences, influences, and events between the time you first became aware of politics and the time you first became active in politics, which were particularly important in moving you in that direction (active in politics)?
That question leads to our next topic—how you actually began a career in public life.

15. Had you ever been elected to a public office before becoming a candidate for a parliamentary seat?   YES   NO   N.A.
(If "YES":)

15-a) What were the(se) office(s)?
(List offices chronologically.)

15-b) Had you ever been a *candidate* for a public office even before you were successful in being elected _____ (title of first office) in _____ (date)?
YES   NO   D.K.   N.A.

15-c) (If "YES":)
What was/were the office(s) for which you were a candidate?
(List office titles and dates:)
(If "NO" to '15', i.e., if respondent says he never held an office before becoming an MP, ask:) "Had you ever been a *candidate* for an elected public office before becoming a candidate for a parliamentary seat?
YES   NO   N.A.
(If "YES":)

15-d) What were the(se) office(s) for which you were a candidate? (List office titles and dates.)
*Check Item*
It is correct to say, then, that the *first* time you were a candidate for an

elected public office was in _____ when you were a candidate for _____?
YES   NO

(If "NO" then correct 'a,' 'b,' 'c.')

15-e) Can you recall how it happened that you first became a candidate for the office? (Repeat name of first office for which he was a candidate and then the date).
(Probe for circumstances, agents involved, whether he volunteered or was recruited, whether he had any opposition for his nomination, and what his motives were.)

16.   Were you already a regular, active party worker at the time you first became a candidate for _____(office) in _____(date)? By an active party worker I mean that you both thought of yourself and were thought of by others as an active, available and reliable worker for a particular party. The affiliation could have continued for more than a single campaign, but it doesn't have to have been with your current party. It could have been with any. If you worked for a party for a few years, then stopped for a while and started again, it's that *first* beginning we're talking about.
YES   NO   D.K.   N.A.

16-a) (If "YES":) "How old were you when you became an active party worker?" (age)

16-b) (If "NO":) "Did you become an active party worker before you became a candidate for a parliamentary seat?"   YES   NO   D.K.   N.A.

16-c) (If "YES":) "How old were you at that time?"

17.   (*Ask only MPs who say they have worked in a party*:)
Speaking of parties, have you ever held a formal party office in a riding, at the provincial level or at the national level?   YES (Local)   YES (Provincial)   YES (National)   NO   D.K   N.A.

18.   Legislators in this country and in other Western democracies have given a variety of reasons to explain why they became active in politics initially. What do you think are the most important reasons people have for getting into politics?

18-a) How about in your case?
(Do not read list.)

| | Applied in his case | Didn't apply in his case | Mentioned for everyone | D.K. |
|---|---|---|---|---|
| Improve business contacts | | | | |
| Improve the federal government | | | | |
| Response to pressures from friends | | | | |
| Improve the local government | | | | |
| Response to pressures from civic and fraternal groups (Elks, Masons, etc.) | | | | |
| Response to pressures from immediate family | | | | |
| Expand one's social life | | | | |
| Response to pressures from more distant relatives | | | | |

| Applied in his case | Didn't apply in his case | Mentioned for everyone | D.K. |
|---|---|---|---|

Response to pressures from
  unions, civil service worker groups, professional associations, etc.
Personal satisfaction, enjoyment, exhilaration
Improve the provincial
  government
Response to pressures from
  business associates
Improve government at all levels
Others

18-b) Was there any particular person or group who encouraged you to enter public life or was this pretty well a decision you made on your own?

19. Thinking now of how you were nominated for a parliamentary seat, had you ever tried to secure a nomination for a parliamentary seat before, but were unsuccessful? YES NO N.A. (If "YES," record date or dates that he had tried to obtain a nomination and ask 'a'.)

19-a) Can you recall what things were important in making you try again to get a nomination?

19-b) (*Ask everyone:*) When you were successful in receiving a nomination, did you stand for a nomination or did you have to run for it? (Record whether respondent had competition, who was pushing his nomination, reasons why he was chosen and his motives for running or permitting his draft).

19-c) (*If not already mentioned:*)
    What in your opinion were the reasons that you received the party's nomination at that time? That is, what were the important factors, people, and organizations that were instrumental in your nomination?

19-d) With respect to the relative importance of the local, provincial, and federal party organizations, which would you say had the greatest effect on your securing the nomination initially?
    Local Provincial Federal Local-Provincial    equally    Local-Federal
    Provincial-Federal   All   None   D.K.   N.A.   (Probe:)   How was that?

19-e) (*If not already mentioned:*)
    Can you recall why you agreed to make the race for a parliamentary seat?

20. Moving on now to the time when you actually were elected to parliament, we have been told that every legislature has its unofficial rules of the game, certain things that members must do and certain things they must not do if they want the respect and cooperation of their legislative colleagues. What are some of these rules?

20-a) I imagine that things could be made rather difficult for anyone who didn't observe these rules. YES NO D.K. N.A.

20-b) (If "YES":) Can you give me some examples of these things?

    (If "YES" to 'a' and 'b' ask:)

20-c) How did you learn of these rules? That is, was there someone who talked to you after the election but before you took office, or did people talk to you after you took office, or did you just learn about them on your own? (Probe for when he learned the rules, and from whom or how he learned of them.)

21. Just before you took office, did you have any ideas about what the job of being an MP entailed? (If "YES," probe for what his expectations were and record fully. If "NO," record why he didn't and skip to Ques. 23.)

22. (If "YES" to 21 ask:) And during your first year as an MP, did things work out just about the way you expected them to or were they somewhat different?

*(Ask everyone:)*
23. Of all the things you did during that first year which did you find were the most gratifying?

23-a) And which did you find the most burdensome and onerous?

24. Did becoming a MP require you to make any major adjustments in your life style? YES NO N.A.
(If "YES:") What were some of the major adjustments you had to make?

25. Apart from looking after your constituents, what are the most important things you have tried to accomplish as a MP?

26. And what are the most important things you want to accomplish in the future?

27. Are there any changes in procedure or in the way the House operates that you think would make it easier for you to accomplish these things?

28. Do you feel there are differences between what you want to accomplish YES NO D.K. N.A.
   a- and what your constituents want?
   b- your party colleagues in the House want?
   c- your local party people want?
   d- your provincial and/or national party wants?
   e- important groups in your riding or province want?
     (Record all elaborations of "YES" answers.)

29. Is there any particular area of work in the House that you feel you have become an expert in? YES NO N.A. (If "YES" record.)

29-a) (If "YES":)
How did you acquire your expertise in the(se) area(s): (Record.)

29-b) (If "NO":)
Is there any particular area that you would like to become an expert in? YES NO N.A.

29-c) (Probe regardless of "YES" or "NO.") Why is that? (Record.)

(Ask everyone other than Cabinet members:)
30. If your party wins the next national election and you are re-elected, what would you say are your chances of becoming a member of cabinet?
    Excellent Very good Good Not so good Poor No chance whatsoever

30-a) Why do you think this is so? (Record.)

31.   From your own experience and based on the experience of others, what
      do you think are the principal criteria applied to select cabinet members?

32.   (Do not ask cabinet ministers. For parliamentary secretaries preface with
      "Other than your own minister, how often do you contact . . . ?")
      Speaking of cabinet ministers, how often do you contact a minister during
      an average month?  Often  Quite often  Depends  Not very often
         Rarely or never  N.A.

32-a) (If Often or Quite often or Depends, ask:) How do you usually contact a
      minister? (If Not very often or Rarely or never, skip to 'f'.) Over the
      phone  Write him  Visit his office  In House lobby, restaurant  At
      social occasions, formal and informal  Party caucus  Through the
      whips  By means of an intermediary  Another member  Other (speci-
      fy)  N.A.

32-b) Which ministers do you contact most often—that is, the ministers of which
      departments? (Record up to five.)

32-c) Are the occasions for such contacts usually constituency matters or with
      regard to the policies of the department(s)?  Usually a constituency
      matter  Usually a policy matter  Both  Neither (Record.)  Other (Rec-
      ord.)  N.A.

32-d) How successful would you say you have been in getting what you have
      asked for, or getting your points across?  Very successful or success-
      ful  Quite successful  Depends on the subject  Not very success-
      ful  Not successful  N.A.

32-e) (If Very successful or Successful or Quite successful or Depends on the
      subject, then ask:)
      How do you determine how successful you have been?

32-f) (If respondent says he doesn't speak to ministers often or contacts them
      seldom ask:) Has it been your experience that there generally is little
      contact between ministers and other members? (Record.)

32-g) (If "YES" to 'f' ask:) Why do you think there have not been more
      contacts? (Record.)

33.   (Do not ask cabinet members.)
      And how about deputy-ministers, how often do you contact deputy-
      ministers or other high ranking civil servants in an average month?  Of-
      ten  Quite often  Depends  Not very often  Rarely or never  N.A.

33-a) (If Often or Quite often or Depends, ask 'd.' If Not very often or Rarely or
      never, skip to 'e'.) How do you generally contact a deputy-minister or
      senior civil servant?  By telephone  Write him  Visit his office  Others
      (Record.)  N.A.

33-b) Which departmental deputies or civil servants do you contact most often?
      (Record up to five departments.)

33-c) Are the occasions for such contacts usually constituency matters or in
      regard to the policies of the department(s)?  Usually a constituency

matter   Usually a policy matter   Both   Neither (Record.)   Other (Record.)   N.A.

33-d) How successful would you say you are in getting what you have asked for, or in getting your points across?   Very successful or successful   Quite successful   Depends   Not very successful   Not successful   N.A.

33-e) (If Depends or Not very successful, ask:) Has it been your experience that there is little contact between members and deputy ministers or other high ranking civil servants?

33-f) (If "YES" ask:) Why do you think there have not been more contacts? (Record.)

34.   (*Do not ask ministers and parliamentary secretaries.*) What about parliamentary secretaries, how often do you contact a parliamentary secretary during an average month?   Often   Quite often   Depends   Not very often   Rarely or never   N.A.

34-a) (If Not very often or Rarely or never, skip to 'e'. For all others ask:) How do you usually contact a parliamentary secretary?   By phone   Write him   Visit his office   In the House lobby, restaurant   At social occasions   Other   N.A.

34-b) Which parliamentary secretaries do you contact most often—that is, the secretaries of which departments? (Record up to five.)

34-c) Are the occasions for such contacts usually constituency matters or with regard to the policies of the department?   Usually a constituency matter   Usually a policy matter   Both   Neither   Other (Record.)   N.A.

34-d) How successful would you say you have been in getting what you have asked for, or in getting your points across?   Very successful or successful   Quite successful   Depends   Not very successful   Not successful   N.A.

34-e) (If *R* says depends, or not very successful, ask:) Has it been your experience that there generally is little contact between members and parliamentary secretaries? (Record.)

34-f) (If "YES:") Why do you think there have not bee more contacts?

34-g) (*Ask only cabinet ministers and parliamentary secretaries.*) How often do members of your own and the opposition parties contact you during an average month?   Often   Quite often   Depends   Not very often   Rarely or never   N.A.

34-h) (If Not very often or Rarely or never, skip to 'l'. For all others ask:) How do they usually contact you?   By phone   In writing   In the House lobby, restaurant   At social occasions   Party caucus   Through whip   By means of an intermediary   Another member   Other (specify)   N.A.

34-i) Do members of your own or the opposition parties contact you most?   His own party   The opposition   About equal   N.A.

34-j) Is the occasion for such contacts usually matters having to do with the member's constituency or the policies of your department?   Usually constituency   Usually policy   Both   Neither   Other   N.A.

34-k) How successful would you say members are in getting what they ask for or getting their points across?   Very successful or successful   Quite successful   Depends on what they want, the subject etc.   Not very successful   Not successful   N.A.

34-l) (If Not very often or Rarely or never to '32,' ask:) Has it been your experience that there is little contact between ministers/parliamentary secretaries, and other members? (Record.)

34-m)(If "YES":) Why do you think there have not been more contacts?

35.    Let's turn for a moment to parliamentary committees. How many committees are you currently a member of? (Record.)

35-a) Which committees are you most interested in? (Record.)

35-b) With respect to (the names of first 2 committees mentioned in 'b'.) "How often do you attend meetings of the _____ and _____ committees."   Very often, often, Fairly often   Depend, too variable to estimate, Sometimes. Not very often, seldom   Rarely, never

35-c) Do you generally stay for the whole or most of the meeting of a committee or do you generally leave early?   Generally stays for most   Generally leaves early   Sometimes leaves early,   Sometimes doesn't, it depends   N.A.

35-e) Which aspect of the (repeat 2 names) committee's work especialy interests you? (Record)

35-f) Why? (If he has not told you in 'e.')

35-g) How do you generally prepare for a committee meeting? (Probe for amount of time he spends preparing, where he gets information and assistance or who helps him to prepare his positions etc.)

36.    Do you think the principal function of House Standing Committees is one of shaping the substance of legislation and influencing estimates, of providing an opportunity to present party positions on substantive issues and estimates, or of giving the individual M.P. an opportunity to participate in a meaningful way in the policy process, or what? (Record fully.)

37.    Has your own work on committees led you to suggest policy changes or additions in any area?

38.    How could the influence of the individual M.P. on a committee be increased? (Record fully.)

39.    Are there other ways, other than committees that is, that individual members like yourself could influence the work of the House? (Record fully.)

39-a) (If Respondent does not mention caucus ask:)
And what about your party caucus, could that help?

39-b) (If Respondent does not mention question period ask:)
And what about the question period, could that help?

40.    Let's think for a moment about your constituency. How about the strength of the other parties in your constituency? Would you describe your constituency as:   Very competitive   Somewhat competitive   Not very competitive   Not competitive   D.K.   N.A.

41. And how about your own party in your riding, how strong would you say it is? Very strong　Quite strong　Not strong or weak　D.K.　N.A.

42. (Depending upon whether respondent is serving his first term in parliament or has been elected for two or more terms ask:) In the last election/ over the years, in federal elections would you say your local party, the provincial party or the national party was the most important in determining the outcome of your election(s)? Local most important　Provincial most important　National most important　Combination important (Record.) D.K. N.A.

42-a) (If respondent cites only one party level ask:)
What are the chief things the ____ party does to help you get elected?

42-b) (If respondent cites more than one level of party ask:)
What are the chief things the ____ and the ____ party do to help you get elected? (Record.)

43. What about after an election, do you think the local party, the provincial party or the national party organization influences the decisions of MPs? (Record.)

43-a) (If respondent doesn't state, probe by asking in which way the party influences MPs, and the magnitude of their influence—i.e. a great deal, some, not much etc.

44. In comparison to other MPs in your party or province did you have to do much campaigning in the last election? YES　NO　N.A.

45. What do you think is the most effective way of campaigning—that is, reaching the greatest number of people in a way that might influence them to vote for you? (Record.)

46. Obviously the cost of a campaign will vary with factors such as the size of a constituency. Still, what do you estimate is the average cost of a successful campaign for a Canadian parliamentary seat? AMOUNT ____

46-a) Generally speaking, what are the major items or areas on which campaign funds must be spent? (Record.)

46-b) In general, what proportion of campaign funds do you think is used for election-day expenses for workers?

46-c) What proportion of an individual candidate's campaign fund do you think comes from: a) his national party; b) his provincial party; c) local fund-raising; d) the candidate's pocket? (Record.)

47. Just a moment ago, I asked you the most effective way to communicate with your constituents during an election campaign. How about after a campaign, do you get much mail from the people in your constituency each week? YES　NO　Depends　D.K.　N.A.

47-a) What is the mail that you do get generally about? For instance, do people write asking about your view on a certain issue, about their stand on a certain issue, do they ask for your help on certain matters such as contacting a civil service official, securing information for them or what? (Probe thoroughly on each of these points.)

48. Do the people in your constituency or province communicate with you in

other ways, such as visiting you personally or telephoning, or sending you telegrams and so on?   YES   NO   N.A.

48.   (If "YES": Have respondent specify in which ways.)

49.   What are these other types of communication about usually? (Record.)

50.   Generally, what types of people communicate with you? Are they average citizens, your friends and acquaintances, business associates, local political leaders, community leaders, spokesmen for special interest groupsl Who are they? (Record.)

51.   And how about you? Do you try to find out how people in your constituency are thinking, especially how they feel about major issues that come before parliament?   YES   NO   N.A.

51-a) (If "YES" to '51':) How do you go about finding out how they feel?

51-b) (If "NO" to '51':) Why is that?

51-c) (For respondents who have answered "YES" to '51.')
Which, if any, of the following do you normally consult if you want information about grass roots feelings in your district? (Hand respondent list F.)

51-d) Which of these do you generally feel give you the most accurate and reliable information?

|  | Consults | Most Reliable source of info. |
|---|---|---|

List F
1. Editorial opinions and letters to editors
2. Party leaders and workers in your riding
3. Business or community leaders in your district
4. Union Leaders in your district
5. MLAs and local public officials in your district or province
6. Ministers or other religious officials in your district
7. Personal friends and acquaintances
8. Others (List)

52.   To which, of any of the following, do you consider yourself accountable for what you do as an MP? (Hand respondent list G.)

List G
1. Your party colleagues in the House
2. The leadership of your party in the House
3. Your local party organization
4. Your provincial party organization
5. Your national party organization
6. The people of your district who voted for you
7. The people of Canada
8. The people of your district, regardless of whom they voted for

      9. The people of your province
    10. To your conscience
    11. To the House as a whole
    12. Any others (List)

52-a) Which of these is the most important to you?

53. One finds, particularly through political biographies of Canada's leaders, that some MPs are mentioned consistently as being more influential in parliament than others, despite the fact that a number of these were never in cabinet, or even in the front benches of their parties. Who, in your opinion, are the 10 most influential members of this parliament, regardless of party? (List)

53-a) Which of the things on this list would you say contribute most to the influence that each of these men has in parliament?
(Hand respondent list H.)
(Begin with the first name respondent has given you, say:) "How about Mr. _____."
(Repeat the name of each M.P. cited and say:) "How about Mr. _____."

List H
1. His formal position in the House
2. His knowledge of parliamentary procedure and the "rules of the game"
3. His expertise in domestic affairs generally
4. His experience in parliament
5. His personal contacts with influential people outside of the House
6. His persuasiveness—the logical force of his arguments
7. His expertise in foreign affairs generally
8. His willingness to help colleagues in his own and in other parties
9. The importance of his district
10. His feel for public opinion
11. His expertise in a particular area
12. His decency and humanity
13. Other (Specify)

54. Who are the three men, either in your own party or in another party, whose advice, opinions and good judgement you especially value?

55. The following are a number of statements about the Canadian parliamentary system and the nature of parliamentary life that have been made by MP's, by political scientists, historians and by the press. Some of them may appear to be oversimplifications of rather complex matters. Some you will undoubtedly agree with, some statements you will disagree with, and some you may be somewhat uncertain about. That's fine; there are no right or wrong answers, only viewpoints. And we want your views on each statement. So, after reading each statement, would you check whether you agree with it; whether you *tend* to agree with it; whether you are undecided—for example, you agree with part of it and disagree with another part; whether you *tend* to disagree with the statement, or whether you disagree *outright* with the statement. (Hand respondent list I.)

List I

The job of a MP entails being a sounding board for constituency opinion and then acting on it. I always attempt to find out what my constituents feel and make my decisions accordingly.
AGREE.   TEND TO AGREE.   AGREE/DISAGREE.   TEND TO DIS-AGREE.   DISAGREE.   D.K.

It is essential that the Canadian government seek closer trade and cultural ties with all Communist nations even if such policies result in some deterioration in Canadian-U.S. relations.
AGREE.   TEND TO AGREE.   AGREE/DISAGREE.   TEND TO DIS-AGREE.   DISAGREE.   D.K.

I can't see why there is any incompatibility between serving your constituency and the nation. I was elected to serve my country, but this is not and has never been inconsistent with serving my constituency and its people.
AGREE.   TEND TO AGREE.   AGREE/DISAGREE.   TEND TO DIS-AGREE.   DISAGREE.   D.K.

Issues that confront us are often so technical and the time for studying them is so short that ultimately both the Government and the Opposition vote on them without a really adequate knowledge of what they entail.
AGREE.   TEND TO DISAGREE.   AGREE/DISAGREE.   TEND TO DISAGREE.   DISAGREE.   D.K.

Let's face it. Insofar as people care about parliament, what they care about, is what you as a MP can do for them in the way of services and favours; not what comes before parliament in the way of issues and legislation.
AGREE.   TEND TO AGREE.   AGREE/DISAGREE.   TEND TO DIS-AGREE.   DISAGREE.   D.K.

The principal function of procedural rules and structures is to permit the majority, which normally means the Government, to work its will.
AGREE.   TEND TO AGREE.   AGREE/DISAGREE.   TEND TO DIS-AGREE.   DISAGREE.   D.K.

The demands that historically have flowed into parliament, or rather those to which parliament has been most attentive, have come disproportionately from a very small and very narrow segment of the population. The policy decisions that parliament makes, even today, disproportionately reflect the interests of this small elite.
AGREE.   TEND TO AGREE.   AGREE/DISAGREE.   TEND TO DIS-AGREE.   DISAGREE.   D.K.

It is clear that the description of the Canadian parliamentary system as "cabinet government" is not adequate. Canadian parliamentary government is now, and to a great extent always has been, prime ministerial government.
AGREE.,   TEND TO AGREE.   AGREE/DISAGREE.   TEND TO DIS-AGREE.   DISAGREE.   D.K.

As long as a parliamentary leader carries with him the conviction of his party colleagues that he will help them be elected again, his power over them is almost absolute.

AGREE.  TEND TO AGREE.  AGREE/DISAGREE.  TEND TO DIS-
AGREE.  DISAGREE.  D.K.

I am not at all certain that doing favours, running errands, or serving your
constituents, call it whatever you wish, really helps get you elected. I am
certain that *not doing these things* when asked will assure that you are not
elected.
AGREE.  TEND TO AGREE.  AGREE/DISAGREE.  TEND TO DIS-
AGREE.  DISAGREE.  D.K.

The suspicion is that the government is not opposed to extensive backbench discussion of important legislation. Just the opposite. Since the
backbenchers cannot control that legislation, the government is happy to
keep them talking. In conditions where party discipline is at its height,
discussion is a convenient substitute for effective backbench influence.
AGREE.  TEND TO AGREE.  AGREE/DISAGREE.  TEND TO DIS-
AGREE.  DISAGREE.  D.K.

The domination of cabinet by the prime minister has been due principally
to the continued development of both Standing and Ad Hoc Cabinet
Committees that are set up to report on particular problems. Needless to
say, the prime minister selects the committees and determines which
aspects of their work will come before cabinet.
AGREE.  TEND TO AGREE.  AGREE/DISAGREE.  TEND TO DIS-
AGREE.  DISAGREE.  D.K.

Government intervention in the economy, even to the extent of the
imposition of wage and price controls, is imperative if Canada is to achieve
substantial economic growth without inflation.
AGREE.  TEND TO AGREE.  AGREE/DISAGREE.  TEND TO DIS-
AGREE.  DISAGREE.  D.K.

My first duty is to the people of my constituency; they are the ones who
elected me.
AGREE.  TEND TO AGREE.  AGREE/DISAGREE.  TEND TO DIS-
AGREE.  DISAGREE.  D.K.

Parliament's legislative function in the sense of conceiving, amending,
rejecting and accepting bills is far less important today than is its job of
serving as a communications link between the government and the public.
AGREE.  TEND TO AGREE.  AGREE/DISAGREE.  TEND TO DIS-
AGREE.  DISAGREE.  D.K.

Even if a MP wanted to find out what his constituents felt about a major
public issue, it would be impossible. The majority of people don't know.
They don't have any information on these things. The rest, or most of the
rest, simply don't care.
AGREE.  TEND TO AGREE.  AGREE/DISAGREE.  TEND TO DIS-
AGREE.  DISAGREE.  D.K.

In a parliamentary system, your party and your party's public record are
all-important. So it's necessary to vote with your party even if it costs you
support in your riding.
AGREE.  TEND TO AGREE.  AGREE/DISAGREE.  TEND TO DIS-
AGREE.  DISAGREE.  D.K.

In recent years different governments, by neglecting the machinery of parliament, also have neglected their own principal means of communicating directly with the public.
AGREE.   TEND TO AGREE.   AGREE/DISAGREE.   TEND TO DISAGREE. DISAGREE. D.K.

It is not the expectation of rewards nor the fear of punishment by the party or the electorate that explains why the members of the Canadian parliamentary parties act cohesively. It is because they want to act together.
AGREE. TEND TO AGREE. AGREE/DISAGREE. TEND TO DISAGREE. DISAGREE. D.K.

The most important part of a MP's job—that is if he is interested in coming back to parliament—is to go to bat for his constituents in their dealings with government, which usually means the civil service. Even statesmen have to be re-elected and for that you have to look after your constituents.
AGREE.   TEND TO AGREE.   AGREE/DISAGREE.   TEND TO DISAGREE. DISAGREE. D.K.

I really doubt whether over the years the majority of cabinets—not just this one—have had much effect on what ultimately becomes law.
AGREE.   TEND TO AGREE.   AGREE/DISAGREE.   TEND TO DISAGREE. DISAGREE. D.K.

A MP seldom has to sound out his constituents because he thinks so much like them that he knows how they would react to almost any proposal.
AGREE.   TEND TO AGREE.   AGREE/DISAGREE.   TEND TO DISAGREE. DISAGREE. D.K.

The caucus promotes party cohesion in the Canadian parliamentary system in two ways. First it permits a frank exchange of opinions that members *really hold*. Second, the tactics that are planned in caucus help insure smooth and coordinated performance in the House and in committees that individual members find gratifying.
AGREE.   TEND TO AGREE.   AGREE/DISAGREE.   TEND TO DISAGREE. DISAGREE. D.K.

With the progressive exclusion of the average MP from any meaningful participation in the policy-initiation and the policy-evaluation process, his role in parliament has been reduced either to intermittently attacking or to defending policies that have been predetermined by party leaders.
AGREE.   TEND TO AGREE.   AGREE/DISAGREE.   TEND TO DISAGREE. DISAGREE. D.K.

In the Canadian parliamentary system, parties are required to take clearcut opposing positions on all major issues, to structure the alternatives for the public, and if it means delaying or preventing the passage of legislation that really should have had rapid passage through the House, that's part of the parliamentary system.
AGREE.   TEND TO AGREE.   AGREE/DISAGREE.   TEND TO DISAGREE. DISAGREE. D.K.

The average MP today, regardless of party, is bored, restive and frustrated. MP's, again regardless of party, want a committee system in which they can work that really is capable of effectively scrutinizing, investigating, and

criticizing the working of the government and its administrative bureaucracy.
AGREE. TEND TO AGREE. AGREE/DISAGREE. TEND TO DISAGREE. DISAGREE. D.K.

The reason parliament has never dealt with the problem of the American impact on the Canadian economy is that it never really has been considered a problem.
AGREE. TEND TO AGREE. AGREE/DISAGREE. TEND TO DISAGREE. DISAGREE. D.K.

The business of name-changing of government institutions and departments, of getting rid of words like "Royal" and "Dominion," both helps foster a sense of nationalism, of Canadian identity, and appeases Quebec—although not necessarily in that order.
AGREE. TEND TO AGREE. AGREE/DISAGREE. TEND TO DISAGREE. DISAGREE. D.K.

The caucus does not give the backbench MP an opportunity to participate in party policy making. It does, however, provide him with the regular opportunity to bring to the attention of his party colleagues any personal or constituency grievances against them.
AGREE. TEND TO AGREE. AGREE/DISAGREE. TEND TO DISAGREE. DISAGREE. D.K.

A MP comes to parliament expecting to act with, and knowing the public *expects* him to act and vote with, the other members of his parliamentary party. That is what the Canadian parliamentary system is all about. It could not continue to exist if MPs acted as free agents.
AGREE. TEND TO AGREE. AGREE/DISAGREE. TEND TO DISAGREE. DISAGREE. D.K.

On the whole, I think parliament would work better if there were *more, not fewer,* interest groups and lobbies trying to influence legislation.
AGREE. TEND TO AGREE. AGREE/DISAGREE. TEND TO DISAGREE. DISAGREE. D.K.

The provision of expert staff assistance to the individual MP and to the several standing committees would not threaten cabinet government, simply free it from total reliance on, and therefore control by, its own bureaucracy.
AGREE. TEND TO AGREE. AGREE/DISAGREE. TEND TO DISAGREE. DISAGREE. D.K.

Parliament today is neither actively involved in the policy process nor does it effectively oversee the bureaucracy although these are supposed to be its two principal functions.
AGREE. TEND TO AGREE. AGREE/DISAGREE. TEND TO DISAGREE. DISAGREE. D.K.

When you get right down to it, the values of all the parliamentary parties are essentially the same. Consequently, parliament never engages in any dialogues that are meaningful to a majority of the public. It has functioned in the past and continues to function today as a convenient screen behind which the elites who exercise the real power are able to operate.
AGREE. TEND TO AGREE. AGREE/DISAGREE. TEND TO DISAGREE. DISAGREE. D.K.

The continued centralization of power in the cabinet and the prime minister always have been rationalized in terms of increased efficiency and effectiveness of parliament although there is not one shred of evidence to support these assumptions.
AGREE.   TEND TO AGREE.   AGREE/DISAGREE.   TEND TO DIS-AGREE.   DISAGREE.   D.K.

My primary responsibility as a MP is to do as good a job as I can for the country—to act according to my conscience. The alternative is to toady to voters.
AGREE.   TEND TO AGREE.   AGREE/DISAGREE.   TEND TO DIS-AGREE.   DISAGREE.   D.K.

There is a role for contemporary parliament to play, a very vital role. The House must equip itself to do two things: to study, first, the conditions from which the need for legislation emerges; second, it must follow through the consequences of legislation. Put another way, the House must concern itself with the formulation of policy at the pre-legislative stage and the scrutiny of policy at the post-legislative stage.
AGREE.   TEND TO AGREE.   AGREE/DISAGREE.   TEND TO DIS-AGREE.   DISAGREE.   D.K.

My job as a MP entails fighting for what I think is right. It also entails being a representative of the people in my constituency. I accept the fact that I have to deal with their problems but I also have to fight for the integrity of parliament and for a program of legislation that is in the national interest.
AGREE.   TEND TO AGREE.   AGREE/DISAGREE.   TEND TO DIS-AGREE.   DISAGREE.   D.K.

Parliament historically has served a vital function in Canadian society as the institution most responsible for promoting the economic development and modernization of this nation.
AGREE.   TEND TO AGREE.   AGREE/DISAGREE.   TEND TO DIS-AGREE.   DISAGREE.   D.K.

Parliament is primarily a device for mobilizing and organizing consent for public policy decisions rather than a device for opposing and unmaking governments.
AGREE.   TEND TO AGREE.   AGREE/DISAGREE.   TEND TO DIS-AGREE.   DISAGREE.   D.K.

As the Canadian parliamentary system of government now functions, the cabinet—*and only the cabinet*—can play a role in the making of policy.
AGREE.   TEND TO AGREE.   AGREE/DISAGREE.   TEND TO DIS-AGREE.   DISAGREE.   D.K.

If anyone tells you he makes his decisions here in parliament on the basis of what his constituents want, assuming he knew what they want, he is either kidding you or himself.
AGREE.   TEND TO AGREE.   AGREE/DISAGREE.   TEND TO DIS-AGREE.   DISAGREE.   D.K.

When you first come to Ottawa you have all sorts of great ideas about what should be done. Then reality sets in. There is nothing, absolutely nothing, an individual MP can do about getting his ideas accepted in the form of legislation unless he's a member of cabinet.

AGREE. TEND TO AGREE. AGREE/DISAGREE. TEND TO DIS-
AGREE. DISAGREE. D.K.

It is not really reasonable to expect parliament, made up as it is of
individuals who every few years are accountable to the public for their
political lives, to make any positive contribution to the development and
modernization of Canada.
AGREE. TEND TO AGREE. AGREE/DISAGREE. TEND TO DIS-
AGREE. DISAGREE. D.K.

In a democracy, the will of the majority must prevail. The government is
presumed to represent that will. It was never intended that parliament and
its procedures should reflect the interests of minorities.
AGREE. TEND TO AGREE. AGREE/DISAGREE. TEND TO DIS-
AGREE. DISAGREE. D.K.

The decline in the power and authority of parliament with respect to the
formulation of public policy is one of the most striking developments in
Canadian government in the 20th Century. Parliament today is impotent.
It has been stripped of any real function in the policy-making process and
retains only the symbolic vestiges of its former powers.
AGREE. TEND TO AGREE. AGREE/DISAGREE. TEND TO DIS-
AGREE. DISAGREE. D.K.

56. Five things seem to be very much on the minds of Canadians. I am going
to read them one at a time. Please tell me if you think that the four
parliamentary political parties all take about the same stand on these
matters, or do they all take different stands on them, or are some more
alike and others different?

|  | SAME | DIFFERENT | SOME SAME SOME DIFFERENT | DON'T KNOW |
|---|---|---|---|---|
| I. Special status for French Canada? |  |  |  |  |
| II. How big a part the Federal Government should take in improving welfare benefits like health insurance, pension payments and that kind of thing? |  |  |  |  |
| III. The power of the Federal government vis-a-vis the provinces? |  |  |  |  |
| IV. Whether or not major steps should be taken to reduce the volume of United States investment in Canada? |  |  |  |  |
| V. Closeness of Canada's relations with Communist countries. |  |  |  |  |

56-a) (For any issue marked "Some same/some different," ask:)
Let's take a look at this chart for a minute and tell me where the NDP,
Liberal, Conservative and Social Credit parliamentary parties are.
(For any issue marked "Same" *and/or* "Different," ask:)

Where would you place each of the four parliamentary parties on this chart?

I.  Quebec should be treated differently than other provinces _____ 1 2 3 4 5 6 7 8 9 Quebec should be treated just like all the other provinces

Things right as they are

II.  Government should take a bigger part _____ 1 2 3 4 5 6 7 8 9 Government should take less of a part

Government's part just about right

III.  Federal government is too powerful _____ 1 2 3 4 5 6 7 8 9 Provincial governments are too powerful

Federal and provincial powers are just about right

IV.  No major steps to reduce U.S. investment _____ 1 2 3 4 5 6 7 8 9 Take major steps to reduce U.S. investment

Amount of U.S. investment just about right

V.  Expand relations with communist countries _____ 1 2 3 4 5 6 7 8 9 Reduce relations with communist countries

Relations are just about right

56-b) Now where would you place yourself on these five matters? (Repeat charts.)

Just a few more questions and we'll be through. Do you expect to make a career out of parliament?   YES   NO   D.K.   N.A.

57.  Would you run again for a parliamentary seat even if you were defeated in a particular parliamentary election?
YES   NO   D.K.   N.A.

57-a) (If "YES" ask:)
What are the kinds of things, other than defeat at the polls, that make a MP like yourself think twice about remaining in parliament?

57-b) (If "NO" to 57 or D.K. or isn't sure ask:)
Why is that? (Record.)

57-c) Are there any other public offices, elected or appointed, that you would like to hold sometime in the future?
YES   NO   D.K.   N.A.

57-d) (If "YES" ask:)
What are these?

58.   Let us suppose that next week for some reason you had to give up being a MP. What would you miss most about not continuing in office?

58-a) (If respondent says he would miss being a MP ask:)
Are these the things that keep you in parliament?
YES   NO   D.K.   N.A.

58-b) (If "NO" ask:)
What are the things that do keep you here as a MP?

59.   Do you consider your position as a MP your principal occupation?
YES   NO   D.K.   N.A.

59-a) (If "NO" ask:)
What do you regard as your principal occupation?

59-b) *(Ask of everyone:)*
What was your occupation when you entered public life?

60.   All in all, what aspects of a member's job do you think should receive more of his time and attention? (Record.)

60-a) Which aspects should receive less of his time and attention?

61.   During a parliamentary session approximately what percent of your time as a MP do you spend in your:
a) Constituency; b) Ottawa; c) Elsewhere?


## DEMOGRAPHIC DATA

(Ask respondent only for data that you cannot get beforehand on him from parliamentary guide.)

62.   Now a little information about yourself, that I couldn't find in the parliamentary guide, and we'll be through.
Are there any business, professional, civic, fraternal or religious organizations to which you belong?

63.   Are you an officer in any of these organizations?
Organization   Member   Officer   Activity Level

64.   Year born?

65.   Where born?

66.   Where did you spend most of your years that you were growing up, that is was it in a large city (  )   in a small town (  )   on a farm (  )
In which province?____

67.   How many years have you lived in the constituency you represent?

67-a) (If Respondent says he doesn't live in his constituency, ask where he does maintain his permanent residence.)

68.   What is your religious preference?
      Catholic    Protestant    Jewish    None    Other

69.   What was the last grade of school you completed?

69-a) Have you attended a University?    YES    NO

69-b) Which one?

69-c) Do you have a degree from a University?

69-d) Have you attended a Graduate School?
      Any Graduate Degree?

69-e) Have you attended a Professional School (Law, Medicine, etc.)?
      Any Professional Degree?

70.   Have you attended school outside your province?

70a)  (If "YES":) What years or what portion of your school life?

71.   What was the original national background of your family on your father's side?    On your mother's side?

72.   Was your father born in Canada?    Your mother?

73.   What was your father's usual occupation while you were growing up? (Try to get respondent to be specific.)

# NOTES

## FOREWORD

1. Gerhard Loewenberg, Parliament in the German Political System (Ithaca: Cornell University Press, 1967); Duncan MacRae, Jr., Parliament, Parties and Society in France, 1946–1958 (New York: St. Martin's Press, 1967); Robert J. Jackson, Rebels and Whips (London: St. Martin's Press, 1968); Frederic Debuyst, La Fonction Parlementaire en Belgique (Brussels: Centre de Recherche et D'information Socio-Politiques, 1966).

2. Gerhard Loewenberg, "The Role of Parliaments in Modern Political Systems," in Loewenberg, ed., Modern Parliaments: Change or Decline? (Chicago: Aldine-Atherton, 1971), pp. 19, 15.

3. Samuel C. Patterson, "Comparative Legislative Behavior: A Review Essay," Midwest Journal of Political Science, 12 (1968), pp. 599–616; quotations at 602, 604.

4. Donald Searing, "Comparative Study of Elite Socialization," Comparative Political Studies, 1 (1969), p. 485; see also Donald Searing and Lewis Edinger, "Social Background in Elite Analysis: A Methodological Inquiry," American Political Science Review, 61 (1967), pp. 428–445.

5. Malcolm E. Jewell, "Attitudinal Determinants of Legislative Behavior: The Utility of Role Analysis," in Allan Kornberg and Lloyd Musolf, eds., Legislatures in Developmental Perspective (Durham: Duke University Press, 1970), pp. 460–500.

6. Donald R. Matthews, U.S. Senators and Their World (New York: Random House, 1960).

7. James David Barber, The Lawmakers (New Haven: Yale University Press, 1965).

8. Richard F. Fenno, Congressmen in Committees (Boston: Little Brown, 1973); Charles S. Bullock, III, "Committee Transfers in the U.S. House of Representatives," Journal of Politics, 35 (1973), pp. 85–120.

9. Gerhard Loewenberg, Parliament in the West German Political System, pp. 129–130.

10. John C. Wahlke, Heinz Eulau, William Buchanan, and LeRoy C. Ferguson, The Legislative System (New York: Wiley, 1962).

11. See the citations of such studies in Jewell, "Attitudinal Determinants of Legislative Behavior: The Utility of Role Analysis," in Allan Kornberg and Lloyd Musolf, eds., Legislatures in Developmental Perspective (Durham: Duke University Press, 1970), pp. 460–500.

12. Allan Kornberg, Canadian Legislative Behavior (New York: Holt, Rinehart, and Winston, 1967).

13. These points are elaborated on further in Jewell, "Attitudinal Determinants of Legislative Behavior."

14. See Jewell, "A Reappraisal of 'The Legislative System' " (paper prepared for the annual meeting of the American Political Science Association, 1970, mimeograph).

15. A number of examples of such choices can be found in several of the studies in G. R. Boynton and Chong Lim Kim, Legislative Systems in Developing Countries (Durham: Duke University Press, 1975).

16. The following examples illustrate these theoretical approaches to the study of influence: L. S. Shapley and Martin Shubik, "A Method for Evaluating the Distribution of Power in a Committee System," American Political Science Review, 48 (1954), pp. 787–792; R. Duncan Luce and Arnold A. Rogow, "A Game Theoretic Analysis of Congressional Power Distributions for a Stable Two-Party System," Behavioral Science, 1 (1956), pp. 83–95; Sven Goennings, E. W. Kelley, and Michael Leiserson, eds., The Study of Coalition Behavior (New York: Holt, Rinehart, and Winston, 1970); Barbara Hinckley, "Coalitions in Congress: Size and Ideological Distance," Midwest Journal of Political Science, 16 (1972), pp. 197–207; Lawrence C. Dodd, "Party Coalitions in Multiparty Parliaments: A Game Theoretic Analysis," American Political Science Review, 68 (1974), pp. 1093–1117.

17. Donald R. Matthews and James A. Stimson, Yeas and Nays: Normal Decision-Making in the U.S. House of Representatives (New York: Wiley-Interscience, 1975); Michael J. Shapiro, "The House and the Federal Role: A Computer Simulation of Roll-Call Voting," American Political Science Review, 62 (1968), pp. 494–517; John E. Jackson, Constituencies and Leaders in Congress (Cambridge: Harvard University Press, 1974); William Mishler, James Lee, and Alan Tharpe, "Determinants of Institutional Continuity: Freshman Cue-Taking in the U.S. House of Representatives," in Allan Kornberg, ed., Legislatures in Comparative Perspective (New York: David McKay, 1972), pp. 379–406.

18. Donald R. Matthews, U.S. Senators and Their World; Wahlke, et al., The Legislative System; Ralph K. Huitt, "The Outsider in the Senate: An Alternative Role," American Political Science Review, 55 (1961), pp. 566–575.

19. Randall B. Ripley, Power in the Senate (New York: St. Martin's Press, 1969).

20. See, for example, Randall B. Ripley, Party Leaders in the House of Representatives (Washington, D.C.: Brookings Institution, 1967); John G. Stewart, "Two Strategies of Leadership: Johnson and Mansfield," in Nelson W. Polsby, ed., Congressional Behavior (New York: Random House, 1971); John F. Manley, "Wilbur Mills: A Study of Congressional Influence," American Political Science Review, 63 (1969), pp. 442–464.

21. For a systematic examination of influence in the Senate, see Samuel A. Kirkpatrick and Lawrence K. Pettit, "Role Structure and Influence Patterns in the U.S. Senate" (paper prepared for the annual meeting of the American Political Science Association, 1970, mimeograph).

## INTRODUCTION

1. Richard Niemi, "Collecting Information About the Family: A Problem in Survey Methodology," in Jack Dennis (ed.), Socialization to Politics (New York: John Wiley, 1973), pp. 414–490.

2. John Honigmann, "Three Principles of Socialization," in Norman Adler and Charles Harrington (eds.), The Learning of Political Behavior (Glenview, Ill.: Scott, Foresman, 1970), pp. 5–8.

## CHAPTER 1

1. Actually, the procedures adopted were those that had been used by the Legislative Assembly of the United Province of Canada (i.e., Ontario and Quebec).

2. Roman March, "An Empirical Test of M. Ostrogorski's Theory of Political Evolution in a British Parliamentary System," Ph.D. dissertation, Indiana University, 1968. His criteria for classification of members as notables are: (1) the member was the son of a present or a former member of one of the legislatures of the British Empire, or a first degree relative of such a person; (2) the member was a peer or related to a titled ancestor—in the case of a French-Canadian, the member was a seigneur or the son of a seigneur; (3) the member held a commission as an officer in one of the regiments at the grade of lieutenant-colonel or higher; (4) the member was related to a churchman whose rank was at least that of a bishop; (5) the member was related to a justice of one of the superior courts.

3. See inter alia, Allan Kornberg, "Parliament in Canadian Society," in A. Kornberg and L. D. Musolf (eds.), Legislatures in Developmental Perspective (Durham: Duke University Press, 1970), pp. 55–128; and Allan Kornberg, David Falcone and William Mishler, "Legislatures and Societal Change: The Case of Canada," Sage Research Papers in the Social

Sciences, Comparative Legislative Studies Series, No. 90–002 (Beverly Hills and London: Sage Publications, 1973), pp. 1–64.

4. March, op. cit., and Kornberg, Falcone and Mishler, op. cit., pp. 21–24.

5. On this point see March, op. cit.; William Mishler, "Political Participation and the Process of Political Socialization in Canada: A Computer Simulation," Ph.D. dissertation, Duke University, 1972; and R. J. Van Loon, "Political Participation in Canada: The 1965 Election," Canadian Journal of Political Science, 3 (1970), pp. 376–399. See also, Canadian Institute of Public Opinion, July 30, 1974; Richard Simeon and David Elkins, "Regional Political Cultures in Canada," Canadian Journal of Political Science, 7 (1974), pp. 397–437.

6. Allan Kornberg, "The Social Bases of Leadership in a Canadian House of Commons," Australian Journal of Politics and History, 11 (1965), pp. 324–334; Kornberg, Falcone and Mishler, op. cit.; and David J. Falcone, "Legislative Change and Output Change: A Time Series Analysis of the Canadian System," Ph.D. dissertation, Duke University, 1974. See also, John Porter, The Vertical Mosaic (Toronto: University of Toronto Press, 1965), ch. 13; Robert J. Jackson and Michael M. Atkinson, The Canadian Legislative System (Toronto: Macmillan of Canada, 1974), ch. 4; Thomas A. Hockin (ed.), Apex of Power (Scarborough: Prentice-Hall, 1971); Richard Van Loon and Michael Whittington, The Canadian Political System (Toronto: McGraw Hill, 1971), p. 351.

7. David Falcone, Allan Kornberg and William Mishler, "Parliamentary Change in Canada: The Survival of a Null Model in a Longitudinal Analysis," in Mattei Dogan and Juan Linz (eds.), From Notables to Professional Politicians (Cambridge: M.I.T. Press, in press). See also, Roman R. March, The Myth of Parliament (Scarborough: Prentice-Hall, 1974), ch. 2.

8. Kornberg, Falcone and Mishler, op. cit., p. 27.

9. As would be expected, the written portion of the Canadian constitution, the British North America Act of 1867, is an important source of formal parliamentary procedure, delineating, as it does, processes involved in the introduction of money bills, the duties of the speaker and so forth. Certain statutes passed by the several parliaments (as for example, the House of Commons Act, the rulings of former speakers, and the written works of recognized parliamentary authorities) also have been and still remain sources of procedure. Finally, the Standing Orders of the House of Commons, the written rules enforced during every session, constitute probably the most important component of formal procedure. A thorough study of procedural change is W. F. Dawson, Procedure in the Canadian House of Commons (Toronto: University of Toronto Press, 1962). See also J. R. Mallory, The Structure of Canadian Government (Toronto: Macmillan, 1971), pp. 257–279.

10. See for example, Gilbert Campion, Parliament: A Survey (London: George Allen and Unwin Ltd., 1952).

11. Donald Macdonald, a Liberal cabinet minister, puts the matter somewhat differently but still succinctly when he notes that, "almost inevitably the government party and those in opposition tend to have different attitudes toward parliamentary reform. The ministers worry about how they will ever find time to run their departments, to think through policies, and to shape the estimates and bills for the next session. The opposition, realizing that once the House has adjourned, they, unlike the ministers, must go back to their private activities, activities which normally attract little publicity, may want year-round or, at least ten-month sessions. Ministers, therefore, will talk about the waste of time. The opposition, in contrast, will expatiate on the dangers of trying to make the trains run on time." Donald S. Macdonald, "Changes in the House of Commons—New Rules," Canadian Public Administration, 13 (1970), p. 31.

12. The rule changes made in 1969 set aside 40 Mondays and Tuesdays from 5 to 6:00 p.m. for consideration of bills and motions sponsored by private members. The same time, 5 to 6:00 p.m., is available without restriction on Thursday and Friday.

13. For example, bills that have been considered by standing committees no longer need

to be taken up by a Committee of the Whole House. Discussions of the many changes made in parliamentary procedure in the sixties and then implemented in 1969 include, inter alia, Phillip Laundy, "Procedural Reform in the Canadian House of Commons," The Parliamentarian, 50 (1969), pp. 12–16; D. Page, "Streamlining the Procedures of the Canadian House of Commons," Canadian Journal of Economics and Political Science, 33 (1967), pp. 27–49; C. E. S. Franks, "The Reform of Parliament," Queen's Quarterly, 76 (1969), pp. 113–117; and J. A. A. Lovink, "Parliamentary Reform and Governmental Effectiveness in Canada," Canadian Public Administration, 16 (1973), pp. 35–54. See also, J. Lovink, "Who Wants Parliamentary Reform?" Queen's Quarterly, 74 (1972), pp. 505–512; and Jackson and Atkinson, op. cit., ch. 9. Also on Committees generally see, Roddick Byers, "Executive Leadership and Influence: Parliamentary Perceptions of Canadian Defence Policy," in Hockin (ed.), Apex of Power, pp. 163–182; Roddick Byers, "Perceptions of Parliamentary Surveillance of the Executive: The Case of Canadian Defence Policy," Canadian Journal of Political Science, 5 (1972), pp. 234–250.

14. Parliamentary scholar J. R. Mallory has been highly critical of S.O. 75c. "It is difficult to see forcing through the Standing Order as anything but a brutal use of majority power." Mallory, op. cit., p. 208. On the other hand, Mr. Macdonald, who was part of the majority that pushed S.O. 75c through the house—indeed he was in charge of its passage—has defended it thusly, "In my view, this is not a crude rule. In fact, its defect may be that it contains so many safeguards, so much due process, that it will not be effective against obdurate opposition." Macdonald, op. cit., p. 38.

15. Under the Closure rule, any cabinet minister, provided he has given the House 24 hours notice, may move that "further consideration of a question be not further postponed." The motion is not debatable and, if carried, no member may speak for more than 20 minutes on the question to which Closure has been applied. Insofar as parliamentary politics are questions of bargaining and persuasion, the introduction of a motion of Closure serves notice that the "normal" processes have broken down. More important, perhaps, is that (unlike the British House of Commons) a government's use of its majority to enforce Closure in a real sense is a violation of Canadian parliamentary norms. In the British House of Commons Closure is not a dirty word. In the Canadian House it is and the use of this device nearly always imposes severe costs on the governing party, the most important of which is that it may become a central election issue. A second and more frequently used measure is called "putting the previous question." This rule permits a member at any time during debate to move that the "question now be put." The motion is not put to a vote immediately but is itself debatable. However, there can be neither amendments to the motion to put the question, nor to the main motion, and the motion to put the question, if successful, must be immediately followed by a vote on the main motion. See, Allan Kornberg and Barry Cooper, "Procedural Changes in the Canadian House of Commons: Some Reflections," Journal of Constitutional and Parliamentary Studies, 2 (1968), pp. 1–18.

16. In March 1973, the Committee on Procedure and Organization began a detailed study of the uses and abuses of question period. In the fall of that year it produced a 26-page confidential draft report recommending several changes including the removal of the 40 minute time limit for questions on Wednesdays. The draft also recommended that the right to ask supplementary questions be restricted to the original questioners and that the speaker consider the imposition of some sort of sanctions for members who continuously and knowingly ask questions they know are out-of-order. After the committee submitted its report to the House, certain experimental changes in the question period (notably in postponing all questions of privelege and points of order to the end and in taking ministerial statements after question period) have been instituted.

17. Macdonald has summarized the benefits that will accrue from these rule changes as follows. "Almost all draft bills go to one of the standing committees after second reading in

the house. There the clauses are examined and improved or approved. When the standing committee has completed its work, it reports back to the House the text of the bill as adopted and recommended by the committee. . . . The report stage has been made debatable. . . . I believe that there is general agreement that by altering the legislative process in this way – that is, by sending most bills to standing committees and by making it possible for members to move amendments to bills at the report stage – we have made an important improvement. There is now more time for the bills to be scrutinized intensively, for several standing committees can be operating at once. The members on a standing committee have a chance to increase their expertise. And the ministers, the parliamentary secretaries and the departmental personnel are fully available to explain the basic scheme of particular bills." Macdonald, op. cit., p. 35. On the matter of parliamentary committees generally and on the change in the operation of committees implemented in 1969 particularly, see C. E. S. Franks, "The Committee System of the Canadian House of Commons," paper presented to the Annual Meeting of the Canadian Political Science Association, Toronto, June 1969; C. E. S. Franks, "The Dilemma of the Standing Committees of the Canadian House of Commons," Canadian Journal of Political Science, 4 (1971), pp. 461–476; Thomas Hockin, "The Advance of Standing Committees in Canada's House of Commons: 1965–1970," Canadian Public Administration, 13 (1970), pp. 185–202; J. R. Mallory and B. A. Smith, "The Legislative Role of Parliamentary Committees in Canada: The Case of the Joint Committee on the Public Service Bills," Canadian Public Administration, 15 (1972), pp. 1–23; and Michael Rush, "The Development of the Committee System in the Canadian House of Commons," The Parliamentarian 55 (1974), pp. 86–94 and pp. 149–158. Although most evaluations of the changes made in the operation of the committee system are positive, see the series of reports issued in 1971 by the Study Group on Parliamentary Committees and External Relations. Interestingly, the MPs who were members of this study group generally were far more skeptical about the utility of the changes and the ability of current committees to influence legislation – despite the changes – than were members of the group who were not MPs.

18. Allan Kornberg and David Falcone, "Societal Change, Legislative Composition and Legislative Outputs in Canada: Some Empirical Considerations," paper prepared for the Symposium on Ministerial and Legislative Decision Making, Bellagio, Italy, August 23–29, 1970, p. 23.

19. For a general discussion see Lester Milbrath, Political Participation (Chicago: Rand McNally, 1965), particularly ch. 5. Two studies with cross-national data bases relate education and participation [Alex Inkeles, "Participant Citizenship in Six Developing Countries," American Political Science Review, 60 (1969), pp. 1132, 1135, 1137] and [Norman Nie, Bingham Powell and Kenneth Prewitt, "Social Structure and Participation: Developmental Relationships, Part I," American Political Science Review, 63 (1969), p. 371]. For a study of the correlates of Canadian participation in particular, see R. J. Van Loon, op. cit., especially pages 383–386; and William Mishler, op. cit., ch. 4.

20. Norbert Weiner, The Human Use of Human Beings (Garden City: Doubleday, 1959), p. 18.

21. The Library of Parliament, as such, was established by An Act in Relation to the Library of Parliament (S.C., 1871, ch. 21 – now the Library of Parliament Act, R.S.C., 1952, ch. 155, as amended by S.C., 1955, ch. 25).

22. See the Library of Parliament Annual Reports for a concise description of the research they carry out for MPs.

23. For example, the informational resources of legislatures were discussed (January 18–20, 1973) at an international symposium sponsored by the Inter-Parliamentary Union. If the reports on the kinds of information and staffing services available to the legislative bodies of the thirty-three countries represented are accurate, then an interesting but ironic situation prevails. In the more developed countries, a wider variety of information and

technical facilities appear to be available to the members of legislative bodies that have played and continue to play what at best can be described as a very modest role in generating, considering, and implementing policies (e.g., the Supreme Soviet of the U.S.S.R.) than appear to be available to the members of bodies that have played and continue to play a very important legislative role (e.g., the British House of Commons).

24. Edwin R. Black, "Opposition Research: Some Theories and Practices," Canadian Public Administration, 15 (1972), pp. 24–41.

25. The opposition parties also made it clear that they would be more receptive to the procedural changes the government wished to implement if they were given additional staff assistance. Black, op. cit., pp. 25–28. See also, David Hoffman, "Liaison Officers and Ombudsmen: Canadian MP's and their Relations with the Federal Bureaucracy and Executive," in Hockin (ed.), Apex of Power, pp. 146–162.

26. House of Commons, Debates, 28th Parliament, 1st Session, 1968–69, p. 2792.

27. "Tory members remained a gaggle of political private enterprisers who selfishly preferred to pursue their separate ways to the electoral gallows rather than hang together and work as a united opposition. Under such circumstances, it was impossible for the Research Office to discontinue the plethora of daily services provided to the members in favour of concentrated effort on a few party-determined issues. One result was the proliferation of demands on the Research Office on a complete laissez-faire basis . . ." Black, op. cit., p. 37.

28. Another means for MPs to acquire needed information and expert assistance that could affect their reelection became available with the establishment of the Parliamentary Internship Program. This program, which began in 1970, is modeled after the American Congressional Internship Program. It was privately funded and administered jointly by MPs and the Executive of the Canadian Political Science Association. Very briefly, the program annually provides a limited number of government and opposition members with the assistance of ten men and women, ages 21–35, who have backgrounds in the social sciences, law, or journalism. Each intern usually is attached to a MP for an entire parliamentary session. During that period the intern does library research, prepares position papers on various aspects of public policy, and provides the member with questions that he can ask of ministers during question period. Interns also answer constituents' letters, assist MPs in answering requests for assistance from individual constituents and thereby, it is assumed, also improve MPs chances for reelection.

29. Roland Michner, House of Commons, Debates, February 26, 1959, p. 1393. See also, J. R. Mallory, The Structure of Canadian Government, pp. 269–271.

30., For example, The Montreal Gazette of February 8, 1957, noted that "if the opposition backbenchers have not been able to come up with any $64.00 questions, they have apparently decided that sixty-four $1.00 questions will do just as well."

31. There are presently 264 members in the House. However, the Standing Committee on Privileges and Elections is currently examining a system for readjusting the method for determining the number of members from each province. The Committee estimated that in 1981 the number of seats will be 281. In the year 2001 they estimated there will be 307 MPs. See, Minutes of Proceedings and Evidence of the Standing Committee on Privileges and Elections, Tuesday, April 9, 1974, pp. 3:57–3:61. See also, House of Commons, Bill C-36: An Act to provide for representation in the House of Commons, to establish electoral boundaries commissions and to remove the temporary suspension of the Electoral Boundaries Readjustment Act, First reading, November 22, 1972.

32. There also are joint House and Senate committees and in the past there have been sessional committees. The Committee of the Whole, which is not really a committee in the conventional sense, but rather a procedural device involving the whole House of Commons, has taken three forms: The Committee of Supply which deals with expenditures; the Committee of Ways and Means which is concerned with revenue; and the Committee of the

Whole House. Before 1968 legislation that had been sent to and reported out of a standing committee also had to be evaluated, clause by clause, by the Committee of the Whole House.

33. R. MacGregor Dawson and Norman Ward, The Government of Canada, 4th edition (Toronto: University of Toronto Press, 1964), pp. 380–381.

34. A number of empirical studies tend to support Dawson's and Ward's judgment. See the series of studies referred to by Allan Kornberg, "Parliament in Canadian Society," pp. 97–118.

35. J. A. Corry, a long-time student of comparative and Canadian politics, has tended to dispute this point and suggest a number of cogent reasons why committees in British-model parliamentary systems are not likely to become serious rivals of cabinet. See his "Adaptation of Parliamentary Processes in the Modern State," Canadian Journal of Economics and Political Science, 20 (1954), pp. 1–9.

36. Macdonald, op. cit., p. 31.

37. Marcel Lambert, cited in Thomas Hockin, "New Procedural Reforms," in Paul Fox (ed.), Politics: Canada (Toronto: McGraw-Hill, 1963), p. 270.

38. D. M. Fisher, "Parliamentary Committees in the Twenty-Fourth Parliament," in Paul Fox (ed.), op. cit., p. 213.

39. At present the standing committees are: Agriculture; Broadcasting, Films and Assistance to the Arts; External Affairs and National Defense; Finance, Trade and Economic Affairs; Fisheries and Forestry; Health, Welfare and Social Affairs; Indian Affairs and Northern Development; National Resources and Public Works; Justice and Legal Affairs; Labour, Manpower and Immigration; Regional Development; Transport and Communications; Veterans Affairs; Miscellaneous Estimates; Miscellaneous Private Bills and Standing Orders; Privileges and Elections; Public Accounts; Procedure and Organization.

40. Until this most recent change, legislation reported out by standing committees was again considered by Committee of the Whole, a practice which lengthened rather than shortened the time allocated to the passage of any piece of legislation.

41. The Public Accounts Committee has the assistance of the Auditor-General and his staff. The External Affairs and Defence Committee has the assistance of the Parliamentary Center for Foreign Affairs and Foreign Trade and at different times several committees have had the assistance of ad hoc advisors.

42. Franks observes that, "committees paradoxically are more free to express an independent view the less their reports have legal authority; and to give their reports executive force would lead to more government control and less committee independence." Franks, "Dilemma of Standing Committees," p. 469.

43. Hockin, "The Advance of Standing Committees," p. 198. Hockin also noted, despite government efforts to discourage the practice, that some standing committees had begun to amend and to "refine" government bills. He speculated that this kind of activity might increase significantly during periods of minority government, and if it did, the consequences for responsible parliamentary government might be "severe."

44. The most comprehensive and systematic analysis of changes in the structure and composition of the Canadian Cabinet is by R. J. Van Loon, The Structure and Membership of the Canadian Cabinet. Working papers for the Royal Commission on Bilingualism and Biculturalism, 1966.

45. On this point see A. D. P. Heeney, "Cabinet Government in Canada,"Canadian Journal of Economics and Political Science, 12 (1946), pp. 280–301, and W. E. D. Halliday, "The Executive and the Government of Canada," Canadian Public Administration, 2 (1959), pp. 229–241.

46. Bernard Crick, "Parliament in the British Political System," in Kornberg and Musolf (eds.), op. cit., p. 35.

47. See for example, David Butler and Donald Stokes, Political Change in Britain:

Forces Shaping Electoral Choice (New York: St. Martin's, 1969), p. 377. Table 17.3 shows that in the mid 1960s over 60% of the British public either had no feelings about Labour party leaders or, other than Prime Minister Harold Wilson, did not know who were the Labour leaders.

48. Another factor bolstering the prime minister's position in his party is the manner in which the public perceives political issues. Positional issues, despite the fact that they are the very essence of political controversy at the elite level, still may be only dimly perceived by the public. Even when positional issues are visible, the public may not have developed stable attitudes towards them. When this is the case, the public is quite often content to "go along with" the government of the day—and with the prime minister's leadership of that government. Butler and Stokes, ibid., pp. 173–192.

49. See, for example, the polemics by Walter Stewart, Shrug: Trudeau in Power, (Toronto, McClelland and Stewart, 1972), and Denis Smith, "President and Parliament: The Transformation of Parliamentary Government in Canada," in Thomas Hockin (ed.), Apex of Power, pp. 223–241.

50. This argument is made by Joseph Wearing, "President or Prime Minister," in Thomas Hockin (ed.), Apex of Power, pp. 242–260.

51. For literature dealing with some of these changes see inter alia, A. D. P. Heeney, "Mackenzie King and the Cabinet Secretariat," Canadian Public Administration, 10 (1967), pp. 366–375; Marc Lalonde, "The Changing Role of the P.M.O.," Canadian Public Administration, 14 (1971), pp. 509–537; Gordon Robertson, "The Changing Role of the P.C.O.," Canadian Public Administration, 14 (1971), pp. 487–508; and A. W. Johnson, "The Treasury Board of Canada and the Machinery of Government in the 1970's," Canadian Journal of Political Science, 4 (1971), pp. 346–366.

52. It is difficult to estimate the size of prime ministerial staffs before this time because of the practice of "seconding" clerical and staff assistance from other departments of government. Although in theory such staff continued to be members of the public service and to have their salaries charged to the departments from which they were drawn, in practice, their work for the prime minister was political. See also, Fred Schindeler, "The Prime Minister and the Cabinet: History and Development," in Hockin (ed.), Apex of Power, p. 28.

53. Thus, for example, senior members of the prime minister's staff work with senior members of the cabinet secretariat to make certain that the prime minister is thoroughly briefed daily on the main issues involved in any current policy discussions. His attention is drawn to any differences of view between ministers or departments and suggestions are made to him with respect to any implications that require consideration in advance of a decision. This places him at a distinct advantage since even his most knowledgable and hardworking colleagues are not briefed on every major issue in every department.

54. There currently are 10 cabinet committees. Five deal with areas of government activity: External Policy and Defense; Economic Policy; Social Policy; Science, Culture and Information; and Government Operations. Four are coordinating committees: Priorities and Planning; Treasury Board; Legislation and House Planning; Federal-Provincial Relations. In addition, the Special Committee of the Cabinet handles regulations and other proposed orders-in-council that do not require the attention of the full cabinet. Robertson, op. cit., p. 492.

55. Lalonde, op. cit., pp. 514–515, also emphasizes the importance of the prime minister's appointment power. The prime minister has the power to make approximately 400 appointments to the highest public offices in the country (e.g., Supreme Court appointments). He either decides on these appointments personally or else approves prospective appointees suggested by other members of cabinet.

56. Mildred A. Schwartz, Politics and Territory: The Sociology of Regional Persistence in Canada (Montreal: McGill-Queen's University Press, 1974), pp. 64–79.

57. Bruce Hutchison, The Incredible Canadian (Toronto: Longmans Green, 1952) and R. M. Dawson, William Lyon Mackenzie King: A Political Biography (Toronto: University of Toronto Press, 1958), both passim.

58. The single best treatment of the origins of the two old-time Canadian parties probably is Escott M. Reid, "The Rise of National Parties in Canada," Papers and Proceedings of the Canadian Political Science Association, 4 (1932), pp. 187–200.

59. William Morton, The Progressive Party in Canada (Toronto: University of Toronto Press, 1963), p. 288.

60. Kornberg, "Parliament in Canadian Society," p. 95, Table 9. See also, Roman March, The Myth of Parliament, p. 18.

61. Jean Laponce has written an interesting and amusing paper on the several party labels that Canadian MPs have employed at various times. See his "Canadian Party Labels: An Essay in Semantics and Anthropology," Canadian Journal of Political Science, 2 (1969), pp. 141–157.

62. Kornberg, "Parliament in Canadian Society," pp. 73–82. See also, John C. Courtney, The Selection of National Party Leaders in Canada (MacMillan, 1973); D. V. Smiley, "The National Party Leadership Convention in Canada: A Preliminary Analysis," Canadian Journal of Political Science, 1 (1968), pp. 373–397.

63. William C. Hood, "The Canadian Economy: An Overview," in R. H. Leach (ed.), Contemporary Canada (Durham: Duke University Press, 1967), pp. 60–80; and H. E. English, "The Canadian Industrial Structure: An Essay on its Nature and Efficiency," in R. H. Leach (ed.), ibid., pp. 81–103.

64. Dawson, Mackenzie King, p. 319.

65. J. M. Beck and D. J. Dooley, "Party Images in Canada," Queen's Quarterly, 67 (1967), p. 437.

66. Robert Presthus, Elite Accomodation in Canadian Politics (Toronto: Macmillan, 1973), passim.

67. For an interesting, if biased, description of Mr. Diefenbaker's tenure as prime minister, see Peter C. Newman, Renegade in Power: The Diefenbaker Years (Toronto: McClelland and Stewart, 1964), passim.

68. Some of Mr. Diefenbaker's problems during his stormy career as leader of his party and as prime minister may very well have stemmed from the fact that he did opt to be something more than a mediator and conciliator. He had a preference for very definite policies, particularly of the reallocative variety. Thus, even his sharpest critic, Peter Newman, has written of him in describing the dilemma faced by anti-Diefenbaker forces in the Conservative party during the 1967 Conservative leadership convention that eventually overthrew Diefenbaker: "At the heart of the Tory dilemma was the cruel fact that at this point in their history the Conservatives had to seek a man with the capacity both to unite his party and to win the prime ministership of Canada. Yet the lessons of recent Conservative history dictated the difficulty of the choice. In the preceding thirty-two years, the Tories had captured power only under John Diefenbaker, a man who in party terms was an outsider and not really an ideological conservative at all. He had gained office by pressing for welfare-state policies his party had bitterly opposed for decades. His minority wins of 1957 and 1962 and his overwhelming mandate of 1958 were all based on the attraction his personality and policies had for non-Conservatives, particularly in the Prairies and the Martimes." Peter C. Newman, ibid, pp. 152–153.

69. Lionel H. Laing, "The Patterns of Canadian Politics: The Election of 1945," American Political Science Review, 40 (1946), pp. 760–765.

70. Illustrative of Mr. Diefenbaker's success, both in transforming the base of Conservative party support and drawing disproportionate support from social groups who once regarded the party as an anathema, are some statistics drawn from John Meisel's 1968 election study. These indicate, for example, that although only 7.1% of the Catholic

population in Ontario voted Conservative, 25.3% of the Catholics in the Prairies and 31.9% of the Catholics in the Atlantic region voted for the Conservatives. With regard to voters of "other" than French or British descent, 52.2% of them voted for the Conservative party in the Atlantic provinces, and 33.0% in the Prairies compared with only 17.2% of this group voting Conservative in Ontario. With respect to voters who described themselves as "lower class," 52.3% in the Atlantic provinces and 33.2% in the Prairie provinces voted for the Conservative party. In Ontario, only 23.9% of the self-styled lower class voted Conservative. These figures demonstrate that the trends documented by an earlier study, Robert Alford, "The Social Basis of Political Cleavage in 1962," John Meisel, ed., Papers on the 1962 Election (Toronto: University of Toronto Press, 1964), tables XI and XIV, have continued.

71. Although the Liberals made substantial gains in the West (particularly in British Columbia) in the 1968 election that produced the parliament on which this study focuses, their strength was reduced in the 1972 election and they continue to be weak in the Atlantic region.

72. See J. A. Irving, The Social Credit Movement in Alberta (Toronto: University of Toronto Press, 1959), and C. B. Macpherson, Democracy in Alberta: The Theory and Practice of a Quasi-Party System (Toronto: University of Toronto Press, 1953).

73. Maurice Pinard, The Rise of a Third Party: A Study in Crisis Politics (Englewood Cliffs, Prentice-Hall, 1971), and Michael Stein, The Dynamics of Right Wing Protest: Social Credit in Quebec (Toronto: University of Toronto Press, 1973).

74. In the 1956 Winnipeg Declaration the party expressed its willingness to tolerate a "mixed" planned/free enterprise economy. For a highly critical account of the transition of the CCF from a radical and socialist movement to a party with modest reform aspirations see Leo Zakuta, A Protest Movement Becalmed: A Study of Change in the C.C.F. (Toronto: University of Toronto Press, 1964). For a more recent study with a different perspective on the party see Walter Young, The Anatomy of a Party: The National C.C.F. 1932–1961 (Toronto: University of Toronto Press, 1969). Also of interest on this point is N. H. Chi and G. C. Perlin, "The New Democratic Party: A Party in Transition," in H. G. Thorburn (ed.), Party Politics in Canada (Scarborough: Prentice-Hall, 1972), pp. 177–188.

75. See S. M. Lipset, Agrarian Socialism: The Cooperative Commonwealth Federation in Saskatchewan (New York: Anchor Books, 1968), a study of the triumph of the CCF and difficulties the party subsequently experienced with an entrenched bureaucracy in attempting to implement its major policy goals.

76. See, Allan Kornberg, Canadian Legislative Behavior: A Study of the 25th Parliament (New York: Holt, Rinehart and Winston, 1967), pp. 126–129.

77. This is a topic that is discussed in ch. 5.

78. Allan Kornberg, "Caucus and Cohesion in Canadian Parliamentary Parties," American Political Science Review, 60 (1966), pp. 83–92; and Kornberg, Canadian Legislative Behavior, op. cit., pp. 129–136.

79. See also Robert Jackson and Michael Atkinson, op. cit., pp. 69–71.

80. To the best of our knowledge, private bills dealing with divorce and the incorporation of companies are not included in these figures. Largely because of the opposition of church leaders in Quebec to legislation that would make divorce easier, up to and including the 23rd Parliament, individual divorce "bills" were routinely introduced into the Commons as a service by Quebec MPs to their constituents.

81. Kornberg, "Parliament in Canadian Society," p. 110, Table 2. Kornberg offers a number of explanations for the decline in "productivity" of more recent parliaments, the most important of which is that the kind of legislation parliament now considers in quantitatively and qualitatively different from the legislation considered by parliament before World War II.

82. Until World War II orders-in-council did not even have to be published. Since the number of such orders increased enormously during the war, the government began the practice of tabling at the beginning of each session all orders that had been passed the

previous session. By the end of the war the practice of publishing delegated legislation was firmly established and was made mandatory in 1947. However, parliamentary scholar J. R. Mallory is highly critical of the current practice governing the scrutiny of orders-in-council by parliament and has called for the establishment of alternative machinery with which parliament can thoroughly review orders and other forms of delegated legislation. See J. R. Mallory, The Structure of Canadian Government, op. cit., pp. 140–146.

83. Kornberg, "Parliament in Canadian Society," pp. 109–11.

84. Kornberg, Falcone and Mishler, "Legislatures and Societal Change," passim; and Falcone, Kornberg and Mishler, "Parliamentary Change and Policy Change," passim.

85. Kornberg, Falcone and Mishler, "Legislatures and Societal Change," p. 32.

86. In support of this point, see David Falcone and William Mishler, "Canadian Provincial Legislatures and System Outputs: A Diachronic Analysis of the Determinants of Health Policy," paper presented at the annual meeting of the Southern Political Science Association, New Orleans, November, 1974.

87. Speech to the Washington Press Club, March 25, 1969, cited in R. J. Van Loon and M. S. Whittington, The Canadian Political System, p. 23.

88. For a synthesis of this literature and a presentation of data pertinent to the argument, see David J. Falcone, "The Canadian Economy," Current History, 62 (1972), pp. 203–209.

89. For literature pertaining to this argument see, inter alia K. D. MacRae, "The Structure of Canadian History," in Louis Hartz (ed.), The Founding of New Societies (Toronto: Longmans, 1969), pp. 219–274; G. Horowitz, "Conservatism, Liberalism and Socialism in Canada: An Interpretation," Canadian Journal of Economics and Political Science, 32 (1966), pp. 144–171; Erwin Hargrove, "Popular Leadership in the Anglo-American Democracies," in Lewis Edinger (ed.), Political Leadership in Industrialized Societies (New York: Wiley, 1966), p. 147; S. M. Lipset, Political Man: The Social Bases of Politics (New York: Doubleday, 1963), pp. 248–273, 515–531; S. M. Lipset, "Social Structure and Political Activity," in B. Blishen et. al. (eds.), Canadian Society: Sociological Perspectives (Toronto: Macmillan, 1968), pp. 289–302; John Porter, op. cit.; R. J. Van Loon, "Political Participation in Canada,"; Robert Presthus, op. cit., ch. 2; S. D. Clark, The Developing Canadian Community (Toronto: University of Toronto Press, 1968), part III, pp. 185–268; S. M. Lipset, "Canadian National Character," Cultural Affairs (Spring 1969) especially pp. 49–50; Joel Smith and Allan Kornberg, "Self-Concepts of American and Canadian Party Officials: Their Development and Consequences," Social Forces, 49 (1970), pp. 210–225; Joel Smith and Allan Kornberg, "Some Considerations Bearing on Comparative Research in Canada and the United States," Sociology 3 (1969), pp. 341–357; George Grant, Lament for A Nation: The Defect of Canadian Nationalism (Toronto: McClelland and Stewart, 1965). By way of illustration, Erwin Hargrove has written, "Canadian political society has stressed order, loyalty, and deference to government more than popular assent. Social equality is desired, but with less fervor than in America. Hierarchy in all spheres of life is taken for granted. There is much less drive to improve the lot of all citizens by government actions than in the United States although paradoxically, because there is less fear of government, the minimal welfare state is well developed." Hargrove, op. cit., p. 197.

90. John Porter, op. cit., passim.

91. F. H. Underhill, In Search of Canadian Liberalism (Toronto: Macmillan, 1960), passim.

92. Presthus, op. cit., passim; and Falcone and Mishler, op. cit., 18–22.

93. Presthus, ibid., p. 36.

94. For example, the noted Canadian historian, Frank H. Underhill has called parliament a screen "behind which the controlling interests pull the strings to manipulate the Punch and Judy who engage in mock combat before the public." Underhill, op. cit., p. 168.

95. Porter, op. cit., pp. 425–426.

96. R. Taylor Cole, The Canadian Bureaucracy (Durham: Duke University Press, 1949), p. 269.

97. John Meisel, "The Formulation of Liberal and Conservative Programmes in the 1957 Canadian General Election," Canadian Journal of Economics and Political Science, 26 (1960), p. 571.

98. R. J. Van Loon and M. S. Whittington, op. cit., pp. 406–446.

99. For a compendium of representative expressions of lament on the decline of the Canadian Parliament see Roman March, "An Empirical Test of M. Ostragorski's Theory of Political Evolution in a British Parliamentary System," ch. 4.

100. Norman Ward, The Public Purse (Toronto: University of Toronto Press, 1962), p. 50.

101. K. C. Wheare, Legislatures (New York: Oxford University Press, 1963), p. 233.

102. Gerhard Loewenberg, "The Role of Parliaments in Modern Political Systems," in Gerhard Loewenberg (ed.), Modern Parliaments: Change or Decline? (New York: Aldine-Atherton, 1971), p. 15.

103. John P. Mackintosh, "How Much Time Left for Parliamentary Democracy?" Encounter, 43 (1974), pp. 48–52.

104. For further elaboration on this point, see William Mishler and David Lindquist, "Political Socialization and Legislative Behavior in Canada and Germany," paper presented to the annual meeting of the Southern Political Science Association, Atlanta, November, 1973.

105. Mallory, op. cit., p. 261.

## CHAPTER 2

1. See for example, J. A. Laponce, People vs. Politics (Toronto: University of Toronto Press, 1969); John Meisel, Working Papers on Canadian Politics (McGill-Queen's Press, 1973); and Richard Van Loon and Michael Whittington, The Canadian Political System: Environment, Structure and Process (Toronto: McGraw-Hill, 1971), especially ch. 12.

2. There were only thirteen Social Credit-Creditiste (we shall use these two labels interchangeably) MPs and twenty-five NDP MPs elected to the 28th Parliament.

3. The percentages reported are based upon the party standings in the House at dissolution. The standings at that time were: Liberals 150, Conservatives 71, New Democrats 25, Creditistes 13 and Independents 3. There were two seats vacant. The shifts from the standings following the 1968 General Election are a result of numerous by-elections and the crossing of party lines by some members, most notably Messrs. Perry Ryan and Paul Hellyer of the Liberals and M. Roche La Salle of the Conservatives.

4. Our failure to interview more Liberal and Creditiste MPs from the province of Quebec stemmed both from our inability to secure and train qualified bilingual interviewers and from the idiosyncratic preference of some French-Canadian MPs not to be interviewed. But, regardless of the province they represented, some MPs undoubtedly refused to participate in the study because they had learned from already-interviewed colleagues that the interview required from an hour and one-half to two and one-half hours.

5. Allan Kornberg and Hal Winsborough, "The Recruitment of Candidates for the Canadian House of Commons," American Political Science Review, 62 (1968), pp. 1242–1257, and James S. Lee and Allan Kornberg, "A Computer Simulation Model of Multiparty Parliamentary Recruitment," Simulation and Games, 4 (1973), pp. 37–58. In these two reports we used the Duncan scale to code MP occupations. The two digit scores in this scale range from 00 to 96. This scale is almost perfectly correlated (.94) with one developed by Bernard Blishen, "The Construction and Use of an Occupational Class Scale," Canadian Journal of Economics and Political Science, 24 (1958), p. 523 and "A Socio-economic

Index for Occupation in Canada," Candian Review of Sociology and Anthropology, 4 (1967), pp. 41–53. We did not use the Blishen scale because the Duncan scale was somewhat more complete. The rationale and method for computing scores in the Duncan scale are described in Albert J. Reiss, et al., Occupation and Social Change (Glencoe: The Free Press, 1961), pp. 109–138. For other data on the social background of Canadian legislators see Harold D. Clarke, Richard Price and Robert Krause, "Timing and Agents of Legislative Role Socialization: The Case of Canadian Provincial Legislators," unpublished paper, Department of Political Science, University of Windsor, 1975; Terrance Qualter, The Election Process in Canada, p. 68; Martin Robin, "A Profile of the B.C. Legislature," Canadian Dimension, 3 (1966), pp. 26–28; and David Hoffman and Norman Ward, Bilingualism and Biculturalism in the Canadian House of Commons, Document #3 of the Royal Commission on Bilingualism and Biculturalism (Ottawa: Queen's Printer, 1970).

6. Kornberg and Winsborough, op. cit., p. 1248.

7. Standard references to this literature include Herbert Hyman, Political Socialization (Glencoe: The Free Press, 1959); Kenneth Langton, Political Socialization (New York: Oxford University Press, 1969) and Richard Dawson and Kenneth Prewitt, Political Socialization (Boston: Little Brown, 1968). With reference to the Canadian experience see Jon Pammett, "Political Orientations of Public and Separate School Children," M.A. Thesis, Queen's University, 1967, and William Mishler, "Political Participation and the Process of Political Socialization in Canada: A Computer Simulation," Ph.D. dissertation, Duke University, 1972; Allan Kornberg and Norman Thomas, "The Political Socialization of National Legislative Elites in the United States and Canada,"Journal of Politics, 27 (1965), pp. 761–775; Jean Pierre Richert, "Political Socialization in Quebec: Young People's Attitudes Toward Government," Canadian Journal of Political Science, 6 (1973), pp. 303–313; D. E. Smith, "The Recruitment, Role Perceptions and Political Attitudes of Saskatchewan MLA's," paper presented at the Canadian Political Science Association Convention, 1970; and R. Van Loon, "Political Participation in Canada: The 1965 Election," Canadian Journal of Political Science, 3 (1970), p. 390.

8. See, for example, Fred Greenstein, Children and Politics (New Haven: Yale University Press, 1965); David Easton and Jack Dennis, Children in the Political System (New York: McGraw-Hill, 1969); and Robert Hess and Judith Torney, The Development of Political Attitudes in Children (Chicago: Aldine Publishing Co., 1967).

9. As children, 66% said they were personally acquainted with public office-holders and 70% recalled being "close" to people who were active in politics. Our data on the political backgrounds of MPs are comparable to those reported for a group of 252 members of the ten Canadian provincial legislative assemblies. In a preliminary report of a study carried out in 1972 Clarke, Price and Krause note that 32% of the provincial members of parliament (MLAs) had fathers who were "very interested" in politics and 8% had mothers with a similar level of political interest. 31% said there was "a great deal of political discussion" in their homes when they were children and 36% had relatives who were or had been elected public officials. Before their election to the legislature 79% had been active in political party organizations and fully 50% had held an elected public office of some kind (e.g., school-board, city council, etc.). See Harold D. Clarke, Richard Price and Robert Krause, "The Role Socialization of Canadian Provincial Legislators: A Note on a Neglected Topic," unpublished paper, 1975.

10. A nineteen page bibliography appended to a recent evaluation of the state of the art of studying political recruitment cross-nationally makes clear that the recruitment process has been the subject of intensive investigation in virtually every developed country in the world. Moshe Czudnowski, "Political Recruitment," mimeographed paper, 1974. See also William Mishler and Allan Kornberg, "Recruitment to the Twenty-Eighth Parliament: A Preliminary Analysis," in Harold Clarke and Richard Price (eds.), Recruitment and Leadership Selection in Canada (Laurentian University Press, forthcoming). See also, T. Qualter, op. cit., ch. 2.

11. Allan Kornberg, Canadian Legislative Behavior: A Study of the 25th Parliament (New York: Holt Rinehart and Winston, 1967) and Hoffman and Ward, op. cit.

12. Allan Kornberg, David Falcone and William Mishler, Legislatures and Societal Change: The Case of Canada, Sage Research Papers in the Social Sciences (Beverly Hills: Sage Publications, 1973).

13. Kornberg, op. cit., pp. 42–62.

14. Donald Matthews, U.S. Senators and their World (New York: Vintage Books, 1960). See also, Herb Asher, "The Learning of Legislative Norms," American Political Science Review, 67 (June 1973), pp. 499–513.

15. John Wahlke, et al., The Legislative System: Explorations in Legislative Behavior (New York: Wiley, 1962). Malcolm E. Jewell and Samuel C. Patterson, The Legislative Process in the United States (New York: Random House, 1966), chs. 15 and 16.

16. Allan Kornberg, "The Rules of the Game in the Canadian House of Commons," Journal of Politics, 26 (1964), pp. 358–380.

17. The remaining 20% acknowledged that they "really didn't know what to expect" (e.g., "I didn't even know what the salary was"). The latter figure is somewhat higher than the 13% of the members of the ten Canadian provincial parliaments who indicated that before taking office they knew "virtually nothing" about their jobs. One half knew a "few things" while 36% indicated they knew "a great deal" about their jobs before their election. See Clarke, Price, and Krause, "The Role Socialization of Canadian Provincial Legislators."

18. In another report of a study of 50 freshmen members elected to Canada's 30th Parliament, Price, Clarke and Krause indicate that prior to their election, constituency representation, constituency service, and the performance of ombudsman functions were the expectations most frequently held for the position by the 50 new MPs. See Richard G. Price, Harold D. Clarke, and Robert M. Krause, "The Role Socialization of Freshmen Legislators: The Case of Canadian M.P.s," a paper presented to the Annual Meeting of the American Political Science Association, San Francisco, Sept. 5, 1975.

19. This also seems to be the case for members of provincial parliaments. Clarke, Price and Krause observe that "most legislators enter parliament without being aware of the intricacies and significance of parliamentary procedure and the order of House business . . . . Caucus serves as an important medium for imparting the complex of information and norms that comprise the legislative role." More specifically, they report that 34% of the MLAs cited attendance at caucus as the "most important" agent of post-incumbency role socialization. Participation in House debates was regarded as most important by 28%, talking informally with parliamentary colleagues by 17%, interaction with interest group representatives by 14%, while 13% indicated that participation with colleagues in committee work was the most important agent of their learning about the role of legislator. See Clarke, et al., "The Role Socialization of Canadian Provincial Legislators," Table 6.

20. Identical questions and coding procedures were employed in the studies of the 28th and 25th parliaments. In each instance the questions asked were open-ended in format. All responses to the questions were recorded fully and were coded according to the typology here discussed. For further discussion of the methodology employed see Kornberg, "The Rules of the Game," pp. 359–366.

21. Kornberg, ibid.

22. Five of the MPs refused to answer the question.

23. Kornberg, Canadian Legislative Behavior, p. 79.

24. In comparison, only 34% of the Conservatives and none of the Creditistes perceived differences with two or more groups.

25. Heinz Eulau, et al., "The Role of the Representative: Some Empirical Observations on the Theory of Edmund Burke," American Political Science Review, 53 (1959), pp. 742–756.

26. Kornberg, Canadian Legislative Behavior, pp. 105–118.

27. Roger Davidson, David Kovenock and Michael O'Leary, Congress in Crisis: Politics and Congressional Reform (New York: Wadsworth, 1967).

28. Variations in representational role-taking also were found to be related to differences in cue-taking in hypothetical conflict situations involving the constituency on the one hand and personal and party preferences on the other.

29. More specifically, we utilized a five point Likert-type scale ranging from: (1) "agree"; (2) "tend to agree"; (3) "agree and disagree"; (4) "tend to disagree"; to (5) "disagree" to code responses to the above statements. In reporting the results below, we have collapsed the "agree" and "tend to agree" responses and the "disagree" and "tend to disagree" responses into single categories.

30. Among the best examples of the use of this approach is Joseph Schlesinger, Ambition and Politics (Chicago: Rand McNally, 1966).

31. Kornberg, Canadian Legislative Behavior, p. 55.

32. Not one NDP MP responded in this manner, however.

## CHAPTER 3

1. Standard references to the study of power include, inter alia, Bertrand Russell, Power: A Social Analysis (New York: Norton, 1938); Herbert Goldhamer and Edward A. Shils, "Types of Power and Status," American Journal of Sociology, 45 (1939), pp. 171–182; Harold D. Lasswell and Abraham Kaplan, Power and Society: A Framework for Political Inquiry (New Haven: Yale University Press, 1965); Floyd Hunter, Community Power Structures (Chapel Hill: University of North Carolina Press, 1953); Herbert Simon, "Notes on the Observation and Measurement of Power," Journal of Politics, 15 (1953), pp. 500–516; James March, "Measurement Concepts in the Theory of Influence," Journal of Politics, 19 (1957), pp. 202–226; Robert A. Dahl, "The Concept of Power," Behavioral Science, 2 (1958), pp. 201–215; Robert A. Dahl, Who Governs? Democracy and Power in an American City (New Haven: Yale University Press, 1961); Dorwin Cartwright (ed.), Studies in Social Power (Ann Arbor: Institute for Social Research, University of Michigan, 1959); Felix Oppenheim, "Degrees of Power and Freedom," American Political Science Review, 54 (1960), pp. 437–446; Peter Bachrach and Morton Baratz, "Two Faces of Power," American Political Science Review, 56 (1962), pp. 947–952; Samuel J. Eldersveld, Political Parties: A Behavioral Analysis (Chicago: Rand McNally, 1964); John Porter, The Vertical Mosaic: An Analysis of Power and Social Class in Canada (Toronto: University of Toronto Press, 1965); Katherine West, Power in the Liberal Party: A Study in Australian Politics (London: Newnes, 1965); and Robert Jackson, Rebels and Whips (London: Macmillan, 1968); and Wallace Clement, The Canadian Corporate Elite: An Analysis of Economic Power (McClelland and Stewart, 1975).

2. In this study the concept of political leadership has been broadly defined to include MPs who held formal positions in the 28th Parliament (i.e., cabinet ministers, opposition party leaders, house leaders, party whips, and standing committee chairmen); MPs who occupied seats in the Conservative opposition frontbench; and MPs who had held a cabinet position in a previous parliament. Defined in these terms, the leadership cadre in the 28th Parliament comprised about 30% of its membership. The figure undoubtedly includes not only the great majority of the "real" holders of power and influence in this parliament, but also a number of MPs who possess little or no influence. Assuming this is the case, many of the differences that will be reported between leaders and nonleaders are particularly impressive.

3. Included among the better known studies are: Floyd Hunter, op. cit.; Robert O. Schulze, "The Role of Economic Dominants in Community Power Structure," American Sociological Review, 23 (1958), pp. 3–9; Robert A. Dahl, Who Governs? Democracy and Power in an American City; Roscoe C. Martin, Frank J. Munger and others, Decisions in Syracuse (Garden City: Doubleday and Company, 1965); Robert Presthus, Men at the Top: A Study in Community Power (New York: Oxford University Press, 1964).

4. There have been a few studies of power and influence in U.S. legislative bodies. Among these are: Heinz Eulau, "Bases of Authority in Legislative Bodies: A Comparative Analysis," Administrative Science Quarterly, 7 (1962), pp. 309–321; Raymond Wolfinger and Joan Heifetz, "Safe Seats, Seniority and Power in Congress," American Political Science Review, 59 (1965), pp. 337–349; William Riker and Donald Niemi, "Stability of Coalitions on Roll Calls in the House of Representatives," American Political Science Review, 56 (1962), pp. 58–65; David Kovenock, "Communications and Influence in Congressional Decision-Making," paper delivered at the American Political Science Association meeting, Chicago, 1964; and Kovenock, "Influence in the U.S. House of Representatives: Some Preliminary Statistical Snapshots," paper delivered at American Political Science Association meeting, Chicago, 1967. Also there is a voluminous body of literature on legislative coalitions and game theory most of which is based upon the analysis of roll call votes. Some of this literature speaks at least obliquely to the question of the distribution of power and influence in legislative bodies.

5. Gerhard Loewenberg, Modern Parliaments: Change or Decline? (New York: Aldine-Atherton, 1971), p. 3.

6. Eulau, "Bases of Authority," p. 314.

7. Ibid., p. 310.

8. The relative power of these regions has been of great interest and concern among students of Canadian politics and society. See for example, Mildred Schwartz, Politics and Territory: The Sociology of Regional Persistence in Canada (Montreal: McGill-Queens University Press, 1974); Paul Fox, "Regionalism and Confederation," in Mason Wade (ed.), Regionalism in the Canadian Community, 1867–1967 (Toronto: University of Toronto Press, 1969), pp. 3–29; Donald Putnam (ed.), Canadian Regions (Toronto: J. M. Dent and Sons, 1954); and P. Camu, E. P. Weeks and Z. W. Sametz, Economic Geography of Canada (Toronto: Macmillan, 1964).

9. As is well known, the controversy generally has revolved around whether the issue analysis or reputational approach is the more appropriate method of delineating holders of power or influence. Although we have opted for the reputational approach there obviously is some merit in the claims and charges of the partisans of both techniques. The basic lines of the controversy were drawn in Dahl, "The Concept of Power," ; Nelson Polsby, "The Sociology of Community Power: A Reassessment," Social Forces, 37 (1959), pp. 232–236; Nelson Polsby, "Community Power: Some Reflections on Recent Literature," American Sociological Review, 28 (1962), pp. 838–854; Raymond Wolfinger, "Reputation and Reality in the Study of 'Community Power,'" American Sociological Review, 25 (1960), pp. 636–644; William D'Antonio, Howard Erlich and Eugene Erickson, "The Reputational Technique as a Measure of Community Power: An Evaluation Based on Comparative and Longitudinal Studies," American Sociological Review, 28 (1962), pp. 362–376; and Thomas Anton, "Power, Pluralism and Local Politics," Administrative Science Quarterly, 7 (1963), pp. 425–457.

10. The finding with respect to the influence ascribed to NDP members is consonant with the findings of Michael Rush. In a private communication Rush, who has conducted an intensive investigation of the committee activity of Canadian MPs, notes that "the NDP parliamentary delegation has taken a very systematic and organized approach to their committee work in particular and their House participation in general. One consequence of this approach is that they have more influence than the size of their group warrants" (private communication, 2 July 1975).

11. Eulau, "Bases of Authority," p. 317.

12. In the Atlantic region we include Nova Scotia, New Brunswick, Prince Edward Island, and Newfoundland while in the West we include British Columbia, the Northwest Territories and the Yukon as well as the three Prairie provinces.

13. The late Professor H. McD. Clokie, a student of Canadian political institutions, observed that the most notable feature of the Canadian Cabinet was the representative nature of its membership. He argued that the cabinet had become, to a unique degree, "the grand co-ordinating body of the divergent, provincial, sectional, religious, racial and other interest in the nation." H. McD. Clokie, Canadian Government and Politics (Toronto: Longmans Green, 1944) p. 214. Generally every province is entitled to representation in the cabinet with Ontario and Quebec receiving the largest number of positions. One of the Quebec ministers by custom is an English-speaking Protestant while one of the Ontario ministers is a Catholic. Provincial representation is further elaborated in that a number of portfolios customarily are regarded as the special preserve of certain regions (e.g., Agriculture to the Prairies or, at times, to Ontario, and Fisheries to British Columbia or to one of the Atlantic provinces). The federal character of the cabinet is again emphasized in the practice of ministers discharging their conventional functions as provincial representatives. The late R. M. Dawson, Canada's foremost political scientist, noted that each minister is constantly concerned with the interests of his province. "In Cabinet councils he will be expected to advise, not only on matters within his particular department, but also on any topic whenever it concerns his province; and his opinion, by virtue of his superior knowledge of that locality, will merit exceptional consideration." R. M. Dawson, The Government of Canada (Toronto: University of Toronto Press, 1944), p. 134.

14. With respect to accomplishments in the past, we found that other than for former Prime Minister John Diefenbaker, members of his cabinet who still were MPs were ascribed relatively little influence.

15. It is interesting to note, although Prime Minister Trudeau and two of his senior French-speaking cabinet colleagues from Quebec received 248 nominations while three English-speaking senior colleagues from outside of Quebec received only 117 nominations, that the latter were cited for their "decency and humanity" 23 times whereas the former's influence was explained in these terms only 17 times. Of these 17 citations, fully 15 came from other French-Canadian MPs. Of course, it may be the case that the power and influence of Mr. Trudeau and his two French-speaking colleagues derive from sources other than their decency and humanity. Alternatively, if they are decent and humane, these qualities may be visible only to other French-Canadians.

16. Fully 64% said that representing the "proper province" was a principal criterion of selection and another 24% felt it was "being a member of the right ethnic or religious group."

17. With regard to affection, the reader should note that a number of times individuals first were nominated by a respondent and then had their names struck off the list of nominees at the request of the respondent because he disliked them (e.g., "Take ____'s name off. I can't stand his phoney piety"). Since some of the MPs were not nominated because of negative affective feelings toward them, we may assume that others were nominated for the opposite reason (i.e., because of positive affective feelings toward them).

18. Bernard Crick, "Parliament in the British Political System," in Allan Kornberg and Lloyd D. Musolf (eds.), Legislatures in Developmental Perspective (Durham: Duke University Press, 1970), p. 35.

19. The use of the coefficient is discussed in Hayward R. Alker, Mathematics and Politics (New York: Macmillan, 1965), pp. 23–53. See also Hayward Alker and Bruce Russett, "Indices for Comparing Inequality," in Richard Merritt and Stein Rokkan (eds.), Comparing Nations (New Haven: Yale University Press, 1966), pp. 349–372. Gini coefficients measure the degree to which any phenomenon is unequally distributed along a range from zero (the most equal distribution) to one (the most unequal distribution).

20. Mildred Schwartz, op. cit., pp. 64–82. For the most detailed systematic study of cabinet recruitment over time, see the aforementioned work of Richard J. Van Loon, The Structure and Membership of the Canadian Cabinet, working paper for the Royal Commission on Bilingualism and Biculturalism, Ottawa, 1966.

21. John Porter claims that prime ministers, particularly Liberal prime ministers, sometimes have resolved this problem by going outside parliament to co-opt individuals who supposedly were more able than sitting MPs. Of course, such co-opted individuals first had to be nominated by a constituency party and then elected in a by-election. See Porter, op. cit., pp. 398–403; also see ch. 8 of this volume.

22. From Memoirs of Sir George Foster, quoted in R. M. Dawson, op. cit., p. 211.

## CHAPTER 4

1. This point is further developed in the introduction to this volume, and in William Mishler and David Lindquist, "Political Socialization and Legislative Behavior in Canada and Germany: Some Problems of Studying A Missing Link in Legislative Research," paper presented at the 45th Annual Meeting, Southern Political Science Association, Atlanta, November 1–3, 1973.

2. An exception to this general pattern is the extensive literature on legislative roll-call behavior in the U.S. Congress, much of which is critically summarized in Ralph K. Huitt and Robert L. Peabody, Congress: Two Decades of Analysis (New York, Harper and Row, 1969), pp. 46–54, and in Duncan MacRae, Jr., Issues and Parties in Legislative Voting (New York: Harper and Row, 1970), passim. Research on the British House of Commons also has benefited from the use of Early Day Motion signatures as a behavioral measure of backbench party loyalty and dissent. See, for example, S. E. Finer, H. B. Berrington and D. J. Bartholomew, Backbench Opinion in the House of Commons, 1955–59 (London: Pergamon, 1961) and Robert J. Jackson, Rebels and Whips: An Analysis of Dissension, Discipline and Cohesion in British Political Parties (New York: St. Martin's Press, 1969). Both roll-call votes and early day motions, however, suffer from the limitation of measuring only a very narrow range of legislative behavior. Moreover, in Canada, given the presence of party discipline and the absence of early day motions, it has not been very practical to undertake research of this kind. To our knowledge, the only broad range empirical study of this aspect of microlegislative behavior in the House of Commons is an unpublished study by Roman March, "An Empirical Test of M. Ostrogorski's Theory of Political Evolution in a British Parliamentary System," Ph.D. dissertation, Indiana University, 1968. On the macro level, research on Canadian legislative behavior is restricted largely to a small but expanding body of literature on legislative policy outputs. An excellent summary of this research may be found in David J. Falcone, "Legislative Change and Output Change: A Time Series Analysis of the Canadian System," Ph.D. dissertation, Duke University, 1974.

3. R. H. S. Crossman as cited in Bernard Crick, "Parliament in the British Political System," in Allan Kornberg and Lloyd Musolf, Legislatures in Developmental Perspective (Durham: Duke University Press, 1970), p. 42. See also, J. Blondel, Comparative Legislatures (Prentice-Hall, 1973), pp. 5–7.

4. Gerhard Loewenberg, Modern Parliaments: Change or Decline? (New York: Aldine-Atherton, 1971), especially ch. 1.

5. Unfortunately, the data we have available for the 3rd and 4th sessions are incomplete and hence are not presented. A speech was defined as a comment by a MP of one or more sentences. However, we did not include comments such as "yes," "no," "boo," "oh" or "hear." The latter comments traditionally have been employed by Hansard to indicate

laughter, cheers, or antagonistic remarks by members. We recognize that our measure of individual participation in debate—based as it is on the number of speeches each member made and their length in Hansard lines—is not as intuitively meaningful as a measure based on the number of minutes or hours of individual speaking. Unfortunately, we knew of no way in which to generate such a time-based measure from the Hansard records that were available to us.

6. It should be remembered that in the case of the NDP Mr. Stanley Knowles served as both House Leader and Whip.

7. For example, the Liberals made approximately 35% of the speeches and used approximately 29% of the House's time in the first session of parliament. The Conservatives, the loyal opposition, made 32% of the speeches that took up 35% of the House's time. The equivalent figures for the NDP were 22% and 24% while for the Social Credit they were 11% and 12.3%.

8. Although our belief is that the government largely has been successful in regulating debate, the fact is that in Canada the government cannot unilaterally control the substance or length of debate. As was indicated in chapter 1, Closure is available but rarely is used. Even the less stringent S.O. 75a, b, and c have been used sparingly since their introduction.

9. Since 1962 the Social Credit-Creditiste parliamentary party has been overwhelmingly or entirely made up of French-Canadian MPs. Thus, it would be hard to label their attacks on cabinet ministers of French descent as "anti-French."

10. Even here, however, there are limits to government control. If the opposition feels it can seriously embarrass the government on a defense issue or a matter of foreign policy, it likely will be unimpressed by the government's claim of privilege and will push vigorously to have the issue included on the agenda for debate.

11. Our analysis of the Speeches, Questions, and Division Votes in the first two sessions of the 28th Parliament included coding each speech, question and vote according to its substantive content into one of eight issue categories. These categories, including brief descriptions of the type of issues they embrace, are as follows: (1) Defense and External Affairs—issues relating to defense, foreign policy and external affairs, questions of sovereignty, and veterans' affairs; (2) Public Finance—issues encompassed by the jurisdiction of the Treasury Board, Ministry of Finance, and Ministry of National Revenue, including the budget, the economy, taxation issues, questions concerning the Price and Income Commission or concerning banking; (3) Social Welfare—issues pertaining to national health and welfare policy, housing problems, consumer and corporate affairs, poverty, medical care, social security, food and drugs, etc.; (4) Legal-Political—issues related to either internal parliamentary procedures or to national law and justice including questions pertaining to elections, constituency boundaries, parliamentary reforms, the Constitution, justice ministry or the solicitor general; (5) Primary Industry-Extractive—issues related to industries directly involved with the exploitation and conservation of natural resources including agriculture, fisheries, forestry, mining, the environment, pollution abatement, national parks and energy; (6) Labor and Secondary Industry—issues concerned with labor, manpower and immigration, industry, trade, commerce, science and technology; (7) Internal Development—issues relating to regional economic development, urban affairs, public works, transporation, communications, etc.; (8) Miscellaneous—a variety of disparate issues including such symbolic issues as bilingualism and the language bill, and such other topics as Expo 70, tourism and rainmaking.

12. The large percentage of the time for debate allocated to issues that are broadly defined as being "legal-political" in nature can be attributed to: (a) the fact that during the first two sessions of this parliament the government was pressing for the institution of rather massive and extremely important changes in parliamentary procedure; and (b) the fact that there always is a great deal of wrangling over procedural issues in any democratic legislative system. Procedures, even when impartially applied, never are neutral in their effect. They

invariably have an impact upon the disposition of substantive issues and are the source of important advantages for various groups within the system.

13. Although question period and debate undoubtedly serve somewhat overlapping functions in practice, in theory, at least, it can be argued that the primary purpose of debate is to facilitate the passage of sound legislation by providing for maximum public discussion of competing points of view. In parliamentary systems, moreover, debate is intended to provide a forum for the official opposition to present alternatives to government policy. Question period, on the other hand, presumably is intended to be an instrument of legislative oversight. In practice, as we have noted, both question period and debate probably serve both of these functions and several other functions as well. The asking of questions of a government began in the British House of Commons. The first recorded question was asked in 1721 but Chester and Bowring state that "Questions in anything like their modern usage are largely a development of the nineteenth century, particularly of the period after 1830." See D. N. Chester and Nona Bowring, Questions in Parliament (Oxford: Clarendon Press, 1962), p. 12. However, by the time Canada became a nation (1867) the practice was well established in Britain and became an integral part of the procedure utilized in the Canadian House of Commons.

14. The theoretical foundations and empirical evidence supporting the various explorations of party loyalty and cohesion in British-style parliamentary systems are discussed at some length in the literature. See, for example, Leon Epstein, Political Parties in Western Democracies (New York: Praeger, 1967); Allan Kornberg, "Caucus and Cohesion in Canadian Parliamentary Parties," American Political Science Review 60 (1966), pp. 83–92; and Allan Kornberg, Canadian Legislative Behavior: A Study of the 25th Parliament (New York: Holt, Rinehart and Winston, 1967). See also, Lawrence Leduc, Jr. and Walter L. White, "Opposition and One-Party Dominance," Canadian Journal of Political Science, 7 (1974), 96–100.

15. Question practice in the Canadian House of Commons differs somewhat from the British. In Canada the terms "oral" and "written" refer to notice (i.e., written questions appear on the Order Paper, oral do not). In the British House of Commons all questions (with the exception of Private Notice questions) are written. They appear on the Order Paper as either starred or unstarred questions. A starred question indicates that an oral response is desired whereas an unstarred question indicates that a written response will suffice. Written answers–including answers to questions put down for oral replies which were not reached during question time–appear daily in Hansard.

16. In Canada, as in Great Britain, ministerial responsibility is the standard test applied to all questions by the Speaker. Although generally the test is loosely applied, it results in some questions being ruled out of order. Assuming the question is not ruled out of order, a good rule of thumb is that the more precisely it is worded the more difficult it is for a minister or his parliamentary secretary to avoid answering. Veteran parliament-watchers enjoy the performance of ministers who appear to be answering questions openly and completely but in reality are saying little that is substantively important. However, as the data in tables 4.6 and 4.7 indicate, ministers will not play even this little game about 10% of the time.

17. In describing the impact that asking the right questions can have on the career of a British MP, Chester and Bowring note that "questions are a continuous source of publishable information and news stories for the national dailys, for the provincial press, for the thousands of specialized periodicals and for the newspapers of other countries. . . . When reported in one of the dailys, quite often the questioner's name is mentioned and it will certainly be mentioned in his local newspaper and usually in any specialist periodical." See Chester and Bowring, op. cit., p. 177. To a somewhat lesser extent, asking the right questions can have similar consequences for the careers of Canadian MPs.

18. Members of the cabinet are excluded from the Questions measure for the obvious reason that cabinet members answer, but do not ask, questions. We have recorded the

number and length of Cabinet replies to questions and present these data at the bottom of tables 4.6 and 4.7.

19. Lord Bryce, Modern Democracies (New York: Macmillan, 1922), ch. 8, and Loewenberg, op. cit., passim.

20. All bills introduced into the House either are public or private. A private bill is just that; its subject matter can concern an individual, a group, or even a locality but it will not affect the general public (e.g., a bill incorporating a company or altering the charter of an existing corporation). Public bills, in contrast, are intended to have a general or public purpose. A public bill that is part of a government's program and is introduced by a cabinet member is termed a government bill. A public bill that is not a part of a government's program and is introduced by a MP who is not a member of the cabinet is referred to as a private member's public bill or simply as a private member's bill. Although a private member's bill has a public purpose (e.g., a bill to regulate lobbying activity) it cannot deal with a subject that will have the effect of raising or spending money. In order for a private member to introduce a subject which will have a financial impact, he must introduce it in the form of a resolution which urges the government to "consider the advisibility of . . ."We term such debatable resolutions "DRs" in table 4.9. A bill that has been passed by parliament becomes an act. After it has been signed by the Governor-General, it becomes a law.

Private members' bills normally do not need to be heavily promoted since so few of them ever reach second reading. An analysis by Stewart Hyson of the fate of private members' bills introduced into the 24th, 26th, and 28th parliaments bears this out. Some 73% of all such bills "died" on the order table. An additional 18% were talked out during second reading (i.e., no decision was reached on the bill by the end of the hour and it was placed on the bottom of the list of bills). Approximately 5% reached the committee stage. Slightly less than 2% were ruled out of order or defeated on second reading and slightly over 2% became law. In the 28th parliament, 780 private members' bills were introduced and 22 were enacted into law (approximately 2.8%). See R. V. Stewart Hyson, "The Role of the Backbencher: An Analysis of Private Members' Bills in the Canadian House of Commons," Parliamentary Affairs, 27 (1974), pp. 262–272.

21. The written portion of the Canadian Constitution, the British North America Act, provides that "questions arising in the House of Commons shall be decided by a majority of voices other than that of the Speaker and when the voices are equal, but not otherwise, the Speaker shall have a vote" (S.49). When debate on a question is over, the Speaker puts the question to the assembled members. The latter vote by voice "yea" or "nay" and the Speaker then announces his interpretation of the vote, an interpretation that rarely is accepted by the losers. Accordingly, at least five members will rise to demand a recorded vote. The Speaker will have the division bell rung for approximately ten minutes to summon members to the House. Customarily, the summoned members, government and opposition alike, will enter the House in a body, bow to the Speaker, and take their seats. The Speaker again will put the question, asking members in favor to rise. Beginning with the leader, the members of each party will rise as their names are called by an Assistant Clerk. The Speaker then will ask all those opposed to rise and the division proceeds as before. The Clerk of the House who keeps the official record of the division announces the results to the Speaker who then formally decides the question under consideration. For a detailed account of voting in the House see William F. Dawson, Procedure in the Canadian House of Commons (Toronto: University of Toronto Press, 1965), pp. 181–192.

22. Van Loon and Whittington make the following assessment of the value of private members' bills: "The MP can put on the record his point of view on a certain policy area. Furthermore, by introducing a bill which favors interests in his constituency he can publicize problems which exist there and which are perhaps unique. In this way, the MP can use the private member's bill as a device to assist him in the performance of the representative or ombudsman function. . . . Thus it is a useful device for criticizing the government's

policy priorities and for publicizing special problems and needs within certain regions and constituencies of the country." Richard Van Loon and Michael Whittington, The Canadian Political System (Toronto: McGraw Hill, 1971), p. 485.

23. As was just noted, approximately 2% of the private members' bills introduced into parliament become law. See Hyson, op. cit., pp. 262–272.

24. We did find indirect support for the thesis frequently encountered in the literature that a governing party tends to be more cohesive than an opposition.

25. The magnitude of this correlation coefficient also increases our confidence in the reliability of the content analyses of both speeches and divisions. Since the magnitude of the correlation coefficient is inversely proportional to measurement error (other things being equal), the size of this coefficient indicates a minimal level of measurement or coding error.

26. However, some MPs introduced as many as 42 PMBs in a single session.

27. Hyson's data which include only private members' bills indicate that in the 24th, 26th, and 28th parliaments, members of the Liberal party introduced 27.3% of all private members' bills. The Conservatives introduced, on the average, 26% of such bills; the CCF-NDP MPs introduced 42%; and the Social Credit-Creditiste MPs introduced approximately 6% during the 26th and 28th parliaments. They were unrepresented in the 24th parliament. See Hyson, op. cit., p. 267, Table 3.

28. Hyson has estimated a ratio of bills introduced per party member by dividing the number of private members' bills the members of each party introduced into the three parliaments by the size of their parliamentary delegations in each parliament. In the case of the governing party, cabinet ministers were excluded. His findings are consonant with our own. That is, the NDP ratio is the highest (2.77). The Conservative party is the lowest (.27). The Creditiste party (.44 for the 26th and 28th parliaments only) and the Liberal (.35) fall in between, but are much closer to the Conservative than to the New Democratic party. Hyson, op. cit., p. 267, Table 4.

29. Of course, committees also provide members with an opportunity to investigate various matters that are neither the subject of prospective legislation nor related to the magnitude and distribution of estimates. For example, committees may concern themselves with how a particular governmental department is being administered, how and why problems arise in particular departments, and so forth—in other words committees provide the opportunity for the performance of what generally is termed the "oversight" function of parliamentary bodies.

30. Liberal MP Mark MacGuigan wrote at the end of the first session of this parliament: "Whether or not the Government yet accepts the fact, it made a fundamental change in our system when it introduced the legislative committee. . . . The change is a fundamental improvement because it enables the individual member to make a more creative contribution to the law-making process. . . . The only loss is the power of the executive." Mark MacGuigan, "Backbenchers, the New Committee System and the Caucus," in Paul Fox (ed.), Politics: Canada (Toronto: McGraw-Hill, 1970), p. 381. Supporting this assertion MacGuigan notes that "Liberal members have on several occasions themselves moved amendments to government bills, or voted in support of Opposition motions or amendments. The most notable instance occurred in the Justice Committee on March 25, 1969, when an amendment to the breathalyzer section of the omnibus Criminal Code Bill was proposed by a Liberal MP and, despite the opposition of the Minister of Justice, was carried, with five Liberals and four Conservatives out-voting two New Democrats and the poor Liberals who voted for the government version." Ibid., p. 380; Dorothy Byrne, "Some Attendance Patterns Exhibited by Members of Parliament during the 28th Parliament," Canadian Journal of Political Science, 5 (1972), pp. 135–141, also deals with House and committee attendance.

31. In the first two sessions of parliament, three of the twelve Liberal MPs in the subsample did not make a single speech in the House and in the fourth session two of them

were silent. None of the opposition members failed to speak in the House in all four sessions of parliament.

32. See, for example, Nicholas R. Masters, "Committee Assignments in the House of Representatives," American Political Science Review, 55 (1961), pp. 345–357; Charles Bullock, "Freshmen Committee Assignments and Reelection in the U.S. House of Representatives," American Political Science Review, 66 (1972), pp. 996–1007, and Malcolm E. Jewell and Chu Chi-Hing, "Membership Movement and Committee Attractiveness in the U.S. House of Representatives," American Journal of Political Science, 68 (1974), pp. 433–441.

33. Van Loon and Whittington suggest one reason for the relatively low prestige of the Public Accounts Committee. They point out that the basic weakness of the Public Accounts Committee is that the government usually chooses not to heed its recommendations. "The committee reports directly to the House, as do all standing committees, but the report does not produce any debate; the report is simply received by the House and forgotten or ignored by the government." Van Loon and Whittington, op. cit., p. 479.

## CHAPTER 5

1. See Gerhard Loewenberg (ed.), Modern Parliaments: Change or Decline? (New York: Aldine-Atherton, 1971).

2. See, Allan Kornberg, "Caucus and Cohesion in Canadian Parliamentary Parties," American Political Science Review, 60 (1966), pp. 83–92.

3. For a more elaborate theory of constituency communication see Ian Budge, et al., Political Stratification and Democracy (Toronto: University of Toronto Press, 1972) and Ian Budge and Cornelius O'Leary, Belfast: Approach to Crisis (London: MacMillan, 1973).

4. See table 5.14 for response categories.

5. See table 5.15 for response categories.

6. Allan Kornberg, Canadian Legislative Behavior: A Study of the 25th Parliament (New York: Holt, Rinehart and Winston, 1967), pp. 129–131.

7. Richard A. Van Loon and Michael S. Whittington, The Canadian Political System: Environment, Structure and Process (Toronto: McGraw-Hill, 1971), p. 456.

8. Ibid., pp. 244–245.

9. J. W. Pickersgill, The Mackenzie King Record (Toronto: University of Toronto Press, 1960), p. 9.

10. Mark MacGuigan, "Backbenchers, The New Committee System and the Caucus," in Paul Fox (ed.), Politics: Canada (Toronto: McGraw-Hill, 1970), p. 382.

11. Kornberg, Canadian Legislative Behavior, op. cit., p. 133.

12. Ibid.

13. A number of British parliamentary scholars have argued that textbook explanations of the cohesion exhibited by British parliamentary parties place too much stress on the concept of discipline. Such explanations, in their view, do not sufficiently emphasize the extent to which cohesion is a product of mutual accommodation and a spirit of give and take between the front and backbenches. See for example, Robert E. Dowse and Trevor Smith, "Party Discipline in the House of Commons–A Comment," Parliamentary Affairs, 16 (1963), pp. 159–164; Robert J. Jackson, Rebels and Whips (New York, 1968); Norman Hunt's interview with Martin Redmayne in Anthony King (ed.), British Politics: People, Parties, and Parliament (Englewood Cliffs, 1966), pp. 142–147; and Allan Kornberg and Robert C. Frasure, "The Management of Cohesion in British Parliamentary Parties," Journal of Constitutional and Parliamentary Studies, 6 (1972), pp. 9–22.

14. Because of their position in the House, cabinet members were not asked these questions but instead were asked how often they were contacted by members. Neither, for obvious reasons, did we ask parliamentary secretaries about their communication with themselves. However, we did ask them about their contacts with both ministers and deputy-ministers.

15. Donald C. Rowat, "Why We Need an Ombudsman" in Fox (ed.), Politics: Canada, op. cit., p. 393.

16. Mitchell Sharp, "The Expert, the Politician and the Public" in Fox (ed.), Politics: Canada, ibid., p. 432.

17. Admittedly, the policy-oriented content of Social Credit communications contradicts this general pattern. However, given the very small number of Social Credit MPs, percentages based on the Social Credit data are rather unstable. Consequently, the unexpected pattern in the Social Credit data detracts very little from the validity of the observed relationship between representational roles and communication content.

18. As a further test of the proposition that the content of communications in parliament is related to individual representational roles, we correlated a summary measure of representational style and focus (described in Appendix C) with three variables that measure the extent to which member communications with ministers, deputy-ministers and parliamentary secretaries were concerned with constituency matters as opposed to public policy issues. The correlations (Pearson's r) between representational roles (constructed so that delegate-servants scored high, Burkean-trustees low, and politicos in between) and constituency service communications ranged from .24 (p < .001) for communications with ministers to .13 for communications with deputy-ministers (p < .01) and parliamentary secretaries (p = ns). Although these correlations are quite modest (and despite the fact that the correlation for parliamentary secretaries is not statistically significant) their direction is consistent with our expectations and provides a modicum of additional support for the proposition.

19. Measures of success based upon the subjective perceptions of those being questioned have certain shortcomings. Respondents may misperceive a situation, they may engage in self-deception or they may restructure their goals in light of their perceived accomplishments. Given these possibilities the data on the relative success of MPs in dealing with ministers, ministerial assistants and high echelon bureaucrats should be viewed with a certain amount of caution.

20. On the other hand, our inability to find data that support the assumption that opposition MPs are more successful in their dealings with deputy-ministers than with members of the cabinet may be due to the fact that we did not ask respondents who did not communicate regularly with deputy-ministers whether they felt they had been successful in achieving their objectives. However, we did ask them why they did not communicate more with deputy-ministers and their responses suggest that had we asked them if they were successful, they probably would have said "no." They generally said they did not communicate more because it was "useless to do so," that "there was little or nothing to be gained" from such communication, and so forth.

21. There were no differences in the success rates with respect to parliamentary secretaries.

22. The question asked here was, "What is the mail that you do get generally about? For instance, do people write asking about your view on a certain issue, about their stand on a certain issue; do they ask for your help on certain matters ... or what?" Because all responses were recorded, the percentages reported in the text add to more than 100%.

23. Because of the small size of the leadership groups in the Creditiste and New Democratic parties we did not include the two minor parties in the analyses presented in tables 5.9, 5.11, and 5.13.

24. This finding is not unexpected in view of recent work on interest groups in Canada.

See Robert Presthus, Elite Accommodation in Canadian Politics (Toronto: Macmillan, 1973), passim.

## CHAPTER 6

1. In the case of the Liberal party, this measure includes all the government bills introduced by the members of the cabinet. It also includes the aforementioned private and private members' bills and debatable resolutions (see Appendix C, Section II).

2. The construction of the participation variable employed here and throughout the remainder of this chapter is discussed at length in Appendix C. Very briefly, however, the "number of speeches and questions" and "number of bills and debatable resolution" variables are weighted factor score indices derived from a principal components factor analysis of eleven participation variables. Although a third factor, labeled "committee activity," also emerged from the analysis, the loadings of the committee variables on this factor were marginal prompting us to ignore this factor and to use, instead, the single variable, "percent attendance at committee meetings" as the primary measure of committee participation. Similarly, because neither of the cabinet communications or bureaucratic communications variables loaded on any of the dimensions derived from the factor analysis, these variables are included in this and all subsequent chapters in their unrefined form. The "Frequency of Constituency Communications" variable was derived from two questions: (a) Do you get much mail from constituents? and (b) Do constituents frequently contact you in any other way? Respondents who answered yes to both questions were scored "1." Those who answered no or undecided to either or both, were scored "0."

3. As is well known, multiple regression analysis is a technique that allows the simultaneous assessment of the independent effects of a number of independent variables on a single dependent variable. For a very readable discussion of this technique see Hubert Blalock, Social Statistics (New York: McGraw-Hill, 1960), pp. 273–358.

4. See, inter alia, W. W. Cooley and P. R. Lohnes, Multivariate Procedures for the Behavioral Sciences (New York: Wiley, 1962); and Harry E. Anderson, "Regression, Discriminant Analysis, and a Standard Notation," in R. B. Cattel, ed., Handbook of Multivariate Experimental Psychology (Chicago: Rand-McNally, 1966), pp. 153–173.

5. Indeed, there is a strong negative correlation (−.31) between being a committee chairman and speaking frequently in the House.

6. Regression analyses conducted only for cabinet members reveal that ministers who received a considerable number of influence and good judgment nominations were distinguished from their colleagues who were not recognized in this manner by the fact that the former spoke more frequently and introduced more legislation into the House than did the latter. However, only frequency of speaking was a significant predictor of influence (Beta = .67), and good judgment (Beta = .70).

7. Members of the Cabinet were not questioned on the extent of their communication with deputy-ministers.

8. There seems to be some carry-over betweeen participating on the floor of the House and participating in committees as there is a correlation of .24 between these activities for the 34 members of the subsample.

9. It may be noted that committee attendance, while positively associated with influence and good judgment nominations among opposition MPs considered as a group, is not always positively associated when the opposition parties are considered individually. Thus, for example, in the Conservative party the zero-order relationships between influence and

good judgment on the one hand and committee attendance on the other are negative, but the Betas, although insignificant, are positive. In the NDP both the zero-order relationships and the Betas are positive. In every opposition party frequency of speaking in the House is always positively related (almost always in a significant fashion) to the two dependent variables.

10. A study of fifty MPs newly elected to Canada's 30th Parliament by Price, Clarke, and Krause provides some empirical support for our assumption. The investigators found that the expectation the freshmen MPs had of performing services for constituents was reinforced during the course of the election campaign through contacts with voters. After the election, interactions with their new constituents and with veteran MPs further reinforced the expectation that they would perform services. Indeed, a substantial number of the newcomers reported that they were heavily involved in communicating with constituents and performing services for them before they had "officially" become MPs (i.e., in the three month interim between their election and the opening of the first session of the 30th Parliament). See Richard Price, Harold Clarke, and Robert Krause, "The Role Socialization of Freshmen Legislators: The Case of Canadian MPs," a paper presented to the Annual Meeting of the American Political Science Association, Sept. 5, 1975.

11. Readers may also feel we approve of the situation in both parliament and the academy and, in fact, that we are providing a rationale for the continued existence of these conditions. This is not the case.

## CHAPTER 7

1. For an elaboration of this point see, Lester Milbrath, Political Participation (Chicago: Rand McNally and Company, 1965), ch. 1, pp. 29–38.

2. Oliver Woshinsky, The French Deputy: Incentives and Behavior in the National Assembly (Lexington: Heath, 1973), p. 3.

3. John Wahlke, Heinz Eulau, William Buchanan and LeRoy Ferguson, The Legislative System (New York: John Wiley and Sons, 1962).

4. See for example, Roger H. Davidson, The Role of the Congressman (New York: Pegasus, 1969); Weston H. Agor, The Chilean Senate (Austin: University of Texas Press, 1971); and Allan Kornberg, Canadian Legislative Behavior (New York: Holt, Rinehart and Winston, 1967).

5. James David Barber, "Strategies for Studying Politicians," American Journal of Political Science (1974), pp. 443–467.

6. James David Barber, The Lawmakers: Recruitment and Adaptation to Legislative Life (New Haven: Yale University Press, 1965).

7. James L. Payne and Oliver Woshinsky, "Incentives for Political Participation," World Politics (1972), pp. 518–546. For applications of this approach see James L. Payne, Patterns of Conflict in Colombia (New Haven: Yale University Press, 1968), and Oliver Woshinsky, op. cit.

8. Joseph Schlesinger, Ambition and Politics: Political Careers in the United States (Chicago: Rand McNally, 1966).

9. These include one measure of representational style and focus; one measure of specialization/expertise; and six measures of the MP's perceptions of any role conflict between what he wants to accomplish and what other significant individuals or groups in the legislative environment want him to accomplish. All of the variables employed in this analysis are described further in Appendix C.

10. This subsample is considered to be representative of the population of backbenchers involved in committee work.

11. Although the percentage of variance in the three participation variables accounted for by motivations is something less than dramatic, the level of explanation achieved here, we believe, is substantial and compares more than favorably with other studies of elite behavior that rely upon survey data. Indeed, the level of explanation achieved is particularly impressive given the sometimes very crude measures of motivations that we employ.

12. It must be noted, however, that the variables we employ as measures of MP incentives are also rather crude indicators of elite motivations. Moreover, unlike the deputies in Woshinsky's study who were assigned to mutually exclusive incentive categories, all of the MPs in our analysis have been given scores for all of the incentive measures. No doubt some of the differences in our respective findings are due to these differences in our methodologies.

13. For comparative data and a lucid description of the backgrounds and perspectives of U.S. Senate "professionals" see, Donald Matthews, U.S. Senators and their World (New York: Random House, 1960), pp. 92–117. See also, William S. White, Citadel: The Story of the United States Senate (New York: Harper and Brothers, 1956).

14. The subgroups included: (1) Liberal MPs; (2) Conservative MPs, (3) opposition party MPs; (4) minor party MPs; (5) parliamentary leaders; and (6) parliamentary backbenchers.

15. The cabinet ambition variable does not enter the Liberal equation because the question was not asked of cabinet ministers.

16. Chapter 9 addresses the question of whether the influence of environment is direct or indirect.

17. See chapter 6.

18. Although we found that constituency competition was not a significant correlate of debate activity among all MPs, it was a significant determinant of variations in debate among the Conservatives (Beta = −.29), and among both the leadership and backbench subgroups as well (Beta = −.27 and .24 respectively). Note, however, that the direction of this relationship is reversed among the backbench and leadership subgroups. This suggests that our failure to find relationships between competition and participation among MPs as a group may be a consequence of the contradictory relationships between competition and debate among the two leadership and backbench subgroups—a pattern perhaps produced by the tendency of several of the parties to "parachute" higher party leaders into noncompetitive, "safe" constituencies.

19. On the socialization of political elites, see inter alia, William Mishler, "Political Participation and the Process of Political Socialization in Canada: A Computer Simulation," Ph.D. dissertation, Duke University, 1972; Allan Kornberg, Joel Smith and David Bromley, "Some differences in the Political Socialization Patterns of Canadian and American Party Officials," Canadian Journal of Political Science, 2 (1969), pp. 64–88; and Heinz Eulau et al., "The Political Socialization of American State Legislators," Midwest Journal of Political Science, 3 (1959), pp. 188–206. For a general review of the literature on the politicization of mass publics see, Robert Weissberg, Political Learning, Political Choice, and Democratic Citizenship (Englewood Cliffs, N.J.; Prentice Hall, 1974), chs. 4 and 5. The very meager literature on mass socialization in Canada is briefly reviewed in Richard A. Van Loon and Michael Whittington, The Canadian Political System (Toronto: McGraw-Hill, 1971), pp. 67–72.

20. See, with respect to Canada, Allan Kornberg, Harold Clarke and George Watson, "Toward a Model of Parliamentary Recruitment in Canada," in Allan Kornberg (ed.), Legislature in Comparative Perspective (New York: David McKay, 1973), pp. 250–281, and William Mishler and Allan Kornberg, "Patterns of Recruitment to the Canadian House of Commons," in Harold Clarke and Richard Price (eds.), Recruitment and Leadership Selection in Canada (Laurentian University Press, forthcoming).

21. Donald Matthews, U.S. Senators and their World, op. cit., p. 11.

22. Lewis Edinger and Donald Searing, "Social Background in Elite Analysis: A Methodological Inquiry," American Political Science Review, 61 (1967), pp. 428–445.

## CHAPTER 8

1. Allan Kornberg, "The Social Bases of Leadership in a Canadian House of Commons," Australian Journal of Politics, 11 (1965), p. 325.

2. Ibid.

3. We would have liked to extend our comparisons of party leaders to the leadership of the New Democratic and Social Credit parties. Unfortunately, their small number precludes such comparisons.

4. John Meisel, Working Papers on Canadian Politics (Montreal: McGill-Queen's University Press, 1973), pp. 217–252. For data on some of the difference between Liberal and Conservative cabinet ministers, 1896–1960, see John Porter, The Vertical Mosaic (Toronto: University of Toronto Press, 1965), pp. 386–414. For additional comparisons for the period 1867–1968, see Allan Kornberg and David J. Falcone, "Societal Change, Legislative Elite Composition, and Political System Outputs in Canada," a paper presented at a symposium on ministerial and legislative decision-making in parliamentary regimes, Bellagio, August, 1970.

5. Kornberg and Falcone observed that during the first 100 years of Canada's existence the four most significant differences between the legislative outputs of Liberal- and Conservative-led parliaments were: (1) Liberal governments passed more redistributive legislation; (2) Liberal governments passed more foreign policy legislation; (3) Liberal governments expended larger proportions of the national budget on the military, and (4) Conservative governments have been more "productive" in that over the years they have passed more major bills each day in which parliament has been in session. Kornberg and Falcone, ibid.

6. Porter, op. cit., pp. 399–403.

7. This relationship exists if we include all cabinet ministers, front-bench Conservatives, the leaders of the New Democratic and Social Credit parties in the leadership group together with the several chairmen of the standing committees, and the house leaders and the whips of each of the parties.

8. The difference in age was not statistically significant.

9. Samuel J. Eldersveld, Political Parties: A Behavioral Analysis (Chicago: Rand McNally, 1964).

10. See Allan Kornberg, David J. Falcone, William T. E. Mishler, Legislatures and Societal Cnange: The Case of Canada, Sage Research Papers, Comparative Legislative Studies Series (Beverly Hills: Sage Publications, 1973), p. 19.

11. However, the strengthening of the committee system has made the position of committee chairman considerable more attractive than it was in the past.

12. Indeed, they were distinguished in a statistically significant fashion from backbenchers by only four attributes: (1) they were more often businessmen and professionals when they became politically active; (2) they were reared in less politicized environments; (3) they were less aware of sanctions available to enforce adherence to the rules of the game; and (4) they more often feel they will become ministers.

13. Porter, op. cit., p. 403.

14. Ibid., p. 405.

15. Ibid., p. 398.

16. Ibid., p. 396.

17. Ibid., p. 396.

18. Ibid., pp. 406–409.

19. See, for example, the findings of Canadian Institute of Public Opinion Polls reported in "Parliament in Canadian Society," in Allan Kornberg and Lloyd D. Musolf (eds.), Legislatures in Developmental Perspective (Durham: Duke University Press, 1970), pp. 55–58. See also the reports of Public Opinion Polls cited in Price, et al., "The Role Socialization of Freshman Legislators: The Case of Canadian MP's," a paper presented to

the Annual Meeting of the American Political Science Association, San Francisco, September, 1975.

20. See, for example, Gerhard Loewenberg (ed.), Modern Parliaments: Change or Decline? (New York: Aldine-Atherton, 1971).

21. Thus, Schlesinger's data for 1921–1957 are consistent with our own finding that the members of the Conservative frontbench (many of whom presumably would have been members of a Conservative cabinet) had a considerably longer period of parliamentary experience than did the members of the Liberal cabinet. See Schlesinger, "Political Careers and Party Leadership," in Lewis J. Edinger (ed.), Political Leadership in Industrialized Societies (New York: John Wiley & Sons, Inc., 1967), pp. 266–293, particularly Table 9.6, p. 287.

22. See, inter alia, Kornberg and Falcone, op. cit.; Richard J. Van Loon, The Structure and Membership of the Canadian Cabinet (a working paper for the Royal Commission on Bilingualism and Bilculturalism, 1966); and Roman March, The Myth of Parliament (Scarborough: Prentice Hall, 1974).

23. Our impressions are derived from interviews with the Conservative frontbenchers and the members of the Liberal cabinet.

24. John Meisel, "Howe, Hubris and '72: An Essay on Political Elitism," in Working Papers on Canadian Politics, op. cit., pp. 217–252.

25. Ibid., p. 233.

26. Ibid., p. 240. With respect to the ability of the two parties to attract candidates, the reader will recall that a substantial number of the Liberal cabinet ministers were self-starters whereas a number of the Conservative frontbenchers reported being strongly pressured to become candidates.

27. Ibid., p. 241.

28. Ibid., p. 241.

29. When the dependent variable in discriminant function analysis is a "dummy" or binary variable, the results generated by the analysis ought to be identical, or nearly so, with those generated by dummy variable regression. This situation applies to all of our discriminant function analyses except that for the Liberal cabinet-committee chairmen-backbench MP groups.

# CHAPTER 9

1. See, Herbert Simon, Models of Man (New York: John Wiley and Sons, 1957), chs. 1–3; Hubert Blalock, Causal Inferences in Non-Experimental Research (Chapel Hill: University of North Carolina Press, 1964). For more general literature on path analysis see, Sewell Wright, "Path Coefficients and Path Regressions: Alternative or Complimentary Concepts," Biometrics, 16 (1960), pp. 189–202; Kenneth Land, "Principles of Path Analysis," in Edgar Borgatta (ed.), Sociological Methodology (San Francisco: Josey-Bass, 1969) pp. 3–37; and David Hiese, "Problems in Path Analysis and Causal Inference," in Borgatta, Sociological Methodology, pp. 38–73. For the views of those disputing the Simon-Blalock technique see, W. S. Robinson, "Asymmetric Causal Models: Comments on Polke and Blalock," American Sociological Review, 27 (1962), pp. 545–558.

2. Blalock, op. cit., p. 51.

3. Ibid., p. 192.

4. Blalock, for example, found it exceedingly difficult to test all possible linkages even in a very simple four variable model. See Hubert Blalock, "Four Variable Causal Models and

Partial Correlations," American Journal of Sociology, 68 (1962), pp. 182–194. With eight variables and thus more than 20 billion ($3^{28}$) possible models, an exhaustive test clearly is not possible.

5. Two particularly troublesome problems result from our decision to employ only one indicator of each concept. First, although practical considerations necessitated this procedure, it is apparent that no single indicator, regardless of the magnitude of its correlations with other variables, can adequately capture the full scope and complexity of such multifaceted concepts. At best, therefore, our variables tap only a limited aspect of a concept's relationship with individual influence. Second, it seems equally apparent that the use of different measures of the same concept in different models reduces their comparability. With respect to the first of these considerations, although a certain loss of complexity is inevitable in any model, the criteria we have employed to select indicators of each concept help insure that we have included their most salient aspects. Moreover, given the nature of the variable selection process, the appearance of different variables in different models provides valuable information about party variations in the pathways to influence, thereby increasing rather than detracting from the comparability of our models. We elaborate more fully upon this latter point below.

6. Although most of these discussions focus on the validation of computer simulation models, the general strategies proposed are applicable here as well. See, for example, the discussion of validation in Thomas H. Naylor, Computer Simulation Experiments with Model of Economic Systems (New York: John Wiley and Sons, 1971), pp. 153–163.

7. Blalock, Causal Inferences, pp. 44–60.

8. See the discussion on statistical significance and small sample size in chapter 2.

9. The reader will note that we have retained the political socialization to influence link despite its disappearance when committee activity is controlled because we have data of this kind only for the 34 MPs in our special subsample.

10. See, for example, the argument to this effect by Hugh Forbes and Edward Tufte, "A Note of Caution in Causal Modeling," American Political Science Review, 62 (1968), pp. 1258–1264.

11. The substantive implications of these revisions are discussed in the subsequent section on path analysis.

12. See Otis D. Duncan, "Path Analysis: Sociological Examples," American Journal of Sociology, 72 (1966), pp. 1–16.

13. Blalock, in "Causal Inference, Closed Population, and Measures of Association," American Political Science Review, 61 (1967), pp. 130–136, has argued for the use of unstandardized coefficients. As we understand it, he draws a fairly sharp distinction between searching for natural laws and describing populations. Standardized coefficients are useful in the latter but may be confusing in the former circumstance. Since Blalock favors the search for laws as the proper aim of science, he favors unstandardized coefficients. We would argue that the aim of science is the development of laws which operate in populations to a definable (and preferably large) degree. As such, we find the sensitivity of standardized coefficients to "disturbances" useful in comparative work in leading us to inquire into the source of the error and thus, hopefully, to move another step in the process of inquiry.

14. See, Donald E. Stokes," Compound Paths: An Expository Note," American Journal of Political Science, 18 (1974), p. 208.

15. No doubt the surprisingly weak effects of attitudes and motivations on ascribed influence stem as well from the severe limitations imposed on the number of variables that could be included in the models. Because the models include only a single measure of each concept and because, as was noted in chapter 7, more motivational than recruitment, socialization, or social background variables are significantly correlated with participation, motivation probably cannot be represented as well by a single measure as can other concepts in the models.

16. The use of different indicators of identical concepts to describe differences in the pathways to influence in the Liberal and Conservative parties requires further justification. Normally, valid indicators of the same concept must mean the same thing. Strictly speaking, however, what we have chosen to call concepts in our models are properly understood as aggregates of several distinct but related concepts. Social background, for example, is not a single concept but a set of experiences, educational, religious, ethnic, etc., all of which variously condition the individual's development and his later life attitudes and political behavior. Our use of different social background indicators in the Liberal and Conservative models reflects the fact that for different groups of MPs different social background experiences are more useful than others in explaining variations in influence. Because explanation is a principal concern of our analyses, we decided to employ whatever indicators of a concept contributed most to the explanation of individual influence, even if this required the use of different variables in different models. The alternative, clearly less desirable, was to employ identical indicators and to accept a substantial reduction in the level of variance explained.

17. The possibility of testing this assumption in a future study in which the Conservative party would form the government may be rather difficult. As will be argued in the next chapter, it seems unlikely that the Conservatives will win a national election in the not too distant future.

18. The Conservatives tend to view the proper role of parliament as one of agenda-setting and/or establishing national priorities rather than one of formulating or amending specific policies. This may explain why they attach little importance to a structure in which the latter goal can be accomplished.

19. Becoming an expert on some aspect of parliament's work may have become a party norm among Liberals. It is significantly related to early life political socialization, a high level of education, activity in the Liberal party organization in the electorate, and knowledge of the parliamentary rules of the game.

20. The reader also will recall that social background is strongly and directly correlated with their recruitment and with their attitudes and motivations. It also indirectly influences their parliamentary tenure.

## CHAPTER 10

1. Jean Blondel, Comparative Legislatures (Englewood Cliffs: Prentice-Hall, 1973), p. 142.

2. The reader will recall that the cabinet minister who was charged with steering through the House the massive procedural changes that restructured the committee system admitted that the use of the Committee of the Whole device never had given MPs an opportunity to give detailed consideration to a government's proposed expenditures, whereas an item-by-item consideration of the estimates of the several departments of government would be possible if the new procedures on committees were adopted.

The committees, however, have not been able to take full advantage of the opportunity that has been provided because they still lack the expert staff required for systematic in-depth analyses of departmental estimates. Instead, they have been forced to rely on the professional advice of the civil servants who initially proposed the expenditures and who have a very real interest in having the committees accept them. Members of committees also have been hampered by their inability to compel cabinet ministers to defend their departmental estimates and legislative proposals. Committee members, unable to question a minister in committee about a bill or estimate, who have tried to get the information from him in the House, almost always have been referred back to the committee to which the bills or estimates were sent–a runaround that has frustrated and angered more than one MP.

3. Fully 36% of the Conservative and Creditiste MPs, but only 11% of the Liberal and New Democratic parties' members, felt committees essentially were "useless."

4. The tendency of the Liberal and New Democratic MPs to more often view parliament's functions in terms of lawmaking also is reflected in their attitude towards standing committees. 30% of the Liberal and New Democratic MPs but only 6% of Conservative and Creditiste MPs felt the principal function of committees was to amend, modify, improve, and check (i.e., refine) legislation.

5. John Meisel attributes not only the Liberal party's parliamentary style but also its hubris to the fact that it has held power for so much of this century. Meisel, Working Papers on Canadian Politics (Montreal: McGill-Queen's University Press, 1973), p. 239.

6. Fred I. Greenstein, "The Benevolent Leader: Children's Image of Political Authority," American Political Science Review, 54 (1960), pp. 934–943.

7. Both our evaluation of standing committees and our prediction that the number of committee activists may increase in future parliaments are consonant with the conclusions of Michael Rush. Rush conducted an extensive study of the activities of the reorganized committees following the procedural changes of 1968–1969 (private communication July 2, 1975).

8. The three most frequently suggested changes were: (1) the provision of an adequate and independent professional research staff for each committee; (2) the reports of committees conducting investigations should be binding upon the government; and (3) there should be more "free votes" in committees.

9. An analysis of the fate of private members' bills introduced into the 24th, 26th, and 29th parliaments by Stewart Hyson bears this out. See R. V. Stewart Hyson, "The Role of the Backbencher: An Analysis of Private Members' Bills in the Canadian House of Commons," Parliamentary Affairs, 28 (1974–1975), pp. 262–272.

10. Hyson writes, "One cannot help but notice, while surveying the list of private members' bills over the years, that several politicians have their 'pet' projects which they introduce year-after-year in hopes of eventually gaining sufficient support to enable enactment." Ibid., p. 263.

11. In this regard, it is interesting that Conservatives in both the 25th and 28th parliaments tended to view party caucus as a cathartic instrument–one that provided an opportunity for venting grievances against party colleagues.

12. The ability of a parliamentary party to project an image of being good managers and administrators can be an asset at election time. With reference to Britain, Butler and Stokes suggest that the Conservative party's success in projecting an image of being a party "with a capacity to govern" helps explain why, despite massive social changes in the composition of the British electorate, the party has been able to maintain itself in office for so much of the past century. See David Butler and Donald Stokes, Political Change in Britain (New York: St. Martin's Press, 1969), passim.

13. This is a position taken by John Meisel in his overview of the 1972 election. "Scathing imputations of stupidity directed wholesale at opposition MPs; rude words and gestures both inside and outside Parliament; the calling of civil-liberties-minded critics 'weak-kneed bleeding hearts'; repeated invitations to the public to throw him and his government out of office if it did not like them, offended and alienated a large number of Canadians." Meisel, op. cit., p. 229.

14. Hyson's analysis of the fate of private members' bills supports this interpretation. He notes that in the three parliaments he considered "Members of the CCF/NDP have introduced a far greater number of private members' bills per parliamentary member than members of any other party." He goes on to observe that "most CCF/NDP members have tended to perceive themselves as law-makers with the prime purpose of having a major

impact on the policy of the government." Hyson, op. cit., p. 268. Walter D. Young has attributed the policy efforts of the CCF/NDP to their steadfastly held beliefs, to their faith in the rightness of their cause, and to the belief that their actions in parliament would demonstrate to the public that they were members of a responsible and legitimate party rather than a group of wild-eyed radicals. See Walter D. Young, The Anatomy of a Party: The National CCF, 1932–61 (Toronto: University of Toronto Press, 1969), ch. 8. Young's observations are consonant with our own profile of the characteristics of "gadflies," a substantial proportion of whom are members of the CCF/NDP.

15. Allan Kornberg, William Mishler, and Joel Smith, "Political Elite and Mass Perceptions of Party Locations in Issue Space: Some Tests of Two Positions," British Journal of Political Science, 5 (1975), pp. 153–177.

16. Indeed, at the time of this writing a bitter exchange of ad hominems was taking place between Transport Minister Jean Marchand and the Conservative backbench. Mr. Marchand, who suggested that some of the attacks were inspired by racism, called for an end to the attacks, "in the name of the country." Drawing parallels between his situation and the attacks suffered by Messrs. Lamontagne, Favreau, and Tremblay in earlier parliaments, Marchand charged that Conservative backbenchers "are trying to kill me." Suggesting that "everywhere there were French-Canadians they were under attack," Marchand claimed that he was "not anxious to see the resurrection of this spirit of suspicion and racism." Also enduring heavy criticism at the time were two other ministers of French-Canadian origin. See Globe and Mail, Toronto, March 8, 1975.

17. Mr. Trudeau claimed that he did not say what he was accused of saying. He merely said "fuddle-duddle," a comment which inspired the sale of thousands of fuddle-duddle T-shirts during the next few months.

18. That the speculations of media savants have at least some impact on public images of parliament and of the several parliamentary parties and, hence, have some effect on the outcome of elections is a matter that need not be debated here. Suffice to say that many people, including members of parliament, believe that they do.